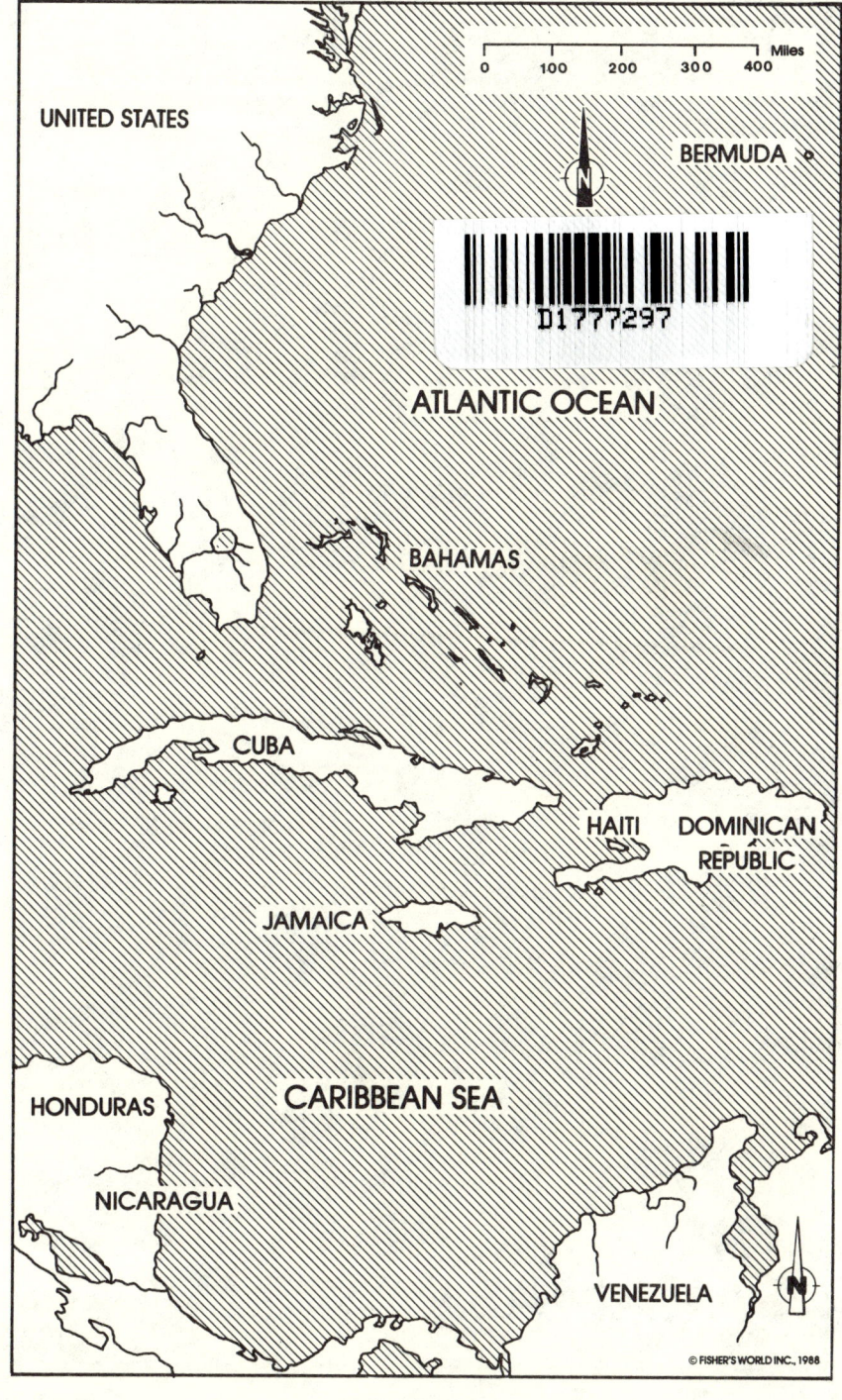

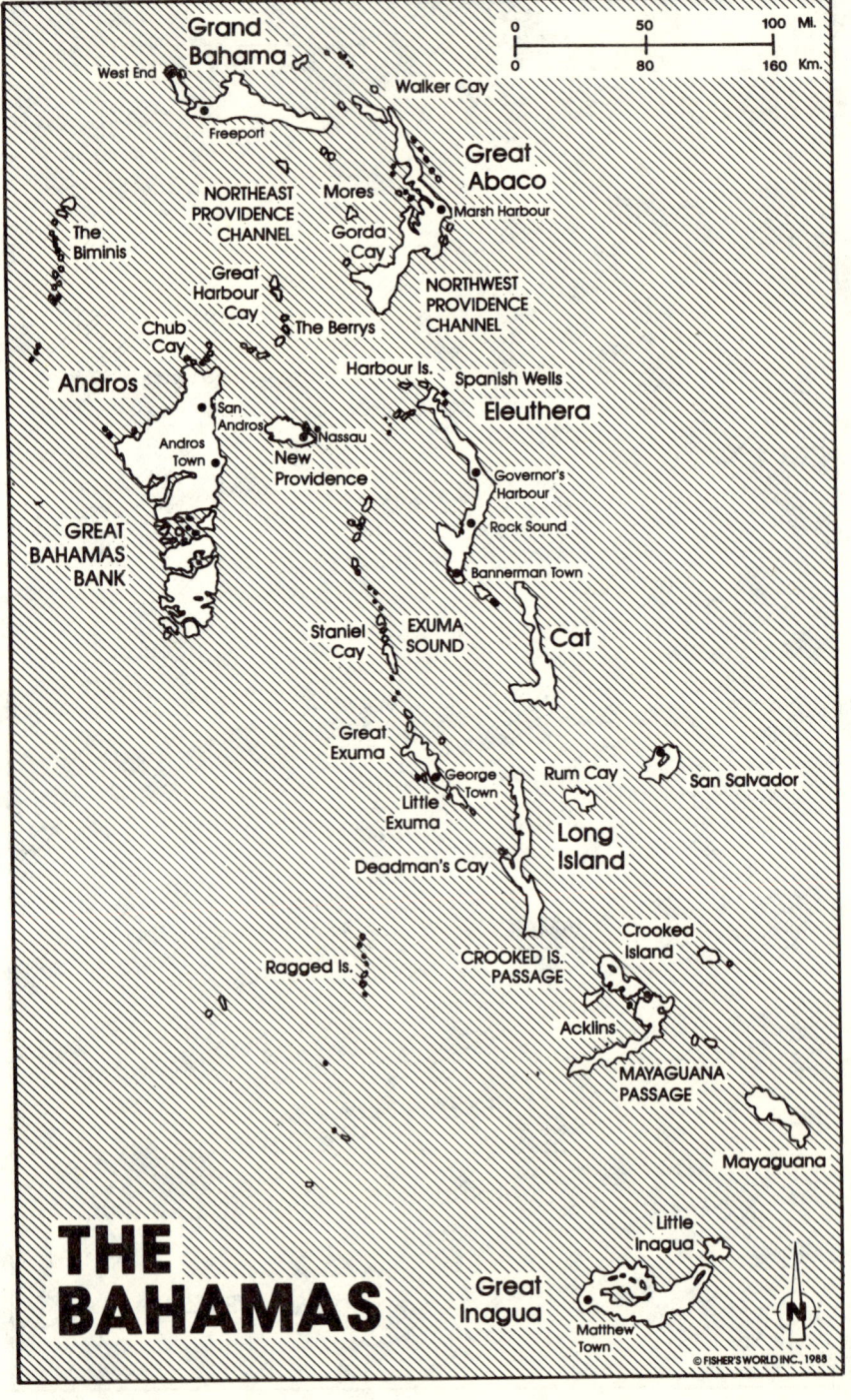

NASSAU
and the

5697

917.296 Lawes, Dianne
L
    Nassau and the
      Bahamas

$14.95

DATE		

IMPERIAL PUBLIC LIBRARY
P.O. BOX 307
IMPERIAL, TEXAS 79743

© THE BAKER & TAYLOR CO.

About the Author

Dianne Nicholson Lawes is a freelance writer who has been visiting and writing about the Bahamas for many years.

Publisher: Frank A. Marshall
Senior Editor: E. R. Grusky
Cover Design & Illustration: Eric Walker
Map Illustration: Salie Clemente

All prices are based on those available at time of writing. It is inevitable that changes will have taken place by the time that this book is published. Please double check so as to be sure of latest figures. We will be delighted to hear from you, whether it be a recommendation or complaint, at World of Travel Publishing, 106 South Front Street, Suite 2E, Philadelphia, PA 19106.

© 1989 by Fisher's World Inc.   ISBN 1-55707-039-3

All rights reserved. No part of this book may be reproduced or utilized in any form or by any means, electronic or mechanical, including photocopying, recording or by any information storage and retrieval system, without permission in writing from the publisher. All inquiries should be addressed to World of Travel, 106 S. Front Street, Suite 2E, Philadelphia, PA 19106. World of Travel is a division of Fisher's World Inc., Nutmeg Farm, Route 17, Laporte, PA 18626.

Table of Contents

Introduction 1
    Goombay Music & Junkanoo 2
    Food & Drink 2
    Seafood Galore 4
    Other Delights 5

Nassau 9
    If You Have Only One Day 9
    If You Have Two Days 11
    A Three-Day Treat 14
    If You Have More Time 15

Author's Choice/Nassau/New Providence Island and Paradise Island 17
    Hotels 17
    Restaurants 24
    Entertainment 26
    Sports 33
    Getting Around 34

Junkanoo *by Lee Hays* 35

Grand Bahama 39
    If You Have Only One Day 39
    If You Have Two Days 41
    If You Have Three Days 43
    If You Have More Time 44

Author's Choice/Grand Bahama 47
    Hotels 47
    Restaurants 50
    Entertainment 53
    Sports 59
    Getting Around 61

Through A Glass Darkly: Test Your Sunglass Savvy *by Frances Sheridan Goulart* 63

The Family Islands 67
    The Biminis 67
        South Bimini 71

- **Berry Islands** 71
- **Andros** 73
  - Central Andros 73
  - North Andros 75
  - Mangrove Cay and Congo Town 75
- **The Exumas** 75
  - George Town 76
  - South to Williams Town 77
- **Long Island** 81
- **The Inaguas** 82
- **Crooked and Acklins Islands** 83
- **Jumento Cays** 86
- **Rum Cay** 86

Author's Choice/Family Islands 87
- **Andros** 87
  - Congo Town, south 90
  - Mangrove Cay 90
  - North Andros 90
- **Berry Islands** 91
- **The Biminis** 91
- **Crooked and Acklins Islands** 93
- **Exumas** 93
  - Great Exuma 93
  - Staniel Cay 96
- **The Inaguas** 96
- **Long Island** 97
- **Rum Cay** 98

Underwater Adventures in the Bahamas
by Renee Wright 101

The Outer Family Islands 105
- **Eleuthera** 105
  - Spanish Wells 107
  - Harbour Island 108
  - North Eleuthera 109
  - Central Eleuthera 111
  - Governor's Harbour 112
  - Southern Eleuthera 113
  - Rock Sound 115
- **Abaco** 115
  - Central Abaco 117
  - Elbow Cay, including Hope Town 118

    Great Guana Cay 120
    Treasure Cay 121
    Green Turtle Cay 122
  Cat Island 125
  San Salvador 127
  Mayaguana 129

Author's Choice/Outer Family Islands 131
  Abaco 131
    Elbow Cay, including Hope Town 131
    Green Turtle Cay 132
    Great Guana Cay 135
    Marsh Hasbour 135
    Treasure Cay 140
    Walker's Cay 140
  Eleuthera 141
    Governor's Harbour, including South Palmetto Point .. 143
    Harbour Island 143
    Rock Sound 148
    Spanish Wells 149
  San Salvador 150

Index 151

Travel Planner

List of Maps

The Abacos 114	Golf Courses I 134
Acklins/Crooked Islands ..84	Golf Courses II 138
Air Transport 100	Golf Courses III 142
Andros 72	Golf Courses IV 146
Bahamas Golf Courses ... 130	Grand Bahama 38
Bahamas Hotels & Restaurants with Key 88-89	Inagua 80
	International Bazaar 54
Bahamas Islands iv	Location Map iii
Berry Islands 70	Long Island 78
The Biminis 68	Lucaya 46
Cat Island 124	Nassau 8
Downtown Freeport 42	New Providence Island 6
Eleuthera, Harbour Island 106	New Providence/Restaurants & Hotels with Key 18-19
The Exumas 74	Paradise Island 16
Ferry System 62	
Freeport 40	San Salvador 126

Introduction

Sprinkled through beautiful multihued seas, the Bahamas comprise some three thousand sun-blessed isles less than a hundred miles off the United States coast. Most of these islets are too tiny to support settlements, but about seven hundred are large enough to be termed islands, and some thirty support towns, industries, tourist fare, and markets for all sorts of products. Two-thirds of the nation's 209,505 people live on minute New Providence, while Andros, by far the largest island, supports less than one twenty-fifth of the population over its 2,300 square miles.

The 209,505 Bahamians tallied by the 1980 census includes blacks whose ancestry traces back to the late 1700s, when Loyalists and their slaves arrived from continental America. There was also direct immigration from Africa. Most white Bahamians are descendants of the earliest settlers of the 1600s, as well as 18th-century Loyalists. There is also a large expatriate population. The majority of blacks in this group are Haitian refugees who, according to government figures of the early 1980s, number nearly 40,000 and occupy the lowest rung on the socioeconomic ladder. White expatriates include many self-employed professionals or business people who now consider the Bahamas their home; there are nonworking retirees and winter residents, and many people employed in short- or long-term positions by government or private industry.

It was 1973 before England's apron strings were snipped to create a Commonwealth country out of what had been, for 335 years, a protected Crown colony. As the old social order went down the drain, the Progressive Labor Party waved a "Bahamas for Bahamians" flag that helped boost national awareness and pride.

Some of the rewards of economic development are already visible. In the not so distant past Bahamians, particularly Family Islanders, were almost totally dependent on gathering herbs and bush-medicine ingredients to treat ailments; Today this traditional practice is complemented by trained medical doctors and nurses who staff government-operated clinics on many islands. There are forms of national insurance, workers' compensation, and old-age benefits. New construction is seen throughout the islands, with more secure concrete-block homes replacing the old shacks. There is a continual effort to improve roads, transportation equipment, and telephone and Telex systems. This work is slow and often brought almost to a standstill for lack of funds, but the government works hard to fulfill its promise to share modern advantages with all the people, no matter how remote their settlements may be. This is a nation that works hard to meet the goals of its chief industry, tourism, while simultaneously guiding its people ever "Forward, upward, onward, together," as the national motto enjoins.

GOOMBAY MUSIC AND JUNKANOO

Ranging from gentle ballads to boisterous rhythms, Bahamian songs tell of island life and traditions. The beat is light, the tempo is up, and the sound is called Goombay—derived from the name of the goatskin drums traditionally used to accompany whistles and cowbells. While Caribbean Calypso tunes are frequently heard, along with popular songs from America, England, and other lands, Goombay is predominant. It reigns with special splendor during Junkanoo.

With the thumping of goatskin drums, the jangling of herd bells, the sound of horns, whistles, and other noisemakers, plus the stomp and shuffle of myriad feet, Junkanoo is launched early in the morning of December 26. Some revelers are "scrappin'"—riotous folk dressed in scraps of cloth and paper. Others seriously compete for prizes by decking out in elaborately fantastic masks and hats, with richly colored costumes that represent months of work. Singly or in groups, participants cavort, dance, and strut through the streets, often with tourists in tow. Days of merriment akin to Mardi Gras celebrations are climaxed by a second parade in the very early hours of New Year's Day. Nassau has the biggest festival, but many other island towns put on good shows, too.

Though archivists trace these revels to the 1700s, the word "Junkanoo" first appears in the 1950s. Before then, the celebrations were tied to the season and starred Johnny Canoe—a famous folk hero among West African slaves in the Bahamas, Caribbean, and southern United States. Most tales describe him as a figure dressed in outrageous rags and tatters, wearing a tall hat and a mask depicting beast, bird, or man. Whether he was a god, a slave or ever existed is unimportant. While the custom of Junkanoo is dying out in other places, it retains a primary place in the heart of the Bahamas.

FOOD AND DRINK

Today's tourist can expect culinary treats in the Bahamas—not just the international fare served in posh restaurants or resorts, but specialties of the Bahamian kitchen, too. Certain favorite island dishes are found in almost all eateries, but it's in the home that they reign supreme. If you can't wangle an invitation to a home-cooked meal, try a native restaurant for a wide selection of local concoctions. This chapter helps guide you to the fixings and flavors of the Bahamas.

Basically British, the diet was adjusted to regional land and sea harvests. When supply ships fell victim to pirates, privateers, reefs, and shoals, or when the soil adamantly refused to foster certain crops, resourceful colonial cooks substituted a dash of this for a pinch of that, and applied it to edibles often unknown to farmers or fishermen of the Old World. As time passed and continental politics prompted Loyalists, Confederates, and their slaves to move here, the newcomers brought along their own foodstuffs as additions to local cookpots.

Southerners from the United States are often delighted to find hominy grits a side order at morning meals in most restaurants. Southerners like them with eggs and bacon, ham, chops, or steaks; the favorite Bahamian breakfast teams them with fish. First broiled with onions, the fish is then laid aside while hard-boiled egg yolk and butter are blended in pan juices; the egg's slivered white is added; and then this sauce is poured over the fish and grits are mounded beside it. Home-cooked breakfasts might also feature corned beef hash, meat or fish pies, pancakes, fritters, fruits, and any of the many delicious Bahamian hot breads and loaves.

Lunch, tea, and dinner are mealtimes when the fare can be hot or chilled, light or heavy. There are interesting salads and soups, sandwiches and burgers, and assorted entrees and vegetables. Peas 'n' rice ranks top among all vegetable dishes, and is made as follows: Tomatoes and onions are fried in bacon or pork fat, then cooked peas of any type are added (pigeon peas are best) along with thyme, salt, pepper, and rice, and all are cooked until the rice is fluffy. Sweet potatoes and yams are popular, too, along with okra, cabbage, pimentos, green peppers, and red hot peppers. And there's more: corn, shallots, cauliflower, pumpkin, Irish potatoes, eggplants, turnips, broccoli, brussels sprouts, carrots, cucumbers, lettuce, watercress, Swiss chard, spinach, and several kinds of beans (peas), plus the imports. Few of these are very unusual to Westerners; it's the Bahamian way of preparing them that makes the difference. Tomatoes and onions are basic to many recipes; the juices of limes, lemons, and sour oranges add piquancy; salt pork is a popular flavoring. Some vegetables become fritters and puddings; others are candied or layered into casseroles. Many end up pickled with mustard or in chutneys and chili sauces; others are cooked into soups, pies, and pilafs, curries and chowders.

Wherever meals are served, in whatever form, you can usually depend on johnnycakes being part of them. They are usually served warm and are always delicious. The johnnycake is noted for it's ability to stay fresh for long periods in the packs of this nation's seafarers and fishermen. And it's those very fishermen who bring in the islanders' gastronomic mainstay: the marine gastropod mollusk called a conch (pronounced konk).

SEAFOOD GALORE

That pretty pink shell cresting the nation's coat of arms is the home of a conch—a large snail of the sea that thrives in Bahamian waters and has become the focus of what I dub conch cuisine. After being deftly extracted from its spiral shell and thoroughly cleaned, the red meat is trimmed away and the conch is ready to eat. The raw meat can be diced and combined with cubed raw vegetables, lemon, and spices to make a tangy conch salad. Or it may be finely chopped, run through a meat grinder, or pounded and beaten vigorously to shred its sinews before cooking.

Many beloved dishes are made from the white, chewy, somewhat bland meat of this mollusk. Famous as cocktail snacks and side dishes, conch fritters are deep-fried balls of ground or chopped conch with flour, onions, eggs, tomatoes, celery, cream, baking powder, and spices. Rich and zesty conch chowder is equally popular. Served as a first course or as a meal in itself, this national treat is a thick blend of cubed conch, potatoes, onions, and tomatoes, bacon or pork, salt, pepper, and the optional additions of other vegetables, bread crumbs, or a shot of sherry. Cracked conch is beaten, rolled in batter and fried. Steamed conch is browned and removed from the pan while onions, green peppers, celery, and tomatoes are sauteed therein, then added to the pan mixture along with seasonings and water and left to steam awhile before gracing the table. Other recipes include scorched conch, conch creole, conch curry, creamed conch on toast, stewed conch, conch pilaf, cream of conch soup, even conchburgers.

Tourists usually find conch cuisine quite enjoyable, but what they most often rave about is Bahamian lobster: the spiny lobster also called crayfish. Sometimes served boiled with drawn butter, it's also made into internationally popular recipes such as lobster Newburg, or whipped into souffles, curries, cream of lobster soup, and traditional favorites like lobster with dill, lobster salad with avocado, or lobster minced with spices and vegetables over rice.

Tasty baked crab may appear on native menus, too, along with varieties of fish that may be broiled, fried, barbecued, or blended into bouillabaisse or fish pudding. Seafood fanciers might also try turtle steaks, turtle soups, turtle pates, turtle stews, and so forth. For real aficionados of sea turtle, we point to a collection of Nassauvians' favorite recipes,—Mrs. Leslie Higgs' *Bahamian Cookbook*—which includes a step-by-step guide for making turtle pie, starting with the do-it-yourself removal of the shell and ending with pouring all prepared ingredients into that shell, sealing it with a pastry cover, then popping it into the oven to bake. The book (one of several great cookbooks sold throughout the country) also explains how to fix whelk soup or stew, how to charcoal sea urchins, and how to prepare several other Old Bahamian seafood specialties.

The sea staple that competes most with the conch isn't any of these. It's the grouper—a smoothly textured fish of few bones and mild flavor, weighing from two to thirty pounds. Fishermen say it's tastiest right out of the water, perhaps grilled over charcoal on the beach or sauteed at the stove of a ship's galley. Most restaurants dish out batter-dipped fried grouper fingers or cutlets to the immense satisfaction of natives and tourists alike. It's also popular baked and done up in stews and casseroles.

OTHER DELIGHTS

When Bahamians want beef, veal, and pork (or dairy products) they most often turn to imports, for little land here can support livestock. Yet chicken is plentiful, and a good many goats and sheep are raised for meat that's indiscriminately labeled mutton. Feasts are made of wild boar that roam some isles, and game birds like pigeons, ducks, and coots are particularly abundant in certain areas. When the Arawak, or Lucaya, Indians lived here before Columbus' era, they looked upon iguana lizards as toothsome dinners, and contemporary Bahamians also eat iguanas, when and if they can find them. But whatever the meat may be, it frequently is uniquely flavored with Bahamian Old Sour—a fermentation of lime juice and salt, often powerfully spiced with ground cayenne pepper or finely chopped little red-hot peppers. These peppers cannot be found in shops or markets, but are handy in most local kitchens and applied to all sorts of food with a generous hand. Meats also take on the fine flavors of local herbs, citrus fruits, bananas, and pineapples.

Fruits enliven many Bahamian meals, and several of these fruits may be new to tourists. Sapodillas grow on a tropical evergreen that also yields chicle, the chief ingredient of chewing gum. Soursop, actually one of the custard apples, is slightly acid with a fibrous pulp. Breadfruit, if baked, looks similar in shape, color, and texture to a loaf of bread, though it really is a member of the mulberry family. There are also local sea grapes, coconuts, guavas, dates, jujubes (Chinese dates), bananas, mangoes, pineapples, passion fruits, and several kinds of apples, plums, citrus fruits, and melons.

Breakfast tables boast many of these fruits raw, as juices, or beaten into batters for breads or pancakes, which well might be spread with luscious coconut butter. Look for preserves of coco plums, gooseberries, and tamarinds; marmalades of sour orange, grapefruit, lime, or lemon; jams of papaya, sea grape, cherry, pineapple, and even sorrel; and jellies of guava, coconut, wine, sweet orange, or mint. Both lunch and dinner can include fruit salads, spreads, or sauces, plus a legion of marvelous desserts like guava duff, a big favorite featured in many restaurants, and other duffs made from dates and coconuts. Puddings feature sapodillas, bananas, pineapples, sweet potatoes, coconut, citrus, breadfruit, and raisins, and fritters are made with bananas or pineapples. There's a scrumptuous list of fruit pies, custards, mousses, tarts, souffles, dumplings, cookies, and candies,

6 Nassau and the Bahamas

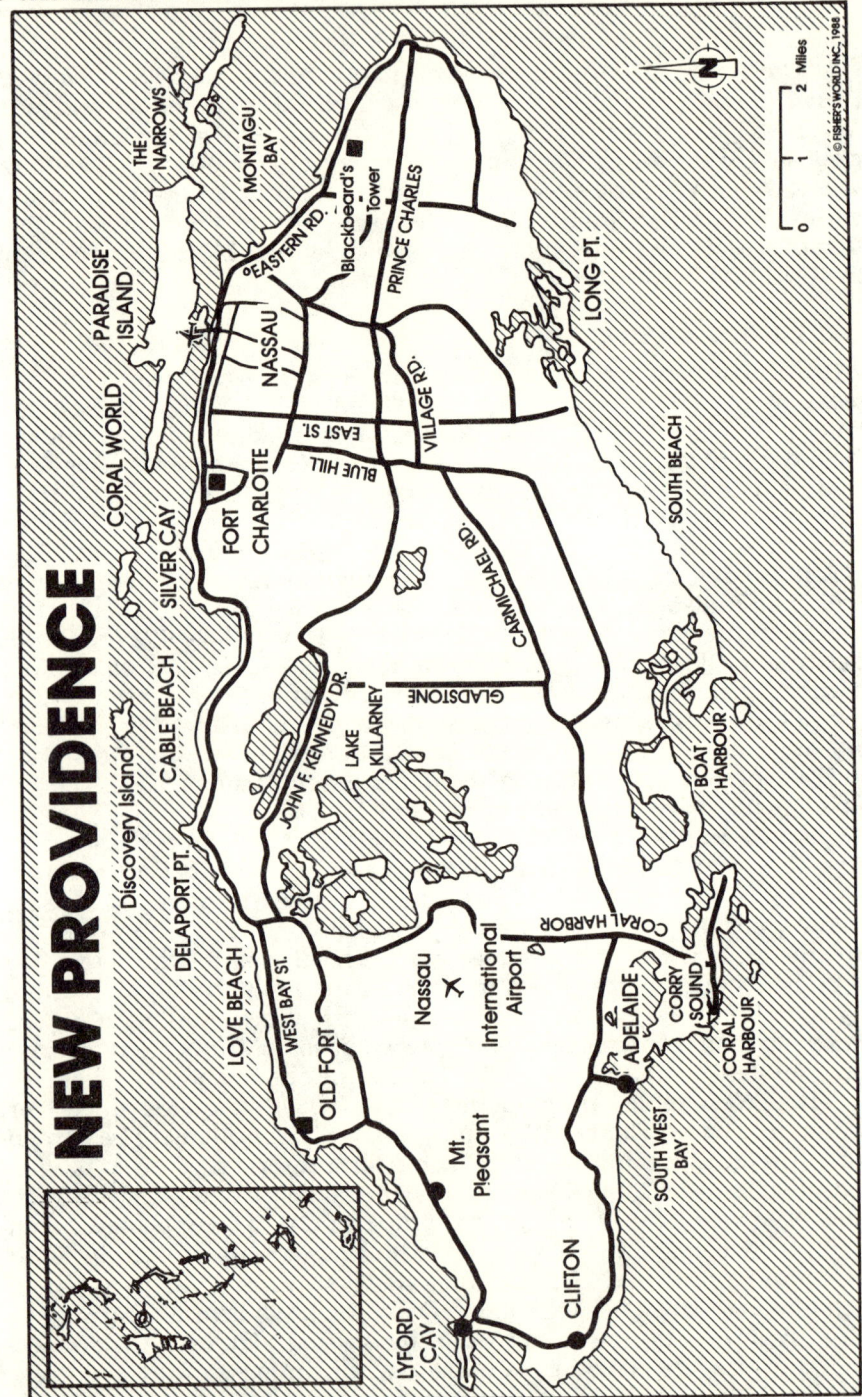

plus ices, sherbets, and ice creams. Mango fool is a dreamy concoction; soursop ice cream is a taste to remember; and Bahamian ambrosia is—what else—heavenly.

These delicious fruits often are singled out or mixed as beverages. Calamondin and other citrus juices stand alone or are used to flavor teas; grapefruit juice sometimes is heated with brandy. Soursops, mangoes, pineapples, and cherries also yield tasty liquids that frequently are spiked with soda water, ginger ale, or alcohol as is a tea derived from tamarind or sorrel.

Fanciful tropical drinks are created with rums, made in the Bahamas and nearby isles, which easily team with all sorts of fruit juices. Distinctively Bahamian is Goombay Smash—a mixture of light rum, coconut rum, sugar, lemon juice, and pineapple juice, with an optional dash of Galliano. If you shake orange juice with creme de cacao (or coconut rum) and light rum, it's a Bahama Mama, sometimes spiked with grenadine or even Nassau Royale as well. Add Triple Sec, Galliano, and light rum to banana liqueur and orange juice and you've got a Yellow Bird, though some people will insist it's better with lime juice and no banana taste. These three favorites are a sample of the long list of island tall drinks that depend on fruit juices and rum, and include Planters Punch, Banana Daquiri, Pina Colada, Cocoloco, Pineapple Smile, Island Sun, Play Girl, plus dozens more. The list of locally flavored spirited drinks includes all the popular imported liquors, whiskys, wines, ales, and beers, plus a fine Bahamian liqueur: Nassau Royale — definitely worth sampling on its own or blended with cool drinks, hot coffees, or flaming fresh fruit desserts.

One more brew to try is made from leaves, roots, and barks. You won't find it in stores or on menus, but you can ferret it out if you're persistent, often by quizzing native bartenders or the staff in restaurants. It's any of a variety of extracts and teas, drunk separately or mixed, which belong to the large collection of local bush medicines. Some brews relieve headaches, fevers, cold symptoms; others are tonics; many are specifics such as those said to be strongly aphrodisiacal. In any case, cheers and bon appetit!

8 Nassau and the Bahamas

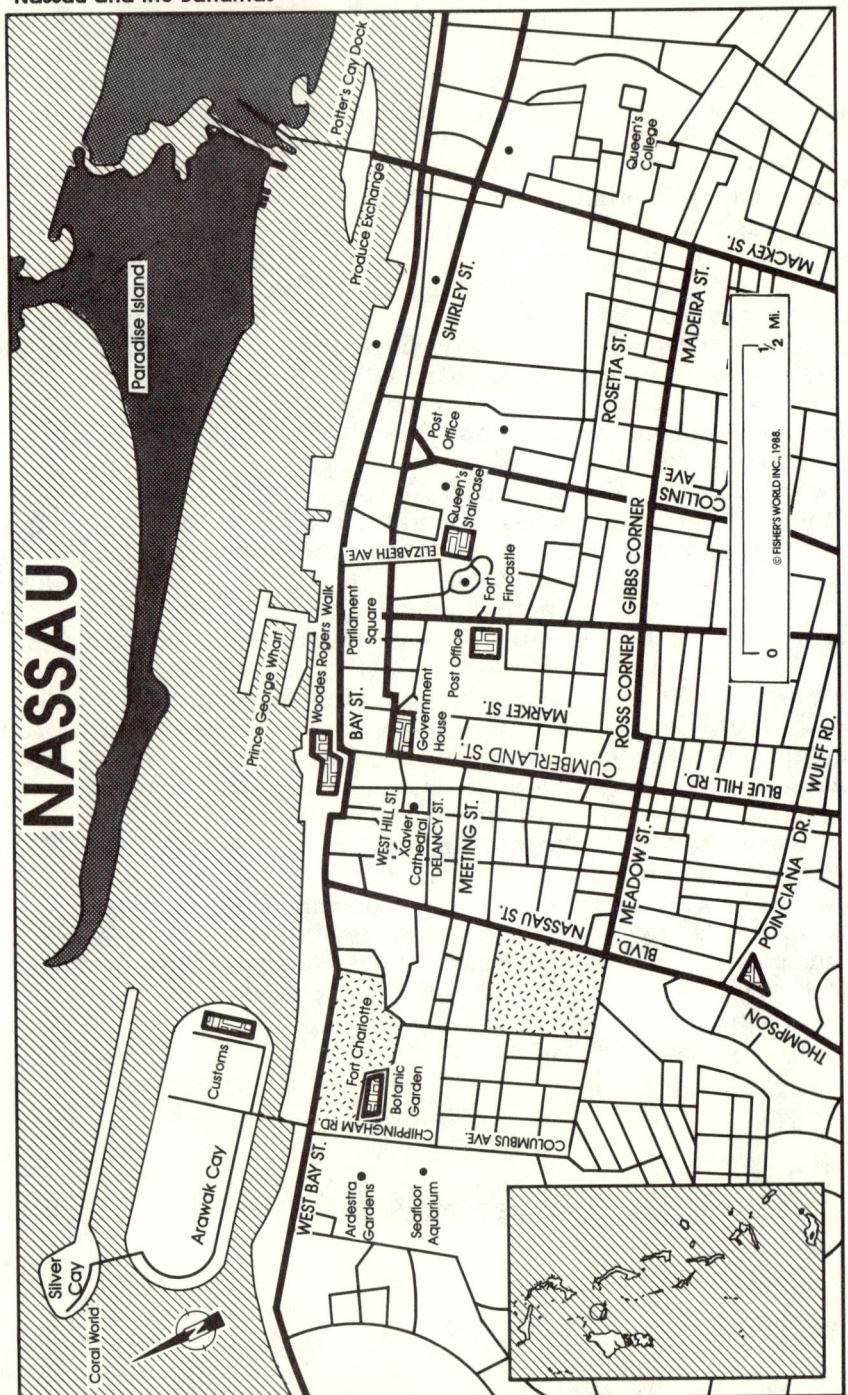

Nassau

As the respected and renowned capital city of the Commonwealth of the Bahamas, Nassau—on New Providence Island—greets travelers from all over the world. As singles, couples, families, and groups, they come to swim in the sea, wander the beaches, stalk the sights, buy native crafts, play in casinos, wine and dine, purchase duty-free international bargains, and enjoy dozens of outdoor sports. Almost anything tourists can imagine doing can be done in and about Nassau, where even the mundane activity often acquires special panache.

IF YOU HAVE ONLY ONE DAY

Start your day in the sunshine with a stroll on the sandy white beach flanking your hotel. Early morning can be the best time for shelling, watching water birds preen, or tracing the trails of fowl and scuttling crabs. You might be lucky and have the entire peaceful scene all to yourself. When the crowds start appearing, you can head back for a leisurely breakfast, preferably on your private terrace, but at least on a terrace or patio dining room where you can savor the morning's marvelously fresh air.

Back on the beach, strip to a swimsuit and unpocket that tanning or screening lotion. The Bahamian sun is probably stronger than your hometown variety, so caution is advised. Bask awhile in the sun and watch the action around you. After some time to digest both what's happening and that breakfast, you may decide to take a swim. If you've never snorkeled, try it. Bring or rent your own gear and enjoy the fascinating sight of brightly colored reefs and assorted marine life, easily visible in the clear waters.

If you're the sporty type, you can rent a small sailboat, or hire a speedy boat for waterskiing. Adventurous types might try parasailing. With a modified parachute securely strapped on, and a strong rope linking you to a powerboat, you'll soar two- or three-hundred feet above the sea, then float gently down to a special landing dock. Though costly and brief, this sport is guaranteed to supply you with unbeatable memories.

Even if you usually eschew dipping under briny water, don't go home without a look beneath this sea's surface. Should getting water in eyes, ears, or hair worry you, head for *Hartley's Undersea Walk*, via the Pied Piper cruises. This excursion welcomes folks of five to eighty-five. You will be outfitted in a shiny helmet, with a see-through pane (no need to remove eyeglasses or contacts) and an individually hosed air supply. Thus protected, you can stroll the sandy sea bottom, in about 10 to 12 feet of water, comfortably gazing at the marine life around you. Another option is to ride a glass-bottom boat, perhaps the *Nautilus*—a 97-foot craft that offers day and night cruises above reefs, wrecks, and the ever changing underwater scenery near Nassau. You also could elect a trek to *Coral World Marine Park*, one of three such showplaces in the world. On Silver Cay, near Cable Beach, it boasts an underwater observatory 20 feet below the sea, and a 100-foot tower with great area views plus a handy bar. There are several nearby specialty pools, tanks, ponds, and aquariums; a nature trail; a hotel; shops; and a restaurant.

When you're ready for lunch, try a Bahamian restaurant locals prefer, maybe even a "take-away" type that serves meals or snacks to go. You could sit and munch these around *Rawson Square*, while watching the sea for a tall ship replica, a working tug, sloops, military cruisers, or fishing boats. Fresh fruit bought from a street vendor makes a dessert treat.

Handicrafts

Near Prince George Wharf, amid honking taxi horns, noisy crowds, and occasional whinnies from horses waiting to give visitors surrey tours of town, you'll find a prime attraction: *Market Plaza*, which houses Nassau's famed straw and crafts market. Passing by and through the building, you'll be entreated to buy wares from Bahamians of all ages, many who call to you and dicker prices without missing a move in the difficult patterns their dexterous hands are weaving.

You'll see jewelry made from shells, coral, shark teeth and colored pods, and local artists' paintings and carvings. But the sheer number and beauty of straw objects overwhelm everything else. In stalls, crowding shelves and tables, or stacked in boxes on the pavement, these handmade items are woven in countless patterns, usually trimmed with bright raffia that forms flowers, palms, shells, figures and letters, sometimes with actual shells added, too. You'll see hats, bags, dolls, toys, fans, baskets, slippers, placemats—and may even have items woven to order.

Sights

Privateer-cum-reformer Woodes Rogers, a particularly colorful governor of the eighteenth century, is shown all ready for a shoot-em-up in the form of a statue on the grounds of the nearby Sheraton British Colonial Hotel. The huge pink hotel rests on the site of old *Fort Nassau*, Rogers' home base, and was used in two Sean Connery 007 epics, Thunderball and Never Say Never Again. It's easily reached by following Woodes Rogers Walk between the water and some shopping arcades, where the Sheraton's Ice Cream Place boasts some tantalizing local confections.

If you're not loaded down with the arts and crafts you've no doubt purchased by this time, and if you haven't overdosed on the sea and sun, spend a lazy afternoon on the streets and lanes nearby. It's easy to be entranced by some of the homes here, whose architecture dates back hundreds of years. Huge mansions sit side by side with much smaller dwellings, not to mention all sorts of guest houses, restaurants, and laundries, and here and there a corner church and graveyard. Everything is attractively, trimmed in the omnipresent greenery and flamboyant flowers.

Within a walkable distance, you'll be able to scout the *Government House* and old *Royal Victoria Hotel*, museums, the library that was once a prison, Parliament and cabinet offices, the original town layout, plus many of the boomtown additions.

Back at the hotel, prepare for a night on the town by taking a snooze. Awake refreshed, and dress for a late dinner. Men will want only a sports jacket with slacks; women can wear pants, but skirts are in vogue here, with short lengths the favored style.

As the evening darkens, it's time to dine in a truly elegant restaurant; one of my favorites is *Buena Vista*. Start with a cocktail or tall island drink, then enjoy a slow procession of exquisite fare, expertly served, in the atmosphere of charm and grace that pervades this fine old mansion. For a change of pace, taxi to the best native show in town, at "Peanuts" Taylor's *Drum Beat Club* on West Bay Street. Then, there's still time to try your luck at a casino.

IF YOU HAVE TWO DAYS

You might be tempted to sleep late after your night on the town, but try to force yourself up and into a swimsuit and beach jacket, to do your snoozing under the shade of a gaily colored beach umbrella, tall palm, or pine. Do it before or after breakfast, and work in a swim or sun bask while you're beachside. But don't linger; there's too much to see and do.

Today's a day to venture farther around town and take in the historic sites and outlying areas you didn't get around to yesterday. You can go by rented vehicle, group minibus tour or taxi hired on hourly rates. Whichever you elect, make a first stop by the tour desk at your hotel and grab a fistful of literature about local sights, plus the free city map. At the same desk, you can sign up for a group tour and get information about renting vehicles and hiring taxis.

The most satisfying, flexible, and comfortable way to see Nassau is by private taxi with a Bahamahost driver. After a look through this book and the free literature, you'll have a better idea of which places interest you most, and should you decide to spend more time somewhere along the way or stop at a spot that happens to catch your eye, your driver-guide can cater to such whims. He can do more, too, because he's trained and tested in a voluminous amount of Bahamian history, folklore, politics, culture, sports, tourist offerings—the works. A Bahamahost can be your inside informer on how to get the most out of your holiday here.

It's worth the time to see the old forts around town, to descend (much easier than ascending) the *Queen's Staircase,* and take the elevator to the top of the water tower for a panoramic view of the island, nearby cays and rocks, and surrounding water dotted with ships. At the eastern end of New Providence, on an extension of East Bay Street called Eastern Road, a footpath leads to the ruins of *Blackbeard's Tower* where, legend has it, the roguish pirate kept lookouts posted. (Perhaps he reveled in its height, too, being a mere five feet four inches himself.) The tower remains are somewhat stubby today, but the view is extensive, and the ride to this site takes you by some of the more posh Bahamian estates, including the Heritage.

Passing Fort Montague Bay, you may see people peering eagerly out to sea, where replicas of old Bahamian working-class vessels skim along in competition, or try to qualify for a regatta. Or there may be signs posted to tout a horse show at *Camperdown.* If so, urge your driver to head inland to this equestrian haunt, and watch the riders put their mounts through the paces of dressage. You might get to see the local elite and notables wrapped in aprons, cooking up burgers to benefit the National Trust.

Back on Bay Street, which runs the length of town, you'll glimpse emporiums both large and small where some of the world's more coveted items are sold. Here, too, you can revel in the diversity of the crowds, where you can spot everything from smatterings of straw vendors to an occasional street singer. The policemen and policewomen are an unforgettable sight, resplendent in their stiffly starched white tunics and their trousers or skirts with red ribbon stripes; their smartly designed white caps bobbing as they direct the traffic.

Driving along West Bay Street, your Bahamahost may explain that the imposing *Xavier's College* near *Fort Charlotte* is actually a Catholic primary school, and those terraced gardens with meandering waterfowl are part of a private estate. Ask about *Arawak Cay,* which was created from harbor dredgings; linked to the shore here, it is home for tanks storing water brought from Andros to supplement Nassau's own supply of fresh and desalinized water. *Caves Beach,* past the Cable Beach area, gets its name from the caves facing the shore. You can pull aside for better investigation of the shallow chambers that may have sheltered seafarers or pirates. By now, you've probably noticed that people name their homes, with selections ranging from quaint to rowdy and stately to poetic.

For more sights of fine homes in beautiful residential areas, turn inland and find quiet streets with large residences painted yellow, blue, pink, and white. Most are edged with lawns, fruit and shade trees, flowers and burgeoning bougainvillea that almost obscures some from view. *Long Bay* is the low, creamy residence of the prime minister, with uniformed guards before its twin gates. A yellow mansion, fenced and also guarded, is named *Saffron Hill*, home of the U.S. ambassador. *Dale House* seems forebiding even now, it's pillared entrance locked and chained. Its owner, Sir Harry Oakes was brutally murdered here in 1943. Though the best investigative minds of the Bahamas, the United States, and the United Kingdom worked on the scandalous case, it remains unsolved.

Over the Hill

Now you can head back via John F. Kennedy Drive—Kennedy created history when he met in Nassau with prime ministers of England and Canada—and Nassau Street. This route will take you through sections "Over the Hill" where old native settlements such as *Bain Town* and *Grant's Town* have expanded to meet Nassau proper. These homes are tiny, of wood or mortar, and often sit on blocks or bricks in close clusters, interspersed with churches, businesses, bars, and the ever-present greenery.

To extend the tour, head for Simms Point via West Bay Street and pass by a recording studio and the exclusive Lyford Cay enclave, around to Adelaide Road and the old village settlement. Stop perhaps at the *Bacardi Rum Distillery* before you head back to your hotel.

Whether or not you extend the trip to circle the island, you might stop for a meal or refreshment at the aptly named *Travellers Rest*, where cheerful Joan Hanna welcomes you to tasty native cooking served in a relaxed yet lively atmosphere with touches of homey comfort. The restaurant overlooks the beach, and you can pause for a dip or spend the rest of the afternoon basking and swimming here. If it's a Sunday, Duke Hanna—head of the musicians' union and also Joan's husband and cohost—will be there with other musicians whose jam sessions bring the townsfolk in droves.

Later, make it an evening in Paradise—the island across the bay. There really is a romantic mood enveloping the *Courtyard Terrace* at the Ocean Club. Palms and flowers, dreamy dance music, and excellent service all add to your enjoyment of the chef's carefully prepared cuisine. Try an after-dinner drink nearby at *Le Cabaret*, while show-girls and troopers pace through a Vegas-style production, then step into the adjacent casino to browse or play. To top off the evening, there are lounges and a disco within the same complex of resorts.

A THREE-DAY TREAT

You can start with a shopping spree along the central region of Bay Street and its arcades. The territory is short in length, but long on renown for its assortment of international merchandise. Even if you're merely window shopping, it can be fun to start at one end of the district and mosey along to the next, crossing again and again to poke around each store and shop, inspecting the offerings. If there's something you particularly want, you're not only likely to find it, but in profusion: watches, cameras, luggage, cashmere, perfumes, liquors, emeralds, diamonds, tobacco, brass, china, crystal—the list is endless. If you're a serious shopper, ducking into all outlets helps you compare stock and prices. Should you be looking for gifts for yourself or the folks back home, the more you see, the more fanciful the selection. And as an exercise in people watching the excursion is hard to surpass.

After Lunch

After lunch, you're within walking distance of the *Royal Victoria Gardens*, on the grounds of an old hotel of the same name, where Confederates, their allies and enemies met those blockade-running days of the mid-1800s. The hotel is closed now (though rumor predicts a renovation soon), but the grand old gardens are still available for all to admire, filled with some three hundred varieties of tropical plants and foliage.

From here, you can see Bahamian medicinal greenery by heading out John .F. Kennedy Drive to the YMCA, where the recently opened *Bush Medicine Gardens* were funded by Swiss gifts. Several special plants—but just a few of those used traditionally throughout the islands to treat illness—were carefully staked with labels under the supervision of Mrs. Leslie Higgs, author of gardening articles and best-known expert in Bahamian bush medicine.

Nassau Botanical Gardens, next on the list, is near *Fort Charlotte*, with eighteen acres of flowers, trees, and shrubs in wide variety. Be sure to visit the grotto of locally quarried stones with its roof of conch shells. While you're in the neighborhood, you may decide to visit *Ardastra Gardens*, especially to see the pink flamingos on parade (no joke) under the strict command of drillmaster Joseph Lexion. Before going there, however, be warned: If women in your party are clad in scanty midriffs, shorts or miniskirts, the drillmaster is equally strict about banning them from the show. I don't know whether his morals or the flamingos' are the determining factor here. But we do know you can extend the day to include yet another show, almost next door, where sea lions and dolphins regularly cavort. The place is *Seaflower Aquarium*, and it's a favorite of folks who want close looks at sharks, manta rays, and other creatures.

For dinner tonight, try the *Nassau Harbour Club*, where you can reserve a table overlooking the yacht marina and waterway. A local favorite here is minced lobster, but whatever you select will be cooked to order and served with a friendly, pleasant deftness. The Drum Beat Club, on West Bay Street, presents fine after-dinner entertainment, and two discos to try are the Palace and Cinnamon's.

IF YOU HAVE MORE TIME

Invest some of your time doing absolutely nothing—in your room, on your balcony or patio, beside pool or beach, in a snug bar or outdoor cafe—enjoying the leisurely pace of the local life-style.

Dip into my descriptions and listings of the local sporting life and try something you already enjoy, or something new—many tourists here never see more than the tennis courts, the golf courses, the gamefish fighting on the line, the topside or underside of these wonderful waters.

Visit the *Archives* and read old papers and see historical artifacts and exhibitions.

Go for a day-long picnic to a nearby deserted island, or take a moonlight cruise—both feature food and music, sea and romantic adventure.

Find a totally different Bahamian experience via a one-day or longer trek to one of the Family Islands.

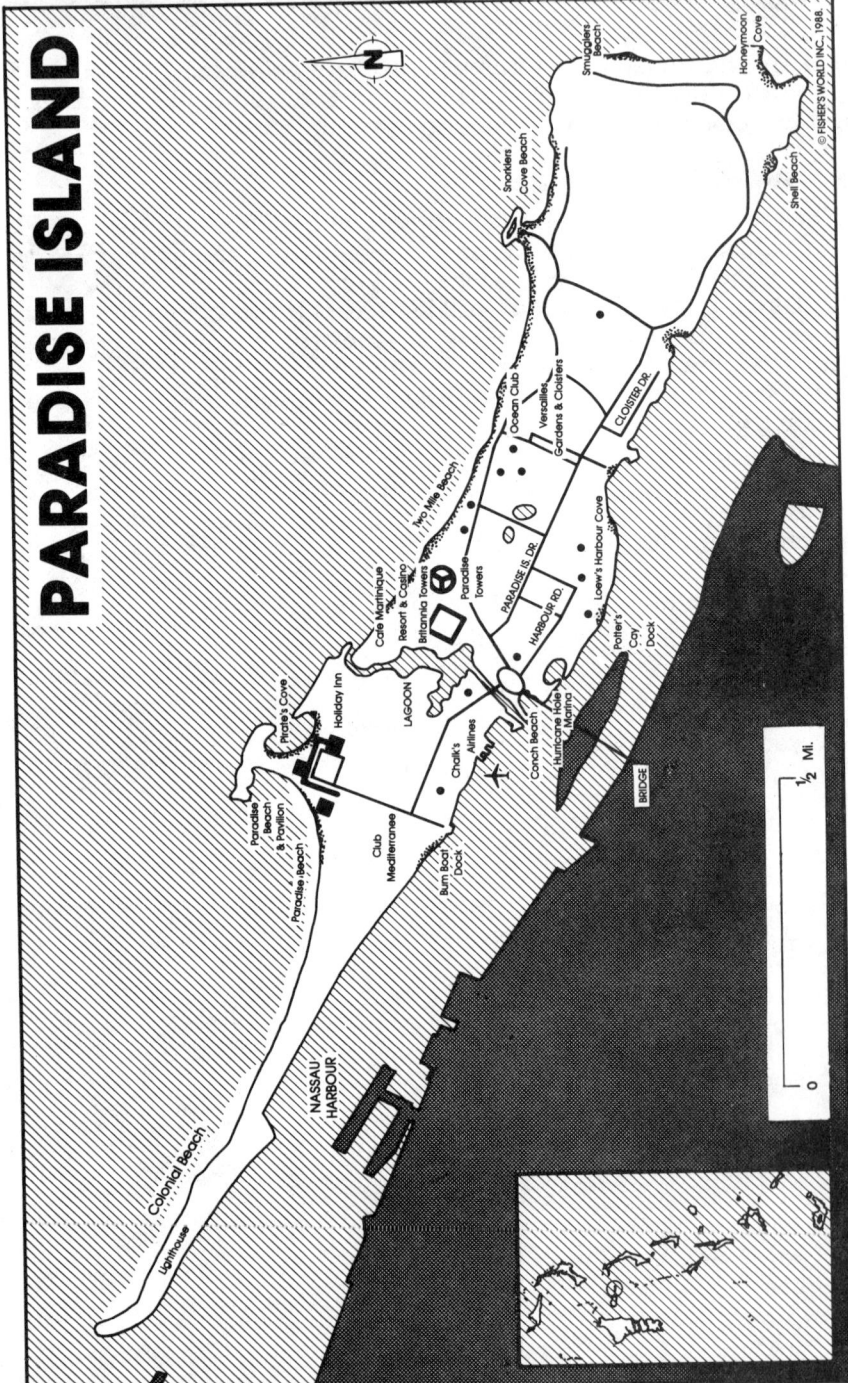

Author's Choice/New Providence- including Nassau, Cable Beach, Paradise Island

HOTELS

See the Travel Planner for explanation of my pricing system.

Britannia Towers Paradise Island. Phone (800)321-3000. Recent $20-million re-do left "city in itself" complex with 600 rooms, health clubs, shops, lagoon pool, maximum sports, snack and gourmet dining (including internationally famed *Cafe Martinique)*, disco, tours, activities, even dolphin shows. Two VIP concierge floors cost a bit more, (53 rooms, 11 suites). June to September *Goombay Festival* features Royal Police Band concerts, cruises, making of Junkanoo costumes and parading in them across isle, cabarets, and folklore performances; all with full tourist participation. *Extravagant.*

Buena Vista Hotel & Restaurant Delancy St. Nassau. PO Box N-564. Phone (809)322-2811 Near the heart of town. This 200-year-old colonial mansion offers romantic exclusivity: only 6 vast rooms are available in a rambling old world estate set amid five acres of gardens. Gracious "family guest" atmosphere. Superior food and service. Five-minute walk to town, beach. *Inexpensive.*

Crystal Palace/Cable Beach Casino Dual Carriageway, Cable Beach. P.O. Box N-4914. Phone (800)822-4200;in Canada (800)631-4200. This "$100-million playground" encompasses 700 oceanfront rooms on

18 Nassau and the Bahamas

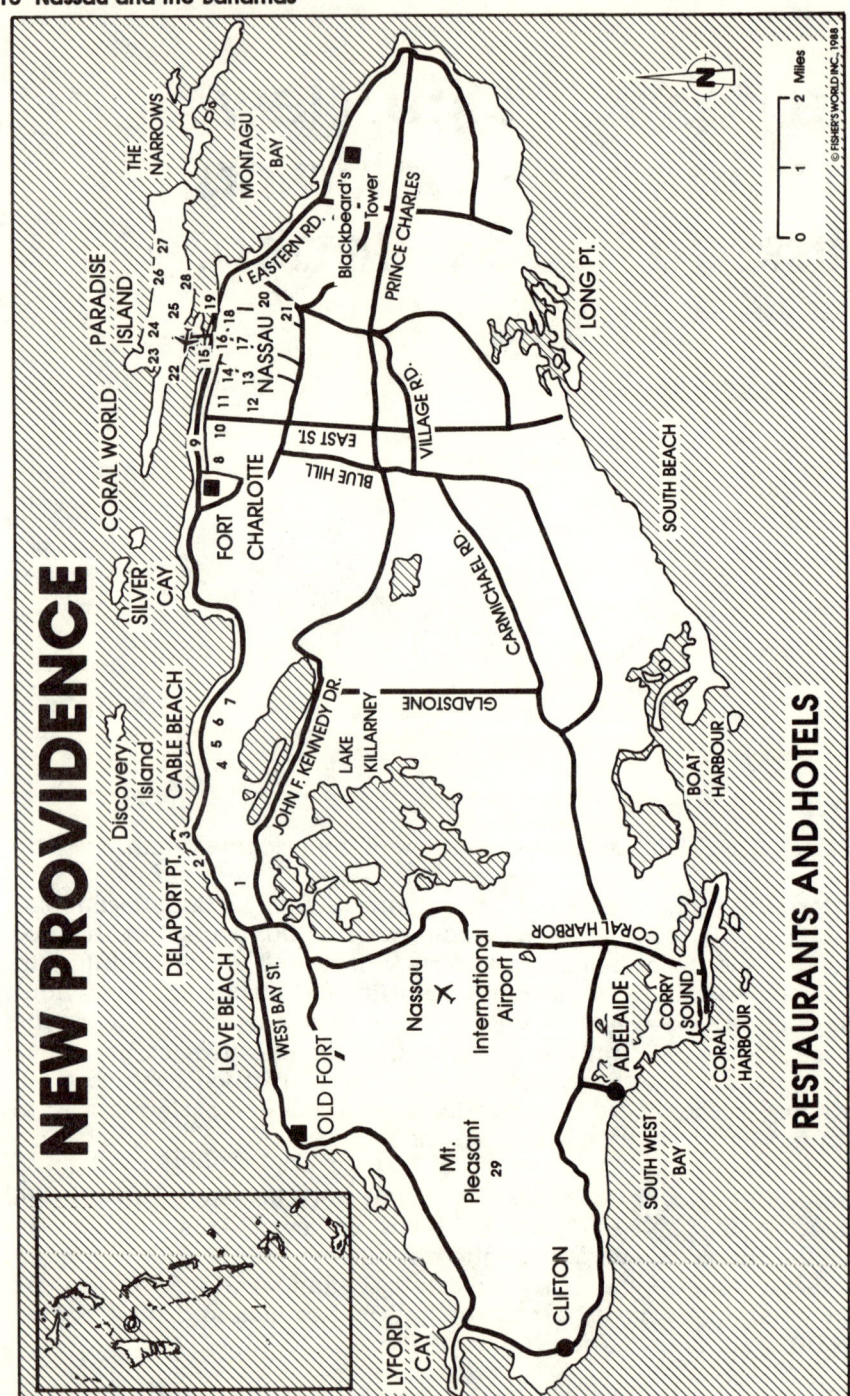

NEW PROVIDENCE

RESTAURANTS AND HOTELS

RECOMMENDED RESTAURANTS
NEW PROVIDENCE ISLAND

- 14 Buena Vista
- 4 Baccarat
- 27 Courtyard Tavern
- 12 Graycliff
- 26 Julie's
- 5 Regency Room
- 10 Ristorante Davinci
- 25 Gulfstream
- 23 Neptune's Table
- 5 Sole Mare
- 7 Rib Room
- 21 The Sun And...
- 24 Coyaba
- 13 Liz's
- 18 Parliament Terrace Cafe
- 11 Rose Lawn
- 8 Travellers Restaurant
- 9 Del Prado
- 15 Green Shutters
- 1 Roundhouse

RECOMMENDED HOTELS
NEW PROVIDENCE ISLAND

- 2 Bahamas Beach Inn
- 24 Britannia Towers
- 14 Buena Vista
- 1 Casuarinas
- 3 Cable Beach Manor
- 22 Club Med
- 5 Crystal Palace
- 12 Greycliff Hotel
- 23 Holiday Inn
- 28 Loews Harbour Cove Hotel
- 6 Nassau Beach Hotel
- 19 Nassau Harbour Club and Marina
- 27 Ocean Club & Tennis Resort
- 20 The Orchard
- 25 Paradise Island Resort & Casino
- 18 Parliament Hotel
- 17 Pilot House
- 4 Royal Bahamian
- 16 Sheraton-British Colonial Hotel
- 26 Sheraton-Grand Hotel
- 29 South Ocean Beach Hotel & Golf Club
- 7 Wyndham Ambassador Beach Hotel

nine floors, including minisuites and special rooms for the handicapped. One wing is devoted almost entirely to 50 extravagant concierge suites, outfitted with huge beds, robes and special amenities in the large baths, champagne and fruit, elegant furnishings, and large private balconies overlooking the beach. The astonishing lobby is four stories high; there are several restaurants and lounges/bars with a variety of entertainments, pools, golf courses, private pier for water sports, children's activities and babysitters. Separate sports complex with tennis, racquetball, squash, health/fitness facilities; separate marketplace for native and international buys, plus arcade shops; 20,000-square-feet of convention facilities with sophisticated extras like eight interpreter booths for simultaneous translations; 20,000-square-feet of casino, plus Vegas-type show. Complex includes the former Cable Beach Casino. *Extravagant.*

Graycliff Hotel Across from Goverment House. P.O. Box N-10246. Phone (312)883-1020; (800)423-4095. Central Nassau. The 235-year-old former pirate's home has 11 rooms (some in cottages) that have been frequented by royalty and celebrities. Spacious and gracious; libraries, parlors, pool, gardens, gourmet food. Relais de Chateaux member. *Extravagant.*

Nassau Beach Hotel Dual Carriageway. P.O. Box N-7756. Phone (809)327-7711: (800)255-5843. Cable Beach. Mature opulence in 408 rooms and suites, including two new penthouse suites and an all-inclusive Palm Club in one wing, with full-time club director to cater to guests' whims. Boasts most water sports (15) in Bahamas, all free; 9 tennis courts, (2 pros), gardens, beach, superb shopping arcade; popular bars, lounges and restaurants; weekly *Barbecue & Junkanoo Feast*; convention haven; small-desk, computerized, fast and personal check in/out. Terrific atmosphere and service. *Extravagant.*

Ocean Club & Tennis Resort Paradise Island. P.O. Box N-4777. Phone (800)321-3000. Pampering is de rigueur in this full-concierge, colonial manse once owned by multimillionaire Huntington Hartford. Champagne is provided in the limo that brings you from airport to resort, where the door to the manse is opened by a top-hatted doorman and each guest is greeted by the manager while checking in. "Preference" reservations at all Resorts International gourmet rooms and facilities, proper afternoon tea, bills presented on the eve of departure. Five villas, 12 tennis cabanas (good buys), and 53 rooms and suites with very personalized service. Ceiling fans and air conditioning plus minibars, terraces, his/her marble sinks, fresh flowers, and probably the only bidets in the Bahamas. Separate tennis club/pool building and 9 HarTru courts that host *Bahamas International Open Tennis* tourney. Private beach, magnificent *Versailles Gardens,* and ancient *Cloisters. Extravagant.*

Paradise Island Resort & Casino Phone (800)321-3000. Britannia Towers, Paradise Towers, and Paradise Club. This vast vacation complex caters to all tastes with 1,100 rooms and suites overlooking the ocean, pool, island, or lagoon via private balconies. Its 14 gourmet and specialty restaurants are flanked by 12 lounges with music and entertainment. There are shopping arcades, a beauty salon, health club and sauna, 12 day/night tennis courts, three miles of private beach, convention facilities, and round-the-clock action that focuses on both outdoor sports and indoor gaming at the casino billed as the "world's largest" of its type. "Paradise" or "Gourmet" Dine-Around Plans, Club Paradise Plus amenities, and assorted package trips are available, plus Vegas-type cabaret and championship golf. For VIPs, there's the three-story, 100-room Paradise Club concierge accommodations in rooms and suites, all with ocean view from private balconies. *Extravagant.*

The Royal Bahamian Hotel & Villas West Bay St. Cable Beach. P.O. Box N-7528. Phone (800)822-4200;in Canada (800)631-4200. A longtime favorite retreat for the rich, famous, royal, and political, this prestigious old hotel has been totally revived after years of collecting sags and wrinkles. Once again radiating "decadent splendor," the former Balmoral Beach has found numerous ways to pamper its guests. Total concierge service (including limos), afternoon tea, a private island, and all the amenities of private clubs. Townhouse villas have maid, butler, room service, pool, whirlpool, and lush garden settings. Deluxe guest rooms (145) in Manor House overlook the ocean. Also available are 23 one-bedroom suites. All sport of all Wyndham resorts nearby, plus shuttles to Crystal Palace/Cable Beach Casino. Magnificent spa with newest equipment; Living Earth mud baths (for great skin, arthritis, circulation, nervous conditions); massage by former therapist to Duke of Windsor, Charles Bowleg. Private beach, gourmet restaurants, 8,000-square feet of meeting space; laundry, valet, gift and sundry shops, and excellent staff. *Extravagant.*

Sheraton Grand Hotel P.O. Box SS. Phone (809)326-2011; (800)334-8484 Paradise Island. New in 1982, 360 beautiful, ocean-view rooms and suites with TV in 14-story, modern deluxe tower located near beach and casino. Also "Grandest" penthouse suite: 7,000-sqare feet, gold fixtures, etc. Full concierge services; 24-hour room service, excellent food, and snacks (don't miss breakfast buffet croissants). Activities program, shops, straw market; pool, private beach; snorkel/scuba gear/lessons; tennis, sports pro shop, rental sailboats, cars, cycles; disco, lounge, entertainment; ballroom, boardroom, conference rooms. *Extravagant.*

Wyndham Ambassador Beach Hotel Dual Carriageway Cable Beach. P.O. Box N-3026. Phone (800)822-4200; in Canada (800)631-4200. Free windsurfing with lessons; sailing, tennis, golf, squash, and racquetball are provided for guests in this 385-room newly redecorated hotel. Good dining, nice beach, straw market, lounges, and the Kid Conch Club (creative center for children). Thoughtful new management. Good packages available. *Extravagant.*

Holiday Inn   P.O. Box 6214. Phone (809)326-2101; toll free in U.S. (800)HOLIDAY. Paradise Island. Friendlier and swankier than many in this chain; 532 rooms view private beach. Friday-night staff show; nightly dancing to music of local and international artists. Floating bar in pool, good sports facilities, activities, great food, cheery staff. *Extravagant.*

Loews Harbour Cove Hotel   P.O. Box SS-6249. Phone 326-2561. Paradise Island. Some of the 250 rooms overlook interesting Nassau Harbour. Clean, neat, pleasant, with TVs in rooms, minibeach, eateries, and nightly entertainment, disco, shops, marina, dock, tennis, water sports, free water taxi to town. *Expensive.*

Sheraton-British Colonial Hotel   1 Bay St. P.O. Box N-7148. Phone (809)322-3301; (800)334-8484. Central Nassau. This stately pink landmark hotel, steeped in history, dominates eight acres with 255 rooms, pool, huge beach, all water sports, arcade with 22 shops including *Ho Jo* and *McDonald's,* fine patio bar/band; other eating and entertainment. Undergoing multimillion-dollar expansion. No room service except Continental breakfast. The 1982 *Never Say Never Again* patio bar was a set for James Bond (Sean Connery) movie filmed here. *Moderate to Extravagant.*

Divi Bahamas Beach Resort and Country Club   Formerly the South Ocean Beach Hotel & Golf Club. P.O.Box N-8191. Phone 326-4391; toll free (800)367-3484. Southwest of Nassau Airport. Located in exclusive area, with 120 rooms and fine facilities. U.S. PGA-rated, 72-par golf course (labeled best in region), hosts international pro-am tourneys. Also notable for its tennis, diving, and fishing. Pool, beach, game room, and TV lounge. Handy bus to town, rental bikes, scooters, cars. Executive conference facilities; packages available. Clubhouse gourmet dining, dancing, and entertainment. Dress code. *Extravagant.*

Cable Beach Inn   Formerly Bahamas Beach Hotel. Phone 327-7341. Over one hundred rooms arranged around a palm-fringed patio. Free bicycles, tennis, snorkeling lessons and gear, game room, health club/sauna, transport to town, many sports, two pools, video game room, liquor store, beach. Dining and popular disco. Casual. Own tours: to nightclubs, even to Haiti or Disney World. *Expensive.*

Cable Beach Manor   Dual Carriageway. P.O. Box N-8333. Phone(809)327-7785. Cable Beach. Pink, neat, and beautiful; a good home away from home, with 34 apartments of 1-3 rooms plus kitchens.

Lovely garden with palms, patio courtyard and pool. Table tennis, game room, TV, movies in lounge. Great beach. *Moderate to Expensive.*

Casuarinas Dual Carriageway. P.O. Box N-4016. Phone (809)327-7921. Cable Beach. Very personalized service. Ultramodern, clean, attractive units with kitchens for 2-6 persons; studios to 3-room townhouses; gift shop, minipool with whirlpool, kids' playground, game room, beach. Excellent, popular restaurants/lounge. Owned/operated by local legends: Nettie Symonette and seven cheery scions. *Expensive.*

Nassau Harbour Club Hotel & Marina East Bay St. Nassau. P.O. Box N-3703. Phone (809)323-3771/8. Fine relaxed, old waterfront haunt of the yachting crowd offers 50 rooms (some with kitchenettes), 65-slip full marina, superior dining, popular pub, lounge entertainment, launderette, and shops. No room service. Owns *Waterloo Lodge* across street, with dining, disco, and beauty shop. *Expensive.*

The Pilot House Hotel P.O.Box N-4941, Nassau. Phone 322-8431. 1985 revamp upgrades this hotel that's now under Buena Vista (five-star) management. On site of old harbor pilot's home, it's favored by yacht owners, race drivers, and sports enthusiasts. Offers 120 rooms including kitchenettes and luxury suites. Has full marina, bank, shops, patio, pool, free glass-bottom boats to town and beaches, dancing, entertainment, bar, and new *La Regatta* gourmet restaurant. *Expensive.*

Club Med P.O. Box N-7137. Phone (809)326-2640. Paradise Island. Internationally-famed vacation site for devotees of group fun. Casual, with intense tennis and many sports. Three hundred rooms. *Moderate.*

The Orchard P.O. Box N-1514, Village Road, Nassau. Phone 323-1297. Near Montague Beach. Extraordinarily pretty two acres of gardens sprinkled with roomy efficiencies and cottages (with kitchens) for 1-6 persons. Pool, laundry, barbecue gear. Casual and cheery. *Inexpensive.*

Parliament Hotel P.O. Box N-7530. Phone (809)322-2836. Across from government buildings near *Rawson Square*, Nassau's oldest still existing hotel (circa 1938), offers 13 rooms in interesting homey building that rises above very popular terrace cafe. *Inexpensive.*

Yoga Retreat P.O. Box N-7550.Paradise Island. Phone 326-2902. Truly for yoga enthusiasts, with 36 rooms/cottages, vegetarian dining, private beach, pool, tennis, snorkeling, and Swami Sankaranada. *Inexpensive.*

RESTAURANTS

Throughout the Nassau/Paradise area, reservations are almost always necessary. These listings are in order of preference. **Note:** Try Dine-Around Plans at both Cable Beach and Paradise Island hotels.

Buena Vista Delancey St. Phone 322-2811. Handsomely prepared superb nouvelle cuisine and Bahamian dishes, served with creative flair, attention to detail, and mellow singing guitarist to boot. Buena Vista offers consistently fine lunch or dinner in a charming atmosphere. Seating on the large enclosed patio amid garden greenery, or in the sparkling indoor cafe. Fine wine list. *Extravagant*—and worth it.

Baccarat In Royal Bahamian Hotel. French haute cuisine with specialties such as sauteed shrimp in creamy dill sauce, duckling consommee, asparagus tips and truffles salad, or iced cream of smoked salmon soup. Jackets required. Reservations a must. *Extravagant.*

Courtyard Terrace Ocean Club & Tennis Resort on Paradise Island. Offers elegant dinner dining under the stars, amid palms and greenery, fountains and soft music. Romantic, tropical setting is matched by delicious Continental fare. Careful, patient service. An investment in pleasure. Jacket required. *Extravagant.*

Graycliff Across from Governmaent House, Phone 322-2796. Delicious Bahamian and Continental fare served to discerning patrons in an elegant old-estate hotel. Wine cellar has Nassau's biggest collection: 70,000 bottles, some dating from the 1800s. Wine prices range from $12 to $5,500. Fabulous desserts and coffees. *Extravagant.*

Julie's Sheraton Grand Hotel. Freshly modern and discreetly luxurious, with fine selections of Continental and Bahamian fare. An extensive wine list. Very attentive service. *Extravagant.*

Regency Room Crystal Palace Resort/Cable Beach Hotel & Casino. Deliciously French. Dinner only. Jackets required. Good wine selection and cheerful, attentive service. *Extravagant.*

Ristorante Da Vinci West Bay St. Central Nassau. Phone 322-2748. Excellent Italian and French cuisine. Homemade pastas, wines from $14 to $250, soft piano and strings, and the best service in the Bahamas. Dinner only. Jackets required. *Expensive to Extravagant.*

Gulfstream Paradise Island Hotel & Casino. Hovering waiters will serve you vegetarian, fowl, beef and other such meals, but seafood really reigns here, from oysters Rockefeller to robust conch chowder. Sinfully rich desserts. *Expensive.*

Neptune's Table Paradise Island, Holiday Inn. Phone 326-2101. Extensive seafood, plus Bahamian and American dishes. Well-stocked salad bar. Live piano music. Jackets required. *Expensive.*

Sole Mare Crystal Palace/Cable Beach. Victorian ambience, soft lighting, superb northern Italian cuisine featuring homemade pastas. Fine wines and service. *Expensive.*

The Pasta Kitchen Wyndham Ambassador Beach Hotel. Charming new restaurant with cosy ambiance. Homemade Italian specialities served with extraordinary friendliness. *Moderate to Expensive.*

Sun And ... Fort Montague area. Phone 323-1205. Walk through a romantic flowered courtyard to enter the intimate bar and posh dining areas of this lovely mansion. Rum cheesecake and a special coffee are a delicious close to a lovely meal. Prompt service. *Expensive.*

Coyaba Britannia Towers, Britannia Beach Hotel, Paradise Island. Phone 326-3000. Headquarters for good Cantonese and Polynesian dining. Good service, ambitious decor. *Moderate to Expensive.*

Liz's Midtown, Elizabeth Avenue. Phone 322-4780. Nice decor, intimate atmosphere in interesting locale. Bahamian dinners and good service. *Expensive.*

Parliament Terrace Cafe Parliament Hotel. Bahamian fare emphasizing seafood specialties served with care to loyal customers and visitors alike. Dine inside or on a terrace amid palms and greenery. Legendary frothy drinks. Try Papa Sam's Chicken and guava shortcake. Old island songs by guitarist. Lunch and Breakfast served, too. *Inexpensive.*

Regata Room Pilot House Hotel. Phone 322-8431. Bahamian, Continental, and American favorites on lunch and dinner menus, and a weekly luau feast that's formidable. Small dance floor and band. Nightly gourmet and seafood specialties. Attentive service amid nautical decor. *Moderate to Expensive.*

Roselawn Cafe Midtown, Bank Lane. Phone 325-1018. Charming, airy old home delights diners at indoor tables or under spreading shade trees on patio. Daily specials, plus antipasto, lasagne, crisp salads, poached salmon, omelettes, even pizzas. Great desserts. Smart service. More elegant at night; also popular for late-night fare. *Moderate.*

Traveller's Rest West Bay Street. Phone 327-7633. It's well worth the ride to visit this special place offering excellent Bahamian food and relaxing, personal service. Open for lunch and dinner, it's even more packed than usual during Sunday jam sessions from about 4 to 8 P.M.

Try conch fritters, turtle steak, and marvelous guava duff for dessert. There is shop on the premises. *Moderate.*

Del Prado El Greco Hotel. West Bay St. Phone 325-0324. Cloister yourself in the ambience of old Spain and devour international fare, often prepared to order at your table. Fine service. *Expensive.*

Green Shutters Parliament St., in central Nassau. Phone 325-5702. A snug pub where home cooking means everything from bangers and mash (the English name for sausage and mashed potatoes), to Bahamian conch dishes. Choose indoor or patio seating for lunch or dinner. *Inexpensive to Moderate.*

Round House Restaurant Casuarinas, Cable Beach. Boasts VIP popularity for good Bahamian cookery (try sauteed snapper and Willie's Surprise). Camaraderie during dinner. Attentive service at breakfast and lunch, too. *Moderate.*

Note: For breakfast or day and night good deli foods, try Cable Beach Casino's *Back Stage Deli.* Many inexpensive, popular restaurants feature consistently good food with a native flair: *Bahamian Kitchen* on Trinity Place, midtown, heads the list. Others are: *Three Queens, Shoal, Poinciana, Fish Net, Reef, F & S Take Away, Jane's Take Away,* and *Casablanca.* At *Captain Nemo's,* savor seafood and native fare while watching harbor activities near John Alfred Wharf. *Smiley's Place* plies you with cool drinks and local treats in a seaside Western Esplande park. For picnic fixings, try local markets, fast food eateries, *Village Gourmet* in Paradise Village Shopping Center, even *Health Corner* or the *Candy Bar* in International Bazaar.

In the Sheraton Arcade, the *Ice Cream Place* has the best ice cream in town and next door sandwiches are tasty and hearty. Nearby are *Dunkin' Donuts, Ho Jo To Go,* and *Howard Johnson's.* You'll find two *McDonald's,* three *Burger Kings, Lum's,* eight *Kentucky Fried Chicken sites* and two *Chicken Unlimited* shops.

Note: Look for new classic French restaurant in Frilsham House, at Nassau Beach Hotel.

ENTERTAINMENT

Performing Arts English chamber ensembles, American opera singers, and European pianists perform here regularly, at the invitation of groups like the Nassau Music Society and Bahamas Music Society. Domestic entertainment features productions by groups such as Bahamas Drama Circle, Nassau Players, Bahamas School of Theatre and the University Players—all amateur.

Domestic singers active around town include the Nassau Operatic Society, the Lucayan Chorale and Diocesan Choral, the Renaissance Singers and Chamber Singers. There are presentations by several gospel groups, James Catalyn & Friends, the Children of Atlantis Dance Troupe, National School of Dance, the Institute of Arts and Nassau Civic Ballet. All of these are worth a visit. Some performances are held in the auditoriums of large resorts, some in the *Dundas Civic Center* (newly renovated on Mackey Street), and Nassau Civic Ballet presents students dancing on the patio stage.

Whether domestic or import, notice of a major performance usually is posted about town and advertised in newspapers, with tickets available to the public.

Gambling *Paradise Island Resort & Casino* gaming room boasts tables for blackjack, American roulette, dice, American baccarat (Punto Banco), plus Big Six Wheels and 1,000 state-of-the-art slot machines. Professionals run this show seven days a week for players who are reputedly heavy rollers. Check out *Salon Prive*—a casino within a casino. The focus is on high stakes. (Jackets required). *Crystal Palace/Cable Beach Casino* , operated by Carnival (Cruise Line) Leisure, Inc., provides 21, American roulette, Las Vegas craps, and American baccarat. Also try Big Six Wheels or any of 585 electronic slots that include nickel machines and a giant Big Bertha. (Both casinos have computerized slots with progressive jackpots.) Clean, modern room draws mixed crowds under its blinking lights and neon signs. Slots open 9 A.M. and tables at noon; closing time varies from 4 to 6 A.M. **Note:** Law forbids Bahamians to gamble in these casinos.

Shows and Revues This small resort city has an amazing number of lively nighttime offerings, including native shows and Vegas-style revues. Native shows typically feature Bahamian Goombay, Caribbean Calypso, and international pop favorites sung and played by local groups, plus limbo contortionists, glass eaters, glass walkers, and fire dancers. The best show in town stars "Peanuts" Taylor, world-traveling master who recently reopened his *Drum Beat Club*, siting it on West Bay Street near the Sheraton, instead of Over the Hill, where it reigned for many years. "Peanuts" presents a professional, well-paced variety show, with fine musicians and talent. Thursdays at the Nassau Beach Hotel are devoted to *Barbecue & Junkanoo Feast* in Pineapple Place restaurant, with dancing after the show. *Le Cabaret*, adjacent to Paradise Island's casino, holds audience attention with a million dollar Vegas-style revue incorporating specialty acts. (Dinner is served). *Les Fantastiques*, at Crystal Palace, skips the gamut from Broadway favorites to modern laser light shows. Dance drama by fine performers mixes with comics, et al, for an all-round fun show. Feast first at the casino's Ristorante Sole Mare (expensive) or Back Stage Deli, or try the elegant supper club overlooking stage and theater seating.

Discos Among the many discos available, two current top favorites are the *Palace* and *Cinnamon's*. Off Bay Street on Elizabeth Avenue, the *Palace* is a big, modern, mirrored bit of elegance with attractive crowds enjoying the ambience from 9 P.M. to about 4 A.M. (except Mondays). In the Nassau Beach Hotel, light and sound reverberate from the lofty ceilings to the sunken dance floor of *Cinnamon's*, where an appreciative audience cavorts from 9 P.M. to about 2 A.M. (except Sundays). Both places cater to a good mix of locals and tourists; both feature fine special performers; both charge $8 to $10 cover. On Paradise Island, try the swinging pace of *Club Pistache* at Britannia Towers, or *Tradewinds Lounge* at Paradise Towers; for more elan, it's the sophisticated *Le Paon*, at the Grand Hotel on Paradise or at the same site, the *Junkanoo Lounge* offers two different shows nightly (10:45 P.M., 12:45 A.M. except Sundays), and dance music from 9 P.M.

Pubs and Bars Nassau Beach Hotel also has a popular *Rum Keg Bar*, with live music and a lively clientele. *Charley Charley's*, on Delancy, is worth a visit. Two local places with ardent regulars are *Green Shutters*, downtown, and the *Poop Deck*, near Paradise Island Bridge. For good music, try the *Never Say Never Again* at Sheraton British Colonial Hotel.

Miscellany Local forms of entertainment include a large variety of fairs and bazaars, gospel sings and church functions, animal shows, and occasional strikes that become massive sing-ins. For an inside look at Bahamian life styles, watch newspapers for notices and attend some of these goings-on. There's also television (local channel with local, U.S., and European shows, plus Miami channels), radio, and a few motion picture houses. Those famous old native night spots that for years drew tourists to neighborhoods Over the Hill have now moved beachside or died out.

SHOPPING The shops I list here are to give you an indication of where to go for specific goods, in case you don't want to roam around.

Antiques For prints, dolls, books, giftware, jewelry and other items, look into *Francis Peek*, *The Heirloom*, and *Balmain Antiques*. (Also see reproductions, often available at $25 to $80 when originals run $100 to $1,000.)

Art Artist Brent Malone operates *The Temple Art Gallery* on East Bay. *Nassau Glass Art Gallery* has a huge selection of originals and reproductions by local and other artists; also frames, packs, and ships art. *Nassau Art Gallery* specializes in originals and prints of known Bahamian artists such as Elyse and Wayde Taylor. Prices range from $250 to $7,500.

Books Extensive selections at *The Island Shops* and *Nassau Shop*. Also try the *Anglo-American Book Store* in Nassau Arcade and the *Paradise Island Drug Store*.

Brass Collector's items, large and small, at *Brass & Leather Shop*.

Cameras Check huge stock around town and at *John Bull, Colombian Emeralds, Jade Dolphin, Pipe of Peace,* and *Patrick's Camera and Watch Shop.*

China, Crystal, Giftware Found in large and small shops all over the city, with good assortments at *Bernards, Solomon's Mines, Treasure Traders,* the *Crystal Shop,* and *Francis Peek.*

Coins and Stamps *Coin of the Realm* carries collector merchandise. The post office has First Day covers and stamp sets. Banks have collectible coins and bills.

Cosmetics Many hotel and specialty shops provide wide ranges of international cosmetics, but for Clinique products, it's only the *Beauty Spot/Perfume Shop.* For Diana Drummond Skin Food and Creams, it's the *Scottish Shop.*

Eyeglasses *Optique Shoppe* and *Imperial Optical* sell sunglasses and prescription lenses with designer frames.

Fabrics and Linens *Bahamas Hand Prints* has a workshop/showroom in Nassau, and its goods are sold in many shops and stores, as are fine Androsia Batiks (try *Mademoiselle).* Other decorative and table fabrics are found at the *Linen Shop, The English Shop,* and *Distinctive Shop.*

Jewelry Gems and "jungque" are sold in *Coin of the Realm, Nassau Shop,* hotel and Bay Street shops, and in international emporiums like *Greenfire Emeralds Ltd., Lords Ltd.,* and *Colombia Emeralds.* Of particular interest is *Black Coral And...* featuring fine black coral pieces created by the noted sculptor Bernard K. Passman; many unique designs set with gems and gold are made to order (also see his sterling flatware with black coral handles). Turtleshell items (you can't take into the United States) and jewelry from conch and whelk shells are well made by Johnson Brothers Ltd., which sells through its own shop and others. Bahamas Conch Shell Jewelry Ltd. items retail at *Sea Garden Shop.* For factory close-out sales, head for *Discount Warehouse.*

Knitwear Cashmeres and European goods are excellent buys at *Trader Vic's,* the *Scottish Shop, Ambrosine, Distinctive Shop, Nassau Shop, Island Shops,* and *Amanda's.*

Leather *Las Tiendas, Brass & Leather Shop, Scottish Shop* and *Pipe of Peace* offer assorted leather goods. Also: *Galaxy Shoes,* accessories.

Liquors and Spirits Though these are sold in many places, *Bahama Blenders, Butler & Sands, Robertson & Symonette,* and *Maury Roberts Co. Ltd.* seem to have large and varied stocks of local and international brands.

Men's Wear *Distinctive Shop, Trader Vic's, Scottish Shop, Nassau Shop, Relax-Sir, Island Shops, Caribah Originals* and *Ambrosine*

Perfumes Almost everywhere. Try *Bahamas Fragrance & Cosmetic Factory, Lightbourne's Perfume Centre, Nassau Shop, The Perfume Shop, The Paris Shop, Island Shops,* and the *Beauty Spot.*

Prescriptions *City Pharmacy* and *Cole Thompson,* both in several locations.

Straw Work Aside from market and street vendors, some shops carry the work of Long Island's Ivy Simms—look for and value it.

Souvenirs *Jackpot* has good selections; also *Pyfrom's*, for T-shirts.
Tobacco *Pipe of Peace, Nassau Shop, Island Shops.*
Watches See stores listed under Jewelry and Cameras.
Women's Fashions M*ademoiselle, Chez Mizpah, Caprice, Coles of Nassau, Caribah Originals, Ambrosine, Nassau Shop, Island Shops,* and *Palm Cottage. The Beautiful Woman,* on Christie Street, specializes in sizes 14 to 32 1/2.

MUSEUMS The fledgling *Archives,* assembles and displays historical exhibitions. There's also an active historical society, with collections of papers and artifacts, and regular publications. The *Junkanoo Art Gallery/Museum* near *Fort Fincastle,* displays old costumes and gives demonstrations of how they're made. There are paintings, prints, souvenirs, gifts, and T-shirts—all carrying out the Junkanoo theme.

HISTORIC BUILDINGS and SITES For more details on these places, stop by Tourist Information Centres.

Museum-quality statuary, and a 14th-century Augustine monastery that was brought here and rebuilt stone by stone, combine to form *Versailles Gardens and Cloister* on Paradise Island. Conceived and completed by millionaire art lover Huntington Hartford, they have been shamefully neglected since the island he developed was purchased by its present owners. Still, they are worth a visit.

Blackbeard's Tower, now in ruins, supposedly was where Blackbeard (Edward Teach) kept lookouts to watch for possible prey. The expansive view from the ground is even better from atop the ruins.

Christ Church Cathedral now occupies the site of Nassau's first parish church (Anglican), c. 1840.

Country villages around New Providence Island include *Adelaide, Carmichael, Fox Hill* and *Gambier,* each settled on land distributed to newly freed slaves.

Fort Charlotte (c. 1787-1789) is the largest of three forts built to defend young colonial Nassau. Guarding the western waterfront, it has open battlements, a moat, dungeons and underground passages, and cannon never fired in anger. Great views.

Fort Fincastle, with its ship's bow design facing the city, was built in 1793 by the governor, the Earl of Dunmore. Used more as a signal tower than anything else, it now stands partially in ruins.

Fort Montague is the oldest of the three existing forts, dating to 1741. (Between here and Montague Beach are areas for concessions, bands and dancing, swimsuit changes, and parking.)

Government buildings congregate around the serene statue of the young Queen Victoria. *Houses of Parliament,* the *Colonial Secretary's Office* and the *Supreme Court* display lasting beauty of colonial design, and a uniquely octagonal, balconied building, now the *Public Library,* has booklined cells that once restricted prisoners in what was the town jail.

Government House is home of Her Majesty's personal representative, the governor general of the Bahamas. Its tall front stairway is interrupted by a statue of a resolute Christopher Columbus, monument to the man who discovered the New World by landing in the Bahamas.

Gregory Arch, also pink and quoined with white, hovers over the entrance to Grant's Town, an Over the Hill settlement built on land given to former slaves. *Jumbey Village*, on Blue Hill Road, is made up of old slave huts, redone and thatched, with outdoor ovens and stony barns. Not far is a little museum, and nearby is *Angelo's Art Centre* with old-time arts and crafts paraphernalia.

Queen's Staircase, cut into solid limestone rock by slaves centuries ago, offered protected escape from Fort Fincastle (see above). Today its entrance is well planted with trees and flowers, and there's a waterfall starting near the top of the 102-foot climb of some sixty-five steps (water shortages usually cut off the cascades of water here).

Sheraton British Colonial Hotel stands on the site of *Fort Nassau*, where both Blackbeard and Woodes Rogers lived for a while (at slightly different times of course). After the fort's completion in 1697, this first building for defense was razed and rebuilt often, eventually becoming a barracks before being torn down to make way for the first hotel that rose here, burned, rose again and was extended to its present, enormous size. The handsome statue of Woodes Rogers here depicts him with full jaw and ankle, though the swashbuckler had lost half of both before arriving to route Nassau's pirates. There's also a replica of *Blackbeard's Well*, where the brigand supposedly hid from officialdom.

St. Augustine's Monastery was designed by Father Jerome, a revered figure whose several churches on Long Island and Cat Island attract many viewers. It is both school and cloister.

Woodes Rogers Walk borders a busy waterfront where that first royal governor stepped ashore.

OTHER SIGHTS The shopping district of *Bay Street*, running from the Sheraton British Colonial Hotel for several blocks eastward, is one of Nassau's most colorful regions.

Rawson Square, is a focus of activity sandwiched between government buildings and Prince George Wharf. You will find horse-drawn surreys for a tour of the area and a plethora of dawn-till-dusk activities.

Seafloor Aquarium features sharks, turtles, and other sea creatures in huge tanks, plus daily shows starring talented dolphins and sea lions.

Straw Market, where natives sell handwoven wares plus other artsy items, recently relocated from open air Rawson Square to the four-storied Market Plaza indoor stalls.

SPECTACLES and DISPLAYS The *Changing of the Guard* is a Nassau tradition accompanied by the Royal Bahamas Police Force Band, which creates its own spectacle wherever it goes, nattily dressed in spiked pith helmets, stiffly starched snow-white jackets, red-piped dark trousers plus an occasional red sash and tigerskin tabard. The band plays as well as it looks and is known for tooting Goombay rhythms as well as military marches. Aside from playing often for royalty, this band bedazzled New York World's Fair visitors, opened the 1968 Olympic Games in Mexico, and twice copped top prize (1978, 1980) in the National Police Parade at Aquidneck, Rhode Island. Don't miss any chance to see these star performers, particularly every other Saturday, when they sound support for guard rotations at government house.

In January, April, July, and October, pomp and ceremony mark the quarterly opening of Bahamian *Supreme Court Assizes*. Done up in the white powdered wig and scarlet robe traditional to British courts, the chief justice of the Bahamas proceeds to the courthouse, stopping to inspect a Royal Bahamas Police Force Honor Guard uniformed like the band mentioned above. Check for exact dates.

Junkanoo is a colorful festival beating out the old year and ringing in the new, literally, with goatskin drums and cow bells December 26 and January 1. January's also the month of the annual *Red Cross Ball*. February brings the *Heart Ball* plus the *Miami-Nassau Yacht Race*, and March hails the *Miami-Nassau Sailing Race*, and the *Red Cross Fair*.

Bahamas *Goombay Holiday*, July through August, is a summer-long fling of concerts, street dances, art and folklore shows, parades, and anything else anyone can dream up that seems like fun and can be accompanied by native Goombay music. During those months, *Independence Celebrations* extend for a week of fireworks and hoopla, and the *Commonwealth Fair* delights all. August's second Tuesday is set aside as *Fox Hill Day*, when residents of that old settlement laud the abolition of slavery a week later than Nassauvians, because back then it took a week for the news of freedom to reach them.

Discovery Day Regatta is Nassau's way of commemorating Columbus each October. November brings *Remembrance Day*, plus pilots from around the world for a *Flying Treasure Hunt*. Then December sports the *Miami-Nassau Power Boat Race* and *Junkanoo*. There are many more special days in Nassau, including sporting tournaments and championships too numerous to list. Check for details with your local Bahamas Tourist Office or the Bahamas Ministry of Tourism. Public holidays for all the Bahamas are listed in the Travel Planner.

TOURS Most hotels have desks linked to one or more sightseeing companies, many of which belong to the Bahamas Sightseeing & Tour Operators Association. According to leaders in this group, the top tourist attraction in Nassau is the city itself, seen on half-day or extended trips to its historic forts, romantic gardens, quaint neighborhoods, and native markets. Other favorites include the *Robinson Crusoe* or *Treasure Island* jaunts to a small island. Nightclub tours are big, too, with samples of the best local entertainment plus drinks, and options of adding dinner and more shows. Water-keyed offerings also rank high and range from a three-hour cruise on a huge catamaran, with swimming and snorkeling, Calypso musicians, and food and drink, to six hours of ocean sailing that include lunch, swims, rum punch, and a chance to try your skills at the helm. Glass-bottom boat trips are always pleasurable here, whether via conventional craft or the streamlined new *Nautilus*. Getting into and under the water, for a closer look via snorkeling and scuba gear, has become so popular that several firms provide adventurous tours. If you yearn to go under but for some reason don't want to get your hair wet, try hard-hat diving with *Hartley's Reef Cruises;* breathe air tubed into the head-covering hat and walk the ocean floor regardless of age or swimming abilities.

All these experiences are available from several firms, including *Majestic Tours*, P.O. Box N-1041, Nassau, and *Tropical Travel Tours*, Official Gray Line Representative and ASTA affiliate, P.O. Box N-448, Nassau. Contact them directly, or through your local travel agent.

SPORTS

Nassauvians have a passion for sports whether played by professionals or amateurs. Professional events, amateur tournaments, championships, and spectaculars are present in seemingly endless numbers. With teams usually sponsored by local firms, and participants of all ages, competitive events are tackled with zest and vigor. There are local and inter-island championships in basketball, baseball, softball and volleyball; the Bahamas Amateur Athletic Association conferences are the talk of the man on the street; the Nassau Darts League alone boasts twenty-two different teams; the Commonwealth American Football League sponsors an annual Bottom Bowl. There also are associations, teams and heavy competition for bowling, boxing, bridge, chess, cricket, cycling, golf, hockey, horsemanship, pool, roller skating, rugby, running, sailing, softball, squash, soccer, swimming (including a 35-mile *Ocean Marathon Swim* from Nassau to Andros), table tennis, whist, and dozens of other favored activities. To watch or even participate in some of these, get more details from your nearest BTO, the Ministry of Tourism/Sports Division, or Nassau newspapers and other media. The same sources can fill you in on which golf, tennis, and boating events bring in top pros from around the world. Nassauvians also keep up with international sports, frequently crowding into bars to watch televised American sports shows.

Active sports fans will find Nassau a true haven, with large collections of facilities and similarly inclined participants—locals and visitors, from novice to pro. Four championship golf courses vie for pro-am tourneys, and there's an additional nine-hole course in town. There are some eighty tennis courts, frequented by top-ranking international players, who seem most at home on the nine courts of the Ocean Club Hotel on Paradise Island. The horse set is found at *Camperdown*; *Happy Trails Stables* offer riding tours.

Many tourists come here strictly for sun and water sports, so there's a proliferation of professionals catering to snorkelers, skin-divers, and scuba enthusiasts, offering everything from rental equipment (including cameras) to certification courses, charter dives, night dives, reef dives, wall dives and exploration of ocean "blue holes." Boating receives equal attention, be it in the yachting or sunfish category, and fishing is superior, whether the goal is a bonefish or a deep-sea giant weighing hundreds of pounds. Topping it all off are waterskiing and its relatives: parasailing and windsurfing. Each type of activity mentioned is the frequent focus of tournaments, championships, rallies, and the like, and a full calendar of these special, often annual, events is yours from the sources noted above.

Shell seekers reputedly find best success on the southern side of New Providence or the eastern tip of Paradise, though you must be early or find every beach picked clean.

GETTING AROUND

In the Bahamas, one form of transport is unique to Nassau: the horse-drawn surrey. This relaxing mode of seeing the town costs $8 to $10 per hour, with lesser rates for shorter time periods, and tips expected. Carriages are easily found, lined up at Rawson Square and off Bay Street on Frederick Street.

Other local forms of tourist transport include taxis, water taxis and ferry services to and from Paradise Island, jitney buses, and rental automobiles, motor scooters and bicycles. Details about all these, as well as current price ranges, are in the Travel Planner section, along with information and rates for renting boats and chartering yachts and aircraft.

Note: Expect a $2 toll when riding over the bridge to enter Paradise Island. From the airport to hotels along the beach, in town, and on Paradise, taxi fares will range from approximately $6 to $18, plus a customary fifteen percent tip.

Junkanoo
by Lee Hays

In olden times, i.e., before television, a large portion of my misspent youth was idled away in motion-picture palaces where, for a few hours and a few cents, one could be relieved of the dreariness of the daily routines of chidhood, specifically school. There, for a dime, in addition to the feature film, one was treated to a vast array of so-called short subjects. These usually included previews of coming attractions, newsreels, cartoons, comedy shorts, serials, and travelogues.

In my recollection, these travelogues always began with a panoramic picture of sea meeting shore bathed in the brilliance of a rising sun, while a disembodied mellifluous-voiced narrator would say something like, "From the beginning of time, the tides of the Indian Ocean have washed the primitive shores of this land. Today, the island paradise of..."

Eventually I grew up and was able to visit an island paradise. On my first trip to the Bahamas, I was extremely fortunate, for I happened to be there the week after Christmas.

In Nassau, on New Providence Island, and in West End, a dozen or so miles from Freeport on Grand Bahama Island, you'll find on Boxing Day and New Year's Day the traditional Junkanoo festival. West End is a small town at the end of the road that leads west from Freeport. Its location means that, if nothing else, you are guaranteed a rather spectacular sunset. With or without the sunset, Junkanoo is spectacular in itself.

As celebrated in the Bahamas, the Junkanoo festival is a not-too-distant relation of Mardi Gras in New Orleans and Carnival in Rio. It is a time of jubilation, reflected in and by the brilliant, humorous, sensual costumes and the background music accompanying them, the Junkanoo music.

The original Junkanoo festivals were one of the few times when the African slaves could drink and make merry legally, and it is said that their wild costumes with the vivid masks and makeup were used by the slaves as a way to disguise themselves while exacting revenge and settling grudges against masters and fellow slaves. Today, however, Junkanoo is considerably more tame and is, in fact, a big, good-natured, joyous party.

The Bahamas, as a series of large and small islands, have abundant harbors sheltered from the wind and sea. This made them a natural haven for pirates who preyed on the shipping between Europe and North and Central America. In more recent times, during Prohibition, rivers of booze were shipped to the States. A great many rum-runners operated out of West End because of its proximity to Miami, about 60 miles due west. And it is at West End, not far from Freeport on Grand Bahama Island, where the most authentic Junkanoo festival takes place. Tourists are encouraged to come for the festivities at West End and in Nassau, but one might say there is a local celebration despite the fact that strangers abound. At West End especially, one can see and hear the collective madness that embodies the spirit of the festival. And one can also join in, if only in a small way, as the all-night party goes on.

At least that was my decision. I wasn't going to just watch all this fun and stand idly by; I felt an uncontrollable urge to participate. Of course

I didn't have a costume, but I quickly realized that not all the revelers were outlandishly outfitted for the occasion. And it didn't seem to be keeping them from having a good time. So I joined the throng dancing in the street. (Mind you, at this point I was completely sober.)

I was pleased to discover that even sans costume I was welcomed with open arms. Literally. Before I could spell Bahamas I was whirling about in a kind of conga line with a crowd of people on a narrow street. It occurred to me that I might be making a fool of myself, but then I thought, Why not? When in Rome, and off I went. The next few hours are impossible to describe adequately. For one thing, I didn't remain clear-headed for long. There was the color and the music and, ultimately, the rum, although God knows where that came from. It was a conspiracy, a conspiracy to see that I, although definitely not a native, had a rip-roaring good time.

The next morning (well, afternoon), I decided to find out more about Junkanoo (albeit in a more sedate fashion). Fortunately, I queried the one person in West End who had the answers.

Austin Grant, who runs one of the hotels, is a dedicated Junkanoo fanatic. He's also one of the organizers of the annual event, preparations for which begin a year in advance. He's also an authority on the music, and he owns one of the largest private collections of Junkanoo costumes on the islands, many of which are on display in his hotel. Grant comes from Nassau and has been involved with Junkanoo since he was a boy.

Most of the costumes are made of paper. "The reason," he explains, "is that originally the people couldn't afford to make their costumes out of cloth and so they experimented with paper." Today the paper is often attached to a wire frame, but the concept remains the same. And, despite the paper, many people take the better part of a year to design and make their costumes. Nevertheless, they only use them once, which makes for a lot of leftovers and Austin Grant's collection.

There are also Junkanoo costume competitions with large cash prizes. Usually groups are formed, often with two or three hundred members, and they spend as much as $10,000 on an entry. This kind of investment is financed by local fund-raising efforts such as bazaars, barbecues, and lotteries. Frequently, an entire village will participate and have only one entry, albeit a quality one.

As for the Junkanoo music, even musicians have a hard time describing it to the layman. Peanuts Taylor, who owns a nightclub in Nassau, is a native Bahamian who spent a number of years in the U.S. as a drummer for Nat King Cole. After a stint in Hollywood, he returned home to open his club where he performs nightly on the native drums.

This is Taylor's description. "The Junkanoo beat is more African. The Calypso you hear in the island, that's more Latin, but the Junkanoo beat is African. It's just drums and cowbells and the drums play the African downbeat and that's why it's so pulsating. It moves and when you hear it, so do you. It's very exciting, especially when the people are in costumes in the streets and the drummers and beating out the rhythm."

Yes, even musicians have trouble characterizing the music. As the saying goes, you have to have been there. But as Taylor adds, with his wide smile and dancing eyes, "Believe me, you'll know it when you hear it."

Taylor holds his hands up in the air when he speaks and you notice they look like shoe leather, a tribute to half a century of pounding tightened goat skin. As a friend of his remarked, "You wouldn't want him to spank you."

What does Junkanoo mean? What is its derivation? Ask three people and you'll get four answers. Actually there may be a dozen, but at least two of them are relatively common and correct. Taylor has one. He says that Junkanoo is an island slang word, used when the natives are kidding around. They'll pin that label on someone who acts like a clown, who makes people happy. The other common explanation is that it comes from a man named Johnny Canoe, who popularized the sound. Either choice is reasonable, but given the concept of costume and music and the sheer pleasure of the occasion, the first option, Taylor's, is the one I choose to believe. It catches the spirit of the occasion.

And somehow, it calls to mind the narration from those old MGM travel films of the 1940s: "And so, as the sun slowly sets into the west, we reluctantly bid a fond farewell to this island paradise."

Corny? Perhaps. But somehow, after you've been there yourself to take in the sunset and the intoxicating vibes of the music, it doesn't seem that way.

Lee Hays is vice president of the Broadcast Services Group of Manning, Selvage & Lee, Inc., an international public relations firm. Author of more than fifty books, he has written speeches, text for videotapes, and copy for such celebrities as Burt Lancaster and Lauren Bacall.

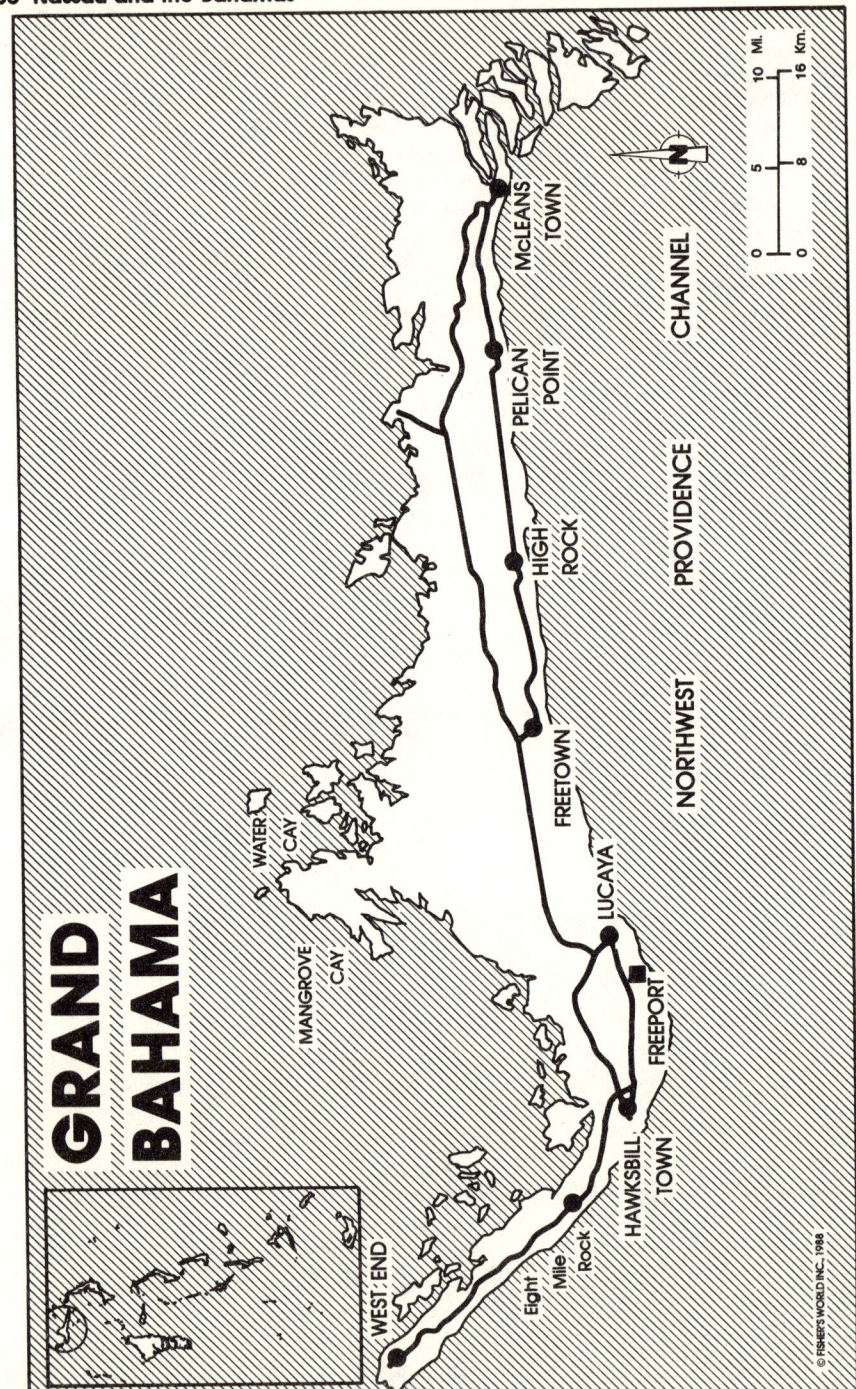

Grand Bahama

It's the Country Club Island, with half-a-dozen championship golf courses, half-a-hundred tennis courts, slews of impressive sea-sports facilities and 60 miles of fine white-sand beaches. It's the nation's industrial center, with oil and steel works, cement and pharmaceutical plants, a world-class harbor, and an international airport. It's open spaces, pine forests, and quaint settlements scattered over 530 square miles that measure 96 miles east to west and comprise the country's northern border and the archipelago's fourth largest island. It's home to 33,102 Bahamians, most of whom live in the central portion that boasts the Bahamas' second most populous area, Freeport/Lucaya—replete with glamorous nightlife, spectacular shopping, gourmet restaurants, sleek resorts, and ambitiously planned additions en route. It's a bit of everything for everybody. And it is, indeed, grand.

IF YOU HAVE ONLY ONE DAY

Start in the sunshine. Whether you're visiting here, in Nassau, or on one of the Family Islands, a good way to start any Bahamian day is with a walk on the beach or along a marina or harbor. Depending on where you walk, it's a fine hour for finding shells, for watching fishermen's waterside activity, or for just being alone with sea, sand, and sky.

After a leisurely breakfast, complete with island fruits, laze awhile in the sun, then take a dip in the water or, if you're ambitious enough, try snorkeling or waterskiing, sailing, or even parasailing or windsurfing. Then, after a shower and perhaps a bit of rest, dress casually and in comfortable shoes and head for the *International Bazaar*.

This ten acre extravaganza offers dozens of shops with heaps of the world's most noted treasures. Each shop is an architectural statement about the country whose merchandise is inside, and each twisting lane imitates shopping streets in other lands. Just strolling

40 Nassau and the Bahamas

through the maze is fun—and a good thing to do before you consider buying anything at any one place. As you wander, you'll come across restaurants with many types of international foods and atmospheres, and after you've browsed a bit, you can choose one for a late luncheon or afternoon snack while you reconsider which shop had precisely the camera or watch, silk shirt or jade carving, emerald ring or formal china service you want. How much time you spend here is up to you, for there's enough to keep you busy all afternoon. Some people come again and again.

Aside from the shops and stores, there's the *Royal Crown Jewels* collection to ogle, and the *Straw Market* artisans to bargain with and watch while they weave and carve beautiful items. Check my shopping notes in this section as a guide to what's available from around the world and from the Bahamas. And before leaving, stop by the *Tourist Information Centre* to collect more information and brochures for another day, or for your next trip to Grand Bahama. Since many airline offices are here as well, you can take time to reconfirm travel plans; a visit to the well-stocked drug and sundry store on the arcade might come in handy, too.

When you finally decide to leave, you'll find taxis lined up to whisk you back to your hotel, or you may opt for the London double-decker bus ride.

A rest is in order before changing for a special night out that starts with cocktails and dinner—try *Ruby Swiss* for a truly elegant meal, the *Captain's Charthouse* for delicious lobster and steak, or any of the restaurants listed later in this chapter. But do keep an eye on the clock, and leave the restaurant with plenty of time to reach *Princess Casino* before the show at *Casino Royale Theatre.* Or swim and shop at Port Lucaya, dining at *Les Oursins*, before trying your luck at the gaming tables—all at *Lucayan Resort & Casino* complex.

It's advisable to make your reservations in advance for dinner at the restaurant and for the show, then have a taxi take you from the restaurant early enough to avoid the end of the line. Those who get in first get the best seats, and often a large group tour or a batch of cruise ship passengers will arrive to swell the line out of sight. Once inside, a waitress will take your drink order; try a Bahama Mama or a Yellow Bird.

As you leave the show, you enter the bustle and pizzazz of the casino. Spend a while watching the action and the "beautiful people," or take a chance on your own luck. And remember, pubs and discos are nearby and open late in case you want to top off the night with a dance or a snack.

IF YOU HAVE TWO DAYS

Take advantage of the fact that you're near the headquarters of one of the world's most prestigious dive centers and the largest such operation in the country—*Underwater Explorers Society* (UNEXSO). Presi-

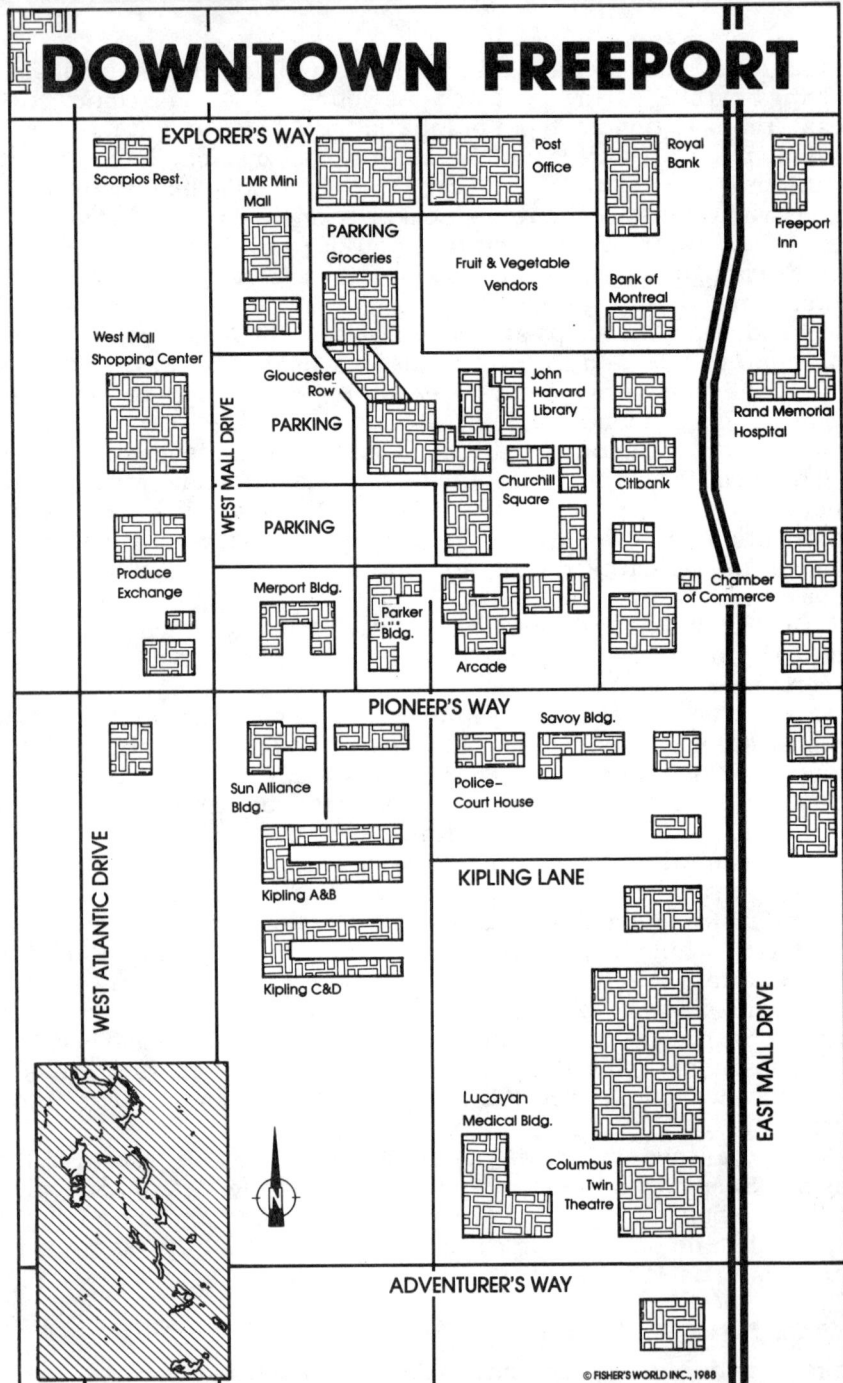

dent John Englander explains that diving is safe for most people, and that only those with histories of lung disease and circulatory problems need check first with a doctor before taking the plunge.

If you've never before tried scuba diving, this is the place to learn. The first day starts with poolside instruction followed by practice of basic skills in the swimming pool and repetition of them in UNEXSO's special 18-foot deep training tank. The next day, your instructor takes you to a shallow reef for a dive in clear warm water full of brightly colored marine life. A second dive in a different underwater locale is part of this introductory package.

For those who have already scuba'ed, there's a choice of a six-dive package that can be scheduled into three dives a day, or a week-long comprehensive course for a certification card from the National Association of Underwater Instructors (NAUI). The course starts the first Monday of each month and includes classroom, pool, and open-water instruction.

If you are not up to scuba, but want to be in the water, UNEXSO has a daily two-hour snorkeling trip for you. With mask, breathing tube, and flippers, you can float on the surface and watch the ocean floor, or dive under for closer looks. For snorkeling or scuba fun, UNEXSO prices include all equipment except wet suits. You should make advance reservations for the activity you prefer: More than 1,000 sport divers sign in here each month, and more than 35,000 have learned to dive here since UNEXSO's opening in 1965.

After a day in the sun, try a night on the water with a sunset cruise that lasts till the moon is high. Back ashore, go for the food and dancing at the *Island Lobster House*, or the relaxed atmosphere of the *Pub on the Mall*, where the food is hearty, the dart games are handy, and the aura is essentially British.

IF YOU HAVE THREE DAYS

Explore the western end of the island. You can go by guided tour, but it's best to hire your own car and driver, which leaves you free from others' schedules and from the toil of often tricky road maneuvers.

Just west of town is *Hawksbill Creek*, where huge piles of conch shells announce the waterside fishermen's market, where conch and fish are sold shortly after being pulled from the ocean's depths. While you're in the neighborhood, you might breeze through the famous harbor area before heading on toward *Eight Mile Rock*, a long and narrow hamlet founded on approximately eight miles of rocky land, with a span of road that measures only twenty-four feet wide yet is dubbed the Queen's Highway. If you've never seen a perfume factory, stop here to tour an island enterprise in what used to be a Baptist church. *Seagrape Village* reputedly has the best breads in the Bahamas; it's surely worthwhile stopping by to taste and test. The next settlement is *Holmes Rock*, and nearby *Hydro Flora Gardens* deserve the time for a tour guided by a top naturalist. On past *Bottle Bay*, there's a bird sanctuary, and it's just a short way farther to *West End*

Point, where on a clear day the fine views include Indian Cay and Wood Cay, as well as *Memory Rock* (a navigation light station).

The sleepy village of *West End* lazes in the sun, with its handful of churches and dozens of bars and lounges, its wooden homes and sprinkling of stores. Pull up to the *Star* and go in for a cool drink. Built around 1945, the Star was Grand Bahama's first hotel, built by Austin H. Grant and now operated by his son and namesake, who usually presides over the bar. Many island tours stop at this weathered wooden building, where rooms are no longer available but where the restaurant offers native meals a round the clock. *Austin's Calypso Bar* is a favorite local hangout. Notice the polished conch shells for sale at half a dollar, the Junkanoo costumes leaning against the wall, the porch posts supporting a second-floor balcony. At night, the dancing goes on until dawn.

If Austin and some of the regulars get to talking, you can hear a lot of tales about this oldest Grand Bahama settlement and its wild rum-running days. If you walk outside to the shore, you can make out old concrete slabs of piers used by the booze boats.

Before the sun gets too low, head back along the highway to Eight Mile Rock and *Harry's American Bar* on Deadman's Reef. Sit on the patio, sip one of Harry's hurricane drinks, try the conch fritters and watch the sun sink into the sea. Then climb back into the car and nose it to the *New Peace & Plenty Restaurant*, where turtle steak or crayfish are superb and Bro Bert's bush brew is not to be missed.

IF YOU HAVE MORE TIME

Set aside leisure hours for the marvelous natural scenery at *Garden of the Groves* and *Rand Memorial Nature Centre*—alike in botanical beauty; different in size, scope, and atmosphere.

Travel eastward to the far reaches of the island. Forgo the bus in favor of a car and driver, and take the Grand Bahama Highway across the Lucayan Waterway and through miles of untamed land, past the U.S.A.F. missile tracking base (the first of four slated for these islands) and on to *McLean's Town*, a little fishing village hardly touched by the years of progress that built Freeport and designed the tracking devices back down the road. The Baptist church is the center of social and community life for all the people who live in these brightly colored wooden homes. The waters of nearby cays and the wide ocean are the source of livelihood for the men and women who go out daily for conch and crayfish, grouper and other varieties of sea life. Only once a year does the village burst its seams with crowds—for the October *Conch Cracking Contest*.

Taking the southern route back, you'll pass through *Pelican Point*, *High Rock*, and *Freetown*.

Go shelling. That is, search out the intricately shaped and colored sea shells that have been popular collectors' items for centuries. Grand Bahama's sixty miles of sandy beach include many stretches that are positioned for superb shelling and isolated enough to assure you of good finds at almost any time of day. Warning: Once begun, this activity can become absorbing to the point of compulsion, even sunburn.

Take advantage of the overwhelming number of fine facilities for all kinds of outdoor and water sports.

LUCAYA

Author's Choice/Grand Bahama

HOTELS

Lucayan Beach Resort & Casino P.O.Box F-336, Lucaya, Phone (809)373-7777; in U.S. (800)772-1227. This name lures the world's wealthy. After a decade of empty silence, and a $40 million rejuvenation, this holiday retreat greets old and new friends with an array of amenities rarely found on one island site. The sprawling complex, five miles from the airport, features another hotel plus complete marina facilities (158 slips), several restaurants and bars, a health spa, night/day tennis courts, and fresh-water swimming pools. Five 18-hole champ golf courses are just minutes away. Of this hotel's 247 rooms with water view, most form a V to one side of the double lobby, canopied terrace, and rows of shops. But 46 branch in the opposite direction, forming a special wing, *International Club Lucaya*, where the expensive price includes spacious rooms, giant beds, color TVs, marble baths, refrigerators, and many extras. Club guests can don resort-provided robes, tuck tanning oils into a complimentary duffle, slide open doors in a wall of glass overlooking the ocean, then step onto the room's private balcony and down its own stairway to reach the resort's wide, 1.5-mile-long stretch of powdery white sand beach. Beach and water sports (swim, sail, scuba, snorkel, parasail, windsurf, deep-sea fish, glass-bottom boat tours). Daily live bands. Day guests play here, too, via the *Cabana Club* which, for a returnable deposit, offers dressing and rest rooms, showers, sauna, lounge, and lockers with keys, from 9 A.M. to 9. P.M. Until 7 P.M., even swimsuited players (no bare feet or tops) can enjoy the 20,000-square foot beachside casino, before it shifts to less casual nighttime gear. There's also a Vegas-type cabaret dinner theater. All guests can enjoy reciprocal service of the sister hotel across the bay, the *Lucayan Marina/Hotel & Spa*, reached by free road shuttle or free 25-passenger, 5-minute ferry ride. Guests can browse, buy, eat, and enjoy the waterside sights at *Port Lucaya*, the international market next-door. *Moderate to Extravagant.*

Atlantik Beach Hotel P.O. Box P.O. Box F-531. Phone (809)373-1444; in U.S. (800)622-6770. Swiss owned/operated, and catering to many Europeans, its 175 rooms have TVs and include 52 units with kitchenettes. Three miles of private beach with boating, snorkeling, parasailing, two pools, *Rum Runners Lounge* with music and dancing, and Continintal and American specialties in the *Spanish Main* dining room. Poolside bar and *Swiss Hut* buffet/cafeteria. Hotel boasts the only *Freeport Windsurfing School*, with simulator and five types of boards. Bus transport and shops. Family packages available. *Moderate to Expensive.*

Bahamas Princess Resort and Casino P.O. Box F-207. Phone in U.S. (800) 223-1818; in Quebec and Ontario Provinces (800)268-7140, other Provinces (800)268-7176; London (01)439-8027. Sister to the Princess Tower and sited in exotic *Princessland*. Offers 800 rooms, 8 villas, 25 studios, and nonstop activities night and day. Its 100 acres of facilities include the $3 million, two-course golf complex designed by Joe Lee and Dick Wilson, six tennis courts, a free-form lagoon pool, assorted sports such as horseback riding, fishing, diving, and boating, a game room, and extensively landscaped gardens. Four dining rooms, a bar, patio, private beach and club, health club, disco ,and elegant showrooms with good native shows, fine foods, and nightly parties. New time-sharing wing. Special package holidays are available. *Expensive to Extravagant.*

Princess Tower Princess Tower boasts a Moorish domed entrance that may well be the island's most photographed structure. A circular lobby continues the Arabian Nights opulence and is flanked by elevators rising toward the 400 tower rooms and suites that overlook almost eight acres of grounds which, in turn, are part of the 2,500 acres of Princessland—complete with flowering tropical gardens, two championship golf courses (each with gourmet dining), a dozen tennis courts, three pools (including the island's largest freshwater pool), and a 20-slip full-service marina. Home of the annual *Bahamas Open Tennis Championships*, and a slew of sports ranging from Frisbee relays to comprehensive indoor, outdoor, and water sports facilities. There is a children's playground with a putting green, and a beach club with a mile of private beach. Two gourmet dining establishments, a restaurant and coffee shop, a bar, lounge, disco and showplace, plus shops and an arcade link to the *Princess Casino* and the *International Bazaar*. Look for gourmet Dine-Around Plan, hot tub, jacuzzi, package holidays, time-share: all part of Bahamas Princess Resort & Casino complex. *Expensive.*

Holiday Inn P.O. Box F-2496. Phone (809)373-1333; in U.S. (800)HOLIDAY. On Lucaya's "hotel row," the Inn has the friendliest atmosphere. An almost tangible cheer prevails from the lobby to the water of its private beach. Its facilities are fine, too: sauna, pool, supervised playground, lovely gardens, and probably the best beach and water sports programs in the vicinity, plus tennis and other activities such as jogging. Large and airy, it has 490 rooms and 16 suites, each with TVs. It has lounges, bars and three dining rooms, where food is tasty and plentiful, whether gourmet or simple. Weekly luaus and barbecues are accompanied by live productions of native shows, with local fashion shows to boot. (Watch for the replica *Lucayan Indian Village* slated for a beachside site here.) Full activities program, children's program, convention service, and group facilities. Daily bus to golf course. Children under twelve stay free with parents. Several packages. *Expensive.*

Xanadu Beach Marina Resort P.O. Box F-2438. Phone (809)352-6782. Recently revamped, posh Xanadu was home to former owner Howard Hughes. Hughes' thirteenth-floor suites are available, as well as 178 rooms on twelve other stories, plus 3-bedroom villas with kitchens. Facilities include a library now containing electronic games as well as walls of books, a pool, private beach, four tennis courts, water sports, boating, marina and dock, dining rooms, lounge, bar, disco, and assorted shops. There's a delightful air of seclusion. Holiday packages are available, children under twelve stay free with their parents. *Extravagant.*

Lucayan Marina Hotel P.O. Box F-336. Phone (809)373-8888; in U.S. (800)772-1227. Sister to the *Lucayan Beach Resort*, this property boasts a $3 million marina renovation and the "finest marine facilities in the Caribbean." Over one hundred slips accommodate 250 boats (up to 169-foot yachts, plus provisions for larger ones), and a 70- to 100-ton lift allows full repair/maintenance boat service. Boaters are offered all hotel services, including telephone and cable TV hook-ups, maid/valet services, and 24-hour room service. Showers, laundry, and ice machines, fuel storage tanks, a ships store and commissary. Boatless vacationers are welcome, too, in 142 air-conditioned rooms, Library, large-screen TV room, electronic games room, pool, jacuzzi, restaurant, snack bar, barbecue pit, and an elaborate spa featuring both Nautilis and Universal equipment, with free aerobic and weights areas. Reciprocal services with the main resort/casino/port, linked via free road shuttle or ferry. *Moderate to Expensive.*

Specialized Accommodations
Deep Water Cay One-half mile out from the Grand Bahama "mainland". A fisherman's paradise, complete with the 10-room Deep Water Cay Club, which features a club house, pool, bar, dining room, and all sorts of special fishing facilities. *Expensive.*

Jack Tar Village Write for information 158 Port Road, Riviera Beach, Fl. 33404. Phone (214)670-9888; toll free in U.S. (800)527-9299. Covering 2,000 acres in West End, and more a private city than anything else, it offers the "largest swimming pool (sea water) in the Western Hemisphere," the Bahamas' "largest pro shop," 27 oceanside golf holes, a 98-slip marina, 16 tennis courts, a shopping complex rivaling the International Bazaar, plus completely self-contained operations for tours, diving, deep-sea fishing, etc, as well as cruises on two authentic Chinese junks, a glass-bottomed boat and a big paddlewheeler. Its own international airport (mostly for its charters), vehicle rentals, native shows and markets, four bars, four dining rooms, a lounge and laundry. There are 580 motel-like rooms—280 now being renovated—including 15 suites and 2 cottages with kitchens. Most guests are U.S./Canadian couples. Average stay is seven nights. There are no age limits, and children under twelve stay free with their parents. No pets.

RESTAURANTS

Visitors will be pleased and impressed with the wide range of eateries scattered across Grand Bahama and the Freeport/Lucaya area. All hotels offer a mix of local specialties and other fare. The International Bazaar lets you pick your favorite country's cuisine. Native restaurants serve everything from home-style meals to gourmet treats. There are several good pubs and a clan of U.S. chains that includes *Burger King*, *Kentucky Fried Chicken*, and *Howard Johnson*'s. There's also a *Pancake House* with authentic Bahamian fare, and *Capricorn Lounge* is open till 4 A.M. serving pizza, burgers, chicken 'n' rice (reservations are recommended).

Les Oursins In the Lucayan Beach Resort. The name means sea urchin, and delicate shells of this marine creature are lighted from within to help create a glowing decor that sets the atmosphere of relaxed elegance. Experienced international chefs create superb fare, and fine wines are available to complement each course. Ladies receive long-stemmed roses; gentlemen may try cognac-dipped Cuban cigars. Deft Service. Jackets required. *Extravagant.*

Cotillion Room In the Princess Tower Hotel. Elegant setting for treats such as caviar, saddle of lamb, Spanish red shrimp Fra Diavolo, and strawberries Romanoff. Fine wine and champagne list. Jacket and tie required. *Extravagant.*

Lucaya Country Club's Famous Dining Room On Albacore Street off Sargent Major Drive. A tasteful room overlooking the golf course, with a large round bar. Lunch features salads and grills. Dinner menu offers oysters Rockefeller and roast pheasant (order 24 hours in advance). Jackets required for dinner. *Extravagant.*

The Rib Room In the Bahama Princess Hotel. Tudor charm and friendly service. Steak Diane is a local favorite here. Jacket and tie required. *Extravagant.*

Ruby Swiss Restaurant At the Bahama Princess Hotel's Ruby Golf Course, this restaurant rightfully boasts the island's largest selection of true gourmet fare, beautifully served in quiet, elegant surroundings, supervised by a Swiss professional. Wines are priced to $150, and selected cognacs and liquers include fifty-year-old Napoleon. Lunch features Swiss bratwurst and Bahamian fare. Breakfast is served, primarily for golfers. *Extravagant.*

Beef Cellar In the Princess Tower Hotel. Fixed-price meals can be prepared over table grills by diners themselves, or cooked to order by the staff. *Extravagant.*

Escoffier Room In Xanadu Beach Hotel. The most expensive restaurant on the island. Provides a beautiful setting, yet the famed gourmet fare on the menu is not prepared by an Escoffier chef. Jacket and tie required. (Note: Tiffany Room here has popular *Sunday Champagne Brunch*). *Extravagant.*

Silvano's The Mall, across from the casino. Bright, airy decor is enhanced by elan of staff. Deft preparation of delicious Italian lunches and dinners. Don't leave without sampling the exceptional homemade pasta. *Moderate.*

Buccaneer Club At Deadman's Reef, Eight Mile Rock. Encompasses a sprawling area with beautiful grounds, a beach and patio, and chalet restaurant with indoor or outdoor seating. The Swiss chef/owner serves superb native and Continental dinners. Lunch and beach grills also served. *Expensive.*

Captain's Charthouse One East Sunrise at Beachway Drive, Lucaya. Here, the soft patter of locals and tourists, plus easy music by Willie Nelson, creates a warm aura for dinner. Menu includes hot homemade breads and very special prime ribs. Good wines; famous *Sunday Champagne Brunch;* popular *Mate's Lounge. Expensive.*

Harry's American Bar Deadman's Reef. A chummy, relaxed atmosphere attracts tourists and locals, who traditionally sip Harry's Hurricane brew and munch conch fritters on the patio overlooking the sea. Step inside for a lunch or dinner that features delicious Bahamian charbroiled seafood steaks. *Expensive.*

Island Lobster House On the Mall. A happy, active place with live music and dancing. Top favorite menu selection: whole lobster stuffed with crabmeat. Early dinner seating has better prices. Good wine and champagne lists. *Expensive.*

Japanese Steak House In the International Bazaar. Operates the only habachi tables in the Bahamas, and these are kept continually busy. Full dinners are complemented by Japanese decor and kimono-clad staff. *Expensive.*

Marcella's Italian Village Inn At East Mall and Kipling. Two dining rooms offer light snacks to full meals, with prices to match. All meats are from Italy; all pastas are homemade, and all foods cooked to order. A large wine list offers rare Italian imports. *Expensive.*

Nino's Fishing Hole Restaurant & Bar Fishing Hole Road (Queen's Highway) on the Bay. Yes, this is the restaurant of Nino Pucillo, author of *Continental Cuisine* and known for Nino's of Palm Beach and Manhattan. In this very attractive, cozy, fireplaced cottage, you can savor real paella Valenciana, and other seafare caught fresh daily on Nino's boat. Continental selections include homemade pasta, bread, and pastries. Moderate.

The Stoned Crab At Taino Beach, Lucaya. Casual and crowded, this is a lighthearted, interesting place where lunch fare features salads and sandwich platters. Good wine list and good bartender. *Moderate.*

New Peace & Plenty Restaurant At Eight Mile Rock. Offers a terrific dining experience in a big old house that opens into a popular native restaurant, where Hilda Williams cooks and serves excellent, authentic old Bahamian specialties, including turtle steak, mutton, pork, fish, conch, and crayfish. Bro' Bert, as Mr. Williams is best known, rules the small bar, mixing tasty international drinks plus native concoctions such as his legendary Health and Aphrodisiac drink. *Inexpensive.*

Freddie's Hunters, just outside Freeport. Reservations please, for this very popular but small restaurant, where you can order lobster and steak, sample delicious native favorites like mutton curried with rice, pea soup and dumplings, soused pigs feet or chicken, all served with cole slaw, peas 'n' rice and johnnycake. Superb food, exceptional service. Lunch and dinner only. *Inexpensive to Moderate.*

Pubs Pubs offer food and congenial camaraderie from early hours through early hours. They are usually best for lunch, but occasionally serve very impressive dinners

A fascinating, multiroomed establishment, *Pub on the Mall* includes the elegant, medieval Baron's Hall for a la carte three-star dinners featuring fine dishes like Cornish game hen, lamb cutlets, lobster, fish, and excellent beef specials. Late snacks (escargots to pizza to prosciutto) are served in the Scotch Corner and Prince of Wales

Lounge, where special events can include *Cowboy Night*, with live country-and-western music. English draught beer, ale, lager, and darts. *Inexpensive to Moderate.*

Sir Winston Churchill Pub, on the Mall, offers island drinks or English favorites, plus a light menu of burgers, sandwiches, even milk shakes, along with fine beef dinners. Darts, electronic games, and regular "Gong Show" events starring tourists keep it lively. *Moderate to Expensive.*

Britannia Pub, at Lucaya Harbour, is hung with portraits of queens and has open fireplaces. Courage on tap and a comfy atmosphere. The menu stretches to include conch, lobster, even "shish kebab alla Greek," as well as traditional British fare. A local favorite place, with darts and electric games. Free fish 'n' chips during happy hour. *Inexpensive to Moderate.*

ENTERTAINMENT

Performing Arts Watch for media ads and posted bulletins announcing current top artists and musicians imported from around the world under the auspices of Freeport Friends of the Arts. For theater productions such as *A Man for All Seasons* or *Fiddler on the Roof*, check for performances by the Freeport Players Guild in the modern, 400-seat Regency Theatre, built with profits from the moderately priced tickets. The Grand Bahama Players, an amateur group, is noteworthy for presenting traditional productions in Bahamian lingo— which many visitors find interesting, if somewhat unintelligible.

Gambling Two magnificent casinos vie for players' action in Grand Bahama. The newest is a revamp of the isle's first gaming arena: *Lucayan Beach Casino*, recently reopened after being closed a decade. Its Freeport rival, *Princess Casino*, offers the same games—slot machines computerized for progressive and link jackpots, Big Six Wheels, tables for baccarat, craps, blackjack, and roulette—within a great amount of space: 20,000-square-feet. Yet there are differences. In the heart of Freeport's tourist area, Princess Casino promises interior posh to match its fantastic, exterior Moorish dome. Lucayan Beach Casino is equally elegant, but more casually sophisticated, and it is beachside. More vacationing masses seem to hit the Freeport casino, while the beachside site caters to international individuals with "high energy" professional/industrial careers. Both casinos establish guest credit lines on-the-spot or in advance. Ask about Lucayan Beach's *Comcheck* the card that allows customers to draw cash against Visa or Mastercard credit. Both casinos offer packages ranging from one day to weeks; both offer instructions in gaming; both have adjacent fine restaurants and entertainment. Also, both are part of multimillion-dollar resort complexes. In Freeport, it's the Bahamas Princess Resort & Casino; in Lucaya, it's the Lucayan Beach Resort & Casino. **Note:** Neither Bahamians nor tourists under twenty-one are allowed in casinos.

54 Nassau and the Bahamas

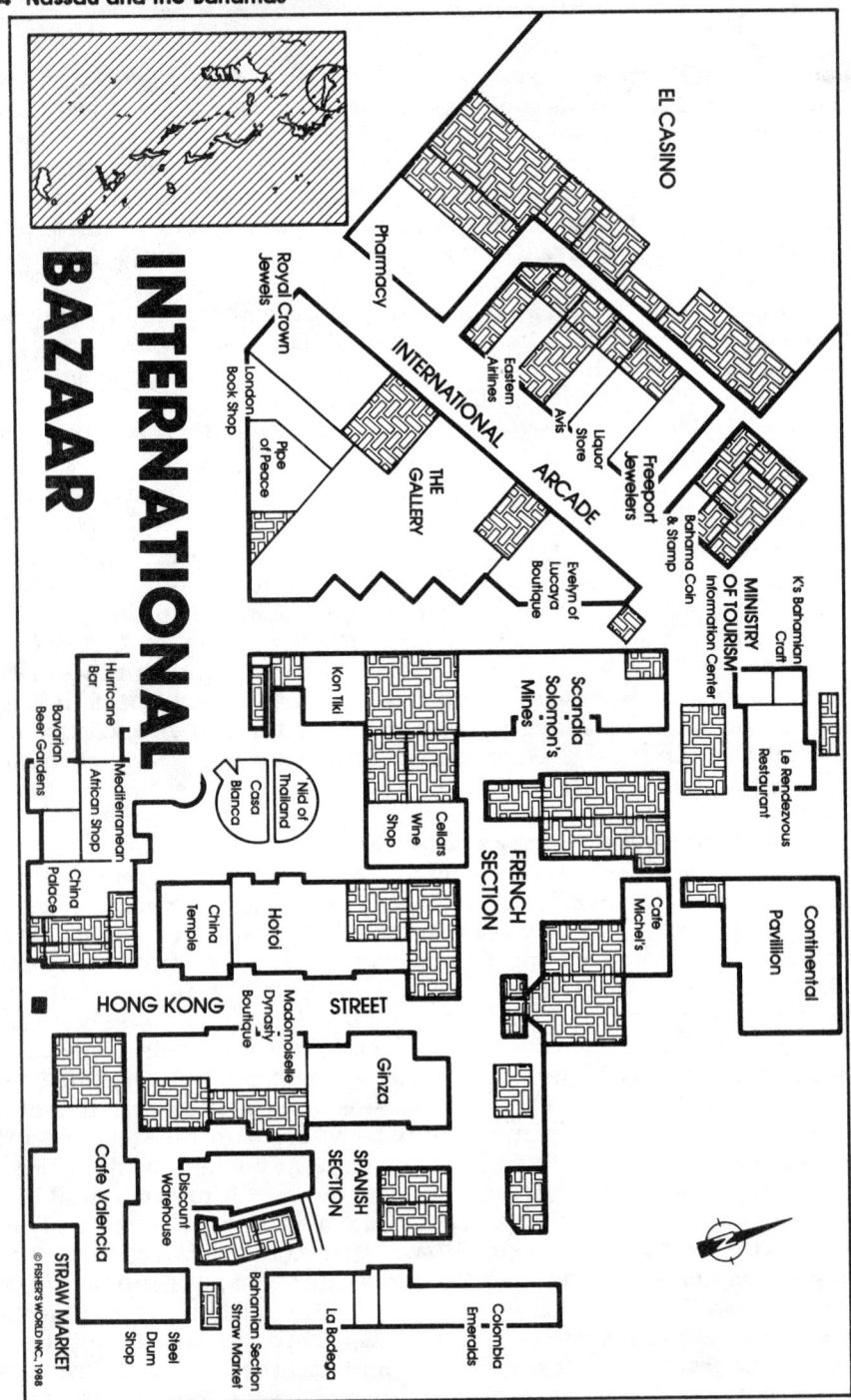

Shows and Revues *Casino Royale Theatre*, in Princess Casino, offers two shows nightly (except Mondays), a production with everything from topless dancers and plotted scenarios to specialty acts and zany antics.

Palm Pavillion, in the Bahamas Princess Hotel, keeps active with live shows and festival-type productions. The first-rate native show features good musicians and singers, an excellent fire dancer and glass eater. Dinner shows are special treats because the food is spectacularly displayed in creative arrangements with ice and butter sculptures and the like, plus enormous variety in buffet fare. Both menu and show change to match *Goombay Festival Night, Junkanoo Luau Night, International Night* and so forth, with dinner seatings starting at 6:30 and 7:00 P.M. *Holiday Inn* offers similar festive evenings each week, and *Pirate's Den*, at Lucayan Marina Hotel, also features a native show, complete with steel and congo drums, fire dancer, glass eater, and Calypso singer.

Discos Most discos mix recorded music with live musicians playing Bahamian Goombay plus Caribbean Calypso rhythms. The dancing starts out around 9 P.M. and spins down around 3 A.M. *Tipsy Turtle Disco* swings at Holiday Inn; *Coral Cove Discotheque* is cozy at Bahamas Princess Hotel; *Desserts & Disco* dishes up sweets and special coffees at Xanadu Beach; *Sultan's Tent* accommodates more than three hundred at the Princess Tower Hotel. All mix disco with live entertainment. *Studio 69* is a favorite spot for locals and tourists. *The Sandpiper* is crowded every night; some drink, some dance, some play backgammon or compete in disco and game tourneys. *Orbit Club Disco* specializes in serving Bahamian seafood and native fare. *Village Calypso Disco* alternates recorded music with Friday and Saturday night live shows featuring local artists and native foods served from its ringside restaurant. *The Back Room* has recorded and live music; breakfast, lunch and dinner; 25-percent tourist discounts.

SHOPPING I do not rate vendors listed here, but merely list them as suggestions of where to find different kinds of merchandise. Aside from the *International Bazaar*, goods are available at the *Hawksbill Shopping Plaza, East Sunrise Shopping Center*, and *Town Centre, Churchill Square*. Unless otherwise noted, shops listed here are in the International Bazaar.

Antiques *The Old Curiosity Shops Ltd.* is the only antique place in town. **Note:** A few other shops occasionally carry antiques.
Art *The Gallery.*
Bahamian Gifts *The Straw Market, the Beachcomber, Bahama Mama, K's Bahamian Crafts, the Happening, the Linen Shop, Little Sparrow Steel Drum Shop*, and *Rhona's Gift Shop*. Stores and streetside stalls in Lucaya and the various island villages and settlements.

Blown Glass Designed by artist Sidney Pratt, the items range from 50 cents to $500; they're also made-to-order. In *Arcade* area.
Books The *London Bookshop* carries books and paperbacks from the Bahamas, the U.K. and U.S., for adults and children. It also carries newspapers, magazines, cards, and postcards.
Brass *Bombay Bazaar, China Temple, India House, Mid-East Emporium, Sabra Shop.*
Cameras *Ernie's Studio & Camera Center Ltd. (Parker Building, downtown) Ginza, Hotoi Ltd., Pipe of Peace. Fast Foto Xanadu Beach Hotel Arcade* sells and rents cameras and also does 60-minute color film developing.
Candy *Chocolate Box, Mortimer's Candy Kitchen.*
Carvings *Higgs Brothers, China Temple, Colombian Shop, India House, Mediterranea, Nid of Thailand.*
China, Crystal, Giftware *Scandia (Solomon's Mines), Midnight Sun, Casa Miro, China Temple, Continental Pavilion Jewelry, Tang's Art Work.*
Children's Clothing *Cardan's Tot and Teens, Caprice.*
Coins and Stamps *Bahama Coin & Stamp Ltd.*
Copperware *Casa Simpatico, Colombian Shop, Sabra Shop.*
Eyeglasses *Optical Boutique El Casino* (sunglasses and prescription lenses plus designer frames).
Fabrics and Linens *The Linen Shop, Kon-Tiki.* (Local and imported fabrics are great buys.)
Gourmet Items *Midnight Sun.*
Jewelry *Royal Crown Jewels* (reputedly the most exclusive jewelry shop in town) *Freeport Jewellers Ltd., Colombia Emeralds, Greenfire Emeralds of Colombia, La Tienda, the Rock Shop (La Tienda II), Continental Pavilion Jewelry Shop, Anata-O Shop, Casa Simpatico, Bombay Bazaar, Bengazi, Charm Chest, El Galleon, El Rondel, Hotoi Ltd, Mediterranea, Nid of Thailand, the Plaka, Kon-Tiki, Azteca de Oro, Mid-East Emporium, Sabra Shop, Belle Bagaille.*
Knitwear *Lee's Hong Kong Shop, London Pacesetter Boutique, Evelyn of Lucaya Boutique.*
Leather *Leather & Things, Casa Miro, Fantastico, El Mercado Mexicano, Mediterranea.*
Liquors and Spirits *Arcade Liquor Store, Carib Liquor Store, Cellers Wine Shop.*
Lingerie *Continental Pavilion Lingerie Shop, Playgirl Ltd.*
Men's Wear *Executive Men's Shop, John Kendrick's Fashions for Men* (Churchill Square), *R. P.'s Men's Boutique, Caprice, Hong Kong Tailor, the Plaka, Bombay Bazaar, Nid of Thailand, Sabra Shop.*
Perfume Almost everywhere, including *Parfums de Paris, Continental Pavilion Perfume Bar,* and drugstores, department stores, shops.
Pewter *Midnight Sun.*
Prescriptions and Sundries *City Pharmacy, Grand Bahama Pharmacy* (E. Sunrise Shopping Center), *L.M.R. Drugs* (Churchill Square, Town Centre).

Records *Sounds Unlimited.* (Bahamian records are great souvenirs.)
Silver *Casa Simpatico.*
Straw Goods *Straw Market,* at stalls along roadsides, and at many stores and shops.
Toys *Cardan's Tots and Teen, L.M.R. Drugs* (Churchill Square, Town Centre), *Hawksbill Fashion & Department Stores* (Hawksbill Shopping Plaza).
Watches *Mademoiselle Dynasty, Bahama Coin & Stamp Ltd., Continental Pavilion Jewelry Shop, Ginza, Hotoi Ltd., Freeport Jewellers Ltd.*
Women's Wear *Evelyn of Lucaya Boutique, Caprice, London Pacesetter Boutique, Dynasty, Love Boutique, Sabra Shop, Bahama Mama, Caribana Boutique, Fol-o-Fashions,* the *Plaka, Bombay Bazaar, Azteca de Oro, El Mercado Mexicano, Colombian Shop, Nid of Thailand, Lee's Hong Kong Shop.* Also *Hawksbill Fashion & Department Store* (Hawksbill Shopping Plaza).

MUSEUMS The *Museum of Underwater Exploration,* located at the Underwater Explorers Society in Lucayan Bay Hotel, shares space with sales merchandise selected to meet the needs of diving buffs. The museum consists of glass cases protecting examples of historical underwater gear plus assortments of items and artifacts found on the nearby ocean floor, ranging from Arawak Indian remains and Spanish coins to guns.

If gems and pageantry fascinate you, visit the *Royal Crown Jewels* collection, an interesting, museum-quality replica group, well displayed in the International Bazaar boutique of the same name. Copies of every crown and item of regalia used by the British monarchy since 1066 is authentically reproduced here, including some items not displayed at the Tower of London. The romantic stories behind many of the pieces and gems are detailed in commentary.

PARKS and GARDENS *Garden of the Groves* is named not for orchards, but for Freeport founder Wallace Groves and his wife, Georgette, who presented the site to the community. Charmingly designed, it has shady areas, pools and waterfalls dotted among its five thousand varieties of rare and familiar shrubs, flowers, plants, and trees native to this part of the world. The 11-acre gardens are found on Lucaya's Shannon Golf and Country Club property, and also encompass *Fern Gully* grotto, well-marked paths, a children's playground, a replica of Freeport's original church that serves as an interdenominational chapel, a large community center with a marvelous indoor sunken garden, and the *Groves Museum.*

SPECTACLES and DISPLAYS *Junkanoo* takes the prize as Freeport's most colorful festival. Launched with a parade on December 26, it evolves into a week-long party, climaxed by another parade on January 1 (see the Travel Planner and Nassau section for Junkanoo details). Each fall, usually in September, there's the *Grand Bahama 200,* an ocean powerboat race bringing international competitors. But the most truly Bahamian fete of all causes large crowds of tourists and natives from many Bahamian islands to trek eastward to McLean's Town each October 12 to witness or participate in the *Discovery Day Conch Cracking Contest*. A recent winner punctured twenty-five shells, extracted the creatures and cleaned them within six minutes and twenty seconds!

TOURS Head first for the *Tourist Information Centre* in Freeport International Airport or the International Bazaar, or for your hotel's tour desk, where you can pick up free maps, booklets, and brochures detailing what's to be seen all over Grand Bahama Island. Tour operators offer organized group trips in and around the Freeport/Lucaya region, to the West End and eastern extremity, to industrial areas, gardens, settlements, beaches, and nearby cays. You can take day trips to Nassau and other Bahamian areas, or try a few nights in Miami or Orlando, Florida, via Air Florida's new Freeport services.

To see this town, you can start with a two-hour Freeport/Lucaya jaunt aboard an authentic London double-decker red bus that stops at hotels and the International Bazaar to pick up passengers, who are delivered back to their starting points after riding through residential sections, exclusive subdivisions with celebrity homes, along beaches studded with elegant resorts, into the industrial and harbor areas and the community focal points such as a colorful fresh air market. Twice weekly, the trip extends to cover the *Garden of the Grove* plus a pub lunch.

West End, that rumrunner's haven and the island's oldest village, is the focus of another bus tour that passes through quaint settlements such as Eight Mile Rock, Deadman's Reef, Seagrape, and Holmes Rock, before reaching West End for stops that include the Jack Tar Village complex, where shopping is similar to the International Bazaar and there are places for lunch and snacks. Pick out your own souvenir conch shell from fishermen's toss-away piles before heading home. This three-hour trip can be extended into an eight-hour tour that explores from Freeport/Lucaya through West End and back in one day. Other tours trip just to Deadman's Reef for sunset and dinner, or to Mader Town for a Club Caribe Beach Party.

Boat tours are popular, too, particularly the rides in the *World's Biggest Glass-Bottom Boat*—three daily 90-minute ventures upon the waters around the island, with great views of brilliantly hued fish and coral reefs, a shipwreck and the continental shelf. A diver even feeds the marine life below while you watch. Trimarans offer sailing jaunts complete with snorkeling gear, instruction, and beach picnics, plus sunset and moonlight cruises (some with powerful light for seeing sea creatures at night). Other boat tours are linked to sports and covered in our sporting section.

Details on all are available at your hotel, the Tourist Information Centres, or by contacting:

International Travel & Tours Ltd., P.O. Box F-850. Phone 352-6910; *Playasol Travel Services Ltd.*, P.O. Box F-2585. Phone 352-4811; *Bahamas Travel Agency Ltd.*, P.O. Box F-3778. Phone 352-3141, ex. 1000; *Fun Tours*, P.O. Box F-159. Phone 352-7005; *Cruises via Reef Tours Ltd.*, P.O. Box F-2609. Phone 373-5800.

SPORTS

Probably more than anywhere else in the Bahamas, Freeport locals follow U.S. sporting events, teams, and gossip, tuning into Miami TV and radio sportscasts and devoting local media time to them, too. As in Nassau, sports fans here also have associations and leagues (see Nassau Sports section) for dozens of different activities and almost all ages. A chat with Tourist Information Centre staff will steer you to what's happening where while you're here, so you can watch or even participate. Several times each year, Grand Bahama is the site of important international tournaments in golf, tennis, boating, windsurfing and other activities. The Ministry of Tourism/Sports Division can supply you with a detailed list of events and dates, plus entry requirements. Often called a holiday heaven for sportsmen, Grand Bahama offers year-round activities for tourists.

Note: Golf, tennis, and other sports are available to all tourists, whether or not your hotel has its own facilities.

Boating While small sporting boats can be rented right on the beach at hotel concession areas, sail and power boats of varying sizes are available for rent and charter at marinas. In the Freeport/Lucaya area, only the *Running Mon Marina*—with complete marine service, 40 slips and a Tami-lift to 40 tons, sportfishing charters, taxidermist agency, tackle shop, showers—is not part of an hotel: P.O. Box F-565, phone 352-6834. *Lucayan Harbour Inn Marina* has 155 slips, 32- to 45-foot charter boats, Tami-lift to 30 tons, taxidermist agent, bar, restaurants, laundry, liquor and gift shops, showers: P.O. Box F-2677, phone 373-1677. Xanadu Beach Hotel Marina, offers 36 slips and 28- to 46-foot sportfishing boats, fuel, showers, water, telephone, cable TV, restaurant, liquor store: P.O. Box F-2438, phone 362-6780. On the Grand Lucayan Waterway, there's the *Sir Charles Hayward Yacht Club* with 600-feet of docking space. By checking all these places, you can find out which boats are available where and for what cost. Be sure to reserve your choice as early as possible—months in advance if you want one for the peak season, whether you want it for pure boating or for fishing. The *Jack Tar Village* in West End also has a marina, with 98 slips, transient dockage, repair capability, and sportfishing.

Fishing Try your luck three different ways: in the deeps for the giants, in the shallows for bonefish, on the reefs for varieties such as blue runner, porgy, queen trigger, small spotted grouper, and Spanish grunt. Whatever you're after, the man to see is *Captain Stan Lockhart*, dockmaster at Lucayan Marine/Hotel & Spa. A fishing pro here for years, he knows just where to find the amberjack, dolphin, barracuda, kingfish, marlin, sailfish, shark, and tuna—he's even caught swordfish hereabouts. Though most catches of several hundred pounds are tagged and tossed back into the deep, some are brought in for mounting. Parties of from six to eight can charter a deep-sea fishing boat here or elsewhere on the island for $270 per half-day or $540 per day, with all gear except their food included. It's more for a two-night run farther off shore, and Captain Lockhart highly recommends *Lolfen Cooper* for such treks. He also recommends *Captain Alonzo Lowe*, at Xanadu Beach Hotel Marina, for good sportsfishing trips. At the Running Mon Marina, the *Casper* offers sportsfishing trips in these waters and special cruises to other islands, as well. For reef fishing at $25 per person, boats leave the beach four times daily at *Silver Point Condominium*; phone 373-5018 for reservations. *Jack Tar Village* also offers guests all types of fishing

Golf A super sport on this Country Club Island, golfing is available on seven different championship courses, most of which were designed and produced by Dick Wilson and Joe Lee. All have pro shops and eateries; most have lessons available. All have equipment for rent ranging from balls and shoes to clubs and often mandatory electric carts. Par is usually 72, and greens fees range from $11 to $20 for 18 holes. The courses start with two at the *Bahamas Princess Hotel:* P.O. Box F-207, phone 352-6721. All others have only one course, and include *Bahama Reef Golf & Country Club:* P.O. Box F-1790, phone 373-1055; *Fortune Hill Golf & Country Club:* P.O. Box F-2619, phone 373-4500; *Lucayan Golf & Country Club*: P.O. Box F-333, phone 373-1066; and in West End, *Jack Tar Village*, phone 348-2030.

Horseback Riding Contact *Pinetree Stables* directly (P.O. Box F-2915, phone 373-3600) or through your travel agent to reserve a ride. **Note:** if you weigh more than 185 lbs., you won't be allowed on these creatures. Fees run about $20 for ninety minutes on land and beach.

Parasailing At approximately $20 per six or seven minutes, this exciting new sport is available at *Lucayan Beach Resort, Atlantik Beach Hotel,* or *Holiday Inn,* neighboring resorts in Lucaya.

Scuba Diving and Snorkeling Both underwater adventure sports are available from world famous *Underwater Explorers Society:* Lucayan Bay Hotel, P.O. Box F-2433, phone 373-1244. Snorkeling equipment is for rent at most hotels. Special boat trips are offered on the 38-foot motorboat *Holiday Dream,* phone 373-1333, and the 52-foot *TriWind* sailing trimaran, phone 373-5880. Jack Tar Village also offers both, for guests only.

Tennis Here's a quick look at what courts are where: *Bahamas Princess Hotel* has 6 hard (2 nightlit); *Bahamas Tower* has 3 clay, 3 hard (all nightlit); *Channel House* has 2 hard; *Holiday Inn* has 4 hard, plus lessons; *Shalimar Hotel* has 2 asphalt; *Silver Sea Lodge* has 2 hard; and *Xanadu* has 3 hard (2 nightlit). *Jack Tar Village* boasts 16; 6 clay (all nightlit), plus a pro shop; all for guests only. *Lucayan Beach Resort* also offers 4 courts (nightlit).

Waterskiing Daily fun from many marinas and beaches, particularly via *Holiday Water Sports*, phone 373-1458, beachside at Holiday Inn.

Windsurfing Called the "fastest growing fad" on earth, windsurfing flourishes on Grand Bahama, where Windsurfer World Championships have been held. Try your luck with this speedy sport via *Holiday Water Sports*, beachside at Holiday Inn. At *Atlantik Beach Hotel Windsurfing School* you can earn a basic German (VDWS) or international (IWSS) certificate; take advanced and freestyle courses; have private or group classes.

GETTING AROUND

There's passenger bus service! It won't compete with London or New York, but it does connect the Freeport/Lucaya streets and even ventures to some outposts of the island. Try it for a short ride, or take the double-decker red London bus to and from various parts of the community for sightseeing jaunts. Taxis are usually the favorite means of tourist transport here, as on other Bahamian islands. If you need one and there's no line of them waiting for riders nearby, your bell captain can call one for you, or you can dial 352-6666. Rates and rules on rides are listed in the Travel Planner where all types of transportation are detailed, including rental boats, yachts, and small aircraft. *Hertz* and *Avis* thrive at Freeport International Airport and other locations, as do *Budget, Holiday,* and *Eddie's Car Rental Services.* Motor scooters are rented by *Curtis Enterprises Ltd.*, at Holiday Inn Hotel and Islander Hophone You can rent bicycles from *Ferguson Bicycle Rental* at Freeport Inn. In the West End area, *Jack Tar Village* operates its own vehicle rentals.

Note: Your travel agent can arrange for an air-conditioned limousine to meet you at the airport on your arrival.

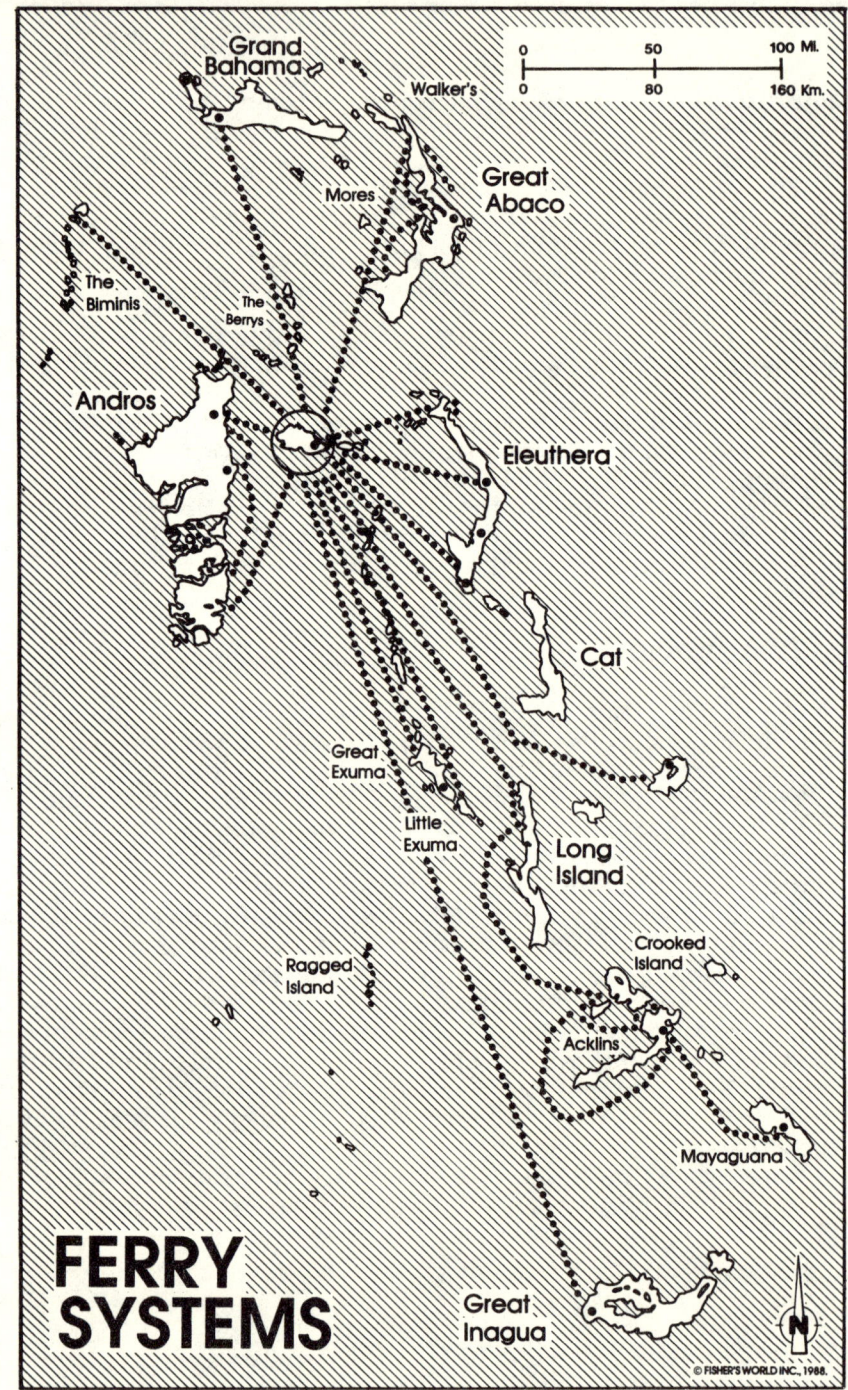

Through A Glass Darkly: Test Your Sunglass Savvy

by Frances Sheridan Goulart

Got your sights set on a new set of fun-in-the-sun specs? Be sure you get a good shady deal. What comes between you and the sun from the fit of the frame to the tint of the lens should be healthy as well as here's-looking-at-you-handsome, cautions Dr. Richard Young of UCLA's Jules Stein Eye Institute.

"Lifetime exposure to sunlight is a major factor in blindness. The eyes deserve protection just as the skin needs sunscreening against wrinkles and cancer."

Ultraviolet light, adds the American Optometric Association, can damage the cornea, the eye's transparent covering, as well as the lens. Long-term exposure to the sun's blue and violet wave lengths can damage the retina at the back of the eye — a condition called age-related mocular degeneration which affects 20-to 30-percent of the population over 50 — and is a major cause of blindness accumulating over a lifetime.

The good news? The right kind of sunglasses can prevent such wrongs. Test your through-a-glass-darkly I.Q. with this quiz on information supplied by The Sunglass Association of America and the American Optometric Association. Give yourself one point for each correct answer.

1. It doesn't matter how dark or light lenses are as long as they're comfortable. T or F?
Answer: False. Lenses should block a minimum of 75 percent of the sun's rays. Here's the through-a-glass-darkly test: With glasses on, stand two feet from a mirror. If you can see your eyes clearly, the lens isn't dark enough. If you can't they're too dark.

2. The only lens coating that blocks both UV and IR rays is...
a) Dietectric b) Mirror
Answer: a. Protects against strong glare from snow or water.

3. UVA rays are the culprits behind cataracts and wrinkling. UVB's are linked to ? and ?
Answer: Cornea burns and skin cancer.

4. Maximum UV protection is ?
a) 400 b) 100 c) 250
Answer: a. As set by the American National Standards Association Institute.

5. Sunglasses are categorized by purpose: Cosmetic, general, and ?
Answer: Special purpose. These are the only ones guaranteed to filter out 99 percent of all ultraviolet radiation. If your specs aren't tagged, ask to see the manufacturers catalog.

6. There are three types of sunglass lens coatings. Name one.
Answer: Antireflective, dietectric, and mirror.

7. A photochromic lens offers the same advantages as a polarized lens. T or F?
Answer: False. Photochromics darken 60 seconds after being exposed to bright light. (In dimmed light the reduction is only 50). Polarized lenses reduce glare but don't necessarily filter out UV rays.

8. What's one disadvantage of gradient and photochromic lenses?
Answer: Both provide only partial protection from UV rays and none from infrared.

9. Infrared (IR) ray protection is essential if you...
a) are a frequent sunbather b) engage in water sports c) do high altitude slope skiing
Answer: All three according to the American Optometric Association.

10. Ultraviolet is no risk during winter months because the UV-screening ozone layer is thinner. T or F?
Answer: True and False. The risk is reduced but not eliminated.

11. If you ski without good sunglasses you're vulnerable to...
a) snow blindness b) sun blindness c) hypothermia
Answer: a and b. The first is caused by UV rays which temporarily overheat and swell the retinal blood vessels. The second is similar to sunburn of the cornea.

12. The best way to test dark glasses for distortion is...
a) pay a lab to run the $10 test b) wear them for a week c) run your own distortion test
Answer: c. Here's how: Hold glasses one foot from eyes. Look through lenses and focus on an object. Move glasses up and down. If image doesn't curve or wave, lenses are distortion-free.

13. After quality of the lens, what's critical factor #2 in protecting your eyes from sun damage?
Answer: Size of the frame. The bigger it is (i.e. goggles and wraparounds) the more UV light it filters out. Around the sides and over the top.

14. Plastic lenses are safer and more protective than glass. T or F?
Answer: All sunglasses are required to meet the Federal Impact Resistance Standards. Plastic's plus? It's lighter and tougher, but costlier.

15. It is important to wear your shades as close to your forehead as possible. T or F?
Answer: True according to the *American Journal of Public Health* (Volume 78, No. 1, p.72-4) the amount of UV light that reaches the eyes increases up to as much as 45 percent when glasses are lowered only one-third of an inch down the nose.

16. Antireflective lenses aren't important if you have polychromic sunglasses. T or F ?

Answer: False. Antireflective lenses prevent light from reflecting back into your eyes. Polychrome is a lens coating that darkens in response to the suns' rays.

17. Price is the key to quality and eye protection in dark glasses. T or F?

Answer: False. Don't go for broke. Efficiency plus scratch-and-impact-resistance are available for $25 and sometimes less. The Technical Committee of the Sunglass Association of America recently conducted a study of 800 popular sunglasses, and found that low priced shades screened as much UV light (97 percent of UVA rays and 99 percent of UVB rays), as higher priced types. Pre-88 specimens often fail the optometrics test.

18. What color lenses should be avoided because they interfere with color perfection?

Answer: Blue or rose expose eyes to harmful end of the light-ray-spectrum radiation.

19. Specs for sports should have...
a) industrial strength lenses b) polycarbonate lenses c) bulletproof plastic

Answer: All three, which are interchangeable. (Polycarbonate is industrial strength plastic, which is also used in making bulletproof plastic).

20. The two marks of a top-rate pair of specs are smooth finely-polished lenses and ?

Answer: Distortion-free lenses. Here's a 60 second consumer test: Hold glasses at arms-length, look through lenses and focus on a straight line. If it distorts, quality is poor.

21. Mirror and polarizing lenses serve the same purpose. T or F?

Answer: False. Mirror lenses are coated to protect eyes from intense glare; lenses that are polarized reduce reflected glare.

22. A good-workmanship tip-off in a metal frame is...
a) an even lustre b) a high-gloss finish

Answer: a. (b applies to plastic.)

23. What's the better lens choice, gradient or photochromic?

Answer: Either. Both offer advantages over untreated lenses.

24. What's the best tint for foggy/hazy days?
a) green b) brown c) amber or yellow

Answer: c. Amber absorbs 100 percent of the blue portion of visible light, which is the main component of atmospheric haze as well as UV rays.

25. Which frame gets the most optical pluses?
a) nylon b) acrylic or faceted c) carbon

Answer: a or b. Both are strong but lightweight. c is outdated.

26. In good sunshades lens color should be ? And both lenses should...

Answer: even, match. And if there is a gradient coating it should lighten gradually.

SCORING

Take one point for each correct answer.

26 to 20: your sunglass savvy is 20/20.

19 or less: You're in the dark about shades. Book a shed-a-little-light-on-shades session with your optometrist soon. For enlightening info write: The Sunglass Association of America, 71 East Avenue, Norwalk, CT 06851.

Here's a hocus-focus craft to try: **Sunglasses From Scratch**

The world's first dark glasses were made by cutting slits in strips of birch bark and wearing these as sunglasses. Here's a here and now version. You will need:

the bottom of an egg carton (the styrofoam kind is easiest to work with)

| scissors | felt tip pen | colored paper |
| string | glue | |

Cut the adjoining bumps in an egg carton. Cut a narrow slit across the center of each bump. Punch two tiny holes at the outer edges. Thread and knot a string through each hole (used to keep specs on when you're done). To decorate shades use colored pens and anything you can think of.

Frances Sheriden Goulart's health and consumer "Hints" features are syndicated by New York Times and Los Angeles Times Syndication sales, among others. She is the author of more than a dozen books.

The Family Islands

All the islands in this and the following chapter are usually referred to as the Family Islands (formerly known as the Out Islands). The Biminis, Andros, Berry Islands, the Exumas, Long Island (with Conception Island and Rum Cay), Crooked and Acklins Islands (with Fortune Island), the Inagua Islands and the Jumento Cays; this is the group I cover in this chapter.

THE BIMINIS

Physically, Bimini is not one island but a cluster of islands southeast of Grand Bahama and fifty miles from Miami, Florida. Hugging the Gulf Stream and near Great Bahama Bank, the Biminis start with hooked North Bimini, severed by a narrow ocean channel from larger South Bimini. In the chain of rocks and cays to the south, Gun Cay is nine miles further, and it's just one mile from Gun Cay Light to Cat Cay, which is followed by Ocean Cay, another nine miles away, home of an aragonite sea-mining camp and the most southerly islet in the cluster.

Getting There

By Air

Chalk's International Airlines, Inc., offers regular seaplane service to North Bimini from Miami, Florida, and Paradise Island, New Providence. It also lands regularly on Cat Cay, via the seaplane ramp there. South Bimini has an airport where private and charter craft land.

By Sea

Mailboat *M/V Bimini Mack*—from Nassau Thursdays to Cat Cay and Alice Town (North Bimini).

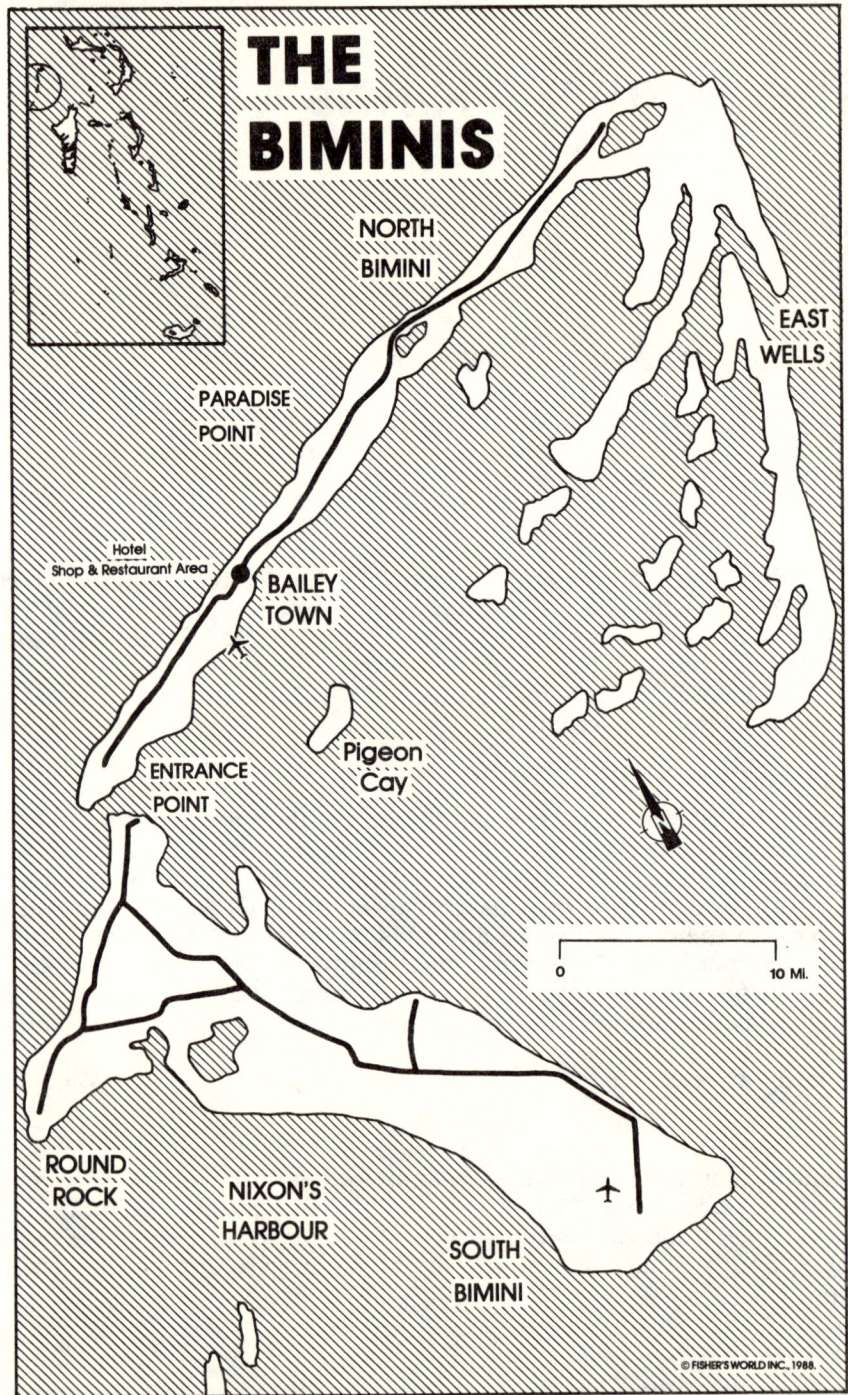

Alice Town is full of boisterous colors and lively action that focuses on tourism. Many visitors arrive on seaplanes that splash down in the harbor and roll up a ramp that literally crosses the main street. When they step onto the pavement, a waiting minibus taxi takes them to hotels, even though all accommodations are within walking distance.

Though Alice Town has a few older homes and hotels commanding spacious lots and beautiful grounds, most shops, restaurants, and bars occupy tiny individual buildings that line the main thoroughfare and climb lanes that link to the beachside road. Souvenirs are offered alongside stores for fishing bait, tackle, and other sporting gear, books and magazines, groceries and liquor, plus a wide assortment of lounges, bars and eateries, where color TVs are often tuned to U.S. sports programs. There's a charming minuscule library that doubles as a post office, with a fine collection of local shells protected by the glass top of a large table used for book and mail transactions. A small branch of the *Royal Bank of Canada* is down the road, and nearby is the fuchsia-colored government clinic, complete with physican and two nurses.

The more you see of North Bimini, the more you notice how crowded everything is. The main street is so narrow that a car must pull over to make room for an oncoming vehicle to pass. Though you might expect the crunch to lessen as you move farther from tourist quarters, it doesn't. The houses almost touch at times, creating a ribbon of old wood and new concrete, colored chartreuse and lavender, pink and gold, lime and yellow. Churches stand out by virtue of their size. A unique Catholic church boasts old mission architecture and has an adjacent elementary school, but there's no high school in Bimini. There is, however, a new *Bay Front Park*, where baseball and softball are played and helicopters occasionally land, even at night, thanks to powerful lights. Because everything is so jammed together, it's hard to know when you've left one town and entered another.

Suddenly, a tall fence barricades the road, posted as private property. Beyond the gates the pavement improves radically and winds through peaceful stretches of shady palms and pines, with deep beds of pine needles covering much of the ground. Soon you see rolling lawns of clipped grass, with gardens, trees, and elegant white and yellow guest homes that stand silent and empty. The road leads past deserted beaches where thousands of pelicans play undisturbed in the water, and gulls float above rocky projections called the *Three Sisters*. Destined to blossom into a fabulous resort complex, this area, formerly known as *Paradise Point*, may remain unchanged for some time. If so, tourists should remember that technically there are no private beaches in the Bahamas—the Commonwealth owns them all.

Back in Alice Town, the government dock is the place to find ferry services to adjacent South Bimini. Approximately every hour, either launches or motorboats transport passengers across the harbor to docks near the *Buccaneer Pointe Club*. The skipper hops ashore with the passengers, climbs into the driver's seat of a minibus and heads for South Bimini Airport. While he checks for newcomers at this end

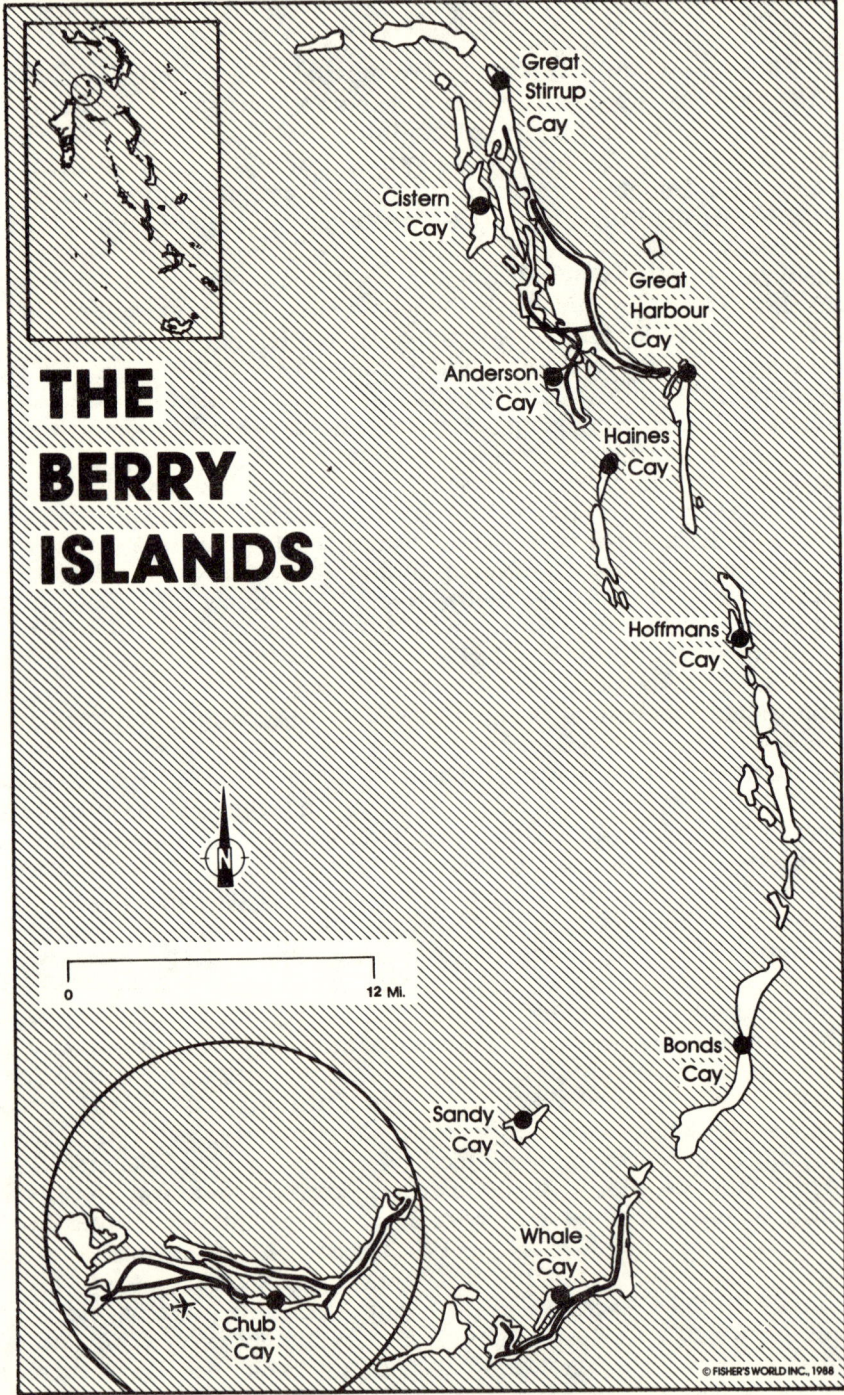

of his transportation line, there's usually time for a quick refresher at the snack bar.

South Bimini

Traveling through South Bimini, you notice the roads are good, usually bordered by thick greenery, with a few modern houses scattered about, many of them closed. If you're curious about the *Fountain of Youth* site, ask the driver to pull over and point the way. A resort lies fallow beyond Port Royal settlement, but there's a sizable group of cottages and modern villas set within a neatly gardened region near some mangrove swamps and natural water channels. Owned mostly by Americans, all but a few of these houses are vacant except on weekends. South Bimini also has some fine beaches and varied birds including pelicans, herons, and white egrets. However, it has only one tourist facility—the hotel near the ferry dock.

Touring around is interesting and spotlights several dichotomies here. Chockablock communities are worlds apart from nearby spacious sanctuaries or lightly populated, heavily thicketed areas. The appealing facades of neat and colorful shops often are offset by piles of litter and refuse, for there's no workable system for collecting trash, and a lack of adequate garbage disposal facilities has turned a great stretch of North Bimini beach into a dumping ground. Hordes of tourists are drawn by the area's superb fishing, and they do find every modern facility and service waiting to aid their sport, though it's often hard to get a hotel room. Yet there's no obvious effort under way to revamp some of the deteriorated resorts, and an official publication actually suggests the local points of tourist interest include hotel ruins left in place since the devastating hurricane of 1926. However, the romantic, historic, sun and fun aspects of Bimini tourism remain undeveloped, unmarked and seldom touted by tour promoters.

BERRY ISLANDS

Getting There

By Air

Private planes land at several private airstrips, and Bahamasair offers twice-weekly service to and from the airport at Chub Cay.

By Sea

Mailboat *M/V Captain Dean*—from Nassau Tuesdays or Wednesdays, to Berry Islands, Sandy Point, and Moore's Island. Also, many yachts cruise the area, where several harbors include northern Great Harbour Cay and southern Chub Cay facilities.

For 150 years, the tides of prosperity and population have alternated between high crests and low ebbs on this close chain of islands

ANDROS

0 — 30 Mi.

Joulter Cays
MORGAN'S BLUFF
NICHOLL'S TOWN
MASTIC POINT
SAN ANDROS
NORTH ANDROS
WILLIAMS ISLAND
STANIARD CREEK
COAKLEY TOWN
ANDROS TOWN
CENTRAL ANDROS
NORTH BIGHT
Big Wood Cay
Yellow Cay
MIDDLE BIGHT
MOXEY TOWN
Mangrove Cay
SOUTH BIGHT
CONGO TOWN
KEMPS BAY
MARS BAY
SOUTH ANDROS
Water Cays
CISTERN POINT
Curley Cut Cays

© FISHER'S WORLD INC. 1988.

bordering Great Bahama Bank's eastern edge. Some thirty miles northeast of Nassau, yet south of the Providence Channel, the entire chain adds up to twelve square miles of land, divided among approximately thirty islets and cays.

Tourist sites have been cultivated here, especially in the northern area, where Great Harbour Cay encompasses an 18-hole golf course and an 85-slip marina. The *Great Harbour Cay Club* may be reopened for business soon, after having been closed a long time. There's an airstrip on this nearly 4,000-acre cay, plus a nightclub in nearby *Bullock Harbour* settlement, and two hotels: the *Sugar Beach Club* and *Fairway Ridge Hotel*. While new investment here may make more facilities available soon, tourists meanwhile continue to swarm to the southernmost Berry isle, where the well known, semiprivate Chub Cay Club is located.

ANDROS

The phrase "only in Andros" could easily become overused, for this island is unique in several ways, even within its individualistic group of the Family Islands.

Getting to Andros

By Air

From Nassau, Bahamasair offers regular daily service to and from northern San Andros Airport, Andros Town Central Airport and, in South Andros, airstrips at Mangrove Cay and Congo Town. Private craft also use these airports, including planes owned by resorts such as Small Hope Bay Lodge, and charters and other airlines listed in The Travel Planner. Seaplanes land at Central Fresh Creek, southern Congo Town, and northern San Andros.

By Sea

Mailboats voyage regularly from Nassau, taking five to seven hours for a one-way trip. *M/V Central Andros Express II* departs Wednesdays for Fresh Creek and Stafford Creek; *M/V Lady Eula* departs Mondays for Mangrove Cay and Kemp's Bay. Both Fresh Creek and San Andros are marine ports of entry. *M/V Big Yard Express* departs Wednesdays for Mangrove Cay; and *M/V Lisa J. II* departs Thursdays for Morgan's Bluff, Mastic Point, and Nicholl's Town.

Central Andros

Andros Town is the small native village that boasts the airport and lies near *Fresh Creek*, *Small Hope* settlement, and *Calabash Bay* village. *Love Hill*, a prosperous settlement with some lovely homes built by and for contractors who live here and work on other islands, is said to have been named by the devout Christians who live here and "believe

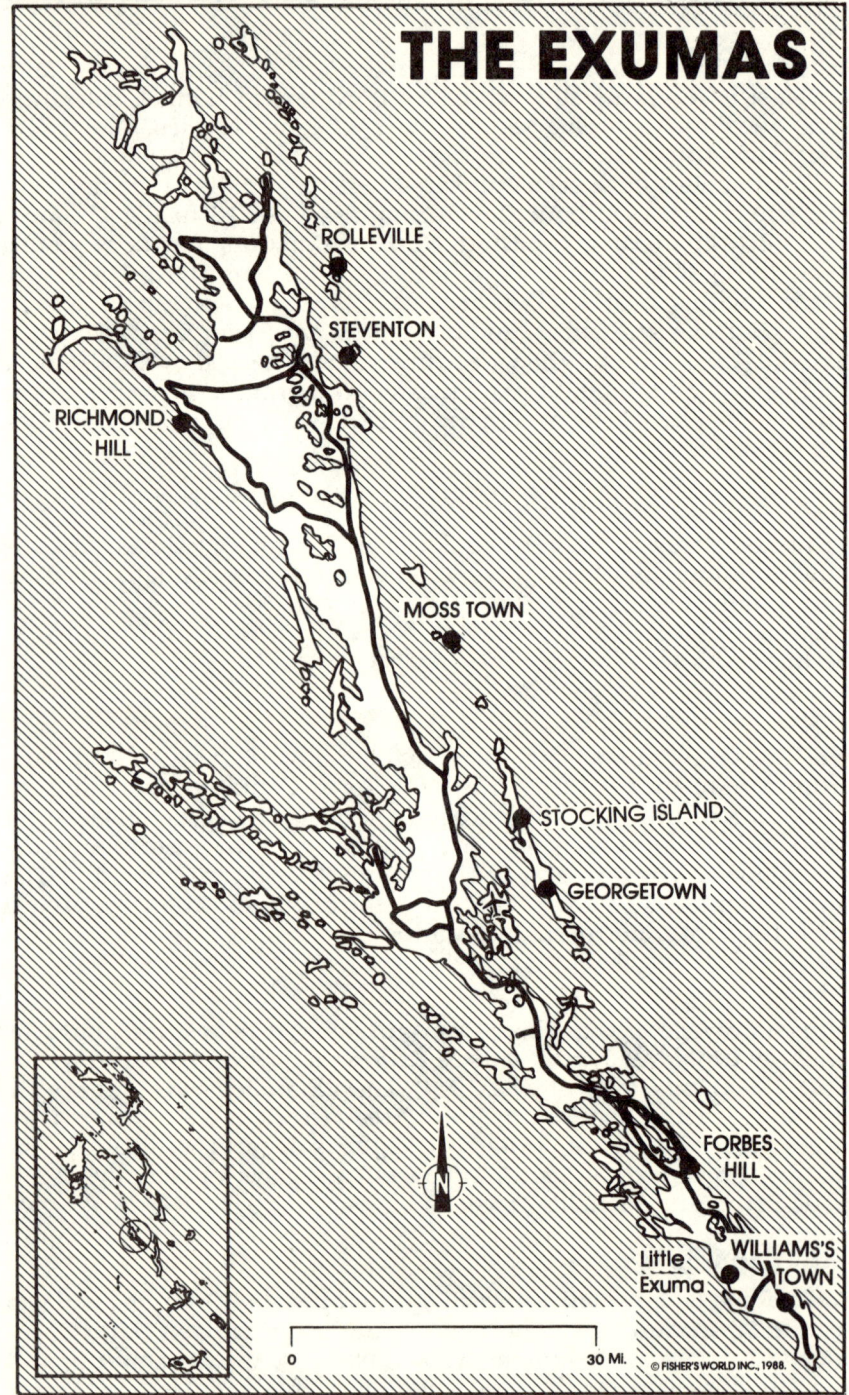

everybody should be loved." There are fine stretches of beach for strolling and shelling.

North Andros

A growing area with several new developments and older settlements, the region includes *Nicholl's Town,* where some half-dozen restaurants with bars feature live band music on weekends. A shopping center supplies native and tourist needs; there are more shops and another restaurant-bar in nearby *Mastic Point,* plus a government clinic. *San Andros,* home of the airport, is in this district, too.

Southern Andros (including Mangrove Cay and Congo Town)

The colorful, annual *August Monday Regatta* brings locals and visitors to watch native skippers vie for awards at Mangrove Cay. All types of fishing thrive here. There are beaches where native master boat-builders set up shop, and tide pools offer superb shelling. Night excursions for land crabs are popular, and many days are spent at little harbors watching cargo boats load and unload. This village and Congo Town are the two southern Andros areas offering tourist accommodations—both sites are far less developed than northern settlements, but have similar sights and activities.

THE EXUMAS

Getting There

By Air

Bahamasair offers direct service twice weekly from Miami, plus regular service connecting Nassau with George Town's airport, where private craft also land, (additional airlines listed in the Travel Planner). At the airport, good food is served for breakfast, lunch, and dinner, as well as snacks and drinks, at *Kermit's Airport Lounge,* open from 7:30 A.M. to approximately 6:30 P.M., according to flight schedules.

By Sea

Mailboat *M/V Nay Dean* departs Nassau on Tuesdays for George Town (also for Long Island's Sims, Salt Pond, and Stella Maris); *M/V The Lady Blanche* departs Nassau on Thursdays for Staniel Cay, Black Point, Farmer's Cay, and Barraterre (all in the Exuma chain of cays).

Whatever they say, they're right—"they" being those who praise Exuma's charm. The only problem is it's hard to find words explicit enough to describe this beauty. Some say you see it best up close, but I marvel at the view from thousands of feet in the sky. It's worth the air fare just to see it. And to make sure you get the best possible view, it's worth checking flight patterns against a map beforehand to determine which side of the plane offers the most advantageous position. Once airborne, press nose to glass and await a spectacle.

When you think you see stripes on the ocean floor, you do. White sand, rippled into patterns by strong currents, is visible because of the incredible clarity of the waters. Suddenly, narrow cays and islets appear, forming a chain that wends southeast, with the deep Exuma Sound pounding eastern banks and the ocean floor rising high and broad from the more distant and westerly Tongue of the Ocean. Through cuts between the tiny bodies of land, currents surge mostly east to west, easily identified since deeper waters are darker in color. Pale greens and aquas are streaked with ultramarines, purples, turquoises—a whole palette of blues and greens, highlighted with white beaches and sand bars, wildly scooped and swirled with unbelieveable underwater formations.

The stunning show runs 140 miles, starting about 45 miles southeast of Nassau, with the Exumas's northern tip curling out of the east to run nearly straight and eventually widen into Great and Little Exuma Islands, which point to, and almost reach, Long Island.

Pilots of small private planes say that they see it best, which is a good reason for making friends among that clan. And yachters have raved for centuries about cruising the Exumas, saying that it is, without doubt, the most beautiful paradise a seafarer could want. Other islands in the Bahamas do offer great natural beauty, they admit, but no other place has a conformation such as these cays create, and no other conformation lies between these two great bodies of water. They also tell you about the exceptional sights you can see from a boat, particularly near the *Exuma Land and Sea Park,* a 177-square-mile preserve founded by the National Trust, where marine life finds sanctuary and thrives to breed with a reckless abandon that enthralls divers, and nature trails and nearly fifty species of birds thrill bird watchers. There are hundreds of virgin beaches; excellent fishing and shelling; plantation ruins and phantom-haunted coves. Don't be content merely to see the Exumas from the sky.

Though private airstrips lace the cays, the public airport is in Great Exuma at George Town. After the plane taxis up to the small buildings and you step out onto the tarmac, you can't miss seeing *Kermit's Airport Lounge.* A green pop-eyed muppet perches over the bar, the namesake of owner Kermit Rolle. Born and bred on the island, he is president of Rolleville, owner of another tavern, local business entrepreneur, and outstanding taxi driver and guide. Although you can stroll through George Town on your own, or rent a car or motor scooter to tour the vicinity, you'll get a better overview if this man introduces you to the towns and tales of Great and Little Exuma. Perhaps, he'll be at the airport and, while driving you to your hotel, can arrange to pick you up later for a day of touring.

George Town

Little George Town snoozes in the sun, crooking an arm to create Victoria Harbour, and stretches its churches, shops and resorts along the eastern shore and around Lake Victoria. If you travel the Queen's Highway from the airport, a 250-foot radio mast reaches skyward to herald your approach to town, and a Baptist church faces assorted stores and eateries as you near the cut of water linking lake to harbor and pass into the center of town. After one or two shops and tourist facilities, the highway bends to avoid a magnificent old fig tree, opposite to a small library and adjacent to a miniature park.

Beyond the fig, George Town's largest and most commanding building rises high, wide, and pink, housing the commissioner's office, courts, police, jail, and other government buildings. Around the road's curve and past a school, three shops and a hotel, St. Andrew's Anglican Church sits on the hill where its doors first opened in 1802. From its wide doors, a sweeping view takes in bits of lakefront, the church community center going up next door, and the tree-lined highway leading past a small rondo of shops, the clinic, and the doctor's house. Go further to two more hotels, or turn inland to drive around the lake, past the Catholic church and a few more buildings, then intersect again with Queen's Highway near the Baptist church. That's George Town, home to some three hundred Bahamians, with facilities for several visiting yachts in addition to about four hundred tourists.

A few thousand people crowd into town each April, drawn by the Bahamian equivalent of the Grand Prix or Kentucky Derby—the *Family Island Regatta*. Also known as the *Out Island Regatta*, it includes about sixty Bahamian vessels—everything from 30-foot Class A racing sloops to 12-foot sailing dinghies—all built by hand and crewed by Bahamians from the Exumas, Abaco, Andros, and numerous other islands. Visitors pack the hotels, bet heavily, applaud the Royal Bahamian Police Force Band on parade, and critically eye the visiting yachts anchored in Victoria Harbour. For a seafaring people who for generations have stretched canvas before the winds, this is the year's most prestigious event.

The race course is the expansive, protected Elizabeth Harbour channel between Great Exuma and seven-mile-long Stocking Island. A chalky pinnacle rises high above the few scattered private homes, still announcing to ships at sea that this is the region of salt flats that meant prosperity from the late 17th through the 19th centuries. For several years, Exuma was the major salt producer of the Bahamas. Today, however, the pillar beckons beachcombers to superb shelling on the eastern shores and to fine white beaches, outfitted with sun shelters and cool drinks, near the little channelside jetty.

North to Rolleville

The Queen's Highway runs the entire length of the island, over lands primarily held in common "generation property" that belongs to five

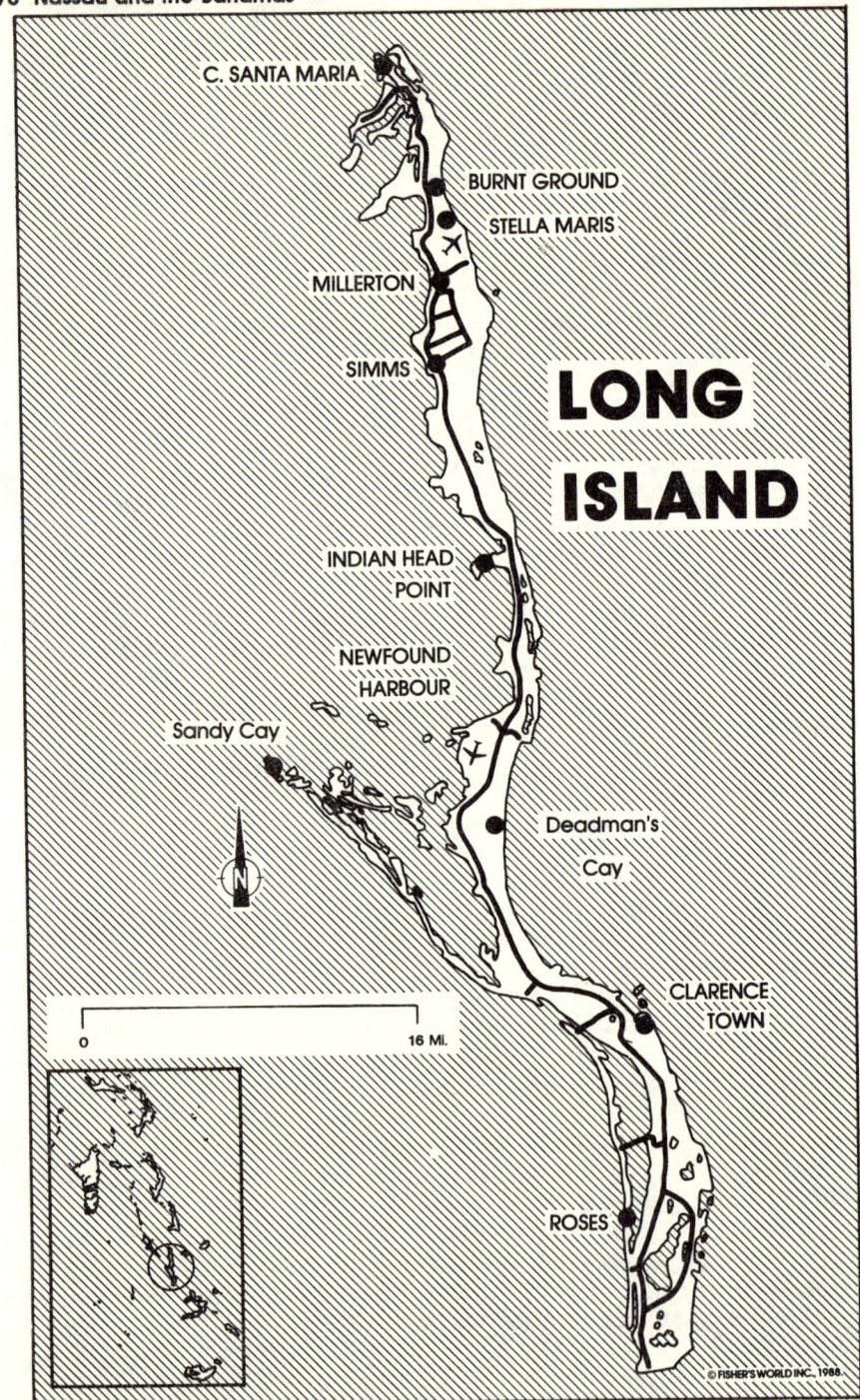

major estates: Ramsey, Mt. Thompson, Steventon, and Rolleville, all north of George Town, and Rolle Town, farther south. Each estate has its own acreage which, says Kermit, combines the best Exuma lands with fresh water, beautiful beaches, and good farming regions.

South to Williams Town

Land development is making slow but sure progress south of George Town, particularly the Bahamas Sound area called *Flamingo Bay*. Here streets are laid out and some houses are already complete, serving their permanent or time-shared owners. A big old white house topping a seaside hill used to be a club, and now acts as a land development office.

Pirate's Point is nearby, just a mile from George Town, straddling a narrow finger of land with views back toward Kidd Cay, and *Kidd Cove* next door. Though the resort is relatively new, the region was indeed a favored haunt of pirates in the early 1700s. The redoubtable Captain William Kidd is said to have preferred this cove and the cay off George Town.

Not far from *Rolle Town* or the Tropic of Cancer, a narrow little bridge joins Great and Little Exuma. Nailed together in the mid-1960s, the bridge took the place of a flat boat in which people barged themselves back and forth across the slim cut of water. There is good land for farming on Little Exuma but its population is sparse. The first region you cross into is called the *Ferry Settlement*, where Red Hill Plantation once was a private home. A thriving establishment lies further down the road, at *Forbes Hill*. The Californians who own and operate this resort call it the *Sand Dollar Beach Club*, but it actually sits on *Pretty Molly Bay*. Pretty Molly was a slave girl who is believed to have grown so despondent about her status that she walked into the bay one moonlit night and never came out. She did not, however, completely disappear, for generations of natives have detailed how Molly frequently returns to the bay and the beach, particularly when the moon is bright. The Americans who bought the place a few years ago claim they've never seen Molly, but locals say perhaps they just haven't recognized her.

If you travel further south almost to the end of the isle, you'll find the *Hermitage*. Built by Loyalist settlers and their slaves, the manor house is still a functioning dwelling—the only old plantation house able to make that claim.

Nearby, in a little Exuma cottage named Tara, lives Gloria Patience, a professional fisherwoman whom most people call the Shark Lady of Exuma. Now sixty-five, she specializes in catching sharks, and has brought in as many as thirty-five in one day. In the evening, she climbs aboard her 13-foot boat, heads for a nearby favorite fishing spot, baits "big hooks with grouper heads on 200-foot lines rigged with chains," then goes home. The next morning she returns to see what she's hooked. "If they're 10 feet or less," she says, "I'll pull them into the boat, but the big babies I have to tow."

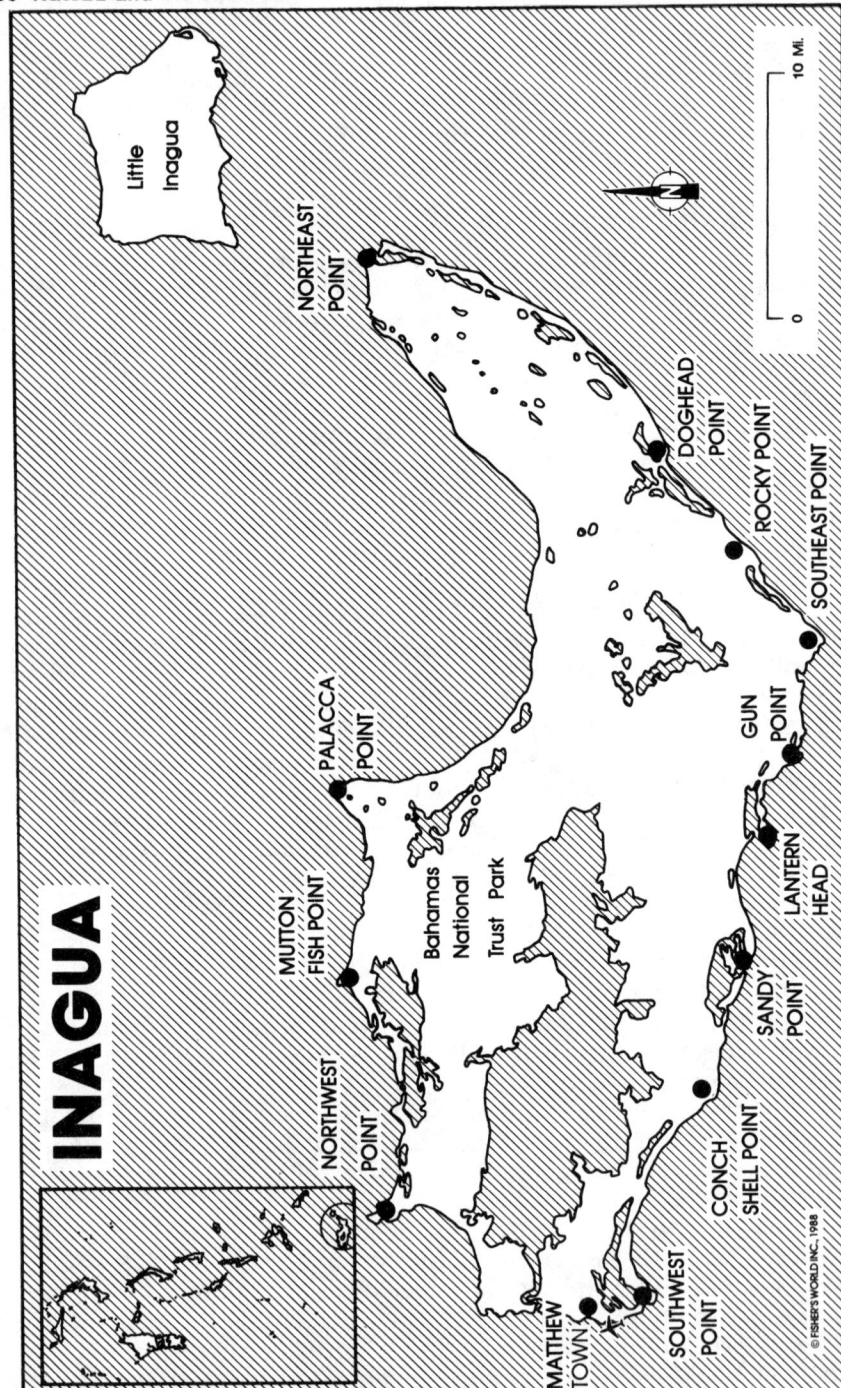

Gloria lives with her husband, George Patience, an artist whose works decorate many hotels and homes. Tourists may visit his studio at Tara and buy paintings and nature collages. They can also ask if Gloria has time to be their guide for an unforgettable fishing trip.

LONG ISLAND

Getting There

By Air

Stella Maris Airport in the north, and central Deadman's Cay Airport are both served regularly by Bahamasair scheduled flights. These facilities are also frequented by private and charter aircraft. Other island airstrips are private, including a northern one on Stella Maris Estates' property and another on the Diamond Salt Company's southern lands.

By Sea

Weekly mailboat service is via the *M/V Bahamaland*—departing Nassau on Saturdays for Clarence Town; also departing Nassau on Fridays for Salt Pond and Clarence Town. Substitute but regular mailboat service to Deadman's Cay and Stella Maris operates weekly and every two weeks via the *M/V Commonwealth* and the *M/V Willmary*.

More than most of its sibling isles, Long Island seems to be a microcosm of this seaswept nation. From generally calm western shallows leading to powdery white leeward beaches, the land rolls up to elevations of 100- to 200-foot crests (Cat Island's 206-foot mountain is the Bahamas' highest peak) that sometimes drop suddenly to the Atlantic shore, where the wind can get choppy and coarse pink sands blanket tiny beaches tucked between rocky formations. These hills flatten out around the southern regions; lakes and ocean "blue holes" dot the land; small cays and islets are sprinkled around the island. Long and thin, its average width is 1.5 miles, and at no point does it span more than 5 miles from shore to shore. From its northernmost tip, which points into Exuma Sound and is severed by the Tropic of Cancer, it snakes southeast to dip into the Crooked Island Passage—a length "officially" measured as 100 miles, or 60 miles, or even 57 miles. Rum Cay and Conception Island stand off its northeastern coast, providing some shielding from direct Atlantic Ocean action, yet from some other two thirds of Long Island, you could look due east and sight no land closer than Africa's shores, thousands of miles away.

As you roam through villages that crop up every few miles all along Rhythm Road (proper name: Government Road), some of the special sights to ferret out include churches. *Clarence Town's* picturesque Anglican and Catholic churches were built by Father Jerome, the priest-architect and Cat Island hermit; the *Bight* boasts the Bahamas' oldest original Spanish church; *Grey's* Catholic Church is special, as are the churches at *Simms*. Houses of worship are as numerous as the bars and taverns.

Deadman's Cay, the biggest village, is home to the Masonic Lodge and Kiwanis Club, and the island doctor's residence and surgery. Nearby are extensive caves, many once homes to the Arawak Indians who left drawings on the walls of tunnels that have never been fully explored by modern man. This village is also the site of plantation ruins. Similar Loyalist-era ruins attract many visitors and are scattered all over the island, with particularly interesting sites at Stella Maris and Grey's. You can check out old and new industry at Hard Bargain, where the Diamond Company harvests salt in June, July, and August. If underwater scenery better suits your fancy, you can choose sites among nearby reefs and waters, or at the famed *Long Island Blue Hole*, where a 900-foot plumb line won't touch bottom. There are coves and beaches of many varieties that offer superb shelling, sporting and views, from the northern cape all the way down to South End, where long and winding Rhythm Road ends right at the surf.

You'll need a boat to visit the smaller Conception Island, which Columbus named Santa Maria de la Concepcion. Today it supports few people but many migrating and regional birds, and the endangered green turtles; it is deemed a sanctuary by the National Trust.

THE INAGUAS

Getting There

By Air
Bahamasair has twice-weekly flights via Mayaguana to Great Inagua's Matthew Town Airport, where private craft also land. There's a ramp for seaplanes, too.

By Sea
Mailboat *M/V Bahamaland* departs Nassau Tuesdays, stops at both Long Island and Acklins Island, then arrives at Matthew Town.

Tiny Little Inagua floats alone and uninhabited, opposite the coast of North East Point. Creating a remote southern border for the Bahamas, Great Inagua lies more than 350 miles from Nassau, and is one of the least visited Family Islands despite its three prime claims to fame: huge flamingos, giant green turtles, and the world's second largest solar evaporation works at the Morton Salt Company complex. To visit these sights on this third largest Bahamian isle means a stay at the island's sole settlement, *Matthew Town* — by itself, a sight to see.

The National Trust arranges tours of *Inagua Park*—287-square miles of wilderness encompassing *Windsor Lake* and constituting a habitat favored by the formerly almost-extinct flamingo. Recently estimated to number about 50,000 here, these neon pink birds share their territory with "nearly every species of bird known to man," to the immense delight of Bahamians, international bird lovers, and members of the U.S. Audubon Society, who keep close tabs on the preserve.

Green turtles are making a comeback nearby. They're busily breeding at *Union Park,* a joint project of the Caribbean Conservation Corp. and the Bahamas Ministry of Agriculture and Fisheries, which restocked these and other waters with thousands of recently hatched green turtles.

After your expedition around Great Inagua, you might sit a spell under the local Lazin Tree or in one of the bars or dining rooms, and query the natives about island lore. They'll tell you, for example, that only one man inhabited Inagua in the beginning of the 1800s; some say he was a slave-killing fugitive from another Bahamian island. Others argue he was Haiti's King Henri Christophe, and they'll offer to guide you to the ruins of a hideaway he built here. You'll also learn about Frenchmen who seriously considered settling here in the mid-1700s, and hear tales of wrecking days as natives point out the lighthouse built in 1870 on Southwest Point. If you ask about the island's name, you'll be told it's but a British bastardization of Heneagua—derived from a term designating a site full of salty water, as Inagua was deemed by its Spanish discoverers.

CROOKED AND ACKLINS ISLANDS

Getting There

By Air

Scheduled weekly, Bahamasair flights link Nassau to Crooked Island Airport, where private planes also land. There is an airstrip on Acklins Island but, to reach Acklins, most tourists take the government ferry that operates between 9 A.M. and 4 P.M. from Brown, Crooked Island, to Lovely Bay, Acklins.

By Sea

Mailboat *M/V Commonwealth* departs Nassau weekly for ports on Crooked Island, Acklins Island, and Mayaguana.

These islands could almost be twins, if only the hump were ironed out of Crooked Island and it was actually land-linked to adjacent Long Cay. As it is, wide headlands of both islands almost kiss at a point called the *Going Through,* then each tapers to form somewhat of a horseshoe around the Bight of Acklins, which opens into the north-south Windward Passage and the southwest-northeast Crooked Island Passage—two key sea lanes. While this position has always had some

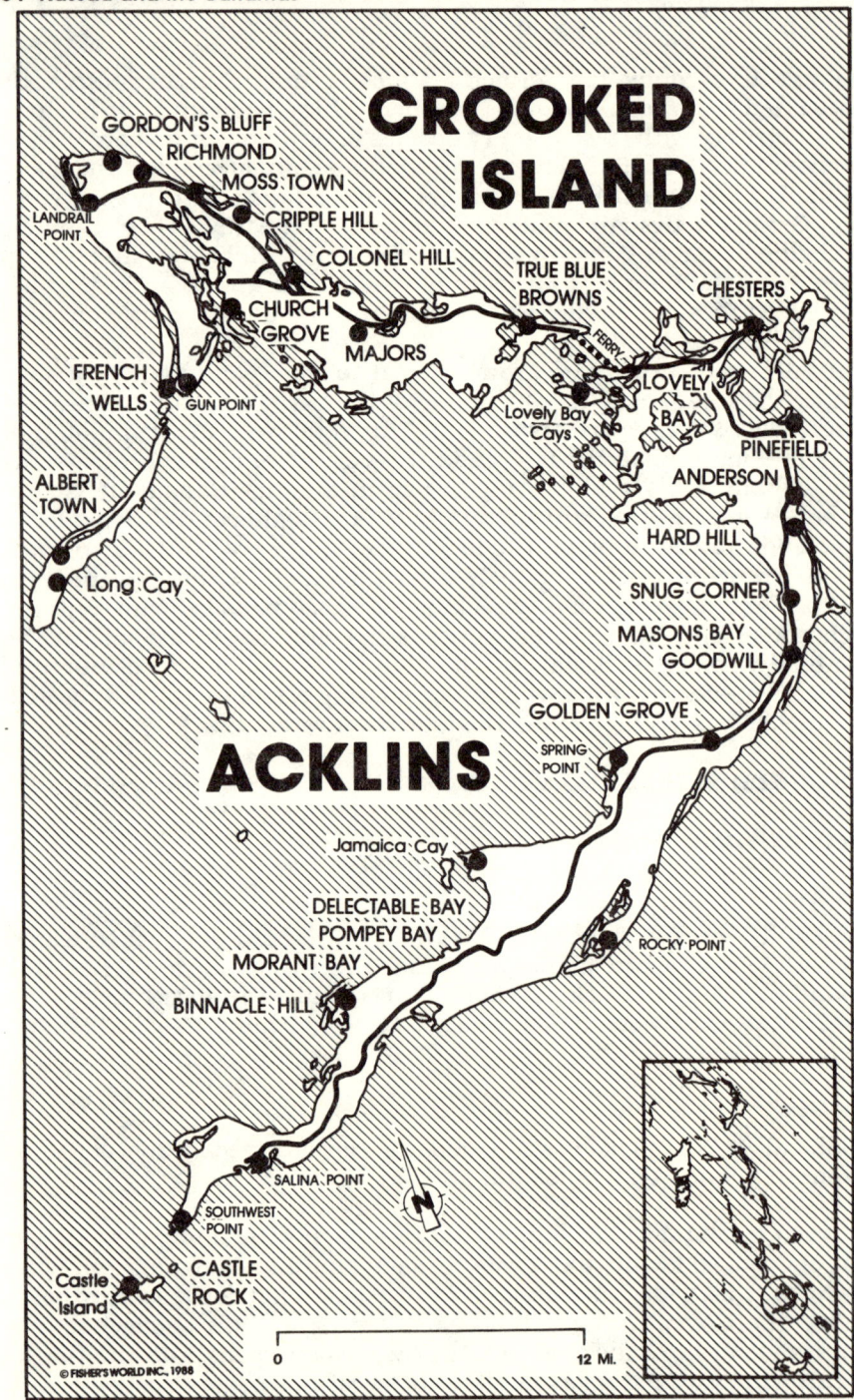

advantages, it has served to sever the island duo from the mainstream of events in Nassau, some 225 miles distant.

The proximity of ocean going vessels probably had a lot to do with Loyalists settling about forty plantations on Crooked Island and a few more on Acklins. They thought it would be easy to ship bales of cotton from the vicinity. That dream was dashed within two decades, however, and most planters had uprooted themselves and abandoned their stakes by the early 1800s. Those who stayed had problems surviving, yet some were part of Crooked Island's volunteer militia, bound and determined to defend whatever they had left during the War of 1812. Most Bahamian militiamen saw action only when their privateering vessels engaged U.S. ships that were stalking British seacraft. The farmer-soldiers here were hard pressed when retaliating American ships raided *Marine Farm*, a British fortification built at the height of old Spanish Main activities.

You can visit the *Marine Farm* site today; then take time to see the *Bird Rock Lighthouse* in the same area. Around 1872 this beacon warned passing ships of shoals and reefs, much to the chagrin of wreckers, who found this region so promising for their salvaging trade that the harbor of Albert Town had become the base of a fleet of independent vessels. The majority of these seafarers also worked the significant sponging grounds in the Bight of Acklins, but they surely worked as wreckers due south off minute Fortune Island, where many of them did, in fact, acquire fortunes. That small southern islet had been an earlier site of salt harvesting after crops failed and planters and their slaves were trying to find ways to stay alive. Fortune Island was again a base for enterprising Bahamians in the early 1900s, for here's where many ocean freighters paused to pick up thousands of stevedores and contract laborers en route to then-developing areas of Mexico and Central America. Later, their temporary assignments completed, the Bahamians would be landed again on Fortune Island, free to take work with the next freighter. World War I brought a halt to this activity. Now classified as a ghost town (according to official literature), Fortune Island nevertheless manages to support a few families.

Back on Crooked Island, there's more to be seen by adventuresome tourists. There are a dozen settlements: From *Colonial Hill* there's a dazzling view of the island and the surrounding bodies of water. *Fortune Hill* is one of the local landmarks, as is *Hope Great House*, which, along with its orchards and gardens, dates from the early 1900s. Across the shallow bay of the Bight, Acklins' is home to fifteen village settlements. The main road winds bayside through *Delectable Bay* and *Binnacle Hill* before turning sharply to *Salina Point*, the southernmost settlement, near the island's South Bluff tip. Just a couple of miles offshore is *Castle Island* with its 1867 lighthouse, which briefly served as a base for pirates who plagued ships in nearby waters. Crooked Island is often referred to as one of "the fragrant islands" because it literally smells good—a feature noted by Christopher Columbus. The explorer landed long enough to briefly search for gold, and claim the territory for Spain after christening it Isabella in honor of his queen.

The fragrance of native herbs still floats on the breezes that play over these islands, mingling with scents from the citrus orchards. You'll see many churches on the island, but there is little shopping beyond staples and necessities. There are several clinics scattered around both islands, plus a few native taverns and eateries, particularly in the Church Grove/Colonial Hill region of Crooked Island. Scuba diving is a key attraction here, along with fishing for tarpon and bonefish.

JUMENTO CAYS

These emerald islets are rarely visited by tourists, yet are greatly admired by the few yachtsmen who cruise here. In its heyday during the latter 1800s, *Ragged Island* boasted about 350 inhabitants and a thriving salt industry. All this started when Loyalist brothers Archibald and Duncan Taylor arrived to claim a land grant, settle *Duncan Town*, and initiate the business that would carry on for generations, even creating secondary, generalized seafaring work for local ships that hauled salt harvests to Nassau. Today, the chain's minute size, relative poverty, and sparse population have so far inhibited its entry into modern tourism or other industries, as has its isolated site. For adventuresome or curious tourists, there is limited air and mailboat service to Duncan Town.

RUM CAY

Easily the most distant member of the family of all tourist-catering isles, tiny Rum Cay measures a mere thirty miles square, has no government airport or airline service, is separated from its nearest neighbors by twenty miles of ocean, and is home to less than one hundred who live in its one settlement, *Port Nelson*. In the 1700s and 1800s this little colony boasted prosperous farms and orchards, fat livestock, and a significant industry shipping a quarter-million tons of salt in its peak year, 1852. The miniature land mass was a vital "last chance" layover for seamen to stock up on fresh foods, water, and supplies before heading east. Hurricanes in 1903 and 1926 wiped out settlements, salt harvests, evaporation basins, and many homes. Then came the exodus that, by the mid-1970s, left only seventy living on the island. Now the village is experiencing a renaissance, due to a philanthropic entrepreneur, Bostonian David Melville, whose initial visit in 1977 grew into an enduring love for Rum Cay. In 1983, the prime minister and other VIPs came to the opening of Melville's Rum Cay Club—a delight to divers and fishing fans.

Author's Choice/Family Islands

HOTELS

ANDROS

Small Hope Bay Lodge Write P.O.Box 21667, Ft. Lauderdale, FL 33335. Phone (809)368-2014; in FL (305)463-9130; in U.S. (800)223-6961. Rustic comfort without luxurious miscellany. Roomy cabins have showers; some cabins feature water beds. Maximumoccupancy of 40 people. All service is gracious and friendly; dress is casual—no ties allowed. The patio is the site for predinner cocktails and appetizers. After dinner, lodge facilities provide games (including bumper pool and table tennis) and there is access to a varied library. There may be dancing to records inside or on the patio. Drinks are passed out from the *Panacea*, an old boat now docked and stocked as the lodge bar. Party at a nearby native club. There's also night reef fishing.

Some guests frequent the lodge during the daytime, too, but most are combing miles of nearly deserted beach, picnicking, swimming and snorkeling, windsurfing, and tanning all over within thatched shelters. You might prefer to take bicycle or automobile tours of near and far settlements, sail an outboard skiff or a Bahamian sloop, or fish. Perhaps you'd rather soak in the only Family Island hot tub, snooze in hammocks, learn about local greenery on a bush walk with one of the staff, or trek to the inland freshwater swimming hole.

It's the rare guest who doesn't venture under the water. For more than twenty years now, Dick and his sizable dive staff have taught beginners how to feel free in the sea. Together, their certifications encompass NAUI, PADI, ACUC, and YMCA (see Travel Planner). All the equipment is at hand; there's a good balance between the supervision and freedom of the diver, and the safety records stand unblemished.

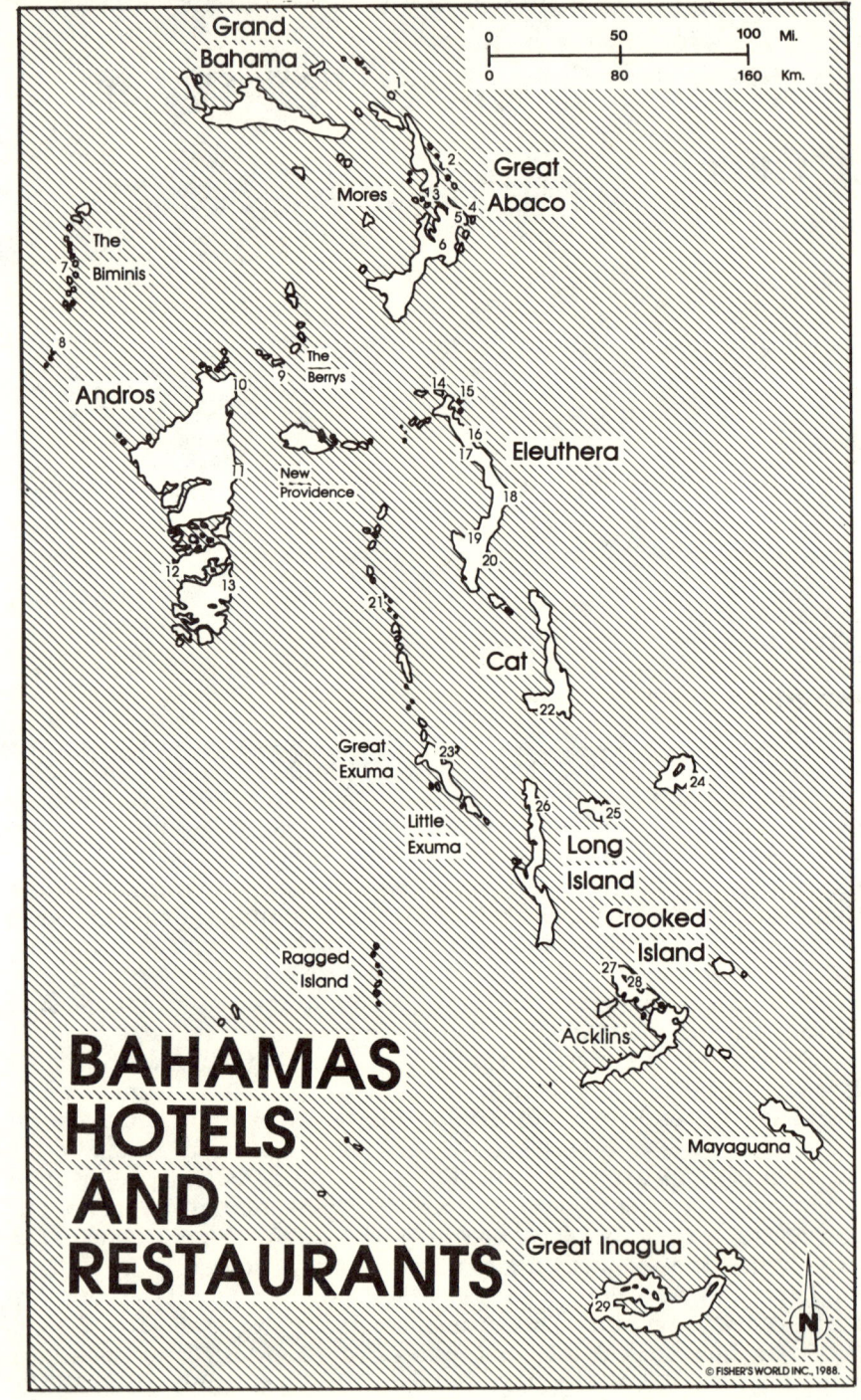

KEY TO BAHAMAS HOTELS AND RESTAURANTS

- 4 Abaco Inn
- 10 Andros Beach Hotel & Villas
- 7 Bimini's Big Game Fishing Club & Hotel
- 7 Bimini's Blue Water Marina
- 8 Cat Cay Club
- 16 Cambridge Villas & Restaurant
- 19 Cape Eleuthera Resort & Yacht Club
- 9 Chub Cay Club
- 18 Club Med-Eleuthera
- 7 Complete Angler
- 5 Conch Inn Resort & Marina
- 15 Coral Sands
- 20 Cotton Bay Beach
- 22 Cutlass Bay Yacht Club
- 5 CYN Thia's Kitchen
- 16 Dunmor Beach Club
- 7 Fisherman's Paradise
- 29 Ford's Imagua Inn
- 5 Great Abaco Hotel
- 2 Green Turtle Club & Marina
- 4 Hope Town Harbour Lodge
- 5 Jib Room
- 5 Keys Bakery & Restaurant
- 13 Las Palmas Beach
- 29 Main House
- 12 Mangrove Cay Guest Houses
- 6 Mother Merle's Fishnet Restaurant
- 2 New Plymouth Club & Inn
- 23 Out Island Inn
- 23 Peace & Plenty Hotel
- 23 Pieces of Eight Hotel
- 15 Pink Sands
- 23 Pirates Point Villas
- 27 Pittstown Point Landings Ltd. Inn
- 7 Red Lion Restaurant
- 23 Regatta Point
- 16 Romora Bay Club
- 25 Rum Cay Club
- 14 Runaway Hill
- 11 Small Hope Bay Lodge
- 14 Spanish Wells Beach Resort & Harbour Club
- 21 Stanlel Cay Yacht Club
- 26 Stella Maris Inn
- 28 Sunny Lea Guest House
- 17 Thompson's Bakery
- 10 Tadwind Village
- 3 Treasure Cay Resort
- 23 Two Turtles Inn
- 15 Valentine's Yacht Club, Inn & Drive Center
- 1 Walker's Cay Hotel & Marina
- 14 Walton's Laugousta Restaurant & Bar
- 20 Windermere Island Club

*For Grand Bahama and New Providence Islands see the Freeport Map and the New Providence Hotel Map.

Minimum diving age of 14 is somewhat negotiable (the oldest diver to date was 91). *Moderate.*

Andros, CONGO TOWN, south

Las Palmas Beach Hotel P.O.Box 800. Phone (809)329-4661. Perfect spot for vacationers who really want to be far from the crunch of commerce yet within civilized, modern environs. Situated two miles from the airport, the 20 double rooms are in air-conditioned cottages, scattered through gardens that encompass a pool and tiled patio. Tennis courts, small rental boats, and private dockage (no cruising yachts, please), snorkeling, boating, and deep-sea fishing. Dining room, bar, TV area, and lounge with occasional disco dancing. Rental cars, bicycles, and scooters are available. *Inexpensive.*

Two nearby travelers' choices are *Congo Beach Gardens* and *Royal Palm* guest houses. Both are *Inexpensive.*

Andros, MANGROVE CAY

All tourist accommodations are in six guest houses that range from small cottages to two-story facilities where between 4 and 8 double rooms are available. Each offers local water sports and entertainment, native food, and friendly service in neatly maintained sites. Contact them directly or through Bahamas Reservations Service: *Bannister's Guest House* (AP only), *Cool Breeze Cottage, White Sand Beach Hotel, Mangrove Cay Beach Hotel,* and *Moxey's Guest House,* all in Little Harbour; and *Longley's Guest House* in Lisbon Creek.

Andros, NORTH ANDROS

Andros Beach Hotel & Villas Nicholl's Town. Phone toll free (800)327-8150. An attractive, modern place specializing in fine diving. Skin- and scuba-diving fans will recognize Neal Watson, formerly found on North Bimini and elsewhere around the island nation. Watson's diving dedication led to the total revamp of this property and its underwater programs. His expertise undoubtedly had something to do with this hotel being chosen as headquarters for the 1985 inaugural of the annual *Bahamas Freediving (skin diving) Championship.* Some of the 24 air-conditioned and neatly appointed rooms are on a strip; others are in interesting cottages overlooking poolside gardens and the beach, which runs undisturbed for three miles. The bar is nearby, and there's a lounge where a live dance band performs three nights weekly. Boating, waterskiing, snorkeling, fishing of all sorts, and two tennis courts. Dockage is available; yachts find fuel and water available on request. Cars, bicycles, and mopeds can be rented. *Morgan's Bluff* is a fine nearby tour site. *Inexpensive to Moderate.*

Tradewind Villas P.O.Box 4465. Phone (809)329-2040. Also in Nicholl's Town and sharing many of the nearby hotel's facilities, these charming villas are set in a beautifully gardened community, with shopping nearby. Of the twenty-six houses here, twenty-two operate under hotel license, accommodating 2 to 4 people each, with one duplex villa on the beach. There's no glitz and glitter here, just family atmosphere for quiet relaxing and barefoot days. *Inexpensive.*

BERRY ISLANDS

Chub Cay Club Chub Cay. On private island. Phone (809)325-1490. This friendly resort club admits non-members, who sign up to return frequently. A port of entry with customs officials, Chub Cay has its own 5,000-foot surfaced airstrip. The 55 air-conditioned rooms include accommodations in lovely villas, in four private houseboats, and in pretty and trim motel-type rooms; children under twelve can stay free with their parents. There are no historical sites or flashy show-biz revues, just calm and casual unstructured living, with naturally beautiful scenery, extremely well-kept environs, and good food. The *Flying Bridge Restaurant* serves American and Bahamian fare, ranging from snacks to fine dinners augmented by poolside cocktails and music for dancing. Facilities here are excellent, and both fishing and diving offer varied treats for beginners and old pros, including various tournaments such as the annual July *Chub Cay Blue Marlin Competition*. The 75-slip marina is equipped with fuel, water, electricity, showers, ice, Tami-lift, dry-storage facilities, a liquor store, and full commissary. Here's where charter fishing boats await guests, but private yachtsmen should be sure to make advance reservations for dockage. Scuba diving and snorkeling here are marvelous. Rental gear is at hand, and two dive boats are kept busy during daily series of dive site outings. Two all-weather tennis courts, powdery white beaches with great shelling, rental bikes, assorted water sports and the wild bird reserve on nearby *Crab Cay*.

BIMINI

Bimini's Big Game Fishing Club & Hotel P.O.Box 699. Alice Town. This comfortable resort welcomes guests to 35 rooms, 4 penthouses with TV, and 6 cottages. All are oversized, modern, and air-conditioned and have private patios. Large marina with 52 slips for visiting yachts and charter fishing vessels (with guides available), plus fuel, ice, water, showers, power, and a liquor store. There's a patio-pool beside the sprawling dining room, where you'll find varied menu selections and friendly, attentive service. Deep-sea fishing, boating, tennis courts, public beach nearby, snorkeling and waterskiing. This hotel sponsors the annual June *Bimini Billfish Tournament* and others. *Moderate to Expensive.*

Bimini's Blue Water Marina P.O.Box 627. Alice Town. Phone (809)347-2166. Sleep where Hemingway slept by renting the Marlin Cottage: three double bedrooms, all needed paraphernalia plus private garden pool ($195 daily; $1,275 weekly). Six double rooms and suites with ocean views—all modern, neat, and nicely appointed; the *Anchorage Bar and Restaurant*, with verandas overlooking the sea has a wine list for lunch and dinner. Open from 7 A.M. through 10 P.M. or later, the Anchorage prepares box lunches for fishermen with advance notice. Swimming pool with refreshment bar, and 42-slip marina that offers dockage, fuel, ice, water, power, showers, lockers, deep freeze for your catches, plus charter boats and skippers for deep-sea, bone-, and bottom-fishing. This is home for the annual *Hemingway All-Billfish Tourney* in April, and for other competitions, too. Accommodations range from *Inexpensive to Moderate*.

The Compleat Angler P.O.Box 601. Alice Town. Big on nostalgia, this hotel boasts 12 rooms and one 2-room apartment; all are spacious, air-conditioned, clean and simple. A popular restaurant and bar operate on the ground floor, and the front-yard bar circles an old almond tree towering among flowered greenery. Rental bicycles and scooters are available, and there's a meeting room with projector, screen and other equipment. Rates are good for boating and deep-sea fishing. Tennis, diving, snorkeling, and marina docks are nearby, and other sports can be arranged.

Also Recommended Cat Cay Club Further south, on Cat Island, this elegant private resort reportedly accepts membership applications and caters to luxury-conscious internationals.

RESTAURANTS First, I highly recommend restaurants of the *Compleat Angler, Bimini Big Game Fishing Club & Hotel*, and *Bimini Blue Water's Anchorage Restaurant*. Aside from these and the ones listed, there are other places offering snacks and full meals.

The Red Lion Inn This restaurant has a bayfront dining room and an air of jolly England. Steaks, seafood, and barbecues are on the menu and prepared so well that most locals rate this food Bimini's best. Go for conch fritters or crab legs plus a Love Machine or Between the Sheets brew while you watch TV in the bar (if the Miami Dolphins are on, that's what you'll watch). *Inexpensive to Moderate*

Fisherman's Paradise Restaurant and Bar Three daily meals with native flavor. All food is prepared to order and served by a friendly staff; sandwiches and take-out specials are prepared for fishermen, Television plus a jukebox provide entertainment. *Inexpensive to Moderate*

SPORTS Other than marinas listed as part of hotel operations, this mecca for sportsfishing and boating also has *Weech's Bimini Dock*, with 15 slips, ice, water, electricity, showers, and charter craft. Dive master Neal Watson offers full scuba equipment, lessons, and great dive trips from his *Underwater Adventures* at *Brown's Marina*, where there's a fine 22-slip marina offering all marine services, boating, and deep-sea fishing. Fishing equipment is available and there's access to the public beach.

HISTORIC SITES South Bimini is where you'll find the *Fountain of Youth* Ponce de Leon searched so long to discover—a taxi can show you the site. Also, several scientists and modern adventurers claim to have found the fabled lost ruins of *Atlantis* under waters off Bimini shores. Another, newer site lies between here and Cat Cay—a concrete boat that ran rum during Prohibition, and served as a bomb site for WW II training aircraft. It now is a favorite dive area. Nearby, the famed *Flight 19* executed a bombing practice before its five U.S. Navy *Avenger TBM* aircraft flew into oblivion—lost without a trace, prompting writers to create *The Bermuda Triangle.* That was in December, 1945. Contemporary political events are linked to Bimini's Big Game Fishing Club Hotel's dock, where a piling plaque marks the Gary Hart Memorial Dock. In the Court passageway leading to Brown's Hotel dockside bar, restaurant, and office, you'll see large plagues honoring former New York politician Adam Clayton Powell and Captain Sam Yolen, commemorating their outstanding contributions to big game fishing in the Bahamas, and honoring Captain A.B. Chalk of Chalk's International Airline.

CROOKED AND ACKLINS ISLANDS

Pittstown Point Landings Limited Inn Though quite new, this self-sufficient resort at Landrill Point, Crooked Island, already has earned an exclusive rating among well-heeled guests who frequently pilot their private planes to land on the inn's own 2,400-foot airstrip, or cruise into harbor aboard their own yachts. No matter how they arrive, they unpack casual gear in one of the 14 double rooms, then usually head for the office to sign up for the daily scheduled series of dives among coral gardens and reefs, about the barrier reef, or into the depths of dropoffs. Even nondivers enjoy snorkeling off the private beach. Closed all of September. *Expensive.*

Also Recommended Tourist facilities are few, far between, and not rated in this region. However, some do exist. In Crooked Island's airport town, Colonel Hill, *Sunny Lea Guest House,* carefully maintained by Eunice Deleveaux, has four rooms accommodating 12, with marvelous views encompassing the entire island. Three miles away in Cabbage Hill, *T & S Guest House* offers six rooms plus cottages, where beach privileges are two miles distant, but scooters, bikes, and cars can be rented. On Acklins Island, Williams Hilltop View has four guest rooms, a wide private beach, boating, fishing, and rental cars.

EXUMAS, GREAT EXUMA

Out Island Inn P.O.Box 49. George Town. Phone (809)336-2171. Exuma's largest tourist facility is intimate in concept, offering 80 air-conditioned rooms. One- and two-story rustic hotel buildings are part of a villagelike cluster of structures, each named for Rolle family settlements. The main dining room has its own site, overlooking beach and harbor, where three daily meals feature American, Continental, and Bahamian cuisine. The ocean-viewing *Reef Bar* is open each evening. Two tennis courts (rental racquets and balls in the *Tennis Shop*), private beach, and swimming in the freshwater pool or by the beach here or on Stocking Island (order a box lunch and spend the day). The marina offers windsurfing, waterskiing and other sports activities, a twice daily ferry to nearby Stocking Island beaches, and 30-slip dockage. Games are available in the Exuma Room. Volleyball and shuffleboard courts. Rental boats, cars, scooters and bicycles. Casual atmosphere. Children under twelve stay free with parents (great place for kids). *Nova Scotia Bank* and shops are here, too. *Inexpensive to Moderate.*

Peace & Plenty Hotel George Town P.O.Box 55. Phone (809)336-2551/2; toll free in U.S. and Canada (800)327-5118. This once was a private home where part of the property was a sponge loft. Its quaint bar, a favored yachters' hangout, supposedly was once the kitchen of a plantation slave compound. A hotel since 1958, the property has evolved into 32 rooms with air-conditioning, telephones, and balconies. Recently refurbished, this charming resort is built around a pool and patio overlooking Stocking Island, where its beach club is accessible via daily boat trips. If you're a seafood fan, the fare is good, otherwise it's marginal and priced high. Some families bring their own fixings or eat elsewhere. Though the service is inconsistent, laughter seems always to be rolling from the kitchen. Boating, fishing, scuba, tennis and other sports can be arranged and paddle boats, sunfish sailboats, and windsurfing equipment are available. Stop by the desk to rent cars, cycles, bikes, sail or motorboats. The biggest attractions here are privacy, snorkeling, and bonefishing. No children under six allowed. *Inexpensive.*

Pieces of Eight Hotel George Town P.O.Box 49. Phone (809)336-2600. Island rock, bleached wood, and climbing vines set the scene for this two-story hilltop hotel overlooking Elizabeth Harbour and Stocking Island. The 32 rooms are air-conditioned, with balconies and nice furnishings. Central swimming pool and patio with great views. The dining room, where American, Continental, and native meals are served, is walled by windows on three sides and flanked by the neat, nautical *Pirates Den Bar*, which opens before lunch and features occasional evening music. Guests may cross Queen's Highway and enjoy all facilities at the *Out Island Inn* sister resort, where they also can eat and sign the check. Recently refurbished. Rental bicycles available. *Inexpensive to expensive.*

Pirates Point Villas P.O.Box 23, a mile south of town at Kidd Cove. Phone (809)336-2554. Well-designed, attractively furnished, modern villas. Air conditioned and constructed of local stone, each split-level villa can accommodate a small family, and features a well-equipped kitchen plus a covered terrace overlooking the bay. Marina, dock, and private beach with barbecue facilities and snorkeling equipment. Beautiful palms, gardens are well tended. Amenities include maid and laundry service, rental vehicles, and arranged sports. By the time this is published, some of the new time-share and rental construction may be complete, including 33 villas, a restaurant, bar, and swimming pool. *Inexpensive.*

Regatta Point Phone (809)336-2206. Five roomy and quite attractive efficiency apartments of one and two bedrooms are set among the trees, lawns and gardens of this Kidd Cay retreat that offers the best views of sailing activities. This secluded holiday site caters to ninety percent repeat business from North America and Europe. Its friendly owners supply daily maid service and arrange sports. There's a private beach. Guests bring or buy their own provisions. *Inexpensive.*

Two Turtles Inn George Town P.O. Box 51. Phone (809)336-2545. Offering 14 rooms that include 4 efficiencies with cooking facilities, this wood and stone establishment has satellite TV for all rooms. There's an interesting bar, and a restaurant featuring good local food with service indoors or in the courtyard. A gift shop is on the premises. Bikes are free for guests, who can ride them to the nearby beach, or try the boat to Stocking Island ($5). Sports can be arranged, as can vehicle rentals. *Moderate.*

SPORTS

Snorkeling and Scuba Diving In George Town, *Exuma Divers* is owned and operated by Wendle McGregor, who rents and sells scuba and snorkel gear. An Andros native who has been diving some eighteen years, McGregor provides beginner and certification courses; he also gives tips to underwater photographers and rents cameras they can use. He has his own dark room to develop their shots. He offers a number of dive trips aboard three custom-made boats that accommodate four to eighteen divers each. Ask about special reef, blue hole and cave dives, night dives and four-day packages of assorted dives. McGregor also operates special fishing charters, waterskiing facilities, and dive cruises to nearby wrecks, dropoffs, islands, and undersea parks.

Fishing If it swims in Bahamian waters, *Clifford Dean's Charter Fishing Service* in George Town knows its habits and can lead you to the right spot to catch it. Likely, that'll be nearby—Dean lists catches of huge marlins, dolphins, kingfish, sailfish, sharks, barracuda, bottom fish, and bonefish. He'll even teach you the ropes or, rather, the lines, of fishing aboard his fully equipped 30-foot *Gemini II*. Dean also provides boat sightseeing trips and cruises.

Boating *Minns Water Sports* rents small sailboats, outboard skiffs, and 16-foot Boston whalers. Bonefishing trips are also available, along with light marine repairs, marine and electrical supplies, and a full marine store. Small dock, no slips.

Exuma Docking Services supplies water, electricity, fuel, laundry, showers, ice, and marine accessories for yachtsmen (6-foot draft at low tide). Fishing trips can be arranged here, and there's an outboard mechanic on duty.

Getting Around Taxis and rental vehicles are available through hotels. In George Town, try *R.R. Maynard Car Rentals. Sam Gray* rents cars and scooters from an Out Island Inn site.

Exuma, STANIEL CAY

Staniel Cay Yacht Club Phone Florida for information (305)467-6850. It's only six rooms, with a bar, dining room, and beach privileges, but oh, what a fine relaxed atmosphere. There's a 12-slip marina with fuel, electricity, water, ice, laundry, dockage, and full boat repair, even including marine electronics. Windsurfing boards and scuba gear are rented here, fishing is great with local guides, and the small dive operation has many fans. Yachters around the world quite likely know of the tiny village of Staniel Cay, a haven for sailing folk. You may have seen its *Thunderball Grotto* in that James Bond film of similar name. You can see it again, up close, even without a yacht, for there is transportation available up to this cay from George Town Airport. FAPonly. *Moderate.*

Getting Around *Exuma Flotilla, Ltd.* offers bare-boat charters, provisioned boats, captained and flotilla cruising on request. c/o P. O. Box N-910, Nassau.

INAGUA

Further from the crowds than most islands, and less developed for tourism, Inagua nevertheless manages to attract some visitors by air and some by sea. Only two establishments exist for travelers, and reservations for each are via direct contact. Both can arrange tennis or fishing trips for guests. Both are in or near Matthew Town, home of the Great Inagua Airport. Neither is rated.

Ford's Inagua Inn Two-story concrete-block white and bright, with five neat rooms above dining room/bar. Closed part of the year. *Inexpensive.*

Main House Open year-round, offering eight double rooms and modern, comfy dining. *Inexpensive.*

SPORTS *Matthew Town Dock* Here's where you can find deep-sea and bottom fishing guides; boating fuel and water on request. However, as there's no dockage, visiting yachts must drop anchor in the bay.

LONG ISLAND

Stella Maris Inn, Marina/Yacht Club and Estates P.O.Box 105. Phone (305)467-0466. A large complex that encompasses a good chunk of northern Long Island, this resort combines comfort with beauty, adding fine food and services and a management that asserts itself trying to discern and meet guests' needs and whims. Here you can choose nicely decorated, air-conditioned hotel rooms adjacent to the lodge, or hotel-serviced rooms, studios, suites, apartments, townhouses, and villas scattered around the property. The resort is picturesque, with high standards in evidence everywhere. The attractive lodge includes offices, a comfortable bar with an expert bartender, a patio for dancing and barbecues, a gift shop, and a dining room where a huge 17th-century anchor rests against a textured rock wall, facing three walls of windows. Meals are prepared by an educated chef who takes extra steps to please, and served by an attentive, cheery staff. The food is delicious at the *Marina/Yacht Club*, too (Sunday guitar concerts). There are rooms and apartments here, plus cottages on a channel leading to fine, leeward bonefishing and bottom-fishing grounds, and a dockside houseboat that sleeps 8 and is yours as a bareboat charter or with a skipper. Yachts can dock and find full services and repairs here, plus all marine supplies. The 12-slip marina's own fleet includes a 15-passenger glass-bottom boat, several small rental boats, and large sail and power vessels for deep-sea charter or cruising, plus dive boats with custom platforms. Soon final touches should be complete on the 62-foot boat that's being built to take 20 passengers overnight to Rum Cay and Conception Island, or on longer trips. The *Dive Shop* with free snorkel gear and rental scuba equipment for 50. Four dive masters offer courses ranging from beginner through instructor (PADI), employing the 18-foot checkout pool, and tests in classrooms and underwater. It's this dive operation that attracts many internationals to Stella Maris, where highly touted dive sites include wide varieties of shallows, reefs, wrecks, walls, caves, blue holes, and regular encounters with shark.

Naturalists also enjoy this resort, where winter strolls along the many roads reveal several species and color of delicate, tall-stalked orchids. The year-round abundant greenery includes wild almonds, gnarled trees, and seven-year apples that locals say are poisonous only every seventh year, but they're not sure of the years' count now. There are many beautiful wild and cultivated flowers, dazzling views of water from cliffs and beaches, the fascinating old ruins of *Adderley's Plantation,* and a marvelous, huge, weathered cave. Slabs of rocks have been positioned into tables, benches, buffet servers, a bar and a bandstand, and truly memorable weekly parties are held here. Weekly dances, barbecues, and parties are also held at the tennis clubhouse or the lodge, where rental cars, jeeps, and bikes are available. Several tennis courts, three swimming pools, three miles of protected beach, children's swings, and small sailboats. Waterskiing, jet skiing, windsurfing. Small aircraft can be rented at the resort's own landing strip, which doubles as the regional airport. *Stella Maris Charter Service* travels between here and the Fort Lauderdale International Airport ($260 round trip). Several package holidays are available. *Inexpensive to Moderate.*

RESTAURANTS Both dining facilities of *Stella Maris Inn and Marina/Yacht Club* are highly recommended. Also recommended is the *Hibiscus Inn* restaurant, offering good native food in a new building with a relaxing atmosphere. Service is available on the tiny patio, or inside among a mini-museum exhibition of old guns, bottles, belt buckles, and other oddities dredged from the ocean floor nearby. At *Thompson Bay Inn Patio and Grill*, the native food is good and the ambience is lively, with an active room sporting electric games, a pool table, a bar and jukebox, and weekend conviviality echoing through to large adjacent dining rooms.

Getting Around Taxis are available at both airports, and there is one island jitney. Rental vehicles are arranged through hotel and guest-house offices.

RUM CAY

Rum Cay Club Write P.O.Box 22396, Ft. Lauderdale, FL 33335. Phone Florida collect (305)467-8355; toll free in U.S. (800)334-6869;or Bahamas Reservation Service (800)327-0787. In this island nation where holiday experiences hinge so often on a resort's management, it's hard to find a host as committed to the guest's comfort and pleasure as David Melville. He combined his business acumen with large dollops of faith, and hope to create "the finest possible" facility—which simultaneously provided an economic base for the islet, jobs for all able locals, and a vacation site fabled for diving (fascinating for fishermen and beachcombers, too). Its cluster of new, casually elegant and roomy accommodations features very large rooms with two double beds, full bathrooms, carpets, rattan/wicker furnishings, small anterooms with desk, light table and magnifying loupe for easy scanning of your latest underwater or landside photography efforts, and large, private, ocean-side screened patios. The roomy main lodge boasts sun deck plus hot tub, patio, boutique, video film center, video games, slide-screening gear, paperback/magazine library, computerized office area, an aquarium behind the well-tended bar, and exceptionally comfortable furnishings. Planted walkways lead across sandy landscaped terrain to connect all facilities, including the dining room where the three superb meals are daily treats. Dinners come with complimentary wine and service is pleasantly attentive.

Color film (E-6) is developed overnight in the photo lab. You can rent underwater cameras such as the Nikonos IV, the Nikonos 15 mm U/W lenses, strobes, etc. Experienced dive masters and special experts teach underwater photography. Comprehensive dive facilities, training from beginner through advanced. Super dive sites include virginal reefs (bank and barrier) teeming with marine life, rich corals and black coral forests, giant rays and crabs, sharks and tame groupers, and wrecks such as the 101-gun British warship sunk in 1861. Tunnels and pinnacles, grottos and deep ridges, overhangs and sheer vertical drop-offs—all in water averaging 100-foot visibility.

Shell-strewn beaches also delight collectors and picnic lovers. Inside shoreline caves, contemporary graffiti mixes with pre-Colombian Lucayan Indian carvings, just part of the isle's history to scout via club vehicles, by foot, or via horse. At *Port Nelson Village* are friendly folk, a commissary, a restaurant, and several interesting village sights. Back at the resort, there's basketball, tennis, windsurfing, sailboats, Hobie cats, and a club catamaran. Private pilots enjoy the airstrip where the club planes land and depart. A mailboat visits each week (big day!); yachtsmen come often. Club guests also tour via tram cars sporting red and white striped awnings—the trams are towed by jeeps. FAP. *Moderate to Expensive.*

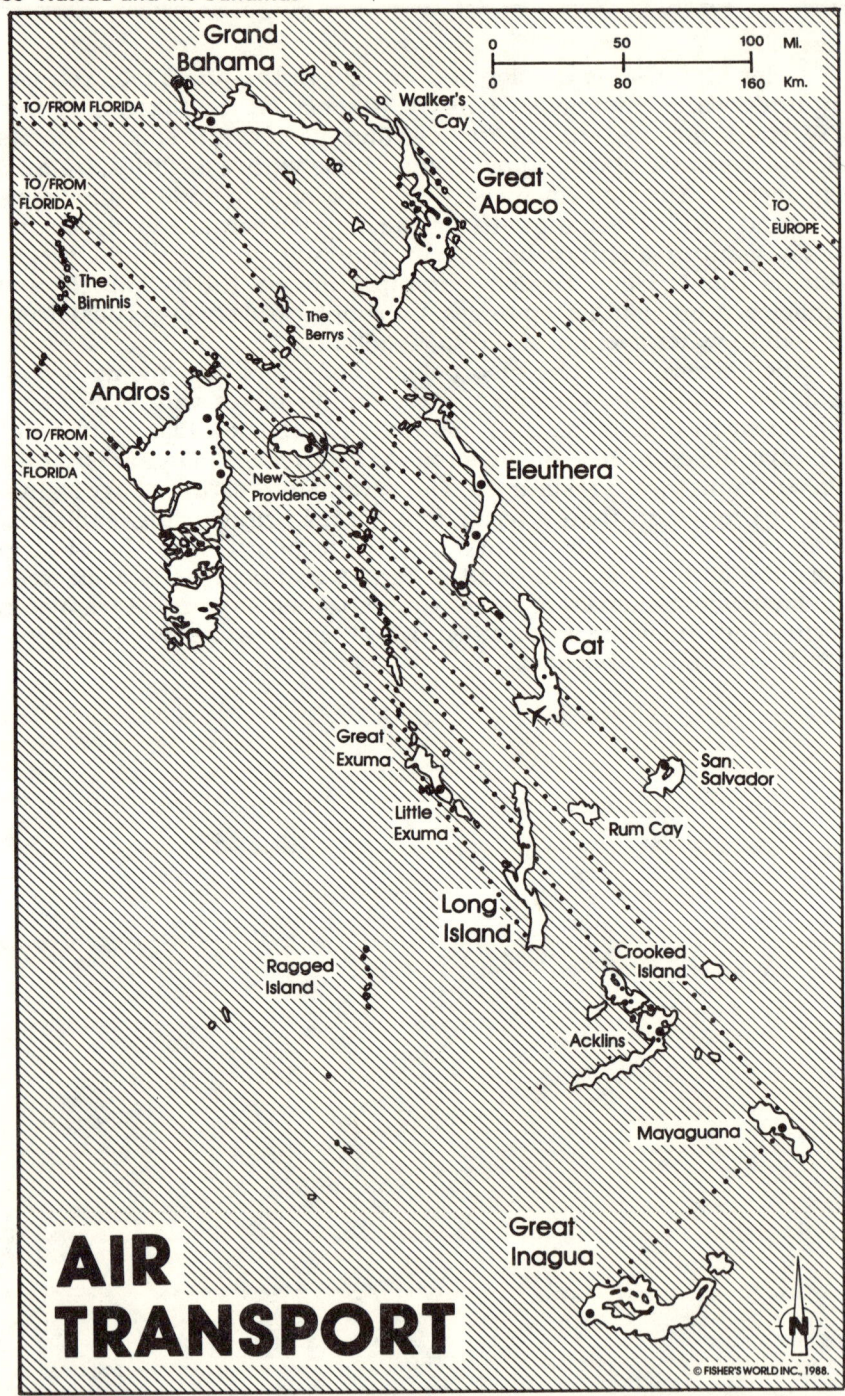

Underwater Adventures in the Bahamas
by Renee Wright

A visitor to the Bahamas who remains above the water misses much of the country's unique splendor. Much of this island nation lies below water. Only 700 small landmasses, many of them just rocky outcrops or sandbars, break the surface. The rest of the Bahamas, more than 90,000 square miles of it, lies beneath the waves.

Indeed, the Bahamas take their name from the Spanish word, "bajamar," meaning the shallows. Some claim the islands are the last remnant of the lost continent of Atlantis.

Behind the Mirror

Others call it the Looking Glass World. Like Alice when she stepped through the mirror, visitors enter a new reality when they pierce the water's reflective surface. The Bahamas contain one of the world's most extensive reef systems. Here, lush gardens of violet sea fans wave amid vividly hued cities of living coral.

The weird shapes resemble the surface of an alien planet where different laws of nature rule. Through them swim inhabitants just as surreal: neon bright fish of impossible shape, giant clams colored a violent purple, huge winged creatures flapping lazily with the current, chains of lobsters migrating single file to some mysterious destination.

This vast underwater wonderland makes the Bahamas a hugely popular vacation destination for divers. They come from around the world to visit sites with exotic names and the reputations to match, places like the Devil's Backbone... the Tongue of the Ocean... Shark Reef.

No visitor should pass up the opportunity to peek into this unknown universe. Fortunately, you don't need expensive equipment or prolonged training. Most people can learn to snorkel in minutes. A simple mask, breathing tube, and pair of fins are your passport to the Looking Glass World.

Above the Reef

Coral reefs surround many of the Bahama Islands. The shores of Eleuthera and Great Exuma are close to sea gardens. Less than a mile off the east coast of Andros lies an immense barrier reef, third largest in the world. Often compared to the Great Barrier Reef in Australia, the Andros Reef offers excellent snorkeling locations in clear water only six to twelve feet deep.

Because of its many reefs, Bahamian shores experience little surf. Often you can just swim out from your hotel beach to discover the coral world. Most hotels loan snorkeling equipment to guests, offer suggestions on good locations and conditions, and, frequently, give lessons. The waves break far out, at the edge of the reef, an important consideration for snorkelers. High waves make entries and exits from the shore difficult and stir up the sand, lowering visibility.

In many places, the reefs rise to within three to ten feet of the surface. Since snorkelers spend most of their time floating on the surface, occasionally free diving down to look at something interesting, this is the perfect depth. Snorkel in water too shallow and you invite nasty coral scrapes or find yourself nose to nose with an eel or spiny urchin.

Snorkeling in deep water, on the other hand, is like diving at night: there isn't much to look at. The water gradually filters out the light, with the reds disappearing first. A blue twilight prevails below 30 feet, the bright reds, violets, and oranges of coral and fish are invisible.

Splash Down

You won't forget the first time you lower your facemask into the water at one of the many national marine preserves. The fish in these protected waters do not fear man. A delicately striped butterfly fish, wearing his distinctive black mask, may hover only feet away. Below, yellow sponges and bright blue coral spread an exotic carpet. As you glide by, an iridescent parrot fish, mottled blue, green and red, nibbles at a pillar of coral. Bright red cardinals dodge through schools of the tiny yellow fish called sunshine.

As you wind through a forest of sea fans and fantastically shaped staghorn coral, named for its ressemblence to antlers, light and colors seem more intense, and everything appears larger than life. The water magnifies size by one third.

A white sand path leads you between coral heads. Below, a herd of goatfish scour the bottom with their catfish-like whiskers. A queen angelfish, lips gathered in a pout, darts under a coral ledge. A brown fish with vertical bars hides in a stand of elkhorn coral. Could it be a schoolmaster snapper?

Identifying the many reef fish provides snorkelers with hours of satisfaction. Dive shops sell waterproof cards and books picturing local fish that you can carry into the water.

Another way to "collect" fish species is by recording them on film. The many new watertight 35mm cameras with automatic focus and flash take terrific pictures at these shallow depths, but the less-expensive 110's often available for rent, produce good shots as well. An added benefit: the time it takes to shoot a roll of film seems to be the perfect length of time to explore before you're ready for a break.

Many underwater photographers lure fish into posing for them with food. Tropical fish eat almost anything - bread, chopped fish or shellfish, luncheon meat, cheese, but one of the most convenient things to feed them is frozen green peas. A bag is easy to carry into the water and the green peas make a nice contrast to the fish in your photos. A bright blue wrasse may take a pea from between your fingers.

Best Wet Bets

The waters of the Bahamas are generally clean and clear with underwater visibility up to 200 feet, even around the most populated islands. On Paradise Island, you'll find good snorkeling at the reefs and coral heads on the south side of the island. Reach them from the Adelaide or South beaches. While exploring Paradise Island by moped, ride down the little road that runs along the north side of the Paradise Island Golf Course. Here, a secluded tree-fringed cove offers the casino isle's best shore snorkeling.

Other good spots, like the Rose Island reefs, lie further off-shore, a short sail away. Many charter boats invite you to spend a day as a castaway on a private island where you can snorkel, sun, or lie in a hammock slung beneath shady trees, sipping island rum from coconut shells.

In Freeport, you can find out where the underwater action is at the Underwater Explorers Society (UNEXSO). Drop by their clubhouse next to the Lucayan Bay Hotel to see films of local dives in their free museum and mingle with divers in the Tides Inn lounge.

Near Freeport, many fish make their home in Peterson's Cay National Park, reached by boat. Follow the underwater trail here past convoluted strands of brain coral and families of blue grunts. You may see a pair of these blue-striped green fish pressing their lips together in a "kiss." Actually, this unique behavior is aggressive rather than affectionate; the fish with the larger jaw wins.

Another turn in the trail brings you face to face with a large midnight parrotfish, named for his dark color and large, bird-like beak. Don't worry; he only uses it to crunch coral. Parrotfish feeding habits helped produce the Bahamas' many sandy beaches.

Several of the Family Islands also have national marine preserves near their shores. Most are accessible only by boat but, since travel on the Family isles is largely by motor launch and water-taxi, a ride to the area is usually no further away than the town dock.

The Exuma Land and Sea Park contains over 175 square miles of sea gardens, most only three to ten feet down. Here slender trumpetfish hang upside down waiting for prey to come close enough to be sucked into their hungry snouts.

With islets and cays strung over 100 miles of ocean, the Exumas offer many good snorkeling sites. Some conveniently located to the resorts at George Town include the long white sand beaches at Ocean Bight and Stocking Island, the ocean side of Staniel Cay, and the sea gardens off George Town itself.

The eastern side of Aboco boasts two marine preserves: Fowl Cay Sea and Land Preserve, north of Marsh Harbour, and the 2,000 acre Pelican Cay National Park, south of Marsh Harbour. Both feature shallow reefs and good snorkeling. Not to be missed by the snorkeler visiting Aboco: Great Guana Cay where an offshore reef stretches for seven unbroken miles along the cay's ocean side.

Wrecking

Besides their beauty, the Abocos reefs are famous for something else-shipwrecks. Generations of islanders made their living as "wreckers," salvaging what they could from ships that came to grief on the reefs. Several wrecks in the area lie close enough to the surface for the snorkeler to visit. The remains of the union warship USS *Adirondack* lie in ten to twenty feet of water. Most of the wooden superstructure has rotted away, but the cannon still point at vanished enemies. Near Marsh

Harbour, two big-wheeled locomotives lie on their sides, clearly visible at fifteen to twenty feet.

The trains, like other wrecks, provide a home for numerous sea urchins, crabs, anemones, and spiny lobsters. Divers call lobsters "bugs" and lure them from their hiding places by tickling their tails with a thin stick. When the lobster emerges, the hunter grabs them behind the antennae with a heavily gloved hand. If you decide to try catching one of these local delicacies, remember that spiny lobster are only in season August 1 to March 31 and must be quite large before you can eat them legally. Think twice before you grab a lobster who points one antenna back. Divers say this indicates he's sharing his home with a moray eel.

The reefs of the Bahamas have been responsible for an estimated 1,600 major wrecks and uncounted smaller ones since the 1500's. Snorkelers may come across a drowned ship, frozen in time, almost anywhere.

More than a dozen sunken ships are known to lie off South Bimini. The *Sapona*, a 300 ft. WWI concrete ship, sits upright in the water, making it a popular snorkeling site. It was used as a floating club by bootleggers during Prohibition until a 1929 hurricane drove it ashore. Today, it's main inhabitants are huge schools of zebra-striped spadefish.

The Devil's Backbone, a vicious reef running along the north shore of Eleuthera, claims many victims. The Lebanese freighter *Arimora* ran aground on a coral bar in 1971. Three-quarters of her hull lies above the water line; below, she teems with sea life, including a giant grouper who acts as official greeter and tour guide.

Endless Summer

To voyagers into the undersea realm, the Bahamas offer almost unlimited vacation opportunities. To see the offshore sights, snorkelers often choose to charter a yacht, either with a crew or "bareboat." Lodging, meals and inter-island transportation are taken care of in the rental fee and the yacht takes you directly to the best reefs and wrecks.

There's always something new to see beneath the Bahamian waters. You may come home a millionaire, even if your luck isn't in at the casinos. In 1965, divers found over $1 million in silver coins in a wreck just one-half mile off Grand Bahama.

Renee C. Wright has been a freelance writer and editor since 1985. She has also taught desk-top publishing and ballroom dancing.

The Outer Family Islands

All these islands have at least two things in common: They're part of the Outer Family Islands, and they're bordered to the east by some three thousand miles of Atlantic Ocean. Their western boundaries vary. This group of the Outer Family Islands includes Abaco, Eleuthera, Cat, San Salvador, and Mayaguana, but I started with Eleuthera because it's the site of the first Bahamian settlement.

ELEUTHERA

A bit quite old, much that's new, a name that's borrowed and some things blue—and even pink—all help to make Eleuthera what it is today: a wedding of twentieth-century progress to centuries of survival expertise.

Less than two miles wide as it arches on the fringe of the archipelago, the 110-mile-long island widens at each end to encompass in the north the original Bahamian colony site, and at its southern cape one of the nation's newest tourist colonies. Around and in between are sprinklings of villages and byways ranging economically from poor to nearly the world's highest per-capita income. There are resorts for royalty and the wealthy international elite, specialty sports establishments, and accommodations catering to families on tight budgets, or singles with loose laughter and swinging styles. Eleuthera boasts world famous pink-sand beaches and a few land-bound "blue holes" of ocean water—one of these apparently bottomless wonders measures over 100 square yards. There are caves encrusted with crystals, and there are enclaves of fiercely loyal citizens whose ancestors settled and named the island ("Eleuthera" is Greek for freedom).

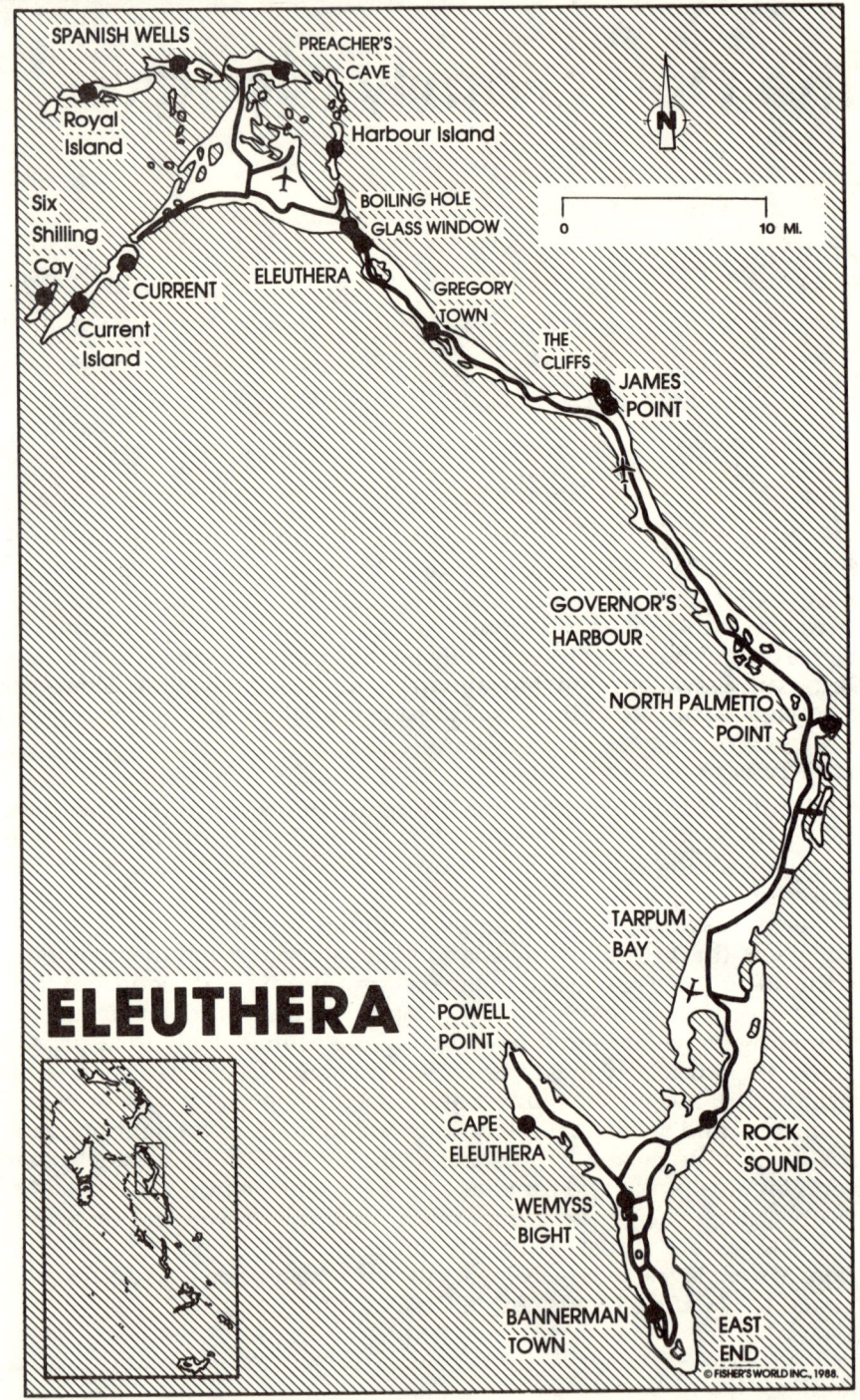

Getting There

By Air

North Eleuthera, Governor's Harbour and Rock Sound have public airports served daily by Bahamasair flights to and from Nassau. See the Travel Planner for other scheduled and charter service flights to/from these airports and private air strips such as the one at Cape Eleuthera.

By Sea

Regular service comes from mailboats that ply to and from Nassau each week, taking approximately seven hours for a one-way trip and usually staying overnight at the island port. The boats and their ports of call are: *M/V Bahamas Daybreak II*—from Nassau to Harbour Island and North Eleuthera; *M/V Lady Blanche*—from Nassau to central Eleuthera; *M/V Current Pride*—from Nassau to Current Island and Current Village.

SPANISH WELLS

From North Eleuthera Airport, it's a mostly unpaved, narrow, fiercely potholed road leading to docks where ferries offer service across the waters to the small safe harbor of Spanish Wells, on St. George's Cay.

This tiny island was well known to Spanish explorers, who for centuries made it their final stop on the way home. Ponce de Leon recorded his stopover at Spanish Wells after his frustrating failure to find the Fountain of Youth. It's joked that here he at least found potable water to see him home, probably by the usual method of sinking wells some two feet into the sands. Today, however, the island's drinking water is piped over from Eleuthera's "mainland."

Stepping off the ferry puts you at *Ronald's Crayfish* operation, which employs a fleet (about twelve) of modern freezer craft to scour Bahamian waters and return with 90 percent of the nation's catch of langouste—the spiny crayfish or clawless lobster that's craved by and shipped to world markets. Other seafare is brought in here, too, and there's a bevy of ladies waiting to dress and box it all, plus giant on-dock freezer buildings to hold it for regular export. With agriculture ranking second in local economy, the people of Spanish Wells produce prime winter crops of tomatoes, onions, cucumbers and other vegetables, citrus and, so they boast, the "world's finest pineapples."

Just past the busy harbor, there's a profusion of flowers, full and stately evergreens, and quaint New England-style saltbox houses which still shelter the families whose ancestors built them along these sandy lanes and roads. Newer homes rise farther from the docks, secure in their concrete block construction, clipped lawns, and abundant flowers and greenery.

HARBOUR ISLAND

A good stretch of road from North Eleuthera Airport deadends at a dock where small ferries and smaller powerboats transport you and your baggage across the narrow channel to Harbour Island. Replete with pink beaches, abundant bonefish, and superb snorkeling and scuba sites, the tiny island on Eleuthera's windward shore has a reputation much broader than its not quite two-mile-square area. Its proud history reaches back more than three hundred years to settlement by Eleutherian Adventurers.

Wandering this tiny hilly isle can be like tripping back decades, even centuries, in time. There are small but fine old homes, built mostly of clapboard and trimmed with elegant gingerbread, some faded and crumbling, but most painted in brilliant tropical colors, standing staunchly on sand swept avenues bare of sidewalks. Built by colonialists, Loyalists, prosperous planters and shipwrights, even those not recently treated with a new owner's loving care are made fetching and picturesque by rainbow splashes of blossoms and greenery such as coconut palms, figs, pigeon plums, casurinas, and citrus.

When you see the masses of jasmine, hibiscus, bougainvillea, occasional orchids, and other flowers, it's hard to believe there's an acute water shortage. Government engineers are working to correct the shortage, but as it hasn't been overcome, do tell your hotel if you spot a leaky faucet. Tap water can get quite salty at times, and as your body chemistry can react unpleasantly, more conscientious hoteliers caution tourists not to drink it and supply bottled or filtered rainwater. Energy is problematic primarily because it costs about four times more than in the United States. Some resorts ask you to observe "comfortable conservation." Energy costs are the main reason most hotels and resorts have maids do guests' laundry, rather than let guests operate coin machines (there is a coin laundry in town).

You may, however, operate assorted vehicles to tour around. Yet since the island is only 3 miles long and 1.5 miles wide, most tourists opt to hike its cliffs and stroll through quaint *Dunmore Towne*—so named when the feisty, fort-building Bahamian governor, the Earl of Dunmore, kept summer quarters here as the 18th century phased into the 19th.

Briefly the capital, Harbour Island of course owes its name to a natural haven that helped it to become the country's second largest city for generations; as early as 1817, it boasted 2,500 residents.

Some islanders toiled for the shipbuilding industry, constructing single-masted privateering craft and 50-ton sloops and schooners. Early in this century, the fourmast *Marie J. Thompson*, weighing in at 696 tons, was launched from the island—the largest vessel ever built in the Bahamas. Sadly, although the record still stands, the industry does not. It petered out by World War II, and the population virtually followed suit; there were only about 750 residents left by the early 1940s.

Some things, however, have been continuous since Dunmore's days: *St. John's* (c. 1768), the oldest Anglican church in the Bahamas, still opens its arched doors for regular services, as does the *Wesley Methodist Church*, built in 1848. There are old guns from the late 1700s, though never used, and other historic sites listed below. Today, there's also a library, a resident doctor, nurse and clinic, a seamstress, bank, beauty parlor and barber shop, some garages and several other churches of interest. The post office, commissioner's office, jail, and police and fire departments cluster together; several bars and taverns are scattered about.

If you want bazaars, gaudy souvenir stands or advertising billboards, you're in the wrong place. But the small neat shops and markets do carry locally made souvenirs and gifts, as well as local and imported clothing and dry goods, plus Eleutherian fruits and vegetables known for their quality in many world ports. These edibles are grown in part on the island, but mostly on a "mainland" tract of six thousand acres bestowed on Harbour Islanders who joined Eleutherians and Loyalist militants to rescue occupied Nassau in 1783.

Today, the island continues to make history as a favorite with tourists from all over the world. They come for prebreakfast beach-combing and shelling on the Atlantic shore, where protective reefs break high-rolling waves, and the soft pink sand is framed by shrubs. Sea grapes and palms fringe rising dunes, and the air is clear and sweet. They're here to stroll the gardens and paths where chickens strut freely and the loudest noises usually come from an occasional sheep, horse, or donkey, or from the many birds that find sanctuary here. They come to drift across shallows in pursuit of fishes, or dive the depths for underwater adventures; to lob tennis balls, and to laze on harborside verandas sipping tall island drinks while watching the bustling government dock fall quiet under the spell of a sunset that's as indescribable as the surrounding waters and all they encompass. They come to sleep with windows open to the pervading sweet scent of night-blooming flowers drifting on prevailing trade winds.

NORTH ELEUTHERA

This area includes North Eleuthera Airport, Preacher's Cave, Bluff, Current, Current Island, and Glass Window.

North Eleuthera Airport

Like most Family Island airports, the one at North Eleuthera consists of a runway where aircraft can taxi until almost touching the small building that's used for tickets and luggage processing. Small craft doze in the sun; a group of passengers and taxi drivers await each landing. Across the road is *J. B. Snacks*, a miniature emporium of light foods, straw works, T-shirts, inexpensive souvenirs and such, where owner J. B. Barry posts this homemade sign: "Love your enemy. It will drive him crazy." J. B.'s blue mini-bus is there, and the man himself, in sunglasses and visor cap, is waiting to take you to your hotel, or for a tour. This man has traveled and been on TV around the world, promoting his island and tourism for the Bahamian government. There are many other taxi tour guides, but he's the most colorful, without doubt.

From the airport, roads lead northeast to Harbour Island ferries, and north to Ripley Head (or Bridge Point), where they branch southwest for Spanish Wells ferries and east to Preacher's Cave. These roads are sometimes well paved, but most are so bad that no comprehensive insurance is available for cars.

Preacher's Cave

Shipwrecked with no provisions, those indomitable Eleutherian Adventurers of the mid-1600s sheltered in this cave that's similar to an amphitheater with a small back room. A central rock formation was later shaped into a rough pulpit for religious services. Holes in the high roof admit shafts of sunlight—two of them so close together they're called "the binoculars."

Bluff

Traveling south again, you learn that much of the land is farmed year round for vegetables, citrus, and other fruits. The farmers ride trucks to the cultivated land, and live in small villages like Bluff, which is reached by a road that becomes the hamlet's main street, lined by clapboard houses and occasional churches. Watch for dome-shaped outdoor ovens for baking bread, and for kitchens located in separate buildings, as is common in villages throughout the Family Islands. This is J. B.'s hometown, and he proudly shows off its new schoolhouse and a restaurant that attracts many tourists, *Arlie's Place*. Just a few years old, attractive and neat, Arlie's is roomy and airy, with fishnet tablecloths in the dining area, a game room with pool tables and a bar that sometimes features "rake and scrape" music played by the owner and friends on bucket, saw, and other implements. The food is home grown, Bahamian, and delicious. Try conch fritters or cracked conch, fish and lobster, fried green tomatoes, or the house specialty, Cabbage Eleanor.

Current

Farther south, at the settlement of *Lower Brogue*, a road winds southwest to Current Village, severed by the Current Cut (a narrow waterway) from Current Island, where fisherfolk live as they have since the days of Bahama's Lord Proprietors. The commercial fishing boat dock is a big attraction in this 200-year-old village. There are food and general stores, a bicycle rental place, and two shops where interesting crafts and gifts are available: *Doreen's* and *Monica's*. Here, too, are tourist accommodations.

Lower and Upper Brogue Villages

Passing through Lower and Upper Brogue villages, the road follows island curves as it crosses a bridge where the surf thunders against a backbone of high limestone cliffs. The spectacular view encompasses the Atlantic's dark, frothy waters on one side, and the multicolored green-blue-white Bahamian waters on the other. The island is almost divided at this point, where erosion formed a portholelike giant window in the rocks, then continued its work till the top portion collapsed. In the eastern waters nearby, the mooing sound created by the wind playing around two rock formations resulted in their being named *Cow and Bull.*

CENTRAL ELEUTHERA

This area includes Gregory Town, the Cave, Shark Hole, Sweetings Pond, Hatchet Bay, Governor's Harbour Airport, Governor's Harbour, and South Palmetto Point.

On the Atlantic side of the road, a large pond reflects a pink color from the bauxite beneath its water, but it's more notable as a source of salt for local folk—evaporation in warm weather dries some of the water, leaving salt deposits that people collect for home table use. Nearby, a large *Oleander Gardens Project* is under way, and there are pineapple farms in the area.

Gregory Town

More prosperous than many villages, this small and aged town welcomes many guests to its awakening tourist industry. A pretty collection of frame houses punctuated by an old stone Catholic church and a newer Baptist church, with a picturesque crescent cove, the settlement boasts a supermarket and a quality bakery. Nearby beaches beckon surfers with what have been called the "second best waves in the world." Vanderbilt and Roanoke seniors come here yearly, and other young people can be seen strolling the roads, surfboards tucked under their arms, at almost any time. People also come to see pineapple rum being made and to go spelunking in nearby caves.

The Cave

Back on the road, watch for a large fig tree standing alone in a field of coarse grass. Locals vow it was planted by pirates in the early 1700s, when the Bahamian waters were notorious for harboring brigands. They supposedly wanted the tree to screen an entrance to a cave where they hid both themselves and their ill-gotten gains. Blarney, you say? Possibly. In any case, the tree covers a narrow hole leading to a huge cavern, which should be explored only with a guide carrying flashlights with fresh batteries.

As you'd expect, tiny bats have taken up residence here, but don't worry—they're used to tourists. A seven-by-ten-foot wide tunnel slopes down to a straight drop of ten feet; here you'll find a ladder with steps hacked out of the rock. It leads into a huge cavern filled with stalactites and stalagmites; two of these meet to form a natural pillar in a chamber that resembles a primitive kind of cathedral.

Further on are more tunnels and caverns, which end rather dramatically at the edge of a cliff that towers eighty feet above the blue-green sea. Where this tunnel ends there's a hole in the rock through which one can crawl to a pond where, according to the locals, tiny blind fish once swam. Others say that this pond goes directly to the sea. It opens into a lake with a beach where you can snorkel at low tide. The whole maze is several miles long and is believed to have been formed during the last Ice Age.

Hatchet Bay (Including Shark Hole and Sweetings Pond)

A long and winding road leads through scrub and vacant lots and farms, past the *Hatchet Bay Plantation*, built in the early 1900s to produce poultry, livestock and feed; today the government runs it solely as a poultry farm. Four times a day, the workers take the unsalable chicken parts and toss them into the Atlantic, where a bevy of ravenous sharks have learned to gather punctually for this tasty freebie; consequently, the place is known as *Shark Hole*. The poultry farm is also worth a stop, if for no other reason than to visit *Sweetings Pond*. The pond has served as inspiration for scores of legends that center on the mammoth sea turtles and other creatures that are believed to hang out in the pool.

During the plantation's rosiest days, its employees built homes in nearby *Hatchet Bay*, where you will find not only colorful architecture but many outlets for such essentials as food, fashion, and liquor. Sailors still tie up here for a meal or for several days of R and R.

Governor's Harbour Airport

Set in the middle of Eleuthera, this small facility serves resorts and villages to the north and south with daily Bahamasair flights to and from Nassau and other points. It's also used by small airlines, charters, and private craft.

Governor's' Harbour

Popular legend tells of a group of colonists called the Adventurers making their first landing in the New World here—where they had a bit of trouble. It seems that some of the male colonists became entranced not only by the beauty of Cupid's Bay but by the not inconsiderable charms of the native women. Being an upright, churchgoing gentleman, Captain Sayle took a dim view of this; he managed to reassemble what was supposedly the monogamous majority of his passenger list and set sail for nearby Harbour Island, only to founder along the way when a fierce storm ripped the sails of the *William* to shreds.

Residents of Cupid's Bay are experts at fishing, farming, and raising goats and sheep. The bay, also known as Cupid's Cay, faces Governor's Harbour, the capital of Eleuthera, and is connected to the center of town by a 150-year-old bridge.

A thriving port for generations, the bay is where Nassauvians once came to buy fancy imports from the same ships that carried Eleutherian produce to other markets. Later, ships came for crates of turtle meat tinned by the first cannery in the Bahamas. The heavy harbor activity that once existed may be hard to visualize today, especially after you take in this drowsy town with its genteel old houses, an aged Anglican church and graveyard dotted with stately trees, and the tall coconut palms and casurinas that line the roads.

The modern world is very much in evidence, though, with medical and dental clinics, the Jeans Scene and other shops, and the sight of dozens of fresh-faced Boy Scouts proudly marching to church.

As you leave town in the evening, you'll see butterflies and moths dancing in the blue and scarlet sky; in the distance, one can see flocks of egrets coasting over fields where hordes of cattle once grazed.

SOUTHERN ELEUTHERA

This area includes Windermere Island, Tarpum Bay, Rock Sound, Winding Bay, Cotton Bay, and Cape Eleuthera.

The main government road, also known as the Queen's Highway, continues south with a crossroad veering west to the banks of Exuma Sound, and east to the settlement of Savannah Sound. The next branch heads for the bridge crossing to Windermere Island, stretching between Savannah Sound Beach and the Atlantic, and buffeting the coast here. En route, bugle shaped, bright yellow bell roses seem to be everywhere among the dense greenery and occasional houses.

Tarpum Bay

Named for the excellent fishing in nearby waters, this is another village just beginning to actively welcome world tourists with a spate of accommodation facilities and activities. Tarpum Bay also boasts G. MacMillan Hughes, a part-time resident artist-sculptor who's also known as a philosopher, lecturer, and clairvoyant. Hailing from Belfast, Northern Ireland, Hughes transplanted himself some twenty years ago, but skips away part of the year to handle exhibits in the U.S. and Great Britain. He paints scenes of the undersea world and lifelike village vistas, and frequently strolls around barefoot, canvas and easel in hand, searching for new inspiration. Should you meet the artist in the street or at his hilltop studio near the water tower, chances are you're in for fascinating conversation, and perhaps an oracular tip from the Irish mystic.

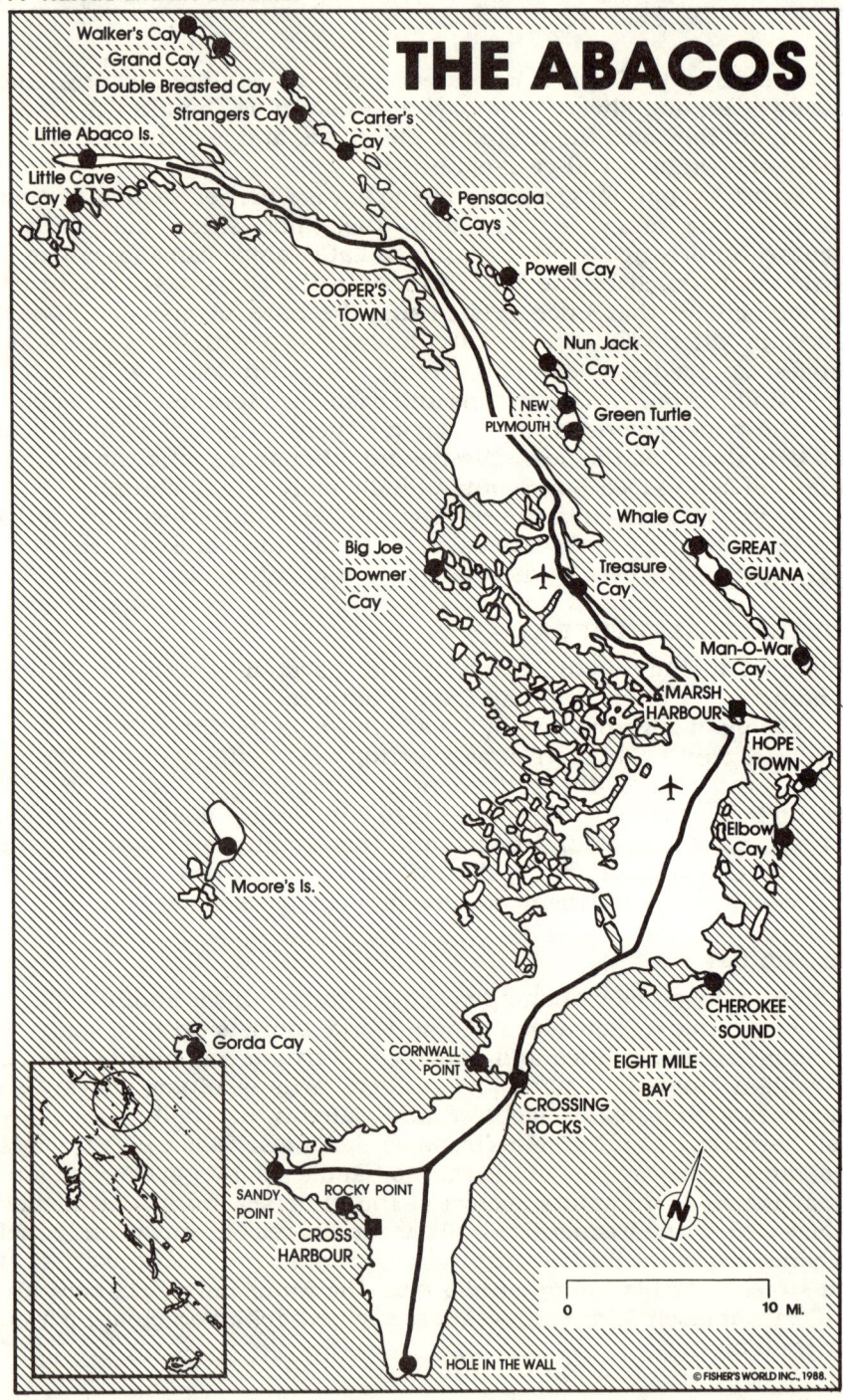

Rock Sound

A huge portion of Eleuthera carries a Rock Sound address label, starting with Windermere Island and including all points south, even the cape. More prosperous than many settlements, it's known as the island's largest town, and is your best bet for a duty-free shopping spree. The modern shopping complex offers food, gifts, liquor, and other goods—all in contrast to some of the older buildings in this more than 200-year-old town. Neat homes with whitewashed picket fences line narrow paved roads, and the old church and graveyard are worth a visit. Another place that attracts tourists is *Ocean Blue Hole*, just east of town. Apparently bottomless, it's home to several varieties of tropical fish just waiting to be fed and photographed.

Rock Sound Airport

Looking newer and more substantial than many Outer Family Island airports, this one sports palms and gardens, daily Bahamasair service to and from Nassau and other destinations, and regular runs by small airlines plus charters and private craft. The field is radio beaconed, which is rare in the territory. Automobile rental can be arranged here, too.

Green Castle

From Cotton Bay, it's a short ride to *Green Castle*, a small town that mixes crowded old shacks with new buildings. A service station and supermarket flash by as you drive through town; then the road continues to the settlement of *Bannerman Town* on the southernmost tip of Eleuthera, and branches west through *Wemyss Bight*, *David Harbour*, and the centuries-old villages of *Water Ford* and *Deep Creek*. The government road then gives way to the private entrance of a huge, modern resort complex, the Cape Eleuthera Yacht Club—now closed, but slated to reopen soon.

ABACO

Secret hideaway for celebrated politicians, film and television stars, and even country and western entertainers, Abaco has its own annual November festival, summer regattas, frequent tourneys in fishing, tennis and golf, and other adventures atop and beneath its waters. It's famous for extensive farms and forests, wild horses and boars, expert shipwrights and sailors, and a unique enclave of artists and quaint villages that contrast with supermodern resorts.

The second largest Bahamian island, Abaco rises from a southern terminus called Hole-in-the-Wall. It expands northeast to jackknife at Marsh Harbour, third largest Bahamian town, and continues to Walker's Cay, the archipelago's most northern edge, which points toward Fort Pierce, Florida, some 100 miles to the east. According to confusing official statistics, Abaco covers 650 (or 776) square miles, stretching to a length of 130 (or 120, or 150) miles with a breadth of

15 (or 5, or 25) miles. There's little disagreement, however, about the many marshes and mangroves that march down the western shores, or about the chain of islets that follow most of its eastern coast to create a protected "inland sea" for some of the finest sailing in the territory.

Cooler than most of the Bahamas, Abaco's winter temperatures supposedly never dip below 50 degrees F, and its summers generally range from 80-85 degrees F. While its cays are coral based and residents fight to capture and preserve rainwater, the "mainland" has a limestone foundation pocketed with ample supplies of fresh water. Mostly flat and low, Abaco also has rolling areas crested by rises of 100 to 200 feet, and records note its more than 200 species and subspecies of birds. Covered by pine, madeira, sea grape and other trees, Abaco also boasts many astonishing ferns, vines, and wildflowers that include serveral varieties of slender-stalked orchids. Back in 1790, the island's soil was reportedly so shallow that in the dry season the sun heated the rock underneath and burned up any vegetables that had been planted. Today, that same white, black, and red earth is famous for fruits, vegetables, and ornamental plants produced for export by farms large and small.

The water around the island is a spectacle in itself, shading from deep blue and smoky purple through emerald, turquoise, and chartreuse, with the darker colors indicating greater depth or underlying reefs and vegetation. It's so calm, clean and clear that you can follow the journey of a sea creature on the ocean floor. These waters are streaked with colorful fishes, studded with amazing corals, and make a favorite playground for friendly dolphins that sometimes swim alongside your boat, and occasionally leap into the steady, gentle trade winds. For fishermen, there's the dolphin fish, as well as sailfish, sharks, and a long list of gamefish that attract international competitors. There are also excellent bonefish grounds in the shallows and marshes and around *Bahama Palm Shores.*

Abaco's waters wash over hundreds of miles of fine uncluttered beaches, many of them totally deserted, pristine, printed only by the tracks of gulls, sandpipers, and other birds, and an almost encyclopedic variety of shell life. Scholars and museum staffs have been coming here for almost a hundred recorded years to scour these beaches for collection-quality sea shells. The local island expert is Colin Redfern, who covers shelling regularly for *Abaco Life.* It tells of the more than 625 different shallow-water species found here to date, including some quite rare and some that were thought to exist only in other parts of the world. Noting that most well-known shell families are here in abundance, several in assorted species, Redfern points out that there are at least 16 species of Wentletrap shells, adding that he personally collected 263 Wentletrap shells in just one day. It's not uncommon for Abaco beachcombers to find items such as glass floats from the nets of fishermen from Portugal and Japan.

From the island's jackknife, on the Atlantic side of the string of cays, there's a barrier reef (technically a fringe reef) running north almost unbroken to the tip of the Bahamian territory. You'll recognize its parameter by the foamy crest of waves breaking in the seascape. Known as the realm of some spectacular diving, it vies with nearby underwater reserves and parks as the favorite haunt of snorkel and scuba buffs, who are beginning to storm the region, guided along by a crop of professional facilities, including a branch of UNEXSO (see Freeport section) and the Chambered Nautilus operations. Those reserves are fostered by the Bahamas National Trust, which also sponsors a woodsy sanctuary for the Bahamian Parrot.

Getting There

By Air

Marsh Harbour and Treasure Cay have public airports with restaurants. Daily service is provided to and from Nassau by Bahamasair, with frequent flights by other scheduled airlines and charter firms.

By Sea

The only regular service is by mailboats, which take about seven hours to complete a one-way trip. More information about such travel is in the Travel Planner section. Two boats and their ports of call are: *M/V Deborah K II*—from Nassau on Wednesdays to Cherokee Sound, Grand Cay, Green Turtle Cay, Hope Town, Man-O-War Cay and Marsh Harbour; *M/V Lady Dean*—from Nassau to Sandy Point each Tuesday.

CENTRAL ABACO

This area includes Marsh Harbour Airport, Marsh Harbour, Elbow Cay (Hope Town), Man-O-War Cay, and Great Guana Cay.

Marsh Harbour Airport

More prosperous than many Outer Family Island airports, this one is the home of a restaurant that serves anything from cold drinks to hot meals. Bahamasair flies here daily, as does Air Florida. Small airlines that offer service to and from the United States and Abaco include Trans Island Airways and Mackey, of Fort Lauderdale, Florida. Fort Pierce Flying Service offers Florida-Abaco charters, and Abaco Air Ltd. provides charters throughout the islands and to and from the United States. Taxis await all flights, alerted of late arrivals via the trustworthy CBs.

Marsh Harbour

It's true that this town is booming, but that doesn't mean its pace resembles a boom town anywhere else. After all, this is the Bahamas, and a Family Island, and these facts naturally eliminate the hurried ado, reducing the boom to a rationally easy speed.

Among the riot of greenery around town are coconut palms usually transplanted from Andros, madeira trees whose steely wood is prized for boat frames, and something called fiddle vine (or "wine" as locals pronounce it). The vine sends profusions of thin shoots to blanket shrubs and such, and they in turn act as mattresses that which cushion the jumping descents from lofty limbs by small children. Where beautiful old homes flourish, the greenery is controlled and trimmed. Some of the homes are charming cottages; others are large and elegant, but the most impressive of all is a castle. Cresting a hill and flaunting vivid aqua crenellated heights visible by land or sea, this tiny castle is L-shaped, has pillows, arches, and white trim, and is still called home by the family of the late Dr. Evans Cottman. Locals say the doctor wanted something different—and got it. They also tell many a fascinating tale of this American scientist whose book records his experiences as the *Out Island Doctor*.

No doubt Cottman would be relieved to see that Marsh Harbour now has two licensed medical doctors, plus dentists and a government nurse. There's more, too: streets lined with service stations, shopping centers, stores and boutiques, hairdressers and barbers, laundries and cleaners, supermarkets and bakeries, banks and churches and assorted businesses. Hanging where two of the streets cross is the single traffic light, though the flow of traffic hardly seems to warrant it. Whatever vehicles are around, be they on land or sea, most are equipped with CB radios, as are hotels, restaurants, service areas and homes, here and in the neighboring cays and villages of Dundas Town and Murphys Town. Those radios are standard means of communication, and in case of any emergency they can be used to summon help quickly.

Elbow Cay (Including Hope Town)

Sparsely populated, Elbow Cay does indeed bend at its thinnest point. Sprinkled with cottages and villas, its southern regions include *Dorros Cove* and *Aunt Pat's Bay* (where balladeer-actor Burl Ives has a retreat). The northerly route up the coast passes both White Sound and Hope Town, which shelters in the elbow's bend as the cay reaches out a narrow strip of land pointing north.

Hope Town is marked by a tall candy-striped lighthouse. The monolith towers over a tiny harbor littered with boats and almost encircled by the small township that tiers on two streets: Up Along, tracing the higher levels, and Down Along, by the water. Only several feet wide, both resemble sidewalk paths between the buildings, but Up Along's real name is the Queen's Highway, and Down Along is known to accommodate automobiles venturing harborside for supplies and passengers. Bicycles can be rented to maneuver these lanes, but it's best to meander along on foot, pausing frequently to admire the charming old clapboard homes, many with dormer windows, picket fences, shingle roofs, and green shutters. A fine example of Loyalist architecture is the *Wyannie Malone Historical Museum*, open to the public and filled with memorabilia and artifacts of Hope Town's existence since the arrival of settlers such as the Widow Malone, who came with her offspring in 1875, and whose descendants still live here. Don't hesitate to talk to villagers here; they may tell tales of the far past, or of the thirty-foot German motor launch that drifted ashore in 1914. They're sure to point out where you can rent a bike or boat, and which local ladies whip up simple breads, fritters, and pies you can buy for a picnic on the fine Atlantic beach.

As you stroll this quaint seafaring village, you'll come across two grocery stores, two gift shops, and two restaurants: *Anchors Aweigh* serves American and Bahamian dishes, with an emphasis on seafood; the *Village Inn*, where breakfast, lunch, and dinner are available, requires reservations for dancing and dining.

Man-O-War Cay

There's something about these remote, industrious villages that stirs the souls of rat-race runners. There are no automobiles here, and no alcoholic beverages are sold. There is no crime and no jail.

Yet the village is a mix of past and present that is not always obvious at first glance. Walking the two paved paths and connecting lanes, you find everything neat, clean, and well maintained. There are old frame houses, some with graceful gingerbread trim, but also many newer ones, securely shaped of concrete blocks; tall television antennas sprout over both. There's a tiny library, a bright schoolhouse and a sports field with wooden bleachers backed by pretty wildflowers along the road. Gnarled old trees stand beside older homes, and one front yard flaunts huge cabbages. Many lawns are cultivated with flowers, fruit trees and shrubs, but some stand stark. In the beachside graveyard, white sands drift over palm-shaded old and new markers of wood and stone, and the nearby sweep of deep sand and rock-fringed beach is washed by age-old waves and twentieth-century debris. But the sea breeze is fresh and sweet smelling, and the shelling is excellent.

As you walk, you see residents putting by on golf carts. More of these electric vehicles are parked here and there, some wearing decals with messages like: "What do you miss by being a Christian? Hell." Similar messages, only more lengthy, rhymed and printed, are free in places like the Bite Site, a harborside shop for hot dogs, hamburgers, and slushies, as well as conch fritters. Outside, you'll note that someone took great care to press large leaves into wet concrete to make interesting patterns for the stepping stones, and that old and weathered wood forms a table and bench under low trees. Nearby, a craftsman makes boats, and beautiful half-models mounted on plaques. The Sailmaker is around the corner, and the *Sail Shop* stocks canvas bags and sailing jackets. Near the busy boatyards, where shipwrights have been turning out fine work for about two hundred years, there's a lime green wood hut labeled *Sally's Sea Side Shop*, where you can buy fine denim overshirts, sun dresses, sunsuits, and other items made by Sally on her aged sewing machine. *Albury's Harbour Store* is here, too, a minisupermarket that carries an assortment of frozen TV dinners. There's also *Weatherford's* neat little store for groceries, dry goods, and religious records, and *Patsy Lee's shop*, with a variety of souvenirs.

At *Man-O-War Hardware*, you can buy snorkeling and fishing gear, while *Albury's Bakers* offers sweets and short orders to go—all the fixings for an afternoon on the beach. There are a few small boats for rent, and if you stop in *Albury's Ferry Service* office, in the long, low building near the dock, it's likely that Marcel Albury will direct you to them—he smilingly acknowledges that his office is an "unofficial information center." Before you leave the prosperous and pretty cay, you can have a hot and tasty meal at *Dock n Dine*, just steps away from the dock. Dinner is served from 6 P.M., but reservations must be made by 4 P.M.; light fare needs no advance notice.

Great Guana Cay

Just seven miles long, this islet has no roads. It does have *Kidd Cove* (named for the pirate), a small settlement of approximately one hundred people, one Anglican church, two small stores and a one-room schoolhouse. Cruising yachtsmen have made this a favorite port for many years. Known as the home of Abaco's longest, most beautiful beaches, Guana Cay offers excellent shelling and superb snorkeling—particularly over the reef, where exciting marine life attracts divers and underwater photographers.

Back on the land, there are places to stay, including Bay View Apartments with one-bedroom facilities, and Pinder's Cottages and Gift Shop, with fully equipped, kitchened cottages that offer views of both bay and ocean. Then there's the Guana Harbour Club, with a marina and dock, and sixteen rooms—each comfortably furnished in a different style and some air-conditioned (Children under twelve stay free with parents). You set your own pace here in activities and dress, with the focus on relaxation and the marvels of nature. Dress for a tasty dinner by candlelight, or sit around in old boating gear; fish, swim, dive, and boat, or saunter through the coconut grove to sprawl on the private beach. Nightly party time features a washboard "scrub and scrape" band and a drink aptly called the Guana Grabber.

Two Villages

Just outside Marsh Harbour, en route to Treasure Cay, are the colorful villages of *Dundas Town* and *Murphys Town*. They were established by the government some forty years ago when it was deemed necessary to gather in many swamp-living, far-flung families and village residents to provide central schooling, medical facilities, and such. Each family was allotted acreage and a house, and as the family grew, new houses were added. Many of these people still live traditionally, off the land and sea. Other settled areas in the woodland between the two key regions include the development of Joe's Creek and the Sand Banks community of private lands and farms. You'll also pass Bahamas

Plants Ltd., a 25-acre nursery that ships 100,000 ornamental plant cuttings each week to U.S. wholesalers who, in turn, supply them to outlets such as Sears and K Mart.

Little Harbour

The most southerly ferry stop and a regular port of call for cruising yachts and charter sightseeing trips, this sheltered site is home to natural caves for exploring. One of these caves was an early home for Randolph and Margot Johnston, who sailed their old Bahamian schooner, the *Langosta,* here in 1951 and decided to settle and build a self-reliant life for themselves and their three sons. You can read the details of how this modern Swiss Family Robinson moved from cave to thatched hut to present prosperity and international acclaim for their artistic works, by getting a copy of *Artist on His Island,* available throughout the island. You also can get the story firsthand while watching the work at the foundry Randolph built, where he creates fine bronze sculptures by the ancient lost-wax method. In the ceramic studio, Margot's unique pieces include realistic representations of Bahamian fishermen, boats, birds, and fish. The Johnston's son, Peter, lives nearby with his wife, Debbie, and their two young sons; both he and his wife are talented sculptors and his marine life works have been heralded as among the world's best. Pete is an avid fisherman who can tell stories tall and true. You can visit *Pete's Pub and Gallery*: Built from parts of the *Langosta,* the pub displays family-made art priced in a wide range. In the evenings, guests sit around hearty drinks and often coax Pete into singing a medley of sea chanties, accompanied by his trusty guitar.

NORTH CENTRAL ABACO

This area includes Treasure Cay Airport, Treasure Cay Resort, and Green Turtle Cay (New Plymouth).

Treasure Cay Airport

The first major government-built Family Island airport, Treasure Cay International was built to the tune of $3 million; it has a 7,000-foot runway, is equipped with the latest gear, and has a new small terminal. What's more, new extensions will result in another 1,000 feet of tarmac, which will allow the big jets to land more than two hundred passengers at a time. Meanwhile, there's regular service via Bahamasair and Air Florida, by Trans Island Airways and Mackey, both out of Fort Lauderdale, Florida, and Fort Pierce Flying Service's charter craft out of Florida. Other charters touch down here, as do many private planes. There's a restaurant, and a bevy of taxis waiting to whisk incoming passengers to final destinations in Abaco. A welcoming sign here, repainted many times, promises you that this is Where your Sufficiencies will be Surfancified.

In a woody area outside the resort borders stands a marine store and the *Hilltop Restaurant*, where locals and tourists venture for seafood and traditional Bahamian dishes. Nearby is the 3,000-acre Ken-Sawyer Farms, where mechanized farming employs 25 tractors, 20 trucks, 6 fork lifts, water from 2,000 wells for irrigation via 15 pumps, plus 600 seasonal laborers from January to June. For years, the frost-free farm has shipped some 350,000 bushels of winter vegetables, and around 10,000 bushels of avocados, to Florida. Just recently, 100,000 citrus trees were planted, and their produce will soon be added to the annual shipments stateside. Most likely, this farming industry will have a big impact on the entire Abaco region.

Green Turtle Cay

Time was when *Grumann Gooses* shuddered and splashed down onto the water, then skied up a seaplane ramp onto Green Turtle Cay to deposit supplies and visitors. That was before an airport was stripped onto the "mainland," making it necessary to pick up incoming freight and passengers and boat them to the outlying cay. The service in 1959 was via sailing dinghy; today the craft are new, streamlined motor launches, kept busy moving not only goods and local people from the unpretentious dock, but large tourist groups and celebrities as well.

From this Treasure Cay Airport dock, ferry trips are regularly scheduled to New Plymouth, Black Sound, White Sound, Bluff Cay, and Coco Bay; they're all part of the regular round the ferry makes as it stops for pickups requested through CB channels.

Green Turtle Cay is an enchanting, historic, two-by-four-mile islet, encompassing fine long beaches, sheltered harbors, assorted resorts and what once was the second largest Bahamian town, New Plymouth. Settled in 1783 by Loyalists and their slaves, New Plymouth was the region's key village by the early 1800s, then kept on growing until it claimed 2,500 people, including its own American consul. Back then, New Plymouth traded its pineapples, sponges, and other harvests in world markets, where its ships and sailors also deposited Abaco lumbers.

The seafarers still farm and harvest from the sea, and also export their crayfish to the United States, but tourism is today's economic mainstay. And tourists are delighted by the town's saltbox houses, mostly white with brightwork in trim and shutters, but also painted primary yellow, salmon, aqua, and green, with picket fences and flying flags.

From the public or ferry docks, a leisurely walk down Parliament Street allows one to study the new and old structures lining the narrow pavement. Next to tidy little *Plymouth Rock Restaurant* is a bank topped by rented rooms, followed by shops for hardware, marine items, drugs, groceries and gifts. Among the houses are delightful inns and two sites of note: the *Albert Lowe Museum* and the *Commissioner's Residence*. A library and post office are just a few steps from Glad Tidings Tabernacle and there's a Methodist church nearby. At the end of the street is a graveyard with some large, shining tombstones, and some old, broken and unmarked graves, and a cornered enclosure of old buildings including what seems to have been a jail. The juxtaposition of crumbling historic sites with those restored to a magnificence probably never known during their first life can be startling. It's something to think about over a cool drink or meal at *Miss Emily's Blue* Bee Bar or the *Sea Garden Club and Restaurant,* located in small aqua shacks at this end of town.

By the time you head back to the docks, you've seen the Shell Hut gift shop, and another two eateries: *Mrs. Betty McIntosh's Sea View Restaurant & Bar,* and *Mizpah Sawyer's Restaurant.* Like all eating places in town, they serve both native cookery and U.S.-type snacks and request advance reservations for dinner. They also sell alcohol—a "shalt not" in some of these cays—and there's a wholesale liquor store here.

The *Albert Lowe Museum,* built in the early 1800s, is a two-storied, gingerbreaded old house of astonishing beauty. Its white clapboard exterior, framed by neat, small gardens popular around town, opens to a polished interior with a well-displayed collection of beautifully executed ship models and local artifacts and memorabilia. There are lovely paintings and some bronze busts that will be moved to the *Memorial Sculpture Garden* commemorating the village's 200th birthday.

Sitting on the quiet dock, while gulls drift overhead, it's hard to imagine the action this harbor knew long ago. Yet after dredging for the new dock ferry operators found evidence of that past—an old cannon clearly stamped with the British crown and dated 1804.

POINTS NORTH AND SOUTH

Though Abaco and its cays stretch many miles north and south of those already noted, most of the territory remains undeveloped or idle, with smatterings of towns here and there. To the extreme north, a popular private resort encompasses tiny Walker's Cay, and in the southeast region lies Sandy Point, where hotel plans are brewing.

Sandy Point

The 53-mile road leading here from Marsh Harbour is desperately in need of new paving, as is the local airstrip, but waterside transport finds good docking at the village, where modern fishing boats supply the fish-packing plant recently situated here. It's pleasant to stroll the isolated town, to exchange greetings with the people, to browse in the general store, and to revel in the ever blooming greenery and swaying palms. It's Christmas all year round according to the decorations at the *Crystal Palace Restaurant,* which serves fine Bahamian meals similar to those at *Salome's* or at *Russell's Dockside Restaurant.*

Shell collectors will rejoice in the two miles of fine beach here, and can take trips for even better shelling at Rocky Point or on Gorda Cay,

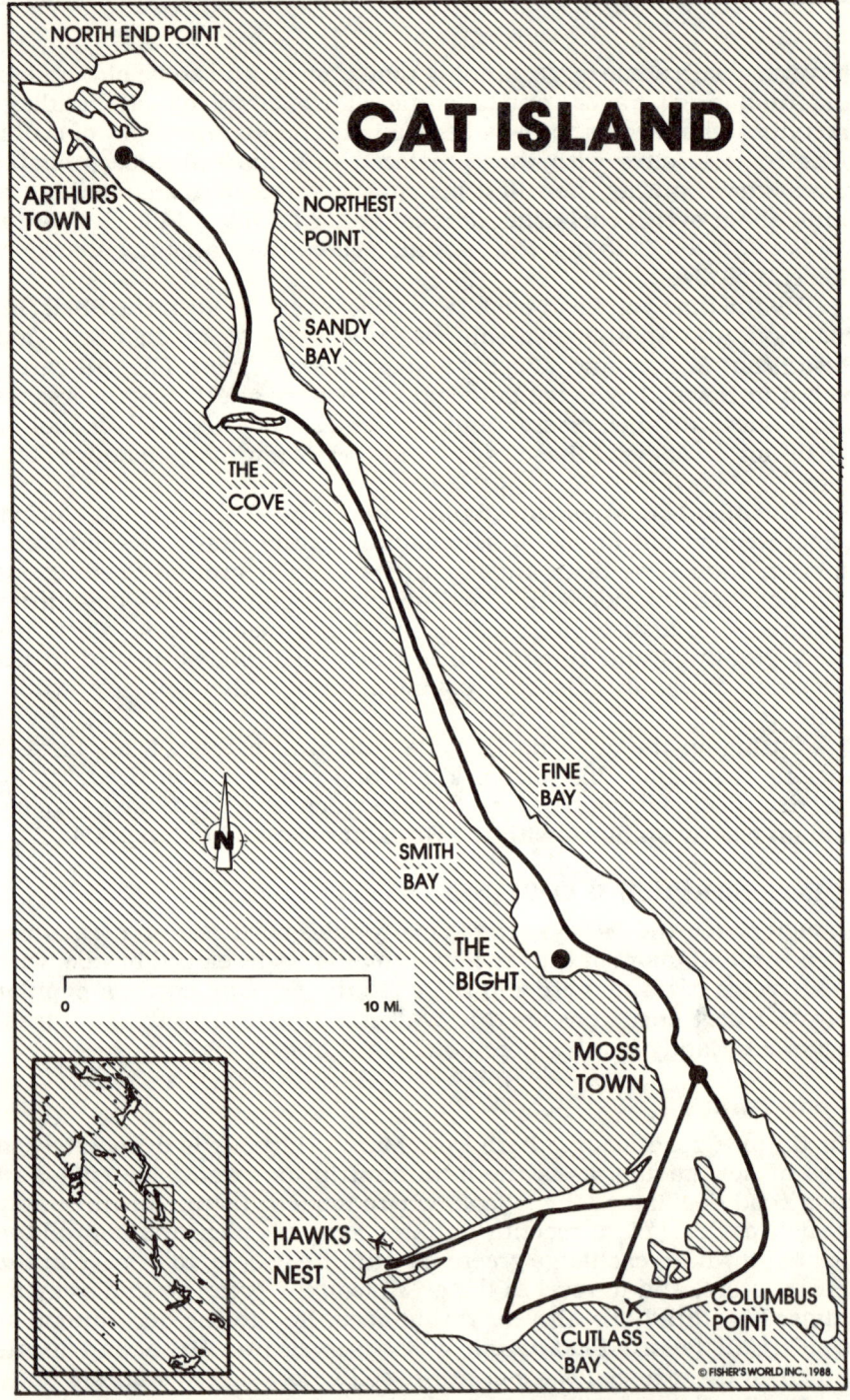

less than ten miles from shore. Those trips also attract fishing fans. Regardless of the type of fishing you favor, it's good in the vicinity: Everything from sharks to bonefish abound. An area of woodland in this region is supported by the National Trust as a sanctuary for the endangered Bahamian parrot, which is only one of the hundreds of birds that attract bird watchers to the area.

CAT ISLAND

Getting There

By Air

Bahamasair offers regular service to and from the island airstrip, which also is frequented by charter and private craft. Seaplane ramp also available.

By Sea

Mailboat *M/V Lady Eula* departs from Nassau to arrive at Bennet's Harbour and Arthur's Town; *M/V Willaurie* departs from Nassau, at Old and New Bight (also sailing to Rum Cay and San Salvador).

Stand on a cliff soaring 206 feet above sea level, and you're at the highest elevation in the Bahamas, on *Mount Alvernia*. From here you can survey both Exuma Sound and Atlantic Ocean beaches. Many of the people in nearby *New Bight* and other island settlements insist that Columbus landed here first. No one seems to have any doubt about the actions of the man buried on this peak: Father Jerome, a legendary Bahamian figure even before his death in 1956 at age eighty. The peak is accessible only after a ride up a rather tortuous road, then a climb up a rock path (where Stations of the Cross are set in cement) that leads to the white stone *Hermitage* of that Roman Catholic missionary who built several noteworthy churches on the island. His grave is in a nearby cave.

Cat Island descends by rolling hills, to wide white beaches protected by outlying reefs. Eighteenth-century pirates are believed to have hid here and some old gold has been found near Bain Town, buried under a weathered tomb. Treasure seekers often revive the search of both land and sea sites. New World colonists first settled this island in the eighteenth century; records show they were murdered or enslaved by Spaniards around 1720. The beautiful and fertile terrain was probably named for Captain Catt, a British seafarer. It was here that swashbuckling Governor Woodes Rogers longed to establish a plantation, but it was Loyalist Colonel Andrew Deveaux who brought that dream to reality and crowned his land grant with an elegantly outfitted mansion. Near *Port Howe*, remnants of his plantation remain, in the form of low walls for borders, all built by slaves. Similar walls are found all around the island. These are reminders of the Loyalists who lived here, many abandoning the island after successive failures

126 Nassau and the Bahamas

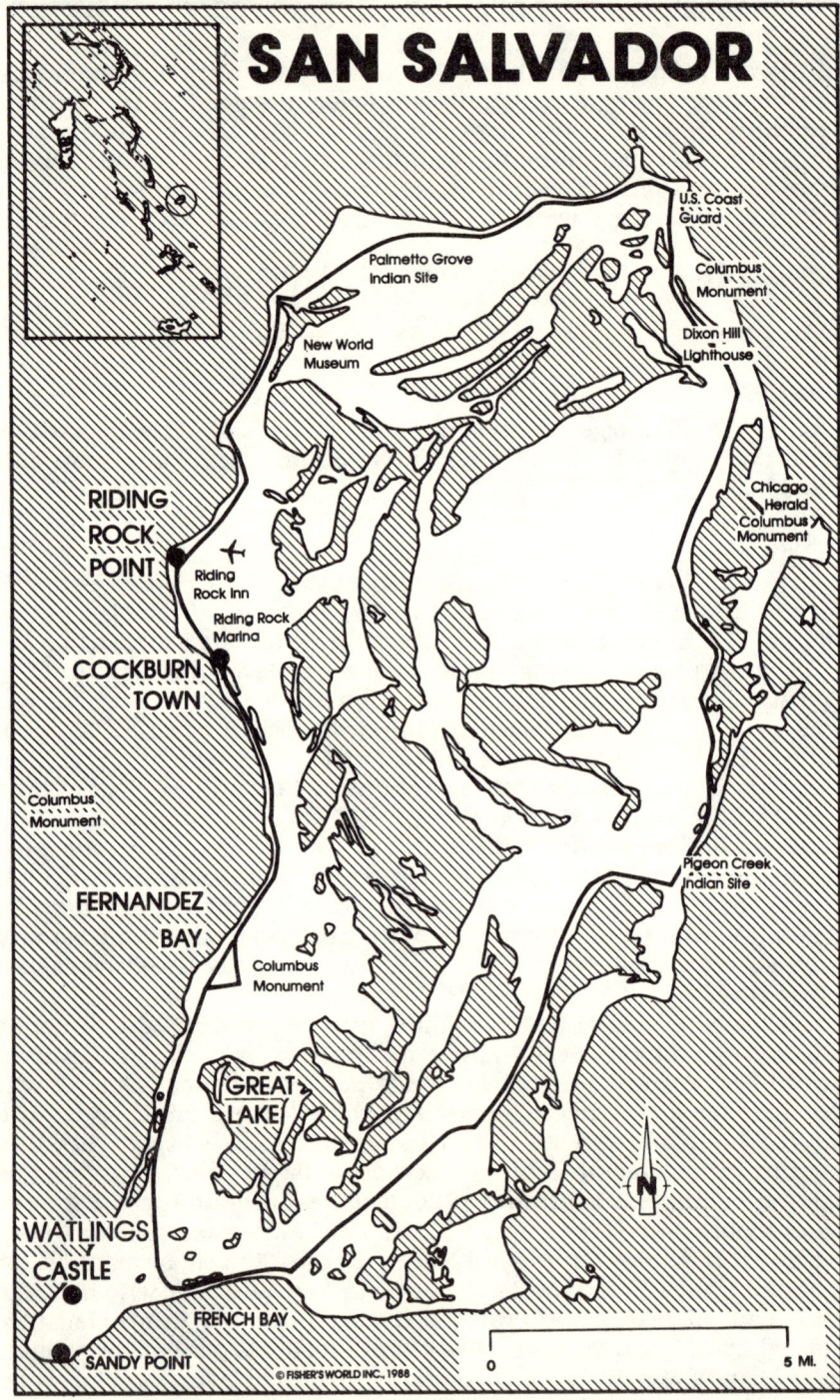

in the attempt for economic security. There are reminders here of the island's original inhabitants, too, with fascinating Indian caves to explore.

Today, an embryonic tourism industry promises sound growth, but progress of all types is slow to show here, and residents still put most of their efforts into fishing and farming for survival. Though the island has long been known as a stronghold of both obeah practices and bush medicine, it now has a resident medical doctor and nurse at the Smith Bay Clinic and nurses stationed at other clinics in Old Bight and Arthur's Town. Throughout the island, there are many small native restaurants, plus *Bridge Inn* at New Bight, where travelers can find snacks and meals. Several small clubs are alive with steel drum, rake and scrape, Goombay, and calypso music; Bain Town even claims the *Gallem* nightery. For long and lonely miles of wild and windy beaches, head for the Atlantic side of the island; beaches on the opposite side are gently washed by the waves of Exuma Sound and are better sites for water sports and picking up fine shells. There's also straw work to take home as souvenirs made and sold at *Hawkes Nest, Old Bight*, and *Arthur's Town*, and assorted gift items are sold at the three tourist facilities.

SAN SALVADOR

Getting There

By Air
Bahamasair has two weekly flights to and from the San Salvador Airport, where charter and private aircraft also land.

By Sea
Mailboat *M/V Pleasant* departs Nassau Tuesdays, stops at Rum Cay and Cat Island before docking at San Salvador.

If Christopher Columbus had only taken the time to erect a lasting marker when he landed in the New World, it would have saved centuries of scholarly debate about the site. But the explorer spent a mere two days here, and to this day no one is certain where he stepped ashore. Documents came to light in the late 1700s, which lead researchers to favor this island rather than Cat Island. In 1926, the Bahamian Legislature agreed, after persuading from a Catholic priest, to officially rename the island San Salvador as Columbus had christened it. Today, four different monuments at four different locations mark the "precise" spot where the explorer planted his cross and claim for Spain, on October 12, 1492. There's even a marker under water, where it's presumed Columbus' ships dropped anchor while he came ashore.

The natives who greeted the Spaniards as gods were a gentle people called Arawak or Lucaya Indians, whose dugouts had brought them to Bahamian islands from South America some hundreds of years before Columbus. Fleeing cannibalistic Carib tribes, the Arawaks scattered throughout the archipelago and numbered roughly 25,000 by 1492. Columbus wrote home telling Spain's rulers that the Indians could easily be subjugated as captive laborers. Within twenty-five years, there were no more Arawaks. These early Bahamians left few traces of their life in the islands, but excavations have unearthed a large village near Pigeon Creek, where shards of shells litter an area that knew successive settlement on this island the Arawaks called Guanahani.

The *Dixon Hill Lighthouse* is a fascinating local sight, built 163 feet above the sea in 1856 and still flashing double beams every twenty-five seconds. Also called the San Salvador Light, this is billed as the only hand-operated, kerosene-burning beacon still functioning. Its 400,000 candlepower can be seen for nearly 20 miles. On the other side of the island, a gentleman named Samuel Edecomber has a routine he's followed faithfully for over half a century: Every day at dusk, he treks to a tree near Cockburn (pronounced Coburn) Town and lights a kerosene lamp to keep unwary mariners away from treacherous shoals.

When the sun is high, the heavy bowers of an almond "lazy tree" offer protective shade, and the wood benches around it provide a comfortable seat for watching activity around this settlement. The tree and its swathe are owned by the proprietor of the *Ocean View Club* across the street, where locals and tourists stop for meals and cool drinks. The two main roads branch off twice, giving frontage for Anglican and Catholic churches, the commissioner's office and residence, the post office and police station. You can't miss the telegraph and clinic building, the courthouse and library, assorted gift shops, and the *Harlem Square Club*, which throbs with a disco beat every Friday. The government dock is near that lazy tree; the public cemetery flanks its other side, with the Catholic cemetery nearby.

Not far south of town are the *Devil Trees*, a group of palms once "fixed" (hexed) to prevent youngsters from sampling the coconuts. Quite near one of the beachside Columbus monuments, this is the most obvious sign of obeah practice on the island, but there's reason to believe such spells and others are still part of local goings-on. Favorite stories are told of "witch babies" who walk the roads, especially around the Easter season. Dressed entirely in black or white, at times going headless, these supernatural beings are bent on troubling mortals, yet can be banished into air if beaten with a switch from a bush named gumalami (or gahalami, depending on who tells the story). This bush is but one of those that grow thickly to cover most of San Salvador. Nearly half the varied foliage here is used to ward off colds, coughs, aches, fevers, and other ailments of a people who had no medical doctors for generations. Many of the older residents were born on a San Salvador that lay isolated and desolate before the twentieth-century military noted its strategic significance.

Though San Salvador has absorbed many facets of modernity, many residents still have no electricity and walk to wells for daily water supplies. In settlements scattered all around the island, these descendants of Loyalists' slaves live mainly by farming and fishing, swapping produce and fish with their neighbors for variety. With families averaging 7 or more members, San Salvador's 804 residents continue to help one another survive as they've done for generations. While many have abandoned their homes here and moved to Nassau two hundred miles away, others are sticking it out, convinced that their island will thrive—and that it's already the best of the Bahamas.

One American firm backs a similar opinion with extensive investments, including land development and the building of several roads, time-shared kitchened villas and luxurious, private beach homes. Known as *Columbus Landings Ltd.*, it also owns and operates the only tourist establishment on San Salvador, and prints a booklet with maps and descriptions of twenty-four island sites and sights, including all four Columbus monuments; the Olympic Flame Monument put up by Mexico in honor of its 1968 games held in the New World Columbus discovered; some explorable caves; and the cays and stretches of fine beach for sunning, shelling and fishing. So far, however, the booklet does not note the huge German tanker astride the rocks at Barkers Point.

MAYAGUANA

Sliced from nearby Crooked and Acklins Islands by the Mayaguana Passage, and from the Turks and Caicos islands by the Caicos Passage, this islet sits amid the famous Windward Passage, far from its Nassau-based government.

The 1980 census counted 464 Mayaguanians, and not one of them claim Loyalist ties, since those early settlers never established themselves here. There are neither industry nor resorts, but Bahamasair does fly to the airstrip. Aside from an occasional cruising yacht, few tourists arrive, and few natives depart. The mailboat journey to or from Nassau is a comfortless ordeal lasting about a week.

130 Nassau and the Bahamas

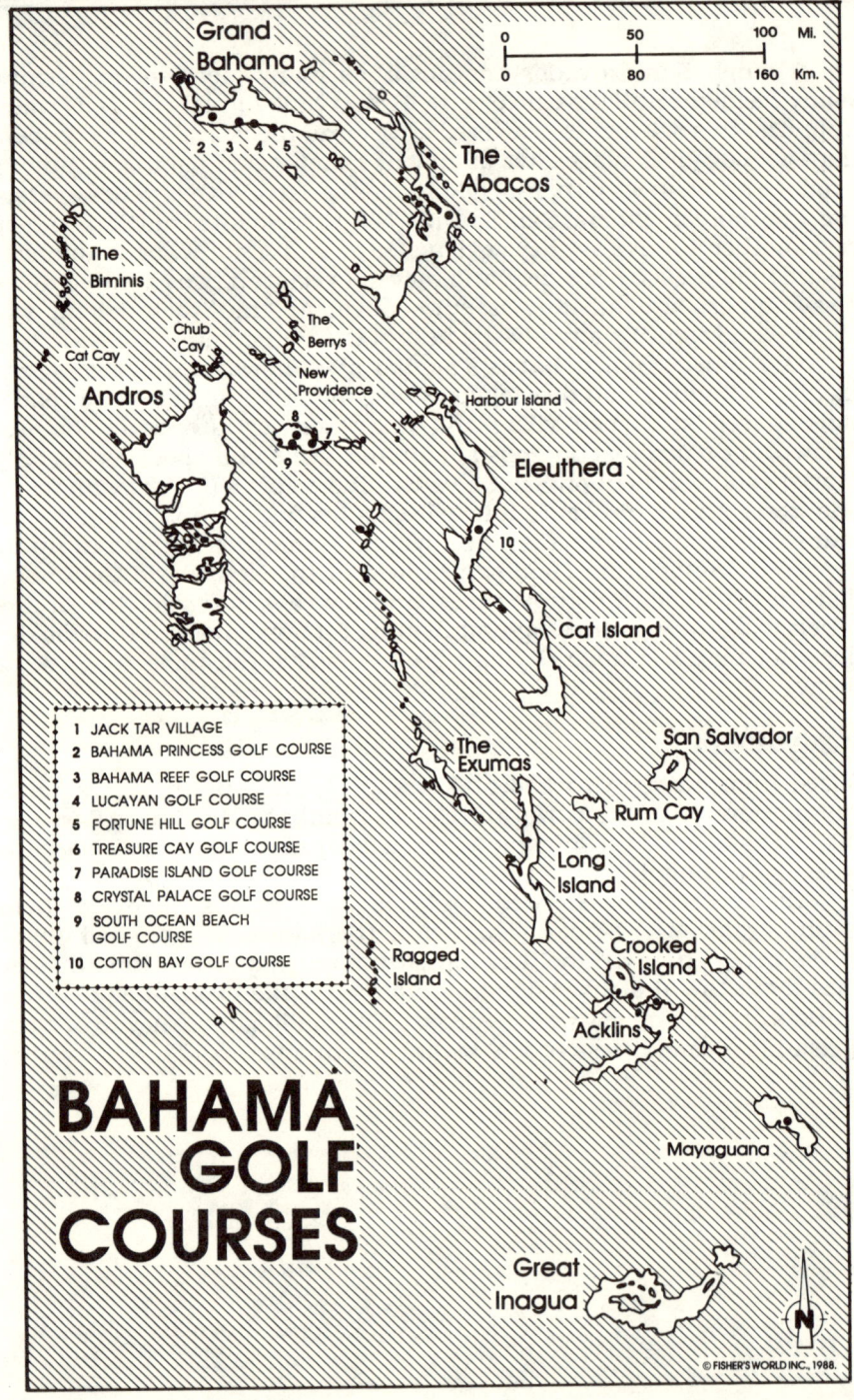

Author's Choice/ Outer Family Islands

IMPORTANT PRICE NOTE FOR OUTER FAMILY ISLANDS

Most Outer Family Island hotels, restaurants, and tourist activities cost notably less than similar facilities in Nassau or Freeport, and this is reflected in my rate classifications. I base hotel rate categories on comparable costs of rooms alone (EP). However, some Family Island establishments supply meals and include food costs in regular rates. Such places are marked (AP or FAP only, or MAP minimum), but food costs were deducted in order to present comparison rate categories, which are defined in the Travel Planner.

AP = American Plan, 3 meals included.
FAP = "Full American Plan," 3 meals included, same as American Plan.
MAP = Modified American Plan, breakfast and one other meals included.

ABACO, ELBOW CAY—including HOPE TOWN

HOTELS

Abaco Inn Six miles from Marsh Harbour Airport. Phone (809)367-2666. A friendly, hideaway on White Sound, reached by automobile over paved and dirt roads, or by an easier walk. A pet donkey unofficially greets those who enter the private enclave where lodge and cottages are fashioned from stone and weathered wood. A favorite four-star retreat for world-weary executives, Abaco Inn is operated by competent, conscientious owners. The three 2-bedroom ocean-front cottages and six harborside double rooms are simple and neat. Rental bikes and barber services are available. Three beaches; up windsurfing, area tours, boating, fishing, snorkeling, and scuba diving. Thatched solarium where you can sun worship au naturel in privacy. Terrace tables and chairs let you enjoy intimate dinners lit by stars and candles, or you can dine indoors; either way, you're in for the treat of creative cookery in five courses. Entertainment in the adjacent bar-lounge. Closed mid-September through mid-November, the inn occasionally accommodates special groups, and often welcomes locals and tourists for fine meals including vegetarian or macrobiotic fare. *Moderate to expensive.*

Hope Town Harbour Lodge Elbow Cay. Twenty minutes from Marsh Harbour Airport. Phone (809)366-0095; (800)626-5690. Overlooking both the harbor and the Atlantic, with steep stairs zigzagging through dense greenery to its hilltop perch. A beautiful old house now expanded into a 13-room main lodge, plus accommodations for eight in the century-old Butterfly House cottage. The cottage has its own kitchen and is situated near the back court, where the gardens open to a pool, a patio snack bar, and the beach. In the main lodge, there are comfortable lounge areas for games and TV, two dining rooms, and two bars that have entertainment, including the very popular *Lighthouse Bar*. The international food is notable, with a Sunday Champagne Brunch bringing crowds for the hot and cold buffet featuring standing rib roast. Marina and dock, beauty shops and barber, complimentary windsurfing and snorkel gear; plus boating, fishing, waterskiing, scuba diving, and sightseeing trips. Lot's of grinning, barefoot tourists here, mostly Europeans. *Moderate to Expensive.*

Also Recommended Private cottages can be rented all over the island, many of them advertised in the local publication, *Abaco Life*. In Hope Town, rentals are available from Sylvia Albury, Ray Swank, and Robert Malone.

MUSEUM Named for one of the cay's founders, *Wyannie Malone Historical Museum* in Hope Town, is a quaint home for memorabilia of rugged island colony living.

Abaco, GREEN TURTLE CAY

Green Turtle Yacht Club & Marina Green Turtle Cay. Phone (809)367-2572. A few minutes' boat ride from town, this White Sound retreat melds the best of vacation pleasures into a five-star treat. Away from the thundering crunch of crowds, it's casual and comfortable. Air-conditioned. Double rooms, villas with 1 to 3 bedrooms and 1 to 3 baths plus kitchens and dining areas, cottages of 2 to 4 bedrooms , also with kitchens and dining rooms, plus patios. Obvious care has gone into their decor and maintenance. The British owners lived in some of the cottages and left behind special items like a treasured old organ for guests to enjoy. A British-trained staff anticipates your needs in a natural manner, whether you're in your own quarters, at the pool, or in the clubhouse. The food is notable, although surpassed by the camaraderie. Jackets aren't required for lawn and patio buffet dinners and dances, but the sportswear is elegant and includes long and lovely tropical gowns for the ladies. Bare feet have been seen, however, in the TV lounge and the delightful barroom that is papered with currency (real bills, signed and affixed by past guests, including a U.S. president. Flags fly from the rafters over and near a huge elm slab hand carved with a depiction of the Mayflower—one of several fine English carvings. All water is rainwater stored in cisterns and used conservatively. The club has a small private beach near the island's other several miles of fine beaches. Tennis, boating, fishing, waterskiing, snorkeling, windsurfing, and scuba diving.

This is also the Green Turtle Yacht Club, prestigiously affiliated with The Royal Yachting Association (British, of course), and Birdham Yacht Club, Florida. Mininmal subscroption covering seasonal membership is added to your check. Its outstanding marina offers gas, diesel, water, ice, showers, laundry, rental boats, sportfishing charters, and scuba tank recharging. Boats from around the world crowd here for July's *Green Turtle Yacht Club Regatta Week*, with races, dances, picnics, and celebrations of Bahamian and U.S. Independence Days. Regatta Week is sponsored by Bacardi & Co., Ltd., which also sponsors the 3-day *Green Turtle Yacht Club Annual Memorial Fishing Tournament* in May. Closed September 4 to November 8. *Moderate to Very Extravagant.*

New Plymouth Club & Inn P.O.Box 462. Phone (809)367-5211. Tropical gardens create a fine setting for this beautiful two-story masterpiece of nostalgia with 8 rooms for rent. There's a pool, dining room, bar, lounge and telephone. Guests enjoy beach privileges and nearby boating, fishing, scuba diving, tennis, and golf. Closed August and September. Reservations urged. MAP only. *Inexpensive.*

Bougainvillea Apartments This is another superbly simple, restored frame building, 150 years old, with gardens that live up to the name. The two fully equipped 2-bedroom apartments are augmented by a dining room and bar. Boating, fishing, and other sports can be arranged. Closed August. *Inexpensive.*

SPECTACLES AND DISPLAYS Look for colorful regattas, fly-ins, sports, and fishing tournaments that bring internationals to compete against Abaco's best. Contact the Ministry of Tourism Sports Division for a list of dates and events. Every November, Abaco Week celebrates island heritage and culture with festivities and an Arts and Crafts Gala that includes paintings, embroidery, needlepoint, crocheting, carving, collage, straw work, shellcraft, model making, and Junkanoo costumes. Don't miss *Green Turtle/Yacht Club Summer Regatta and Tourney.*

GOLF COURSES I

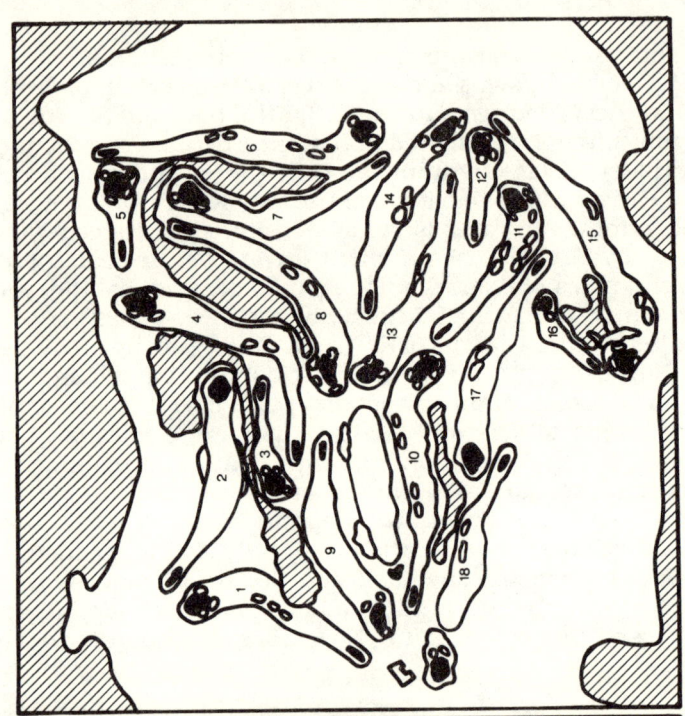

PARADISE ISLAND GOLF CLUB

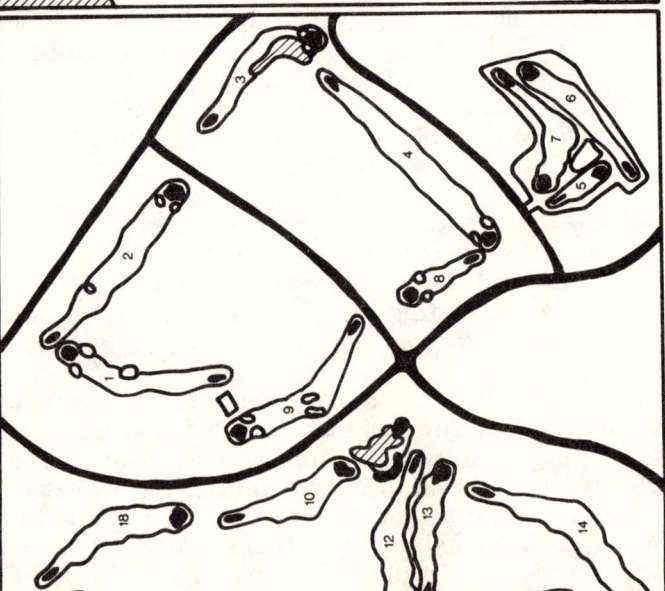

FORTUNE HILL GOLF & COUNTRY CLUB

Abaco, GREAT GUANA CAY

ACCOMODATIONS This away-from-it-all islet offers only the 7-room *Bay View Apartments*, *Pinder's Cottages* (4), and the 19-room *Guana Beach Resort*.

Abaco, MARSH HARBOUR

Conch Inn Resort & Marina P.O.Box 434. Phone (809)367-2800. Marsh Harbour. Plenty of greenery here —huge blossoms of African tulip trees and "poor man's orchid," a tree with orchidlike flowers. A lane leads past these and neat rows of rooms, to the office in the Conch Crawl, where breakfast reigns and snacks and drinks are handy at most hours. Outside and a few steps away is the Conch Inn Marina, with fuel, power, fresh water, ice, showers, laundry, small rental boats, 45 slips, a crowd of yachts, and a special berth for the topsail schooner *William H. Albury*. There's also a raised patio and pool. Ten rooms with water views, two efficiency apartments, and one 2-bedroom cottage, across the street. Air-conditioned, modern, and nicely decorated. Tranquility is what the owners prize. Leisurely tours of the vicinity via rental motorbikes or cars, or taxis with guides. Waterskiing, fishing, snorkeling, scuba diving, beachcombing, boating. Conch Crawl has a radio communications center monitoring UNICOM for aircraft, UHF for boats, and CB for local goings-on, all tucked neatly behind the bar. At the other end of the bar is a telephone with excellent service, particularly on long distance.

Landlubbers come here, too, and one of the reasons they come is to be part of the congenial gatherings in the *Conch Out Bar*, or to sample delicious and carefully prepared foods at the *Conch Inn Restaurant* where the menu includes wild Abaco boar. Ties and jackets are not required. A large lounge area separates the restaurant from the bar, and there's a piano nook in this once-private beach house. *Inexpensive to Moderate*.

Great Abaco Hotel P.O.Box 419, Marsh Harbour. Phone (809)367-2158. High on a grassy hill this two-story facility provides 20 large air-conditioned rooms with patios. Spacious grounds with a freshwater pool, two tennis courts, a terrace where weekly barbecues are held, a gift shop, and a strip of fine beach. Dress can be casual. Dining room with adjacent long, polished bar and musicians constitute one of Abaco's two nightclubs. Dinner features international and local cuisine, and you might even take your own catch to the chef who'll cook it to order. Fishing and fishing charters; snorkeling and scuba diving; rentals of small and large boats; picnics and sightseeing trips by boat; tennis; rental bicycles, mopeds and cars; and bus service to and from Treasure Cay's 18-hole golf course. Many local groups meet here—you might find a gospel sing going on, sponsored by Hope Town churches. *Inexpensive to Moderate*.

Note: Thirteen Abaco hotels participate in Goombay Getaway vacation packages that offer four days and three nights or eight days and seven nights, including air fare, for minimal per person/double occupancy rates.

Watch for the **Boat Harbour & Holiday Houses**-destined to be Abaco's largest marina, with 140 slips, and adjacent 120 two-story townhouses (prices start at $100,000), all on 25 acres next door to the Great Abaco Hotel.

RESTAURANTS Both *Conch Inn* and *Great Abaco Hotel restaurants* are highly recommended. *Moderate to Expensive.* There's a *Kentucky Fried Chicken* chain restaurant in town.

The Jib Room Part of Marsh Harbour Marina, this large, airy restaurant serves dinner on a long veranda overlooking the marina and harbor, or indoors where there is a small saltwater aquarium. A dinghy has been hoisted to the high ceiling and outfitted as a chandelier. Bahamian and American dinners. Frequent outdoor barbecue buffets. Downstairs, the Bilge serves breakfast and lunch. A decked patio offers snacks and drinks by the water. *Inexpensive to Moderate.*

Cynthia's Kitchen In town. Popular for breakfast, lunch, and dinner due to its Bahamian flair and flavor. Open from 8:30 A.M. to 11 P.M. (The place is tiny; Cynthia plans expansions.) *Inexpensive.*

Keys Bakery and Restaurant Eighty-year-old Mr. Key still rises early to mix dough for the first bakings of bread, but daughter Ruthie runs the family-type restaurant. Burgers, salads, and full meals that attract locals as well as tourists. Simple, fresh, and clean. (Closed Sundays) *Inexpensive.*

Mother Merle's Fishnet Restaurant Located in nearby Dundas Town, Mother Merle's high aqua fence opens to a courtyard and dining room, where there is a bar with a jukebox. Bahamian and American specialties, with conch fritters, turtle steak, coconut or pineapple ice cream, and pies topping the list of favorite orders. Mother Merle presides graciously over it all. Dinner only, from 6 P.M. to midnight. *Inexpensive.*

Getting Around

By Land Automobiles can be rented from *H & L Car Rentals*, P.O. Box 507, Marsh Harbour, located at the Shell station. *Western Auto Bicycle Co.*, P.O. Box 507, Marsh Harbour, is the address for rental bicycles and motor scooters. *Jason's Bus Service* operates regularly from Marsh Harbour to Treasure Cay, Spring City, Dundas Town, and Murphy Town and offers charter trips to all settlements; P.O. Box 513, Marsh Harbour. Taxis are the favored tourist transport; they are available by CB call from your hotel desk.

By Sea Having your own small boat is much more important than a land vehicle. When you book accommodations, be sure to arrange boat rental as well—either through your hotel or by contacting *Junior Roberts* (P.O.Box 574, Marsh Harbour), who supplies 19-foot skiffs with 70-horsepower outboard motors.

For boats you can crew alone or charter with a skipper, *Bahamas Yachting Services, Inc.* (BYS) provides fifty 30- to 50-foot sail and power cruising vessels, fully equipped, and also has a full-service marina and 45-slip dock. Abaco's largest bareboat charter firm (cost $700-$1,800 weekly; skipper is $55 extra daily). BYS has tripled its business in a few years. It now offers a unique *Cruise and Learn* course, with eight days of classroom and onboard instruction and practice, a live-aboard instructor, and a final written exam in basic sailing and navigation that qualifies you as a skipper here and with other charter firms, too.

Marsh Harbour Marina also has bareboat and skippered charters, sailboats only, with three 33- to 43-foot vessels, each complete with linens, provisions, ice, and dinghy; booked direct c/o P.O. Box 518, with advance reservations urged for these (cost: $900-$1,400 weekly) and for faster boats or trollers. There's a restaurant, a snack area, and a dive center here, and full-service marina plus dockage available via 40 slips. This marina is a sponsor of annual summertime *Abaco Race Week*, and offers a June sailing course for tyros. Also check out the *William H. Albury*.

By Ferry *Albury's Ferry Service* operates motor launches from its dock near the Great Abaco Hotel, and regularly plys between Marsh Harbour, Hope Town, Guana Cay, and Man-O-War Cay. Its schedules are adjusted to meet airline arrivals and departures, which it monitors and checks by VHF and CB. Charters are available (just radio for a watertaxi): to Treasure Cay, it costs $90 for eight people; to Green Turtle, $130 for eight people; to Hope Town, $55-$80; to Man-O-War, $75-$120. Ferry trips to Man-O-War are $6 oneway, or $8 for roundtrip, same day. Look for special sightseeing jaunts 1 or 2 days weekly via 35-passenger boats which leave at 9 A.M.

Elsewhere in Abaco In Hope Town, *Abaco Bahamas Charters, Ltd.*, offers provisioned and bare-boat charters, plus mooring. *Great Guana Cay* has a 200-foot straight dock that accommodates five yachts. There's also electricity and ice.

TOURS

By Land Check with your hotelier to contact local taxi guides for trips to nearby settlements, or to rent self-drive cars to tour alone. Sample prices for taxis, and one-way trips from North Eleuthera Airport are: 36 miles to Governor's Harbour, approximately $40; 60 miles to Windermere Island, about $65; 98 miles to Cape Eleuthera, $105.

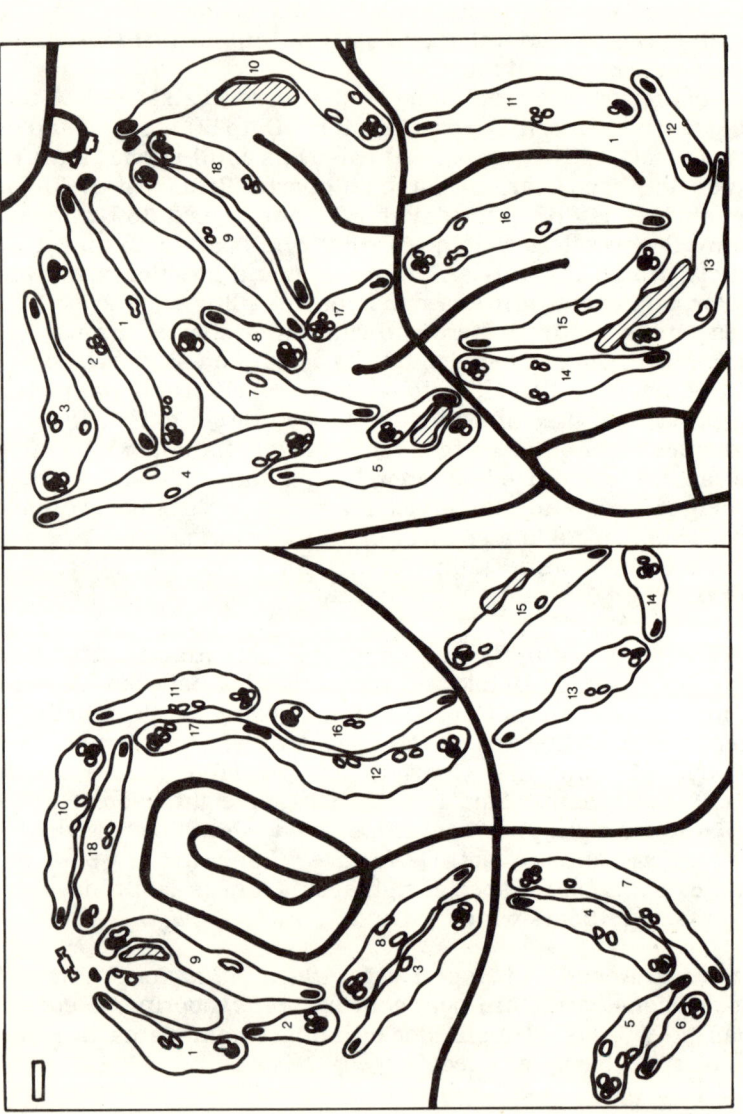

By Sea The best sights are seen by boat, particularly at a gentle speed that allows you to absorb the beauty above and below the water. Many people sail their own yachts here, fly in for cruises aboard crewed vessels, or follow the crowds that have already made this small corner of the Bahamas a world leader in bare-boating. Abaco has more than 100 sail and power yachts, all fully equipped and provisioned for you to captain. If this is a bit more than you're ready for, there are ferries to nearby interesting island villages, and it usually is possible to find skippers who add sightseeing tours to regular services such as scuba trips.

We give top rating to cruises aboard the 70-foot *William H. Albury*, a replica of topsail schooners of the 1800s, lovingly handcrafted in 1963 at Man-O-War Cay, where classic boat building thrives. Skippered by Master Captain Joe Maggio, the *Albury* represents the Bahamas whenever tall ships gather. Most of the time Captain Maggio berths at the Conch Inn Marina to pick up passengers who have booked in advance, then sails away and converts them into cruise crews who enjoy ports of call such as Little Harbour, Elbow Cay, Man-O-War Cay, Great Guana Cay, and Green Turtle Cay. An even dozen passengers can sail together. Current cost is about $600 per person with six people aboard.

Don't miss the area's nature reserves, which include *Pelican Cay's Land-and-Sea Park*, a project of Bahamas National Trust, noted for its underwater caves, coral reefs, fish, plant, and bird life. It's situated between Little Harbour and Tilloo Cay. Further north, between Man-O-War Cay and Scotland Cay, a proposed underwater park is also worth a look.

You may want to make contact with Marsh Harbour Rotary, which meets weekly at Great Abaco Hotel, or with the local Chamber of Commerce, publisher of the twice-yearly *Abaco Life*.

SPORTS Tennis thrives at Great Abaco Hotel. Trips can be arranged for golf on championship greens further north. For boating, fishing, and waterskiing, check with your hotelier or at marinas listed below. Snorkeling is fine just from the beach, and better via trips with boats or dive operations. Dave Gale, certified NAUI instructor, offers scuba instruction and dive trips through his *Island Marine* outfit, on nearby Parrot Cay, which he purchased from the Queen of England several years ago. He also runs a dive shop with rental gear and offers marine repair services. The *Chambered Nautilus*, with Dan Wiltfang at its helm, is a full-range dive center in Marsh Harbour, with facilities at Casurina Point, to the south, and Green Turtle Cay, to the north. A third dive shop is at Marsh Harbour and provides rental equipment, instructions, and a variety of dive trips. *Skeets LaChance*, a legendary local involved with preservation of Fowl Cay and Sandy Cay, operates *Dive Abaco* here and offers skin and scuba lessons, trips, and rental gear (daily or weekly rates) including cameras.

Abaco, TREASURE CAY

Treasure Cay Resort This is really a small city, complete with community associations and a center that includes a grocery, liquor store, beauty salon, bank, resident medical doctor, dentist, pharmacy, and boutique. A nearby taxi stand, library, churches, and a real estate office where people can buy all, or time-shared parts, of local condos, cottages, and apartments completes the city feeling. Many of these accommodations are already built and busy. Very aggressively planned development, eventually will shelter 5,000 people. Management devotes less attention to the two-star hotel and tourist facilities than to development buyers, owners, or potential purchasers. Guests in this three-star complex include Canadians, Americans, Germans, and other Europeans, coming as individuals and in groups as large as 150. Rooms (228) range from simple hotel accommodations to 1- and 2-bedroom villas, apartments, and elegant townhouses, and even duplex villas for large families or couples traveling together. Laundry facilities, a card room, satellite and cable TV for hotel rooms, four freshwater pools, shuffleboard, volleyball, table tennis, two all-weather tennis courts, and an 18-hole championship golf course designed by Dick Wilson. New thirty-two marina units, each with 2 bedrooms, living room, kitchen, plus sleeping loft, with a new pool/patio and the *Jolly Roger* for snacks and drinks. The 75-slip marina has ice, water, electricity, fuel, rental boats and windsurfers, waterskiing, custom wet and dry storage, and a chandlery for yachts. A dive center and shop here is UNEXSO affiliated and offers instructions, certification, dive trips and gear. Miles of powdery, shell-laden beach, where snorkeling gear and sunfish sailboats are free for guests' use. Daily scheduled boat trips for fishing (Treasure Cay has its own bonefish flats) or sightseeing to nearby Green Turtle Cay. There are lists of daily activities for all ages, particularly during November's annual *Abaco Week*, July's *Regatta Week*, and other holiday times. Frequent tournaments in golf, tennis, and bonefishing, pro shops for golf and tennis; and bikes for getting about. The resort hosts the second leg of the annual *International Billfish League Grand Prix* series tourney in summer, other billfish events, and the *Wingding Fly-In* (general aviation) in October. Treasure Cay's three bars feature entertainment. There are two restaurants, where we found the food so poorly prepared and the service so negligent that I resented paying the mandatory 15 percent service charge.

The complex occupies land once farmed by Loyalists who lived in the Carlton community, which in 1884 boasted 219 people before dissension broke up the town, and the residents moved to other settlements such as Green Turtle Cay. *Expensive to Extravagant.*

Abaco, WALKER'S CAY

Walker's Cay Hotel and Marina Phone (305)522-1469. International Game Fish records call sportsfishermen to this self-contained island resort at the northern-most point of Abaco. No ferries ply between the mainland and this cay, but yachts cruise into the 75-slip full-service marina. Aircraft fly between the islet's private landing strip and Fort Lauderdale International Airport, Florida, home of Walker's Cay International Airlines, which schedules flights here and to Bimini. Flights can be booked simultaneously with reservations for any of the 62 air-conditioned hotel rooms with terraces, or the four 2-bedroom villas. Seaplanes can land here and the resort has fuel and tie-downs for the private aircraft that visit frequently. At the marina, you'll find fuel, electricity, water, showers, a taxidermist agency, ship store and liquor shop, tackle shop, laundry. Charter boats are available. Other diversions include wandering the gardens and woods, beachcombing, tennis, boating, windsurfing, and waterskiing. The dive center offers gear and instructions for snorkeling and scuba, plus trips to nearby dive sites. Barbecues are frequent, and there's a dining room where good food can include your catch, prepared to order. The bar and TV lounge are cozy, and secluded places abound for private picnics. Meeting facilities here are often kept busy by corporate executives. *Moderate to expensive.*

ELEUTHERA

CAPE ELEUTHERA

Cape Eleuleuthera Resort and Yacht Club P.O.Box 48. Phone (809)334-2152. This complex rates four stars for its 18-hole championship golf course designed by Devlin von Hagge, six tennis courts, swimming pool, full marina that can dock anything up to 200-foot yachts, large private airstrip, plus fine bed-and-board facilities. Many developments are under consideration for the future, and may be under way quite soon.

Eleuthera, GREGORY TOWN

Cambridge Villas, Restaurant, Bar & Grill P.O.Box 1548. Phone (809)332-2269. Young, active sports buffs are attracted to surfing, cave and beach treasure hunts, and shark feeding treks. *Moderate.* Tourists driving through this region frequently stop for the Bahamian fare, including fish and lobster, pork and barbecue ribs, with desserts of fresh pineapples grown on nearby plantations.

Thompson's Bakery A perfect place for sampling guava and sapodilla cakes, pineapple and coconut tarts, fresh doughnuts, cinnamon rolls and breads. You'll find straw work and souvenirs here, too, and can even rent rooms in the big house on the hill. *Inexpensive*

SHOPPING The *Bahamas House and Gift Shop* provides rental cottages, and works by gifted artist Diane Thompson.

GOLF COURSES III

BAHAMA REEF GOLF & COUNTRY CLUB

TREASURE CAY GOLF CLUB

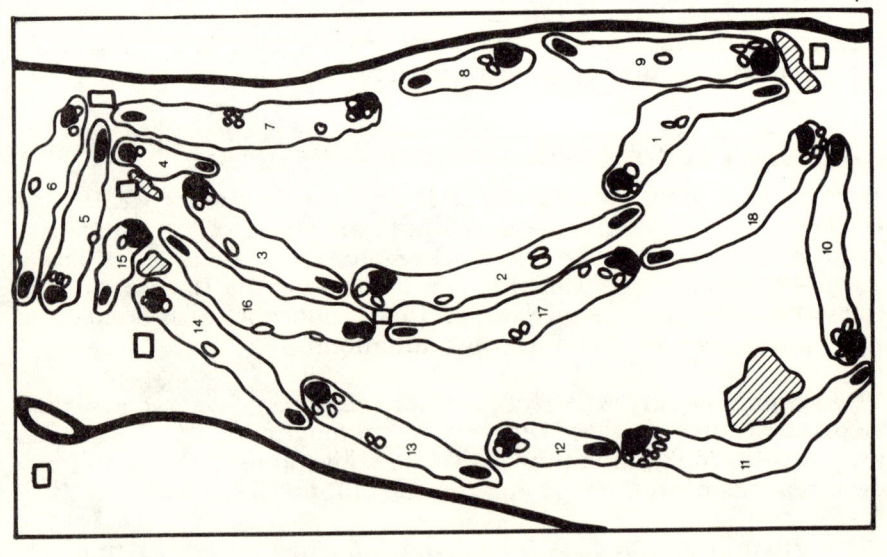

Eleuthera, GOVERNORS HARBOUR (including South Palmetto Point)

Club Med P.O. Box 80. Phone (809)332-2270. On the Atlantic shore site of Eleuthera's first resort, this is one of the Bahamas' two Club Meds. Something like a glorified summer camp for adults—a camp where summer is year-round and one all-inclusive fee eliminates toting cash or figuring tips. All the free French cuisine you want, and nightly cabarets. Snorkel, waterski, sail, swim, scuba with free instruction and gear, including underwater cameras (film is sold), and a photography lab. Or try the large pool, eight tennis courts (two nightlit), volleyball, basketball, calisthenics, yoga, free deep-sea fishing, Atari computer workshop, arts and crafts, daylong picnics, and a multilingual library. There's a boutique, a disco, a marina with cafe/bar; a huge central complex with bar, restaurant, dance floor, stage, and floor-show seats. Neat, twin-bedded rooms with showers, in clusters of buildings with 1 to 3 floors. Parents of youngsters 4 to 12 will praise the year-round MiniClub that's like a glorified day camp, operating 9 A.M. to 6 P.M. Costs run around $700-$800 weekly per person; kids 4 to 7 free; kids 8 to 11 half price. Charter flights from Atlanta, Miami, and New York. Reservations direct or via travel agents.

RESTAURANTS Resorts and clubs in the vicinity that welcome travelers for meals (sometimes only via reservations) include the *Cigatoo Inn*. Also look for *Muriel's Bakery*, Sue Clarie's new restaurant, and *The Blue Room*. Further south, are *Cotton Bay Club* and *Windermere Club*.

NIGHTLIFE Aside from resort action already noted, there's a new movie theater: the *Globe Princess*.

Getting Around *Ronnie's Rent-A-Car*, P.O. Box 118, and *Norma's U-Drive-It*, P.O. Box 136, both offer cars for about $40 daily, sometimes at three-day minimums. Reserve in advance.

Eleuthera, HARBOUR ISLAND

HOTELS This small island offers resorts and rooms for almost every type of traveler, many private homes to rent, and time-share suites or cottages to buy. For toll-free reservations number, see the Travel Planner. Most resorts here eschew tips but add 10 to 15 percent to your tab and divide it among the staff after you depart.

Pink Sands P.O. Box 87, Harbour Island. Phone 333-2030. One of the few Family Island establishments rated five-star. It's a licensed proprietary club that caters first to regular guest-members, then to their friends and others. It has been doing so long enough to welcome the children of married couples who met and played here as youngsters, and to have a mailing list of some 7,000 for two yearly newsletters from second- and third-generation hoteliers.

Charmingly informal, Pink Sands' lodge includes a library, a dining room and comfortable areas for sitting with good company, weekend entertainment and well-prepared drinks. A maximum of 46 couples can stay at the same time, in rooms that actually are cottage suites, with patios, dressing rooms, baths, kitchens and huge rooms furnished comfortably yet conservatively for sleeping, dining, and lounging. All are within individual or duplex cottages scattered among paved paths and tamed flowers and greenery.

Pink Sands' 40 acres here, and another 60 further north, are designated as a bird sanctuary by the *Audubon Society*, whose members come annually to count the fowl. Most guests, however, count the scores at the three corKarpet tennis courts. Tennis is a serious sport here, with British championship Slazenger racquets on loan, balls for sale, and an outdoor tennis lounge for sociable game scrutiny. There's also a barber on duty, beauty-parlor equipment for ladies' use and private label Pink Sands shampoo, moisturizer and lotions for before, during, and after sunning. The famous pink sand beach is outfitted with cabanas, thatched shelters, chairs and tables, plus a small fleet of sailboats and motorboats. All types of fishing are available; bonefishing is superb, as is snorkeling; other water sports are also available, along with rental vehicles and picnics, "simple" American and Bahamian cookery, and a harborside *Pink Sands Lounge.* The atmosphere is casual, but with a dignified informality that calls for clothes of good taste which, after dark, means ties or ascots with jackets (try a crested blazer) for men, dress heels and elegant sports ensembles for ladies (skirts preferred). Closed August to November and part of May; reservations by direct contact. AP only. *Extravagant.*

Dunmore Beach Club P.O. Box 122, Harbour Island. Phone 333-2200. A beautiful place owned and operated by a bachelor from an old island family, the Club welcomes children only if they're old enough to show proper deference and respect for the fine furnishings (no sticky fingers, please). The main building sits high, overlooking pink Atlantic beach sands, and includes a patio with comfortable chairs and tables, lounge areas inside, and a dining room known for serving the best food in town. Sixteen rooms are in charming cottages hidden among trees and shrubs. Dress is informal, and activities include sunning, swimming, and deep-sea fishing, as well as bonefishing. Closed May 10 to August 10. Reservations by direct contact. AP only. *Expensive.*

Romora Bay Club P.O. Box 146, Harbour Island. Phone 333-2325. Offers 25 rooms and two full housekeeping cottages that can accommodate up to six persons. All are air-conditioned, with private patios or balconies that view gardens or the harbor, where there's a dock, several small boats, and a 28-foot sloop. Meals reflect staff training by a Miami gourmet chef, and lunch usually is an extensive buffet staged at the waterfront bar, reached by neat steps traveling down from the higher main house which contains the dining room, library, a comfortable sitting lounge, and a bar. Breakfast can be ordered from room service, and dinner remains casual, but no rowdy clothes or bare feet are allowed. There's a hot tub/jacuzzi spa, a masseur, hammocks for lazing, windsurfing, a resident donkey and parrot, tennis courts and a pro, tennis and snorkeling gear for the asking. You also have several acres of gardens and lawns that reach to the pink beach; bicycles, scooters, golf carts and minimokes for rent; weekly entertainment programs and weekly native musicians. Scuba thrives here with three dive masters, lessons for tyros, and package holiday dive programs. There's an intensive suite/cottage time-share program, and new beach and bedroom units underway. Dress is casual. Closed September 15 to November 1. *Expensive to extravagant.*

Coral Sands Hotel Harbour Island. Phone 333-2350. On the 14 hilly acres, which stretch from the beach toward the center of town, are lawns with fruit and palm trees, profuse flowers and a main lodge that includes dining areas and the *Yellow Bird Bar*, a large balcony and lounge area, a library, and a game room complete with TV and pool table. The outdoor bandstand is dubbed Carnegie Hall by local musicians who play there (and indoors) for Friday night dancing and island events. A path leads to the patio beach bar. Free extras include beach chaises, umbrellas and cabanas, surf riders, snorkeling and gear, sailboats and rowboats, tennis, shuffleboard, table tennis, and badminton. Rental bicycles, golf carts, or cars are available. The food is a fine mix of Bahamian, Continental, and American, deftly served by waitresses who will sometimes sing harmony for you. *Moderate.*

Runaway Hill Club P.O. Box 31, Harbour Island. Phone 333-2150. Classic island architecture, complete with quoins and dormer windows, lends a timeless grace to this inn. Lovely grounds lead to the main house, where the first floor is devoted to public rooms, a restaurant/bar, and a grand veranda for breakfast or drinks with views of the ocean. Upstairs and in an adjacent newly remodeled wing are 8 comfortable rooms, some with patios or balconies. All island sports and activities are available to guests. Dining often attracts guests for expensive, full course, fixed-price gourmet meals. Reservations direct or through travel agents. *Moderate*

Valentine's Yacht Club & Inn & Dive Center P.O. Box 1, Harbour Island. Phone 333-2142. Actively operated by two generations of a Virginia family, the Club has 27 rooms fronting the harbor, a hot tub, swimming pool, barber and beauty shops, and dining room. The *Nautical Bar* glows with copper and features singing guitarists, an international guest list includes many Germans and French. The main lodge reception area is decorated like an old country home, with antiques, Oriental art and hunt club memorabilia. On the Atlantic shore, Valentine's operates *Dunes Club*, with sun deck, game room, showers, changing rooms, lounge, beach attendants, and lunch ser-

146 Nassau and the Bahamas

GOLF COURSES IV

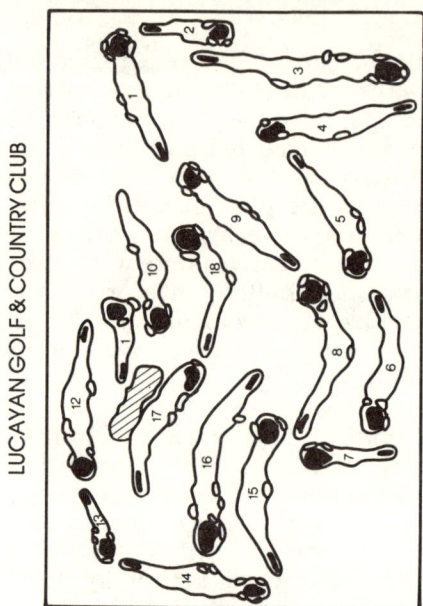

LUCAYAN GOLF & COUNTRY CLUB

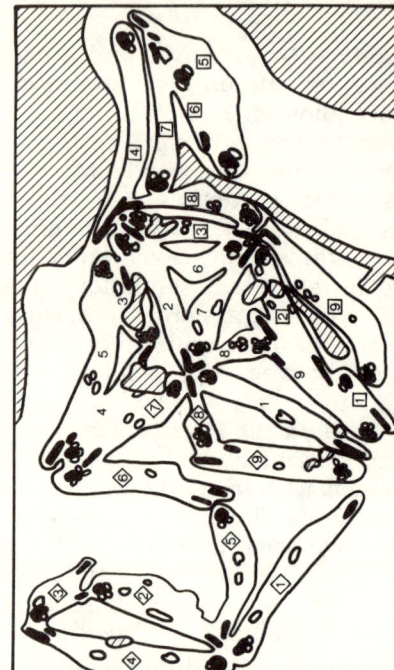

JACK TAR VILLAGE

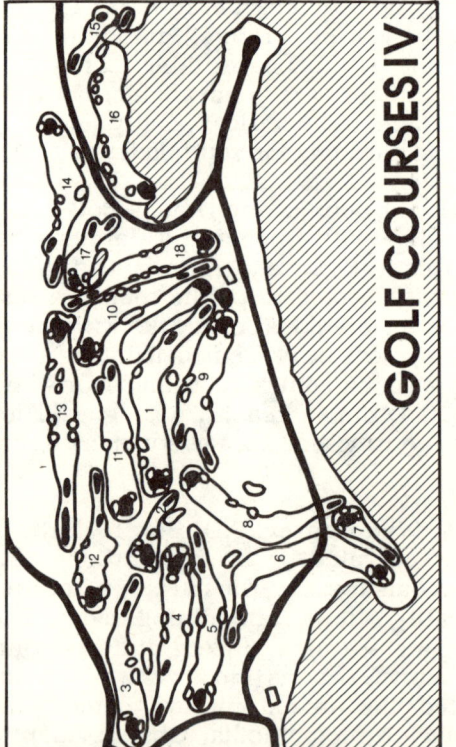

COTTON BAY BEACH & GOLF CLUB

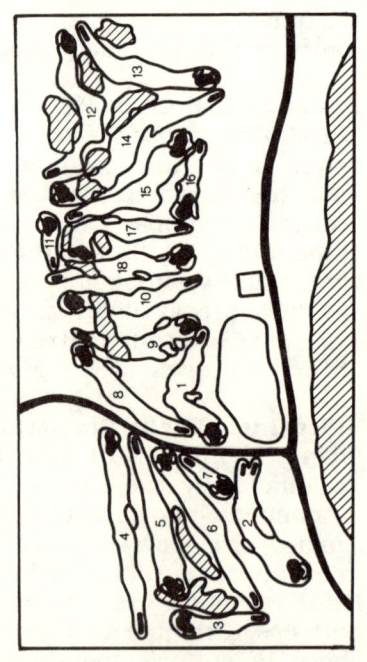

Crystal Palace Golf Course

vice. The harborside marina offers electricity, water, showers, laundry, and a 174-foot dock able to handle seven yachts. The *Dive Shop* is nearby, with newest equipment plus free scuba lessons and two PADI/SSI dive masters. Four dive boats and dive packages are available along with full certification diving courses and shark-cage dives plus underwater photography. Activity is continual and includes everything from kite flying to windsurfing and jetskiing. Rental vehicles are available. Dress is casual. Reservations are direct. *Moderate.*

RESTAURANTS All clubs and resorts cater to guests for meals, but advance reservations are requested, especially for evening meals. Two establishments particularly encourage outside guests: *Runaway Hill* and the *Rock House Picarroon Restaurant.* Both serve light lunches and excellent, expensive, full course, candlelit, fixed-price dinners. *Picarroon* requires reservations by 3 P.M. Try also *Angela's Starfish Restaurant, Major's Everready Cook Shop, Pink Sands'* elegant dockside lounge/restaurant, or picnic fare from local groceries.

NIGHTLIFE and ENTERTAINMENT Each of the clubs and resorts offer live Goombay and Calypso musicians at least once a week, taking turns so that there's somewhere for guests to go every night. Just ask which night the local group plays at which location. *Valentine's Nautical Bar* has nightly music; *Romara* runs a weekly disco night; *Pink Sands Lounge,* harborside, is open day and night for drinks on the veranda. On weekends and special holidays or occasions, something interesting always happens, and each night there are locals and tourists congregating at *Tingum's Nightclub,* the *Vic-Hum Club, Willie's Sunset Inn Bar,* or *George's Billy the Goat Tavern.*

GETTING AROUND Though most people go by foot, rental vehicles are available. Ask at your hotel desk. There are cars, minimokes, golf carts, motor scooters, and bicycles. You'll need a valid driver's license for anything with a motor. Also at hand are taxis—notably *Godfrey and Reggie Major,* and *Percival Johnson*—which usually transport visitors and their luggage to and from the dock, alerted by CB radio.

SPECTACLES and DISPLAYS Watch for sailing events and regattas in the harbor. Check with the Ministry of Tourism/Sports Division for details and dates.

TOURS Your club or resort can ferry you to a nearby deserted cay for a few hours or an all-day tour alone or with friends, with a picnic lunch or a private fisherman-cum-chef—a great way to really get away from everything. You can take a taxi tour of this island, or a boat to Eleuthera, where a taxi or rental vehicle will allow you to tour the "mainland." Or try a boat to Spanish Wells for a half-day tour.

Eleuthera, ROCK SOUND

HOTELS

Cotton Bay Beach, Golf & Tennis Resort Box 28, Rock Sound. Phone (809)334-2101; in U.S. (800)433-5079. World-famed as an exclusive hideaway for fabulously wealthy and powerful movers and shakers, the elegant Cotton Bay Club has evolved into a resort that still beckons some of the former Club's members for casual days (jackets with ties required after 6 P.M.). Nicely decorated and air-conditioned, the 77 rooms are in standard, superior, and suite formats, and in cottages scattered over manicured grounds. Gift shop, hairdressers, and 4 hard tennis courts (resident pros & pro shop), a championship 18-hole golf course designed by Robert Trent Jones, pro golf staff, a golf shop, rental golf gear, and golf course restaurant. Fine beach for sunning, shelling, snorkeling, and swimming, or for sailing and windsurfing. Delightful lounge with windows overlooking the beach.

Trips for deep-sea fishing and bonefishing with native guides available from the resort's David Harbour Marina, where private yachts also dock and find service. The central clubhouse has a round lounge, a first-class bar, and a dining room that requires jackets and ties for dinner. Menus highlight European and American foods, with a few Bahamian specialties. Full room service; picnic boxed lunches. Twice-weekly dancing and entertainment. Direct reservations. Executive conference facilities. New program to "Own a Bit of the Bay" via build, buy, or time-share options. FAP only. *Expensive to Extravagant.*

Windermere Island Club Box 25, Rock Sound Write VSOE Hotels, 1 World Trade Center, NYC, NY 10048. Phone (212)839-0223; in U.S.(800)237-1236; in Canada (800)451-2253. This club is Private with a capital P, with 700 dues-paying members from several countries, primarily the U.S. Nonmembers who stay in the club's 21 rooms, with 20 kitchened suites or apartments with private terraces overlooking the Atlantic, or in 12 of the privately owned villas scattered over the island and available when owners are back home, pay seasonal membership fees. Volleyball, snorkeling (with gear), waterskiing, bonefishing, deep-sea fishing, windsurfing, canoes, a glass-bottom rowboat, sunfish sailboats, and bicycles for guests.

From its casuarina-bordered entrance, past elegant cottages and carefully plotted gardens, right up to its quietly tasteful main clubhouse, everything on this island announces reserved wealth and dignity. Those who stay here are not the type to marvel when British Royalty or heads of state intermingle with financial barons and other guests at the six all-weather tennis courts, in the many-sided pool, on the nearby five miles of isolated beach, or for special island drinks at the polished bar or under towering palms.

A covered terrace is set with traditional white lawn furniture for breakfast and buffet luncheon. The circular lounge offers comfortable wicker seating for cocktails, interesting views, and games such as backgammon—all a floor above the patio-flanked cocktail lounge. There also is a small private card room. French, American, and Bahamian dishes are prepared by a Bahamian chef. Winter evening dress code calls for jackets and ascots or ties for gentlemen, and accepts dress slacks for ladies, who generally prefer such attire rather than long or short gowns. Rental cars and boats are available, as are limited drugstore supplies. There is a gift shop and a pro shop and tennis racquets and balls are at hand, as well as resident tennis pros.

The club accepts visitors for lunch or dinner, but requests advance reservations. Check the bulletin board here for *Windermere Birdwatcher's Life* list. Reservations are direct, with preference to members. Packages are available. AP only. *Extravagant.*

Eleuthera, SPANISH WELLS

Spanish Wells Beach Resort and **Spanish Wells Harbour Club** Box 31, Spanish Wells. Phone 333-4371; toll free (800)262-0621. Scuba is the focus here, and there's an assortment of special package holidays ranging from three to seven nights, handled by travel agents round the world—a true first for the island. Nine specialty dives include daring Current Cut and slews of Devil's Backbone wrecks—even a Union train captured by Confederates and sold to Cuba. Folks of all ages come to try these dives in this tiny, historic township that boasts the world's highest per capita income.

The beach resort offers 21 rooms plus 7 cottages with kitchenettes for one to four guests. There is a dining room and a bar serving snacks, entertainment on weekends, and tennis. A private beach with excellent snorkeling and scuba, and available equipment plus lessons for beginners and for lifetime certification. Two dive masters; the *Dive Shop* is at the Harbour Club, where there are 20 rooms plus dining room and bar/lounge with entertainment. Boating and fishing facilities at the marina, which also supplies dockage, fuel, power, and water.

All sorts of games, plus windsurfing, waterskiing, and sunfish sailing, outboard motorboating, sightseeing and trips by boat, complete with picnic lunches. Half-day trips to Harbour Island. Kitchens of both resorts serve mostly Bahamian cookery, and dinner reservations must be made in advance for nonregistered visitors. Bikes free for guests. Children under twelve stay free with parents. Attire is causal and ties are not allowed. Newly refurbished and restructured, the resorts are very clean. *Inexpensive.*

Walton's Langousta Restaurant and Bar Right on the harbor. Open from 9 A.M. to 3 P.M. and from 6 to 10 P.M., specializing in lunches and dinners featuring the "best crayfish in the Bahamas" as well as luscious turtle, conch, and other seafoods plus beef, pork, and chicken, with all with Bahamian trimmings. You can also have a real Planters Punch, made with key limes, fruit juices, and Myers Rum. Friendly, speedy service. *Moderate.*

The Snack Bar lives up to its name by serving sandwiches, fries, colas, and such, from 9 A.M. to 1 P.M. and 5 to 10 P.M. Roddy's Place serves similar fare. Resorts offer a variety of meals, drinks, and snacks, and groceries stock picnic fixings. All Inexpensive to Moderate.

SHOPPING Head for the ancient wooden *Quilt Shop*, where local ladies gather to turn out one-of-a-kind quilts and other handmade specialties.

SAN SALVADOR

Riding Rock Inn Today, the Inn is well known particularly among scuba divers, who flock here for some of the best diving in the Bahamas. As many as 125 have arrived at once, filling to capacity the 24 two-star hotel rooms and adjacent four-star ocean-front villas, and 1- to 2-bedroom apartments. Divers of all ages come from around the world and are joined by many sport fishing fans who come especially for giant wahoo, blue and white marlin, and bonefish. Unstructured activities include boating, waterskiing, parasailing, windsurfing, surfing, hiking, beachcombing, tennis, and regular tours of the island by hotel minibus, which also takes guests to picnic sites. There are rental cars, bicycles, and motorbikes (which can constitute extreme hazards when paired with the pitted roads). For in-depth sightseeing by land, and for boats and guides to choice sites for fine fishing, just ask at the desk. The marina has six slips, ice, fuel, laundry, water, showers, power, a commissary but no repairs—advance dockage reservations urged.

Underwater sightseeing is guided by *Island Divers Ltd.* Rated as a gold five-star training facility by the Professional Association of Diving Instructors (PADI), Island Divers offers tyro and advanced scuba courses, rental gear, and daily dive series from custom-designed dive boats. There's a complete *Underwater Photo Center* here, too, linked to Skin Diving magazine editor/publisher Paul Tzmoulis, with gear for rent and courses that train you to work it like a pro, plus color film developing and a screening room for viewing your progress. Located dockside, these facilities often host special conference or study programs like the postgraduate Diving Medicine in Depth, which conforms to established Undersea Medical Society criteria and attracts physicians interested in the growing specialty of underwater medicine.

Snorkeling is also special around San Salvador, with lessons and trips available. *Riding Rock* has a freshwater pool for swimming buffs. Near it is the *Straw Market*, where two local ladies sell hats, bags, toys, fans, nested boxes, and other items created by a variety of weaving techniques. Just steps away, the main lodge offers gift items ranging from conch pearls to T-shirts, all near the relaxed dining room, where food and service are good. Reservations direct, by writing or by dialing (809)322-2631. Fly Bahamasair or Riding Rock's charter plane from Fort Lauderdale. *Moderate to Extravagant.*

Index

Abaco, 115-25, 131-41
Acklins Island, 83, 85, 93
Adderley's Plantation, Long Island, 97
Alice Town, North Bimini, 67, 69, 91-2
Andros, 73-5, 87, 90-1
Andros Reef, 101
Andros Town, Central Andros, 73
Ardasta Gardens, Nassau, 14
Artists, 28, 55, 79, 113, 121, 133, 141, 150
Atlantis, 93, 101

Bacardi Rum Distillery, Nassau, 13
Bahama Palm Shores, 116
Bahamas, climate 1, 81; food, 2-7; geography, 1, 81; history, 1, 81, 127; music, 2, 17, 27, 32, 35-37, 127, 147; site of first colony, 105
Bahamahost, 10, 11
Bain Town, New Providence Is., 13
Barraterre, The Exumas, 75
Bermuda Triangle, 93
Berry Islands, 71-3, 91
Bight of Acklins, 83
Biminis, The, 67-71
Blackbeard's Tower, 30
Black Point, The Exumas, 75
Blue Holes, 34, 56, 82, 115
Bluff, North Eleuthera, 110
Brogue Villages, N. Eleuthera, 110, 111
Boating, 21, 33, 47, 48, 49, 50, 59, 61, 77, 87, 90, 91, 92, 93, 94, 95, 96, 97, 99, 120, 131, 132, 133, 135, 137, 139, 140, 141, 142, 144, 145, 147, 148, 149, 150
Bullock Harbour, Berry Is., 71
Bush Medicine Gardens, Nassau, 14

Cable Beach, Paradise Is., 17-27
Calabash Bay, Central Andros, 73
Cape Eleuthera, 107, 113, 141
Casino's, 13, 20, 21, 27, 41, 47, 48, 53, 55
Cat Island, 67, 92, 125, 127
Chub Cay, Berry Is., 71, 73, 91
Churches, historic, 30, 31, 77, 109
Concepion Island, 81, 82, 97
Columbus, Christopher, 82, 83, 125, 127, 128
Congo Town, South Andros, 75, 73, 90
Coral World Marine Park, Silver Cay, 10
Cotton Bay, Eleuthera, 113, 115
Crooked Island, 83, 85, 93
Cupids Bay, 112-13
Current Island, 110
Current Village, 110

Deadman's Cay, Long Is., 81-2
Devil's Backbone, The, 101, 104, 149
Diving, 9, 21, 22, 23, 33, 34, 47, 48, 50, 59, 60, 87, 90, 91, 92, 93, 94, 95, 96, 97, 98-99, 101-04, 108, 109, 116, 117, 120, 131, 132, 133, 135, 139, 140, 141, 142, 144, 145, 147, 148, 149, 150

Duncan Town, Ragged Is., 86
Dundas Town, Abaco, 118, 120
Dunmore Towne, Harbour Is., 108-09

Elbow Cay, 118, 131-32
Eleuthera, 105-115, 141-50
Eleutherian Adventurers, 110, 112
Elizabeth Harbour, Great Exuma, 77
Exuma Land and Sea Park, 76, 103
Exuma Sound, 76, 81, 113
Exumas, The, 75-79, 93-96

Family Islands, The, 67-99, 103
Farmer's Cay, The Exumas, 75
Father Jerome, 81, 125
Festivals, 2, 31-32, 44, 58, 77, 90, 91, 92, 133, 140
Fishing, 34, 47, 50, 59, 60, 71, 76, 79, 85, 86, 87, 90, 91, 92, 93, 94, 95, 96, 97, 98, 108, 113, 116, 120, 123, 127, 129, 131, 132, 133, 135, 137, 139, 140, 141, 142, 144, 145, 147, 148, 149, 150
Fishing Tournaments, 91, 92, 115, 133, 140
Forts, 30
Fortune Hill, Crooked Is., 85
Fortune Island, 85
Fountain of Youth, 71, 93, 107
Fowl Cay Sea and Land Preserve, 103
Fresh Creek, Central Andros, 73

Garden of the Groves, Grand Bahama, 44, 57
Georgetown, Great Exuma, 76-77, 93-94, 95-96
Glass Window, N. Eleuthera, 111
Golf, 20, 21, 22, 33, 50, 59, 60, 115, 135, 139, 140, 141, 148
Goombay music, 2, 17, 32, 127, 147
Government House, 11, 31
Governor's Harbour, 107, 111, 112, 143
Grand Bahama Island, 39-62, 67
Grant's Town, New Providence Is., 13
Great Bahama Bank, 67, 71
Great Guana Cay, 103
Great Harbour Cay, 71
Green Castle, Eleuthera, 115
Green Turtle Cay, Abaco, 121, 122-3, 132-33
Gregory Town, Eleuthera, 111, 141
Gun Cay, 67

Harbour Island, 108-109, 143-147
Hatchet Bay, 111, 112
Hemingway, Ernest, 91, 92
Hermitage, The Little Exuma, 79
Hole-in-the-Wall, Abaco, 115
Hope Great House, Crooked Is., 85
Hope Town, Elbow Cay, 118-119, 132
Hydro Flora Gardens, Grand Bahama, 43

Inagua Park, Great Inagua, 82
Inaguas, The, 82-83

Indians, 49, 81, 127-128

Jet Skiing, 97, 147
Jumento Cays, 86
Junkanoo festivals, 2, 17, 20, 27, 30, 32, 35-37, 44, 58, 133

Kidd Cay, Grand Exuma, 79, 95
Kidd Cove, Great Exuma, 79, 94-95
Kidd Cove, Great Guana Cay, 120

Lighthouses, 85, 118, 128
Little Exuma, 79
Little Harbour, Abaco, 121
Long Island, 81-82, 97-98
Love Hill, Central Andros, 73
Loyalists, 79, 82, 86, 108, 109, 118, 122, 125, 140

Mangrove Cay, South Andros, 73, 75, 90
Man-O-War Cay, 119-20
Marine Farm, Crooked Is., 85
Marsh Harbour, Abaco, 115, 117-18, 120, 135-39
Mastic Point, North Andros, 75
Matthew Town, Great Inagua, 82
Murphy's Town, Abaco, 118, 120

Nassau, 9-15, 17-34
Nassau Botanical Garden, 14
New Providence Island, 9, 12
Nicholl's Town, North Andros, 75, 90-91
North Bimini, 67, 69
North Eleuthera, 107, 109-111

Obeah, 127, 128
Ocean Bight, 103
Ocean Cay, 67
Oleander Gardens, Central Eleuthera, 111
Outer Family Islands, The, 105-150

Paradise Island, 13, 17, 20, 21, 22, 23, 24, 25, 27, 30
Paradise Point, North Bimini, 69
Pelican Cay National Park, 103
Peterson's Cay National Park, 103
Pirates, 11, 79, 83-85, 111, 125, 126
Pirate's Point, Great Exuma, 79
Port Royal, S. Bimini, 71
Preacher's Cave, 110
Pretty Molly Bay, The Exuams, 79

Queen's Staircase, Nassau, 12, 31

Rand Memorial Nature Centre, 44
Regattas and racing, 32, 58, 75, 77, 115, 133, 140, 147
Rock Sound, Eleuthera, 107, 113, 115, 148-49
Rolle Town, The Exumas, 79

Rolleville, Great Exuma, 77
Rose Island Reefs, 103
Royal Victoria Hotel and Gardens, Nassau, 11, 14
Rum Cay, 81, 86, 97, 98-99
George's Cay, 107

Salt Works, 82, 85, 86 111
San Andros, North Andros, 73, 75
San Salvador, 127-129, 150
Sandy Point, Abaco, 123, 125
Savannah Sound, 113
Seafloor Aquarium, 14
Shark Hole, 111, 112
Shark Lady of Exuma, 79
Shark Reef, 101
Shelling, 9, 44, 73, 75, 76, 82, 91, 98, 99, 109, 116, 119, 120, 123, 127, 129, 135, 140, 141, 148, 150
Ship wrecks, 103-04, 129, 149
Shopping, 28, 55-57, 150
Snorkeling. See Diving
South Bimini, 67, 71
South Palmetto Point, 111
Spelunking, 81, 111-112, 121, 125, 129, 141
Spanish Wells, St. George's Cay, 107, 149-50
Staniel Cay, The Exumas, 75, 96, 103
Stella Maris, Long Is., 81-82, 97-98
Stocking Island, 103
Surfing, 111, 141, 145, 150
Sweetings Pond, 111, 112

Tarpum Bay, 113
Tennis, 20, 21, 22, 23, 24, 33, 47, 48, 49, 50, 59, 92, 94, 97, 99, 109, 133, 135, 139, 140, 141, 142, 144, 145, 148, 149
Three Sisters, 69
Tounge of the Ocean, 76, 101
Treasure Cay, Abaco, 117, 120, 121-122, 140

Underwater Explorers Society (UNEXSO), 41-42, 57, 60, 103, 117, 140
Underwater Parks, 10, 67, 103, 117, 139
Underwater Photography, 95, 98, 102, 120, 139, 142, 147, 150
Union Park, Great Inagua, 82

Victoria Harbour, Nassau, 76

Walker's Cay, Abaco, 115, 140-41
Water Skiing, 9, 61, 94, 95, 97, 132, 133, 135, 140, 141, 142, 148, 149, 150
Williams Town, Great Exuma, 77, 79
Wind surfing, 21, 34, 47, 48, 59, 61, 94, 97, 99, 132, 133, 140, 141, 145, 147, 148, 149, 150
Windermere Island, 113
Winding Bay, 113
Windsor Lake, Great Inagua, 82
Wrecking, 85, 103

NASSAU and the BAHAMAS

By Dianne Lawes

TRAVEL PLANNER

INCLUDES —
- **TRAVELERS ADVISORY SECTION**
    - General Trip Planning Information
    - Specific Info On Nassau and the Bahamas

- **ABSTRACT OF AUTHOR'S CHOICES**
    - Where To Stay
    - Recommended Restaurants
    - Things To Do

- **COMPLETE SET OF MAPS**

World of Travel
PUBLISHING

1989

About the Author

Dianne Nicholson Lawes is a freelance writer who has been visiting and writing about the Bahamas for many years.

Publisher: Frank A. Marshall
Senior Editor: E. R. Grusky
Cover Design & Illustration: Eric Walker
Map Illustration: Salie Clemente

All prices are based on those available at time of writing. It is inevitable that changes will have taken place by the time that this book is published. Please double check so as to be sure of latest figures. We will be delighted to hear from you, whether it be a recommendation or complaint, at World of Travel Publishing, 106 South Front Street, Suite 2E, Philadelphia, PA 19106.

© 1989 by Fisher's World Inc.   ISBN 1-55707-039-3

All rights reserved. No part of this book may be reproduced or utilized in any form or by any means, electronic or mechanical, including photocopying, recording or by any information storage and retrieval system, without permission in writing from the publisher. All inquiries should be addressed to World of Travel, 106 S. Front Street, Suite 2E, Philadelphia, PA 19106. World of Travel is a division of Fisher's World Inc., Nutmeg Farm, Route 17, Laporte, PA 18626.

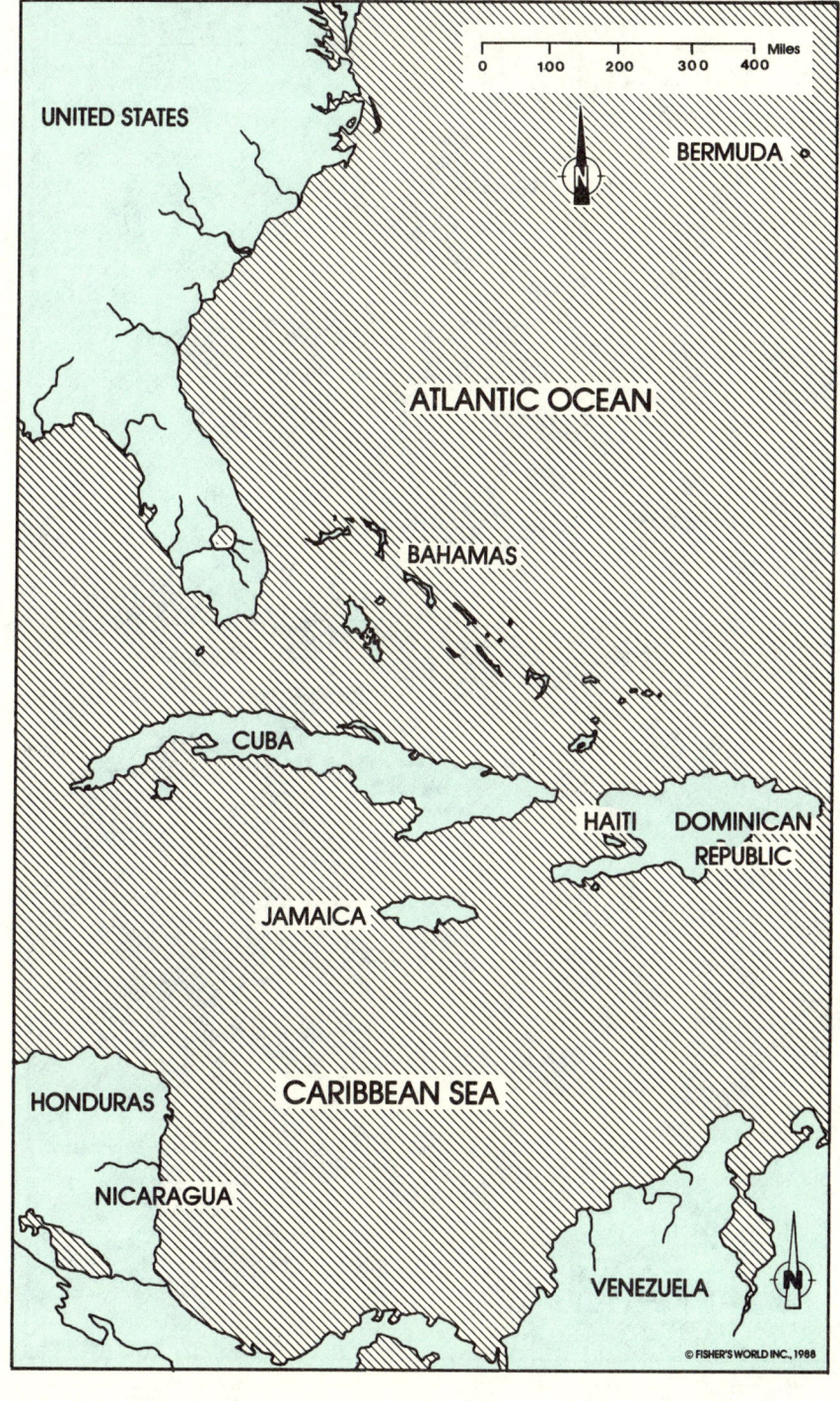

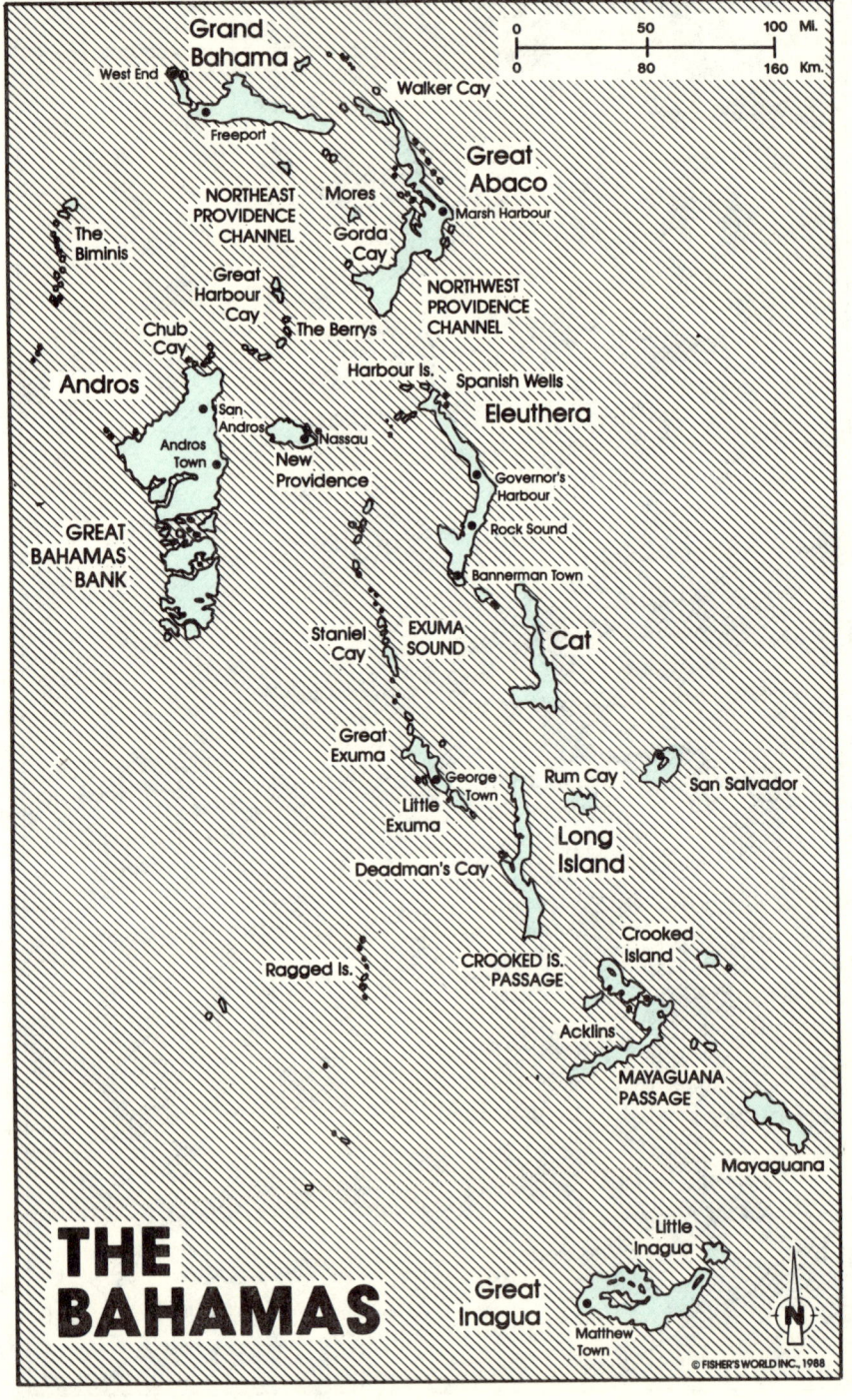

Table of Contents

Travelers' Advisory/Planning Ahead
- Travel Agents and Tour Operators 1
- Travel Bargains Too Good To Be True 1
- Travel Insurance 2
- Emergency Telephone Numbers 3
- Legal Problems 3
- General Airport Tips 3
- Complaints Against Airlines 4
- Handling Money 4
- Security Abroad 5
- Medical Problems 5
- General Health Hints 5
- Senior Citizens 6
- Traveling With Children 6
- American Embassies and Consular Services 6
- Detailed Customs Information 7
- Travel Glossary 9

Travelers' Advisory/Bahamas/Planning Ahead
- Costs 13
- Climate 13
- Sporting Events 15
- Bahamian Holidays 17
- Sources of Information 17
- Package Vacations 21
- Packing 22
- Passports 23
- Visas 23
- Health Certificates 23
- Embarkation Card 23
- Handicapped Traveler 24
- **Getting There** 24
  - By Air 24
  - By Sea 26
- **Formalities on Arrival** 28
  - Customs 28
  - Money 29
  - Getting into Town 29
- **Settling Down** 32
  - Choosing a Hotel 32
  - Restaurants 33

Tipping	34
Clubs	34
People-to-People	35
Bahamahost	35
Business Hours	35
Electricity	35
Water and Drink	36
Communications	36
Medical Assistance	37
Pounds and Kilos	37
Special Cautions	**39**
Drugs/Weapons	39
Sun	39
Insects	39
Poisons	39
Beaches	39
Camera Care	39
Scuba-Diving Precautions	41
Crime	41
Getting Around the Bahamas	**41**
By Air	41
By Sea	42
Ports of Entry	43
By Car	43
By Taxi	44
By Bus	44
Going Home	**45**
Author's Choice	**47**
New Providence/Nassau/New Providence Island and Paradise Island	**47**
Hotels	47
Restaurants	50
Entertainment	51
Shopping	53
Museums, etc	55
Sports	57
Directory	59
Grand Bahama	**61**
Hotels	61
Restaurants	63
Entertainment	63
Shopping	65
Museums, etc.	67

- Sports 69
- Directory 71
- **The Family Islands** 73
  - **Andros** 73
    - Central Andros 73
    - Congo Town, south 73
    - Mangrove Cay 73
    - North Andros 73
  - **Berry Islands** 73
  - **The Biminis** 75
  - **Cat Island** 75
  - **Crooked and Acklins Islands** 75
  - **Exumas** 77
    - Great Exuma 77
    - Staniel Cay 77
  - **Inagua** 77
  - **Long Island** 79
  - **Rum Cay** 79
- **The Outer Family Islands** 79
  - **Abaco** 79
    - Elbow Cay, including Hope Town 79
    - Green Turtle Cay 79
    - Great Guana Cay 81
    - Marsh Harbour 81
    - Treasure Cay 83
    - Walker's Cay 83
  - **Eleuthera** 83
    - Cape Eleuthera 83
    - Gregory Town 83
    - Governor's Harbour 83
    - Harbour Island 85
    - Rock Sound 85
    - Spanish Wells 85
  - **San Salvador** 87

List of Maps

The Abacos 82	Bahamas Islands iv
Acklins/Crooked Islands .. 74	Berry Islands 68
Air Transport 38	The Biminis 70
Andros 66	Cat Island 72
Bahamas Golf Courses ... 12	Downtown Freeport 62
Bahamas/Hotels and Restaurants with Key 30-31	Eleuthera, Harbour Island .84
	The Exumas 76

Ferry System 40
Freeport 60
Golf Courses I 14
Golf Courses II 16
Golf Courses III 18
Golf Courses IV 20
Grand Bahama 58
Inagua 78
International Bazaar 64
Location Map iii
Long Island 80
Lucaya 56
Nassau 52
New Providence Island 46
New Providence/Hotels with
Key 48-49
Paradise Island 54
San Salvador 86

TRAVELERS' ADVISORY-PLANNING AHEAD

TRAVEL AGENTS AND TOUR OPERATORS

You'll save a lot of time if you use an agent or tour operator, even if you plan an independent trip. If you don't know of a reliable agent, get in touch with the American Society of Travel Agents (ASTA), PO Box 23992, Washington, D.C. 20026-3992 or phone (703)739-2782, and ask for the name of an agent near you. ASTA has a Consumer Protection Plan in case a tour operator goes bust on you, among other things.

As for the tour operator, the company should be a member of the United States Tour Operators Association (USTOA). The latter's Financial Security Plan for Consumer Protection insures your payments against loss in case of some financial trouble by the firm. Information at USTOA, 211 E. 51st St., New York City, NY 10022; phone (212)944-5727.

You may wish to enquire whether your travel agent is a Certified Travel Counselor (CTC). There are about 8,000 persons (some owners of agencies) who have earned this title following their names after five years experience and mastering a two-year, graduate-level program, including four 4-hour exams. For more information phone (617)237-0280.

TRAVEL BARGAINS TOO GOOD TO BE TRUE

There are some warning signs an alert consumer will look for when checking out travel bargains advertised by companies whose names are unfamiliar at first. The American Society of Travel Agents says to watch out for:
1. Does the price seem unreasonably low compared to similar offers?
2. Do they ask for your credit card number over the phone or say they will send a messenger to collect your check when the information you seek is being delivered?
3. Will the firm give you its name, address, phone number, and name of their bank?
4. Do they press you to make an immediate decision?
5. Does the firm have a prepared brochure? Will they send you definite information, including total cost, in writing, before you have to commit any money?
6. Do they tell you which airline you'll be flying and which hotel you'll be staying at? ("Major" isn't a good enough description.)
7. Do they quote one price, then ask you to provide additional deposit or join a club?

Most scams involve oral misrepresentation, high pressure tactics, and offers in the $50 to $400 range, determined to be the "affordable" range almost anyone can pay.

TRAVEL INSURANCE

Check your own policies to see if you are covered for medical expenses while traveling, for loss of luggage or other personal belongings, for liability in case of an accident while you're driving a car, rented or otherwise, and see what they provide.

Some coverage, such as trip cancellation, is bound not to be in any insurance policy you have for save normal routine.

Some outstanding firms and the coverage they provide:

Access America, 600 Third Ave., New York, NY 10163; phone toll free (800)851-2800. A subsidiary of Blue Cross and Blue Shield of the National Capital Area (Washington, D.C.) and Empire Blue Cross and Blue Shield (New York). Has two programs, one for North American travel (USA, Canada, Caribbean, Mexico), and another for travel overseas (Europe, Asia, Africa, South America, Australia).

Coverages: trip cancellation or interruption (including terrorist actions), travel delay, medical expenses, baggage insurance, baggage delay, travel accident insurance, collision damage insurance. The firm will even fly medical cases back to the United States if necessary.

If leaving in less than three weeks, enroll by telephone with Master-Card, VISA, American Express, Diners club, or Carte Blanche credit cards.

If leaving later than three weeks, enroll by telephone or mail in completed application with check, credit card, or money order.

There are several types of coverage, ranging from 1-4 days in North America to 24-30 days overseas.

Acess America also provides a Message Center service and flight information and publishes a newsletter for subscribers.

Acess America operates a hotline: call collect (202)822-3948 in Washington, D.C. for overseas emergencies. Inside U.S., Canada, Puerto Rico and USVI call collect (800)654-1908. (Telex 706305 ACCESS WSH in Washington, D.C.)

Travel Guard International, 1100 Center Point Drive, Stevens Point, WI 54481-2849; phone (800)782-5151 (Wisconsin (800)634-0644).

Offers three plans including the following coverages: Airline or tour penalty waiver, trip cancellation (before departure), trip interruption (during trip), default/bankruptcy of tour operator, cruise line or airline, supplemental collision damage waiver, medical expenses, baggage and travel document insurance, emergency assistance, accidental death, travel delay, hotel overbooking, baggage delay.

Underwritten by CIGNA Insurance Company, with offices worldwide.

International SOS Assistance, Inc., POBox 11568, Philadelphia, PA 19116; phone toll free (800)523-8930 (PA or outside USA (215)244-1500).

Services include 22 service centers worldwide, referral to English-speaking doctors, legal referrals, emergency hospital deposits, medical evacuations, medical repatriation, patient monitoring.

Health Care Abroad, 1511 K St. N.W., Washington, D.C., 20037; phone (202)393-5500. Health insurance and medical assistance directory.

World Access, 2115 Connecticut Ave. N.W., Washington, D.C. 20036; phone (202)822-3978. Long-term health coverage overseas.

EMERGENCY TELEPHONE NUMBERS

U.S. Government: State Department Overseas Citizen's Emergency Center, Washington, D.C. 20520, phone (202)632-5225 or 634-3600. Staffed 24-hours for illness or accident abroad.

Bureau of Consular Affairs publications: *Tips for Travelers for (Blank) Country*, a general *Travel Tips for Senior Citizens*, or *Your Trip Abroad*. Write: Bureau of Consular Affairs, Public Affairs Office, State Department, Washington, D.C. 20520. For non-emergency calls, telephone during normal business hours.

LEGAL PROBLEMS

Department of State (see Emergency Telephone Numbers above).

International Legal Defense Counsel, 111 South 15th Street, Philadelphia, PA 19102; phone (215)977-9982, a law firm specializing in problems of Americans abroad.

Weapons and Drugs: Do not bring a weapon to an airport passenger screening point. Do not try to board a plane with a weapon. Do not try to ship a weapon in checked baggage without notifying the airline, making sure it is unloaded, and locking the bag. If you don't do these things and it is discovered through X-raying, you could be fined $1,000 in civil court and miss your flight, plus, if arrested and convicted, fined and sent to prison.

If you get caught on a drug charge while abroad, the U.S. Consular Officer cannot do any of the following: get you out of jail or even demand that you be released; represent you at a trial or give you legal counsel; pay legal fees and/or fines with U.S. government funds. The consular officer can visit you, give you a list of attorneys, notify your friends and family, and relay requests for money or assistance, and intercede with the authorities to make certain your rights under local laws are being observed and that you are treated humanely according to international standards.

GENERAL AIRPORT TIPS

- ☐ Check in early at airport
- ☐ Don't check bags at the curb (harder to trace if lost).

COMPLAINTS AGAINST AIRLINES

Department of Transportation of the U.S. Government likes phone calls rather than letters. Phone (202)366-2220. But you can write them for a copy of *Fly Rights: A Guide to Air Travel in the U.S.*, at Consumer Affairs Division, Room 10405, Intergovernmental and Consumer Affairs, Dept. of Transportation, 400 Seventh St. S.W., Washington, D.C. 20590.

The Aviation Consumer Project, P.O. Box 19029, Washington, D.C. 20036, has a book called *Facts and Advice for Airline Passengers* for $2, which you can carry with you as your travel.

HANDLING MONEY

Many travelers prefer to keep cash to a minimum, using credit cards whenever possible. Not only does one minimize the risk of losing cash in a robbery, but there are many advantages to credit card holders while traveling.

American Express offers (without charge, but you must enroll in the program), its Global Assist program, primarily a referral service, which will transmit messages for you, provide interpreter referrals, bail you out of jail, send items you have left behind, advance up to $5,000 in medical expenses, advise you on visa and innoculation requirements, refer you to doctors or lawyers in case of legal or medical emergencies. *Domestic hotline*: (800)554-AMEX. *From overseas*, call collect: (202)783-7474.

MasterCard (Gold Cards only; some banks issuing cards may not participate). Master Assist program provides medical and legal referral hotline, medical expenses, medical evacuation, and flying a relative or friend to your bedside. Join through your local bank or phone (800)247-4623 to find a local bank that participates in the program.

Rate of Exchange: Credit cards often get you a better rate than cash or travelers checks.

Cash Advances: You can get one of these in the middle of your trip if you run out of money.

Cancellation: If you do not get the goods or services you paid for with your credit card, the chance of getting your money back is greater than if you paid by cash or travelers check.

For more information on this matter, write for the pamphlet *Traveling with Your Credit Card*, BankCard Holders of America, 333 Pennsylvania Ave. S.E., Washington, D.C., 20003-1148. Send fifty cents for handling.

Cash Card: Do not leave home without it. *Citrus Cash Card Network* has 17,000 Automatic Teller machines around North America. *Plus* has about 14,000, as well as a few in Japan. *MasterCard* can be used in any of 8,000 Master Teller machines here and abroad and *VISA* in about 18,000. The wholesale exchange rate, (the most favorable one), is used in dispensing local cash from these machines. No commission, and many of the machines have both the local language and English translations. The *American Express* card can be used in about 20,000 machines in twenty countries for cash advances (You must enroll in the American Express Cash program to obtain a pin number to activate the machines). *Diners Club* says you can get cash advances from their offices and affiliates in 1,700 locations in over seventy countries.

Travelers' Checks: Although they are easy to replace (easier for American Express than for some others), they are still a form of cash, and you do often have to pay a service charge when you buy them or cash them. You can avoid the current exchange rate commission if you buy in the local currency where you are going, but then the rate may turn more favorable after you buy them at home.

SECURITY ABROAD

The same precautions one would take in a large American city apply abroad, with the single difference that in a foreign country you stand out as a target. Your clothes, even haircuts, often mark you as an outsider.

A helpful booklet on the subject is published by American Express, Box 2004, Throgs Neck Station, New York, NY 10465. Ask for *Have a Safe Trip.*

Before leaving, make two lists of your travelers' check numbers, leaving one at home, taking the other with you. Do not leave anything valuable in your hotel room. Professional thieves know all the tricks.

MEDICAL PROBLEMS

IAMAT (International Association for Medical Assistance to Travelers) is a nonprofit, charitable organization which provides, free of charge, a directory of English-speaking doctors around the world. The physicians have all been trained in the United States, Canada, or Great Britain. Because IAMAT relies on donations, it is suggested that you make one if you use them.

Write IAMAT at 736 Center Street, Lewiston, NY 14092; in Canada at 188 Nicklin Road, Guelph, Ontario, N1H 7L5; in New Zealand at Box5049, Christchurch 5; in Switzerland at Gotthardstrasse 17, CH 6300 Zug.

A Guide to Safe Drinking Water, published by the National Safety Council, can be had for $6.50 by writing them at Box 11933, Chicago, IL 60611.

GENERAL HEALTH HINTS

Have a dental check-up before your vacation or business trip.

Take extra pair of eyeglasses or dental bridge/plates with you.

Take copy of important prescriptions with generic names of medicine.

Carry a good supply of needed medications.

If you have serious allergy, this should be on an ID bracelet or necklace.

Make sure you have right vaccinations if going to non-industrial nations.

Review your medical insurance coverage or get some.

If you are really concerned, carry a summary of your medical history with you, and possibly a copy of your latest EKG.

SENIOR CITIZENS

There are hundreds of programs for senior citizens, and even the term has been defined many different ways. You can join the AARP (American Association of Retired Persons) from the age of 50, and even if you aren't retired. For only $5 a year, you get a whole raft of benefits, many of which will assist you in traveling. Call (202)872-4700 or write AARP at 1909 K St. N.W., Washington, D.C. 20049.

National Association for Mature People, Box 26792, Oklahoma City, OK 73118, tel. (405)523-5060.

National Council of Senior Citizens, 1151 K St. N.W., Washington, D.C., tel. (202)347-8800.

TRAVELING WITH CHILDREN

Most travel industry people refer to children under 2 as infants, between 3 and 12 as children, and over 12 as adults, at least so far as fares are concerned. Special facilities for children are available on airplanes (but notify them in advance). There are even special menus, often with several choices, for infants and kids.

AMERICAN EMBASSIES AND CONSULAR SERVICES

1. Register with the nearest U.S. embassy or consulate if you plan to stay in one country for "some time." This will help in replacing a lost or stolen passport or to help evacuate you in an emergency.
2. Don't expect an embassy or consulate to help you as a traveler unless you are in serious legal, medical, or financial difficulties. "Please do not," they say, "expect them to find work, get residence or driving permits, act as travel agents or interpreters, search for missing luggage, or settle disputes with hotel managers."

A free list of embassy addresses, etc. can be obtained by asking the Superintendent of Documents, U.S. Government Printing Office, Washington, D.C. 20402, for a copy of *Key Officers of Foreign Service Posts*.

Before leaving home: You may wish to contact the Office of Citizens Consular Services in Washington if you have questions about the following: Acquisition and loss of citizenship, passport and registration services abroad, claims, child custody disputes, estates, judicial services abroad, federal agencies benefit program abroad, report of birth abroad, third country representation.

Office of Citizens Consular Services itself: (202)632-3666.

If you want a Travel Advisory on a certain country, phone the State Department's Bureau of Consular Affairs, Program Planning and Coordination Staff, at (202)632-3816 or 3732.

DETAILED CUSTOMS IINFORMATION

In addition to basic information on the $400 exemption described later, some niceties about the system include:

Additional duty. After you get $400 worth of goods free, and pay a flat 10 percent on the next $1,000 worth, you go to the Tariff Schedules of the United States, available at any Customs office or better libraries. There are individual rates on specific items. The Customs officials say the average tourist purchase is dutiable at about 12 percent.

Duty rates for liquor above your exempt limit are generally 10 percent of their value. The Internal Revenue tax is $10.50 per gallon on distilled spirits, from 17 cents to $10.50 on wine, and 29 cents per gallon on beer. The Customs agents enforce the law of the state where you arrive concerning importation of liquor, and some states don't allow any, even if you pay additional tax or duty. (New York allows anything in, providing you pay.)

Personal belongings. If you're worried about foreign-made possessions you intend to take abroad, such as a camera, you may register them (if they have serial numbers) with a Customs office before leaving the U.S.

If you mail home your belongings and they're American made, mark the package "American Goods Returned."

Vehicles. If you take your car into Mexico or even overseas, you must present proof of U.S. origin when you return, such as vehicle (state) registration, or aircraft FAA Certificate, or boat's yacht license or motorboat ID. You could also register with Customs before departure if you like, but that is not mandatory.

GSP (Generalized System of Preferences). Goods from certain developing countries are given preference and may enter the U.S. duty-free or at a lower rate of duty than is presently accorded other nations. There is a leaflet available from the Customs people (see addresses below) called GSP and the Traveler, outlining all of these countries and articles so exempted.

Paying the Duty. You can pay in U.S. currency, but not foreign, by personal check (U.S. bank), by money order, travelers checks or government check, provided the amount does not exceed the duty by more than $50.

Duty Free Shops. When you buy at one of these abroad, the phrase means the seller hasn't paid duty to his country on the item, so the price is lower to you. You still have to pay duty to your country on returning home.

Gifts mailed from abroad. You can't send a gift to yourself, so it must be addressed to another person. Liquor, tobacco, and perfume containing alcohol that are worth over $5 retail, can't be counted in the $50 gift exemption. You can't send more than one of these $50 gift packages per day to the same person. Mark the package "Unsolicited Gift" and indicate contents and retail value.

Antiques. To be considered an antique an object must over 100 years of age. To import oject(s) duty free requires documentation of age.

Prohibited Articles:
1. Narcotics and dangerous drugs.
2. Toxic substances.
3. Liquor-filled candy and absinthe.
4. Obscene articles and publications.
5. Seditious and treasonable material.
6. Lottery tickets.
7. Products made by forced labor.
8. Endangered species or their byproducts (tortoise shell, leopard skins, etc.).
9. Monkeys and other primates.
10. Most agricultural products (because of disease or pests).

Restricted:
1. Agricultural items. Contact APHIS, Department of Agriculture, 6505 Belcrest Rd., Hyattsville, MD 20792, tel. (301)436-8411, for leaflets and advice.
2. Money. More than $5,000 in U.S. or foreign currency or coins, travelers' checks, money orders, or negotiable instruments or investment securities in bearer form must be reported to Customs on departure and on arrival. It is not illegal to take amounts in excess of $5,000 out of the country into it, but it must be reported at all ports of entry. Automobiles. Must pass safety and air pollution control standards. Contact Environmental Protection Agency, Washington, D.C. 20406, phone (202)472-9413. or Department of Transportation, Washington, D.C. 20590, phone (202)426-1693. Or ask Customs for leaflet, *Importing a Car.*
4. Cultural treasures, art, or artifacts, especially pre-Columbian. Check with Customs and the country of export for special requirements.
5. Firearms and ammunition. Contact Bureau of Alcohol, Tobacco and Firearms, Department of the Treasury, Washington, D.C. 20226, phone (202)566-7135.
6. Medicines containing narcotics. If you use them, have a prescription or written statement from your personal physician that the medicine is being used under a doctor's direction and is necessary for your physical well being while traveling, and carry the drugs in their original containers.
7. Wildlife and fish are subject to certain restrictions. Contact the U.S. Fish and Wildlife Service, Department of the Interior, Washington, D.C. 20240, phone (202)343-9242, or state authorities. Check with Customs for designated ports of entry, and ask for their leaflet on *Pets, Wildlife and Customs.*

8. Merchandise originating in North Korea, Vietnam, Cambodia and Cuba. Contact Office of Foreign Assets Control, Department of the Treasury, Washington, D.C. 20220, phone (202)376-0443, and ask for FAC Regulations and Cuban Assets Control Regulations.
9. Research materials, like disease organisms, etc. Contact Foreign Quarantine Program, U.S. Public Health Service, Center for Disease Control, Atlanta, GA 30333, phone (404)329-3496.
10. Foreign-made articles. Some may be restricted by trademark owner, especially in the field of perfumes and watches. Ask for the Customs leaflet, *Trademark Information for Travelers*.

Military and other Government personnel may have special exemptions if they are traveling under permanent change of station orders, and should check with their personnel office for details.

Custom Addresses

For Customs leaflets, write U.S. Customs, P.O. Box 7407, Washington, D.C. 20044, or call (202)566-8195.

If you have any questions about your Customs clearance, write the Assistant Commissioner, Office of Inspection and Control, U.S. Customs Service, Washington, D.C. 20229.

Customs regulations and procedures are outlined in a free publication, *Know Before You Go*, available from P.O. Box 7118, Washington, D.C. 20044.

Travelers' Tips on Bringing Food, Plant, and Animal Products Into the United States is the name of a free booklet (in English, Spanish, Italian or Japanese) available from the Animal and Plant Health Inspection Service, U.S. Department of Agriculture, 732 Federal Bldg., 6505 Belcrest Rd., Hyattsville, MD 20782.

A TRAVEL GLOSSARY

Most travelers know what terms like charter, bumping or transfer mean, but there are a few terms that remain somewhat obscure. Here they are, with English translation:

Add-On. A supplement, perhaps to a tour package.
Adjoining rooms does not necessarily mean connecting.
Aft. The rear of the ship, or in that direction.
AP. American Plan, hotel rate which includes three meals a day, almost always breakfast, lunch and dinner. Also called pension plan.
APEX. Advance Purchase Excursion Fare on an airline.
Bareboat charter. Chartering a boat without crew or provisions.
B and B. Bed and Breakfast. Sleeping room in private home or guesthouse, which includes full breakfast. Some hotels call this BP, the Bermuda Plan.
Bow. The front of the ship.
BP. See B and B.

Bulk fare. A bunch of seats acquired by a tour operator, for example, who must then seek to fill them.

Continental Breakfast usually means coffee, roll, butter, and sometimes, juice.

Courier. European term for tour escort.

CP. Continental Plan, hotel rate which includes continental breakfast.

Double can also mean twin-bedded room, as often it means only that room can accommodate two people. Specify double bed if you want one.

Demi-Pension. See MAP.

Direct flight does not always mean nonstop, nor does it always mean on the same aircraft. It only means the same flight number.

Efficiency. Term describing hotel, motel or condominium room with housekeeping facilities, such as stove, refrigerator, sink.

EP. European Plan, hotel rate which excludes meals.

FIT. Foreign Independent Travel. Custom-designed tour for an individual and/or his party.

Forward. At or near the front of the ship.

Interchange flight. A through flight which requires passengers to changes planes on route. Sometimes the old rail term, "change of gauge," is used.

ITX means Independent Tour Excursion Airfare. A fare which includes prepaid land package at destination, but passengers may travel separately.

Joint fare. A special through fare for travel on two or more airlines.

Lanai. A room with a patio or balcony which is close to or overlooks water or a garden.

Lido. A swimming pool and the area surrounding it, unless you're speaking of Venice, where an entire island is called the Lido.

MAP. Modified American Plan. Hotel rate includes two meals, usually breakfast and dinner. Also called demi-pension.

Open Jaw. Essentially a roundtrip, but passenger departs for return trip from a point other than the original destination, or returns to a different point from the point of origin.

Parlor Car most often is on a train, but could be a bus, with individual seats that swivel, and food and bar service.

Pitch. In the plane, the distance between rows of seats, front to back. On a boat, the rise and fall of the ship's bow at sea.

Pension. See AP.

Pool route. Most common in Europe, where airlines flying same routes share equally their total revenues, borrow planes and crews from each other and share check-in counters.

Rack rate. Usually in hotels, the offical posted rate for each room. Can often be discounted, if you but ask, "What is the rack rate?"

Share Fare/Rate. Cost to single person willing to share accommodations with person of same sex, if one can be found by tour operator.

Shoulder. The season between the high (or peak) and low (or off-peak) seasons.

Starboard. Right side of the ship as you face front (bow).

Stern. Very rear of ship.

Tender. When boat can't dock, a tender takes passengers from ship to shore.

Tour Escort/Leader. Often used interchangeably, but a leader is really the expert lecturer or specialist whose reputation attracts tour participants, and an escort is the person who accompanies the tour throughout, making everything run smoothly. The escort is sometimes called Tour Manager.

Value Season. Any season other than peak. Prices are lower.

(Most of the definitions above thanks to the Institute of Certified Travel Agents, Box 56, Wellesley, MA 02181, tel. (617)237-0280. The institute awards the CTC (Certified Travel Counselor) diploma to agents with five years' minimum experience who have completed a two-year travel management course.)

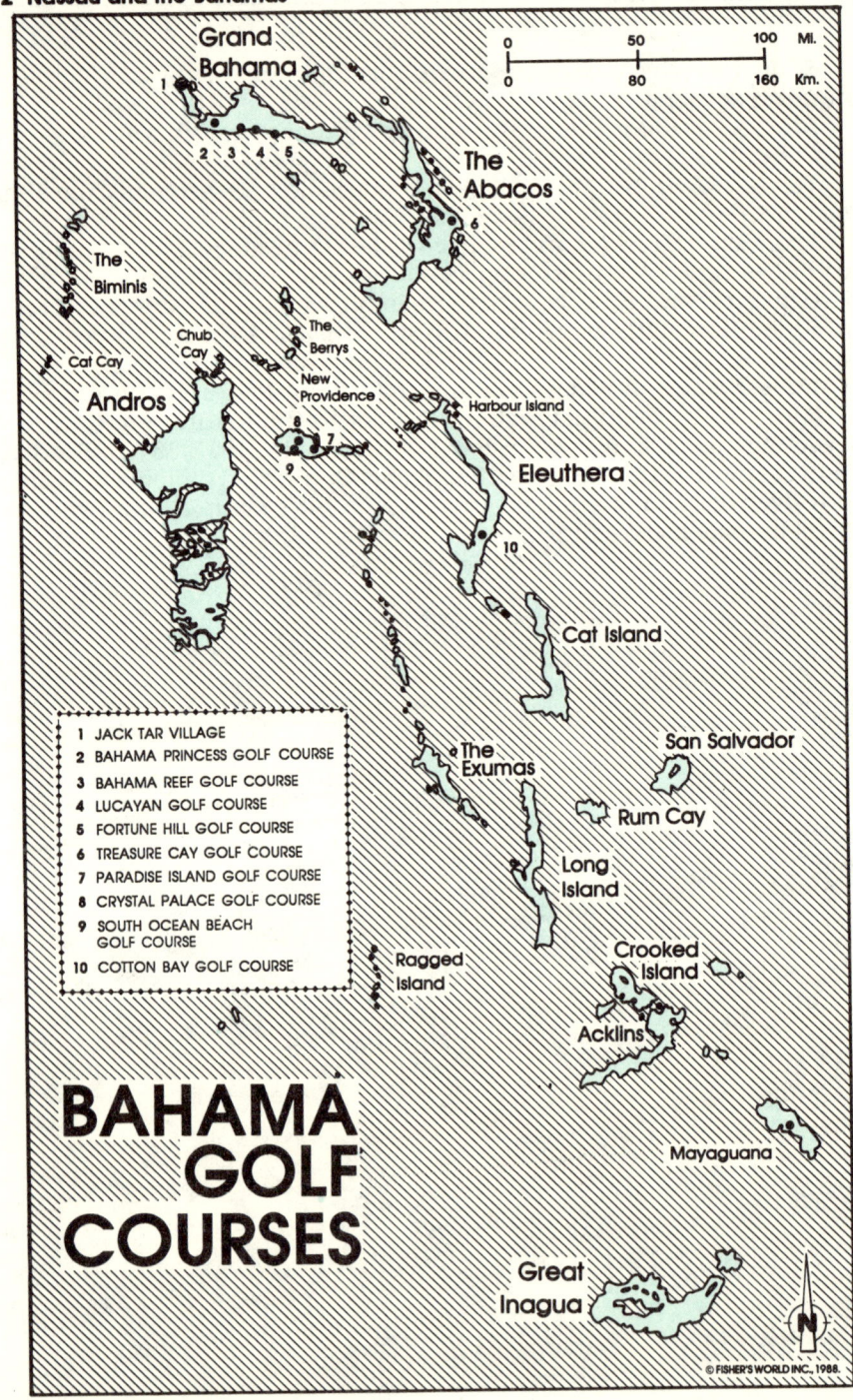

TRAVELER'S ADVISORY- BAHAMAS

PLANNING AHEAD

Costs

The sun and sea may well be free, but everything else in the Bahamas has a fee ranging from moderate to expensive, varying from island to island in specifics.

For a government that collects no income taxes, import duties are a major source of funds. Nearly everything involved in catering to tourism is partially or totally imported, from building supplies and foodstuffs to printed materials and special equipment or vehicles. The heavy levies on "luxuries" often apply to minimal tourist facilities (such as golf carts), which pushes up tourists' costs (that cart rents for $15-$25 per day). Similar duties raise cigarettes to $2.20 and up per pack, a $4 paperback to $8, some beers or cocktails to $2-$6 each and so forth. Most meats and some seafoods are imported, translating to grocery store prices as high as $5 for a 4 ounce bottle of Coppertone, $2 per pound of hamburger, and 99 cents for a tiny tin of "inexpensive" meat spread. Be ready to pay $15 and up for a shampoo, set or cut, from $20 to $40 to visit a medical doctor or dentist, and the proverbial arm and a leg for taxi rides. The fares seem absurdly high until one realizes they must cover not only the cab owner's labor and fuel costs, but also repairs and insurance, which become exorbitant in regions where roads are so bad that only collision insurance is available.

Despite all this, there is another side to the cost coin. All things "native" are decidedly less expensive, including accommodations, foodstuffs and restaurants, entertainment places, and transportation. Shopping sprees can help tourists recoup vacation expenses, with tax-free international bazaars offering 15 to 40 percent off North American and European listed prices for all sorts of goods.

Climate

The year-round mild, balmy weather that attracts tourists today prompted early Western visitors to dub the Bahamas the "Isles of June." Several geographical factors combine to regulate mean temperatures into a 70-83 F range throughout this summer/winter, two-season climate. Severed by the Tropic of Cancer, cooled by trade winds, and warmed by the Gulf Stream, these islands generally are low and flat and constantly buffeted by seas varying from 70 to 80F. Though the mercury can drop into the 40s with the sudden sweep of a winter

GOLF COURSES I

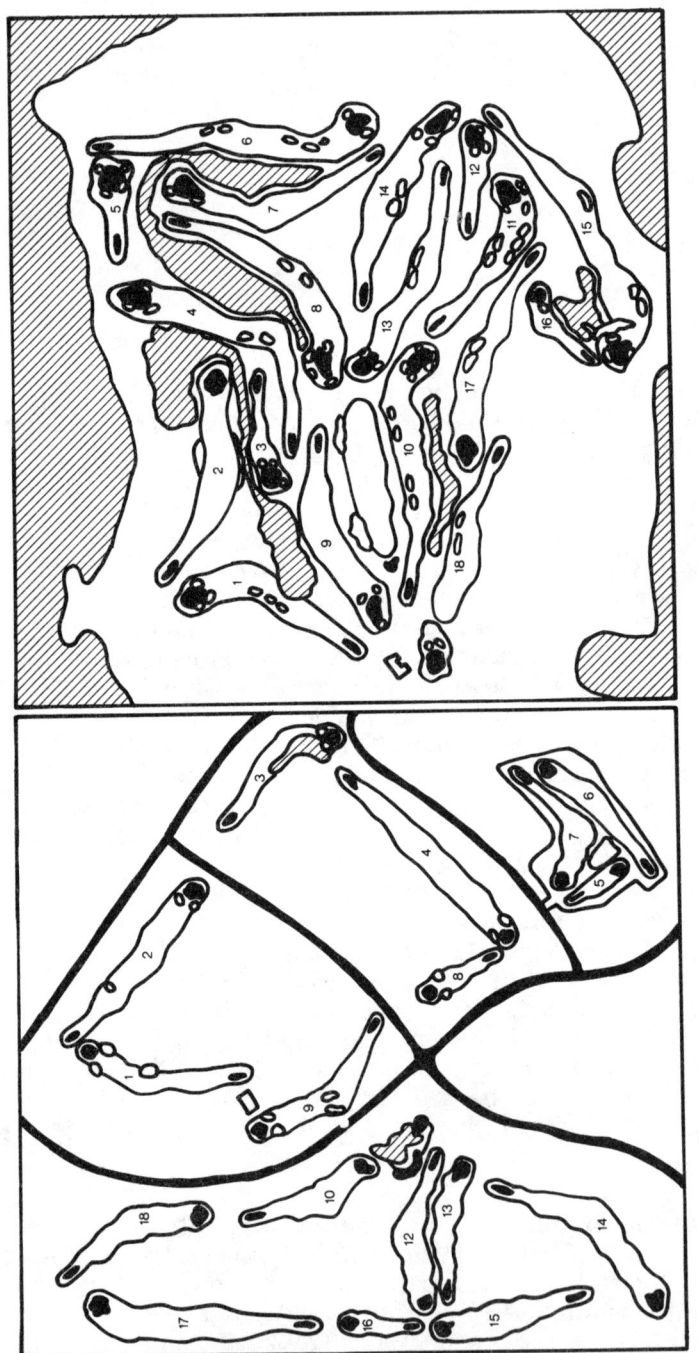

PARADISE ISLAND GOLF CLUB

FORTUNE HILL GOLF & COUNTRY CLUB

cold front that darkens skies and blusters sometimes for a few days, the sun shines at least seven hours daily, even in the rainiest months. Fast-passing showers may spew thunder and lightning, but hurricanes are infrequent (August-November) and their damage is rare enough to warrant local tales for years afterward.

Since weather so strongly affects daily Bahamian life, tourists are assured ample warning whenever carefully calculated charts hint at deviations from the delightful norms. Many Bahamians look to southern Florida for advance predictions, saying the Bahamas average some 10 degrees warmer. Daily newspapers, radio and television provide details; you can dial 915 for Nassau weather. Averages for the entire country are as follows.

Temperature Chart

	Mean Temp.	Mean Humidity	Mean Sunshine	Mean Rainfall
Jan.	69.6	79	7.1	1.72
Feb.	70.0	78	7.8	1.62
March	72.0	78	8.3	1.20
April	74.5	77	8.8	2.16
May	77.0	77	8.4	4.63
June	80.1	79	7.3	8.79
July	81.5	78	8.9	6.36
Aug.	81.9	79	8.6	7.38
Sept.	80.7	82	7.0	6.94
Oct.	78.0	81	6.6	8.07
Nov.	74.2	79	7.4	2.70
Dec.	70.9	78	7.1	1.61

Sporting Events

The Bahamian year is cluttered with special events to woo visitors. Many are sporting competitions to watch or win—such as tournaments with local and international status, geared to golf, tennis, big-game fishing, yachting, powerboat racing, and aviation. The weather is perfect year round for these endeavors—more are slated than we can list, though many are noted throughout this book. However, for the latest information on all such competitions, merely dial the toll-free **Bahamas Sports Line, (800)32-SPORT,** from anywhere in the US. To learn more about sensational skin diving and scuba diving in the Bahamas, or events in parasailing, sky diving, and other favorite island sports, contact one of the "Sources of Information" listed in this chapter.

When it comes to holidays there's unofficial but widespread celebrating of other nations' great days, such as the Thanksgiving Day (late November) and Independence Day (July 4) of the United States. For a timely events schedule, contact the Ministry of Tourism.

16 Nassau and the Bahamas

GOLF COURSES II

BAHAMA PRINCESS HOTEL & GOLF CLUB

Bahamian Holidays and Special Events

January: *Junkanoo Parades* on New Year's Day (Nassau, Freeport, around the islands). *Supreme Court Assizes* opens with great pagentry on second Wednesday in Parliament Square. *Red Cross Charity Ball* and *North American Backgammon Championships.*

February: *Annual Heart Ball*

April: *Good Friday* and *Easter Monday*

June: *Whit Monday. Labour Day*, first Friday. *Goombay Summer Festival*, Nassau and Freeport for approximately four months.

July: *Independence Day*, July 10, marking independence from Britian.

August: *Emancipation Day*, first Monday, marking freedom of slaves. *Fox Hill Day*, one week later in village near Nassau: old-fashioned country fair.

October: *Discovery Day*, October 12, celebrating Columbus' discovery of the Bahamas. *Halloween.*

November: Two annual fund raising events of the Bahamas Humane Societ, *Horse Show* at Camperdown Stables and *Dog Show and Mini-Fair.*

December: *Christmas* (25) *Boxing Day* (26) *Junkanoo* (26)

Most shops and businesses close and assorted festivities are fixed or emerge around these days, but the biggest all-out, bang-up, no-holds-barred partying focuses on the end and beginning of each year: **Junkanoo.**

It's also the highlight of high season for tourists. To participate fully, individuals and groups can contact the *Ministry of Youth, Sports & Community Affairs*, P.O.Box N-10114, Nassau, Bahamas.

Sources of Information

Definitive specifics about the Bahamas and its tourism offerings are yours from its **Ministry of Tourism, P.O. Box N-3701, Nassau, Bahamas.** Main offices and branches are scattered throughout the islands, with special desks at Nassau and Freeport international airports. The Bahamas Tourist Offices around the world are listed by country:

United States

Atlanta: 2957 Clairmont Rd., Suite 150, Atlanta, GA 30345, (404)633-1793

Boston: 1027 Statler Office Building, Boston, MA 02116, (617)426-3144

Charlotte: 4801 East Independence Boulevard, Suite 1000, Charlotte, NC, (704)532-1290

Chicago: 875 N. Michigan Ave., Chicago, IL 60611, (312)787-8203

Dallas: World Trade Center, Suite 186, POB 581408, Dallas, TX 75258, (214)742-1886

GOLF COURSES III

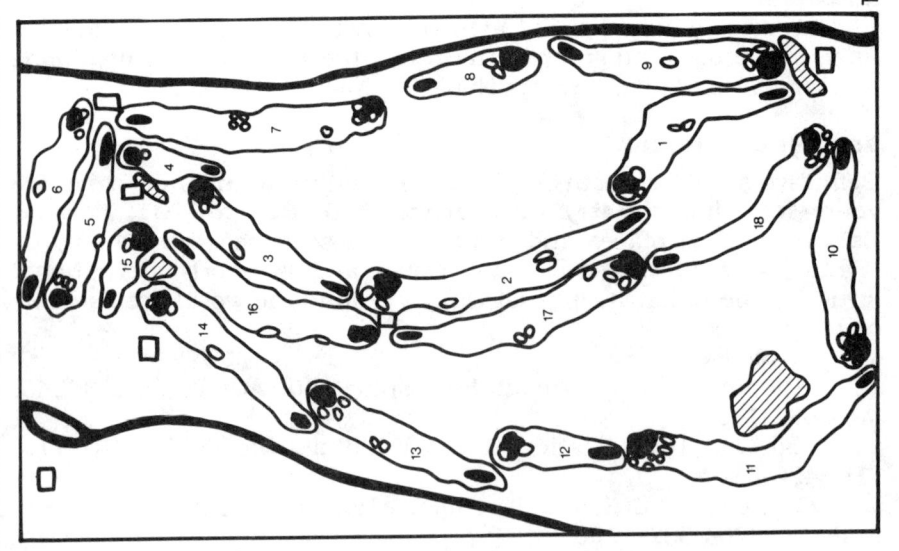

BAHAMA REEF GOLF & COUNTRY CLUB

TREASURE CAY GOLF CLUB

Detroit: 26400 Lahser Rd., Suite 112A, Southfield, MI, (313)357-2940

Houston: 5177 Richmond Ave., Suite 755, Houston, TX 77056, (713)626-1566

Los Angeles: 3450 Wilshire Blvd., Suite 206, Los Angeles, CA 90010, (213)383-9590

Miami: 255 Alhambra Ci., Suite 425, Coral Gables, FL 33134, (305)442-4860

New York: 150 E. 52nd St., New York, NY 10022, (212)758-2777

Philadelphia: Lafayette Bldg., Suite 212, Philadelphia, PA 19106, (215)925-0871

San Francisco: 44 Montgomery St., Suite 503, San Francisco, CA 94104, (415)398-5502

St. Louis: 555 N. Balks, Suite 310, St. Louis, MO 63141, (314)569-7777

Washington, D.C.: 1730 Rhode Island Ave., N.W., Washington, D.C. 20036, (202)659-9135.

Canada

Montreal: 1255 Phillips Sq., Montreal, Quebec H3B 3G1, (514)861-6796

Toronto: 121 Bloor St., East., Suite 1101, Toronto, Ontario, M4W 3M5, (416)968-2999.

Europe

London:, 10 Chesterfield St., London W1X 8AH, England, U.K., 01-629-5238

Paris: 9 Boulevarde de lat Madeleine, 75001 Paris, France, 42-61-61-30/42-61-60-20

Frankfurt : 6000 Frankfurt am Main, Post-strasse 2-4, Frankfurt, West Germany, (069)25 20 29.

Latin America

Contact the Miami office listed under the United States.

Japan

Tokyo: Room 102, Lord-Dom Sanbancho, Chiyoda-ku, Tokyo, Japan, 03-263-7634.

Other offices involved in tourism are:

The Bahamas Chamber of Commerce, P.O. Box N-665, Nassau, (809)322-2145

Bahamas Hotel Association Ltd., P.O. Box N-7799, Nassau, (809)322-8381

Bahamas Family Island Promotion Board, 225 Alhambra Circle, Coral Gables, FL 33134, (305)446-4111

The Grand Bahama Island Promotion Board, P.O. Box F-650, Freeport, (809)352-8356 (also c/o the Coral Gables address above)

Nassau/Paradise Island Promotion Board, P.O. Box N-7799, Nassau, (809)322-8384 (also c/o the Coral Gables address/number listed above).

GOLF COURSES IV

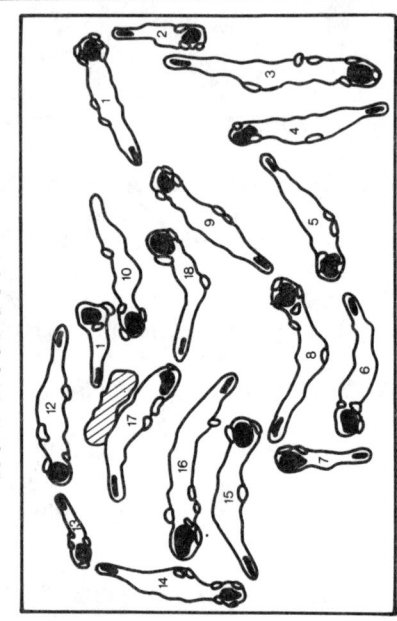

LUCAYAN GOLF & COUNTRY CLUB

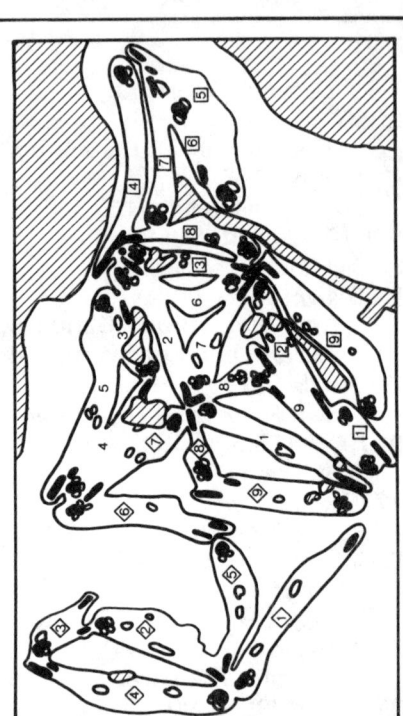

JACK TAR VILLAGE

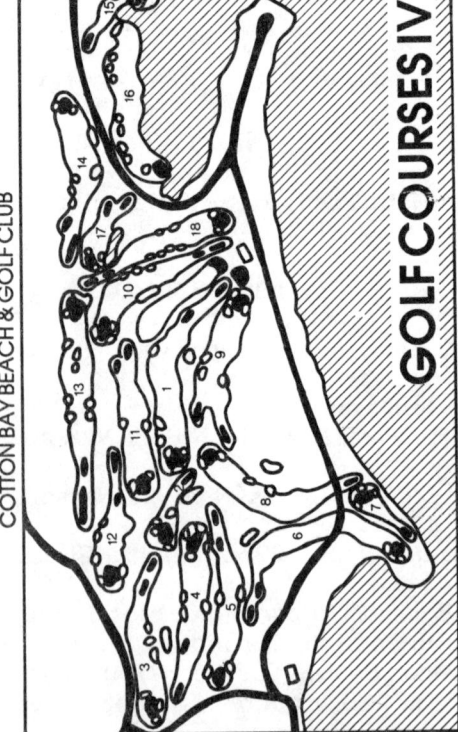

COTTON BAY BEACH & GOLF CLUB

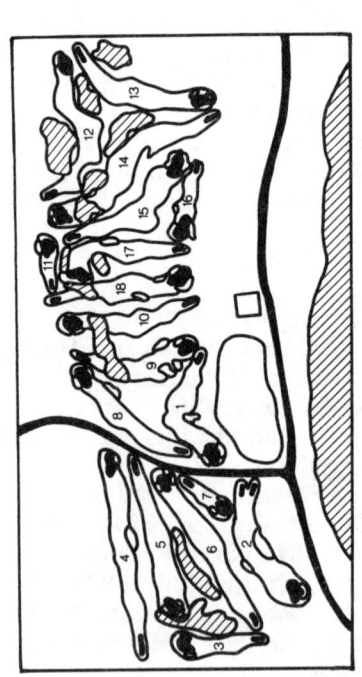

Crystal Palace Golf Course

Package Vacations

Most Bahamian hotels and resorts offer their own special package holidays, and we suggest you investigate through a travel agent or direct call to find the best deal for you.

Sample packages are named *Sun Swingers, Beach Party, Ultimate Singles Experience, Great-est Honeymoon, Taste of Paradise* (gourmet foods), *Fine Fishing, Divers Delight, Glorious Golf, Sports Spectacular;* even *Family Life* and *Great Escape*. You can, for example, try three to seven nights of *Turtle Delight* at $142.50 per person/double occupancy (pp/dbl) plus transportation, at the famous Green Turtle Club, Green Turtle Cay, Abaco, where VIPs and politicians (including a U.S. president) get away from it all. Extras include a boat trip to historic New Plymouth Town, unlimited fishing tackle, snorkeling gear, pool and private beach. Also there are optional boat rentals, sailing excursions, marina facilities, waterskiing, and a chef to cook what you catch on deep sea-, bone-, bottom-, or reef-fishing trips. Or try a *Goombay Winter Fling* of three to seven nights at Nassau's Sheraton British Colonial Hotel, at $119-$279 plus air fare per adult/dbl, with kids under age seventeen free in parents' room, including roll-away beds. Add to your fling unlimited tennis and other resort sports, and $50 to $100 worth of free drinks, plus parties for adults.

Honeymoon specials are big in the Bahamas, and priced well. The posh Lucayan Beach Resort & Casino offers a three days/two nights holiday for $512, including room, champagne, reserved beach/pool chaises, beach bag, tickets to *Pizzazz* show, and more. *Grand Beginnings* at Sheraton Grand Hotel, Paradise Island, start at $347 per couple for four days/three nights, and the Paradise Island Resorts International caters to honeymooners via its various hotels, with sports, parties, and entertainment packages ranging from $380 per couple for four days/three nights, to $1,018 per couple for eight days/seven nights. Deluxe winter honeymoon packages at The Cystal Palace are $624 per couple for four days/three nights (less in summer).

Of all special sports packages, dive trips are probably the most popular in the Bahamas. Small Hope Bay Lodge, in Andros, is one of many resorts with year-round rates: $601 pp/dbl/EAP buys five nights/six days, six dives, including all meals, dive gear, extra fees, beach cottage, and resort facilities; you can opt for extra nights and dives. Add air fare (Small Hope offers transport via its private aircraft from Fort Lauderdale). On Long Island, Stella Maris resort offers three different seven-night/eight-day dive packages priced to $489 pp/dbl EP with eighteen dives, extensive resort facilities and optional extras. (Similar rates apply to a similar package for fishing buffs, and $249 to $279 will buy a regular resort week at Stella Maris.) The Rum Cay Club, Ltd., offers seven night/seven days for $483-$599 pp FAP; dbl add eighteen dives at $250. Included are all fees, dinner wines, dive gear, and resort facilities. Add $250 for from/to Fort Lauderdale transport via the club's own plane. Like most dive resorts, Rum Cay Club rents underwater cameras; it also has a modern color-film processing lab. Other dive packages thrive at Abaco's Treasure Cay, Spanish Wells Beach Resort and Harbour Club, Nassau's fine South Ocean Beach Hotel, Lucayan Beach Resort & Casino in Grand Bahama, and elsewhere.

Big summer excitement focuses now on Goombay holidays with prices for EP hotel rates plus air fares. The word Goombay has been used for years to describe the particular rhythm of Bahamian music, and today it's been borrowed to describe the particular rhythm of any vacation within the Bahamas. *Great Goombay Summer* features Nassau, Crystal Palace, and Paradise Island hotels, with stays of three days and two nights ranging from $45 to $190 pp/dbl, and eight days/seven nights ranging from $140 to $434 (summer prices). Goombay Sundance holidays include Freeport/Lucaya hotels on Grand Bahama, with four days and three nights available at $49 to $272, and eight day/s seven nights for $101-$620. *Goombay Getaway* treats go to 10 different Family Islands, with rates of $45-$252 for four days/three nights, and $105-$560 for eight days/seven nights.

Ask about ever-popular casino vacations from major cities to Nassau and Grand Bahama airports—$199 per person double occupancy buys three nights of Grand Bahama's Princess Casino summer holidays; Lucayan Beach Resort & Casino offers a Casino Express from Newark International Airport three times weekly at $100 to $125 per person including either a night or day/night, round trip fare, $50 in casino chips, $25 in quarters for slots, buffet dinner, and ticket to Pizzazz show.

Also, check into special spring rates, senior citizen, and student discounts. **Note:** Tour details and prices quoted are subject to alteration at any time.

Packing

Comfort should be your first criterion, with casualness the second. This means clothes that are not tight and are preferably of natural fibers or blends that breathe well. Colors can be conservative to gaudy. Where you stay and what you do will influence the contents of your suitcase. Diving devotees take scuba gear, cut-offs, and perhaps little else; high-rollers pack elegant sportswear for casino action. For many evenings at restaurants and clubs, men will need a jacket, even a tie, and women will feel comfortable in a chic dress or sports separates. Cool nights and air conditioning make a sweater or wrap handy; long sleeves and pants guard against exposure to sun, especially at sea. Old outfits are recommended for beaches with oil and/or tar, and sport shoes are a safety device against spiky shells, rocks, or underwater reefs. A lightweight, hooded nylon jacket, doubles as protection against salty ocean sprays or showers. Skimpy bikinis and other swimwear are acceptable nearly everywhere except on main streets, in fine restaurants, and in some shops and lobbies. Beach robes are advised— big pockets can hold ID and tanning lotion.

Handmade straw hats are plentiful, handsome and cheap here, but scarves or visored caps might be needed for boating or shielding hair from constant breezes. Comfortable shoes, at least two pairs, are a must for sightseeing and shopping jaunts. Women may want heels for night spots. If you collect shells, sealable plastic bags are perfect for most finds; a sizable tote makes it easier to hold delicate specimens during the journey home. Film, sunglasses, insect repellent, sun lotions, reading material, and tobacco — all are usually costly and often limited in variety here, so bring your own. Frequent visitors add packs or tins of snacks; families sometimes bring a whole suitcase of edibles.

Passports

None are needed for stays of up to eight months if you are a United States citizen, or for visits of three weeks or less if you are a citizen of Canada or the United Kingdom or Colonies. However, you may be asked to produce proof of ample funds to cover your stay and a ticket or means of leaving the Bahamas. You will be required to show proof of citizenship such as a U.S. Naturalization Certificate, voter registration card, passport, or birth certificate. Passports are required for all other nationals, and U.K. citizens need passports to re-enter the U.K.

Visas

British Commonwealth citizens need no visas, and U.S. citizens need none for visits lasting up to eight months. If you should need a visa, apply at the Bahamian or British Consular Office nearest your home.

United States: the *Consulate General of the Commonwealth of the Bahamas*, 25 Southeast Second Ave., Miami, FL 33131, (305)373-6295; the *Embassy of the Commonwealth of the Bahamas*, 600 New Hampshire Ave., Washington, D.C. 20037, (202)944-3390; *Bahamas Mission to the United Nations*, 767 Third Ave., New York, NY 10017, (212)421-6925; the *Consulate General of the Commonwealth of the Bahamas*, 767 Third Ave., New York, NY 10017, (212)421-6420.

United Kingdom: the *High Commission of the Commonwealth of the Bahamas*, 10 Chesterfield St., London, W1X 8AH U.K., (01)408-4488.

Health Certificates

Minimal Bahamian entry requirements call for certificates of smallpox vaccination and cholera inoculation only if you arrive directly from an area where these diseases have recently been reported.

Embarkation/Debarkation Card

Each visitor arriving in the Bahamas must complete and sign an Immigration Card, and will receive a carbon copy of it to produce on departure.

The Handicapped Traveler

Air and sea carriers to the Bahamas, as well as Bahamian ports of entry, offer special services for handicapped travelers, but specific arrangements and reservations in advance are suggested. Toilet facilities for handicapped persons are available at Bahamian international airports, shopping bazaars, many hotels, etc., primarily in New Providence and Grand Bahama islands. On Paradise Island, hotels with facilities for the handicapped are *Holiday Inn, Britannia Towers, Loew's Harbour Cove* and *Paradise Towers*. In Nassau try the *Wyndham Ambassador Beach, Nassau Beach*, and *Divi Bahamas Beach Resort & Country Club*.

Within the Bahamas, the Ministry of Tourism can suggest further assistance.

Note: Several scuba diving operations are equipped for handicapped people.

GETTING THERE

By Air

There are, of course, the major carriers with their Big Bird-sized airships, but keep in mind that several smaller lines have ferried people from Miami to the islands and back for years. Probably the best known is **Chalks International,** which likes to call itself the world's oldest. Chalks has several daily flights to Paradise Island/Nassau and North Bimini and several weekly flights to Cat Cay, with extensions now in the works. For details, phone (800)327-2521; in Florida, (800)432-8807.

Other scheduled carriers flying from cities in Florida are as follows:
Aero Coach; (800)327-0010
Florida Express: (800)327-8538
Bahamasair: (800)222-4262
Piedmont Shuttle: (800)251-5720
Gull Air: (305)684-1247
Walker's Cay Airlines: (800)327-3714

Delta Airlines; Eastern Airlines; Henson Airlines; Midway; Pan American World Airways Inc.; Trans World Airlines; Turks & Caicos National Airline; United Airlines Inc.

Look for **Caribbean Express** possibly resuming operations under a new name - **Palm Air.**

Treasure Cay Beach Hotel & Villas on Abaco has opened an office in New York to handle its new all-inclusive program, *Treasure Island Club & Cruise*. They offer charter flights from Newark for 3($649 per person), 4($749), or 7($999) nights. From Fort Lauderdale rates average $100 less per program. Flights leave on Fridays or Mondays. For information phone toll free in U.S. (800)327-1584; in Florida (800)432-8257 in Florida; (305)525-0500 in Fort Lauderdale.

Private planes comprise an important part of tourism to the Bahamas, and many services to pilots are available from the Ministry of Tourism, including the *Private Pilot Briefing Centre* with toll-free telephone numbers: Florida only, (800)327-7678; outside Florida, (800)327-7678. Over sixty landing strips in the Bahamas include eighteen airports of entry, and I highly recommend *Pilot's Bahamas Aviation Guide,* which includes charts and detailed flying data updated annually; order direct (approximately $18 total) from Pilot Publications, P.O. Box 9927, Mobile, AL 36609. Many commercial pilots never fly this territory without it.

Charter Air Services and Their Headquarters

Air charter service is available for getting to resorts not serviced by scheduled inter-island flights, for reaching Family Islands on days or at times when scheduled flights don't operate, for small groups or families, or for cases where amphibian plane service is desirable. A select list includes:

* Abaco Air Ltd., Marsh Harbour, Abaco, Bahamas
 Aircraft Charter Service, Nassau, NP, Bahamas
 American Transair, Indianapolis, IN
 *Andros Charter Services, Ltd. Fresh Creek, Andros, Bahamas
 Atlantic Coastal Airways, West Hollywood, FL
 Bahamasair, Nassau, NP, Bahamas
 Beckett Tilford, Inc., West Palm Beach, FL
 Canadian Pacific Airlines, Ltd., Vancouver, B.C., Canada
 Caribbean Express, Inc., Miami, FL
 Challenge International, Miami, FL
 Cherokee Air Services, Marsh Harbour, Abaco, Bahamas
 Emerald Air Inc., Austin, TX
 Executive Jet Aviation, Inc., Columbus, OH
 Eastern Provincial Airways, Nova Scotia, Canada
 Florida Airmotive, Inc., Lantana FL
 Grand Bahama International Airlines, Ltd., Freeport, GB, Bahamas
 Hanger One, Inc., Atlanta, GA
 *Harken Air Services, George Town, Exuma, Bahamas
 Helda Air Holdings, Ltd., Freeport, GB, Bahamas
 Independent Air, Inc., Smyrna, TN
 Jetflight, Miami, FL
 Key Largo Air Service, Inc. Homestead, FL
 Marion Corp., Ltd., Marsh Harbour, Abaco, Bahsmas
 M.D. Air Services, nassau, NP, Bahamas
 Nassau Air Ferries, Ltd., Nassau, NP, Bahamas
 National Jets, Inc., Ft. Lauderdale, FL
 Ozark Airlines, Inc., St. Louis, MO
 Pacific Western Airlines, Ltd., Vancouver, BC, Canada
 Pinder's Charter Service, Ltd., Nassau, NP, Bahamas
 ProAir Services, Miami, FL

Quebecair, Quebec, Canada
Rich International Airways, Inc., Miami, FL
*Seair Airways, Ltd., Nassau, NP, Bahamas
Sky World Airlines, Denver, CO
*Stuart's Fishing Co., Bailey Town, Bimini, Bahamas
Sun Aviation, Inc., Vero Beach, FL
*Taino Air Service, Ltd., Freeport, GB, Bahamas
Transamerican Airlines, Inc., Oakland, CA
Twin Tower Leasing Co., Ft. Lauderdale, FL
Walker's Aviation Services, Inc., Ft. Lauderdale, FL
*Zig Zag Airways, Marsh Harbour, Abaco, Bahamas

* *Inter-Island only*

By Sea

Cruises to the Bahamas

Admiral Cruises

Emerald Seas. Year round: four-night cruises departing Monday from Miami, calling at Nassau, Little Stirrup Cay, and Freeport. Year round: three-night cruises departing Friday from Miami, calling at Nassau and Little Stirrup Cay.

Carnival Cruises

Carnivale. Year round: four-night cruises departing Monday from Miami, calling at Freeport and Nassau. Year round: three-night cruises departing on Friday from Miami, calling at Nassau.

Jubilee. Year round: seven-night cruises departing Sunday from Miami, calling at Nassau, San Juan and St. Thomas.

Mardi Gras. Year round : three-night cruises departing on Thursday from Fort Lauderdale, calling at Nassau. Year round: four-night cruises departing Sunday from Fort Lauderdale, calling at Freeport and Nassau

Chandris Fantasy Cruises

Galileo. November 4 to March 31 - Two-night cruises departing Friday from Miami, calling at Nassau.

Crown Cruise Line

Crown Del Mar. Starting December 16: two-night cruises departing Friday from Palm Beach, calling at Nassau

Dolphin Cruise Line

Dolphin IV. Year round four-night cruises departing Monday from Miami calling at Freeport and Nassau. Year round three-night cruises departing Friday from Miami calling at Nassau.

Holland American Cruise Line

Noordam. November 5 to April 29: seven-night cruises departing Saturday from Fort Lauderdale calling at Nassau and Caribbean ports

Rotterdam. November 10 to April 24: ten-night cruises from Fort Lauderdale calling at Nassau and Caribbean ports.

Westerdam. November 13 to April 23: seven-night cruises departing Sunday from Fort Lauderdale calling at Freeport and Caribbean ports.

Norwegian Cruise Line

Sunward II. Year round four-night cruises departing Monday from Miami calling at Nassau, Great Stirrup Cay, Freeport. Year round three-night cruises departing Friday from Miami calling at Nassau and Great Stirrup Cay.

Premier Cruise Lines

Star/Ship Atlantic. Year round four-night cruises departing Monday from Port Canaveral calling at Nassau and Salt Cay. Year round three-night cruises departing Friday from Port Canaveral calling at Nassau and Salt Cay.

Star/Ship Oceanic. Year round four-night cruises departing Monday from Port Canaveral calling at Nassau and Salt Cay. Year round three-night cruises departing Friday from Port Canaveral calling at Nassau and Salt Cay.

Star/Ship Royale. Year round four-night cruises departing from Port Canaveral calling at Nassau and Salt Cay. (Beginning February 9, ship departing Sundays.) Year round three-night cruises departing Friday from Port Canaveral calling at Nassau and Salt Cay. (Beginning February 9 departing Thursdays.)

Princess Cruises

The Sky Princess. February 8 and February 18: ten-night cruise from Fort Lauderdale calling at Nassau and Caribbean ports.

Royal Caribbean

Nordick Prince. February 18: eight-night cruise departing from Miami calling at Nassau and Caribbean ports.

Windjammer Barefoot Cruises

Amazing Grace. Year round twenty-night Bahamas, Virgin Islands, West Indies, and Grenadines cruises departing the second Sunday of the month from Freeport.

Cruise Line Addresses

Admiral Cruise Lines, Inc., 1220 Biscayne Blvd., Miami, FL 33132, or P.O.B. 010882, Miami, Fl 33101; phone (305)374-1611; or (800)327-0271 toll free throughout the U.S.

Carnival Cruise Lines, 5225 N.W. 8th Ave., Miami, FL 33178; phone (305)599-2600; or (800)432-5424 toll free in Florida; or (800)327-7373 toll free throughout the U.S.

Chandris Fantasy Cruises, 900 Third Ave., NY, NY 10022; phone (212)750-0044; 770 Biscayne Blvd., Miami, FL 33137, (305)576-9900; or (800)621-3446 toll free throughout the U.S.

Crown Cruise Lines, P.O. Box 10265, Riveria Beach, FL 33419; phone (800)841-7447 toll free throughout the U.S.

Dolphin Cruise Lines, 1007 N. American Way, Miami, FL 33132; phone (800)222-1003 toll free throughout the U.S.

Holland America Line, 300 Elliott Ave. West, Seattle, WA 98119; phone (206)281-3535.

Norwegian Cruise Lines, 2 Alhambra Plaza, Fifth Floor, Coral Gables, FL 33134, toll free throughout the U.S. (800)327-7030, Florida toll free (800)432-9696.

Premier Cruise Lines, Ltd., 101 King George Blvd., Cape Canaveral, FL 32920; phone (800)432-2545 toll free in Florida; (800)327-9703 throughout the U.S.

Princess Cruises, 2029 Century Park East, Los Angeles, CA 90067; information phone (213)553-1770: reservations phone (213)553-7000; or outside CA (800)421-0522.

Royal Caribbean Cruise Lines, 903 South American Way, Miami, FL 33132; phone (305)379-2601; or (800)432-6559 toll free in Florida, or (800)327-6700 toll free throughout the rest of the U.S.

Windstar Sail Cruises, Ltd., four-masted computerized schooner offered a series of short cruises (4 to 7 days) this summer. Luxurious accommodation and unusual cruise itinerary. For information on future cruises call toll free (800)258-SAIL in U.S.; (800)341-SAIL in Florida; in Canada, Nordic Tours (800)263-0844.

Many times, a cruise ship can be your best transport, allowing layovers at either Nassau or Freeport; it's something to check as you plan your itinerary. Also, many cruise companies offer special prices for assorted reasons and seasons, and these can save you large portions of regular fares. Call or write shipping lines for the latest brochures and cost details. Firms other than those listed have included Bahamian ports of call in the past, and may add them again; check with your travel agent.

Cruising is a wonderfully relaxed way to travel, but it's usually fattening, too—all ships vie with each other to provide the most delicious foods in enormous amounts, almost around the clock. Ships also feature live entertainers, directed games and parties, gambling casinos, and assorted sports that often include skeet shooting and golf. They usually incorporate duty-free shops.

Charter boats and private yachts are frequent visitors to the Bahamas, where there are many well-equipped marinas and some fine boat builders. Seaports of entry are in Abaco, Andros, Berry Island, Bimini, Cat Cay, Eleuthera, Grand Bahama, Inaugua, New Providence and San Salvador. I highly recommend the *Yachtsman's Guide to the Bahamas,* which is full of valuable data for sailors in these waters; it can be ordered directly from Tropical Isle Publications, P.O. Box 866, Coral Gables, FL 33134.

FORMALITIES ON ARRIVAL

Customs

Arriving tourists are allowed 50 cigars or 200 cigarettes or one pound of tobacco, one quart of spirits, personal effects, and additional purchases (from duty-free shops) totaling no more than $100. For these allowances, or less, an oral declaration suffices; for anything over these allowances, a Baggage Declaration Form must be filled out.

Warning: Long jail stints and hefty fines await those who try to bring illicit drugs, firearms, and illegal fishing devices into the Bahamas.

Money

This may be a British Commonwealth country, but its currency is strictly dollars and cents, divided precisely like U.S. money and freely exchanged on a par with American dollars and cents. All similarity between the two ends there, however, for Bahamian money is beautifully designed, with pictures of native flowers, fish, birds, shells, sailboats, and such. Bills are printed in bright colors and coins pressed into unusual shapes. The 10-cent piece with fluted edges often becomes a souvenir, and even collectors avidly hunt for the hard-to-find square 15-cent piece with rounded corners, plus coins worth $1, $2, and $5, and bills worth 50 cents and $3.

If travelers bring along Yankee dollars, there's no need to exchange them. American travelers checks are usually accepted throughout the islands. Other currencies, in cash or travelers check, are usually accepted by hotels. If not, desk clerks can give you the locations and hours of nearest banks. Since the Bahamas ranks as a major international banking center, there'll be no trouble with any exchange, but plan to pay small commissions for conversions.

American, Canadian, and European major credit cards are honored throughout the Bahamas by many hotels, shops, restaurants, and vehicle rental agencies. Several U.S. gasoline company cards are honored here. But since some places take only certain cards, check beforehand.

Getting into Town

At most Bahamian ports of entry, you can reach your destination by taxi, rental automobile, or transportation provided by your hotel. Some public bus service is available. Taxis wait at terminals, but other transport must be arranged in advance (see Getting Around). If you're visiting an Out Island, it's likely you'll take a scheduled inter-island flight via Bahamasair, though some resorts operate private plane service for guests, either from Nassau or southern Florida. There are destinations, such as Harbour Island Eleuthera, that require several transfers before you arrive. Check chapters on individual destinations for details.

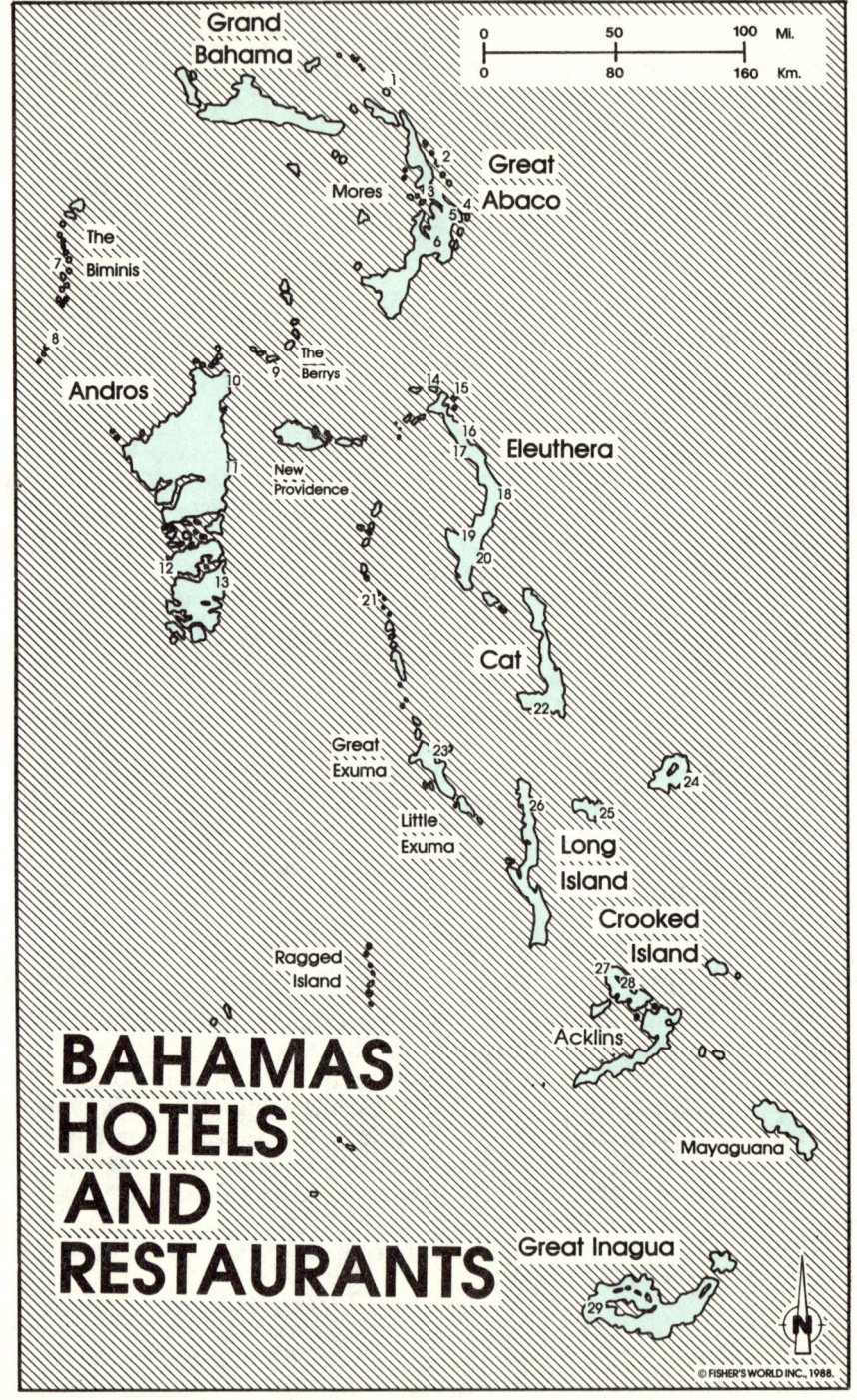

KEY TO BAHAMAS HOTELS AND RESTAURANTS

- 4 Abaco Inn
- 10 Andros Beach Hotel & Villas
- 7 Bimini's Big Game Fishing Club & Hotel
- 7 Bimini's Blue Water Marina
- 8 Cat Cay Club
- 16 Cambridge Villas & Restaurant
- 19 Cape Eleuthera Resort & Yacht Club
- 9 Chub Cay Club
- 18 Club Med-Eleuthera
- 7 Complete Angler
- 5 Conch Inn Resort & Marina
- 15 Coral Sands
- 20 Cotton Bay Beach
- 22 Cutlass Bay Yacht Club
- 5 CYN Thia's Kitchen
- 16 Dunmor Beach Club
- 7 Fisherman's Paradise

- 29 Ford's Imagua Inn
- 5 Great Abaco Hotel
- 2 Green Turtle Club & Marina
- 4 Hope Town Harbour Lodge
- 5 Jib Room
- 5 Keys Bakery & Restaurant
- 13 Las Palmas Beach
- 29 Main House
- 12 Mangrove Cay Guest Houses
- 6 Mother Merle's Fishnet Restaurant
- 2 New Plymouth Club & Inn
- 23 Out Island Inn
- 23 Peace & Plenty Hotel
- 23 Pieces of Eight Hotel
- 15 Pink Sands
- 23 Pirates Point Villas
- 27 Pittstown Point Landings Ltd. Inn
- 7 Red Lion Restaurant

- 23 Regatta Point
- 16 Romora Bay Club
- 25 Rum Cay Club
- 14 Runaway Hill
- 11 Small Hope Bay Lodge
- 14 Spanish Wells Beach Resort & Harbour Club
- 21 Stanlel Cay Yacht Club
- 26 Stella Maris Inn
- 28 Sunny Lea Guest House
- 17 Thompson's Bakery
- 10 Tadwind Village
- 3 Treasure Cay Resort
- 23 Two Turtles Inn
- 15 Valentine's Yacht Club, Inn & Drive Center
- 1 Walker's Cay Hotel & Marina
- 14 Walton's Laugousta Restaurant & Bar
- 20 Windermere Island Club

*For Grand Bahama and New Providence Islands see the Freeport Map and the New Providence Hotel Map.

SETTLING DOWN

Choosing a Hotel

Most accommodations cluster around Nassau and Freeport, while others are scattered throughout smaller towns or sited remotely on a far-flung isle. They may be camplike bungalows, or tiny, posh villas in a row, or high-rise and huge, but the norm is a new or newly modernized building of some 60 to 150 rooms, fitted out to provide at least as much comfort as the average U.S. facility. Some chain establishments are more elegant here than elsewhere, and many hotels are luxuriously appointed even by strict international standards.

Service, however, is something else. It evolves around what's fondly termed Bahamian Time, coupled with the average hotel employee's lack of exposure (despite training courses) to efficient operations abroad. The result: Service is slow and easy—whether for telephone calls, maintenance, food, luggage toting, or errands. There's no peevishness about it; it's generally quite friendly, and irritation evinced by guests merely baffles the employees. A good way to circumvent frustration is to head for moderate-and-above establishments that accommodate 40 to 60 guests, where service becomes more akin to personalized catering. Otherwise, plan to exercise a lot of patience.

In this island nation, the success and scope of your visit is pretty much set by where you stay. Whichever most fits your fancy, it's here, and you can usually buy it through one of several different official plans: **European Plan** (EP) is room only; **Continental Plan** (CP) is room and light breakfast; **Full American Breakfast** (FAB) covers a hearty breakfast plus room; **Modified American Plan** (MAP) is a room plus breakfast and one other meal; **American Plan** (AP) is described as a room and three meals, and **Full American Plan** (FAP) is the same as AP. Since food is rather expensive in the Bahamas, the most economical stays call for rooms plus some food. On the popular MAP option, some hotels have the Dine-Around Plan that allows guests to eat in several outside restaurants, adding variety to economy. Some Family Island hotels operate only on MAP or FAP rates, primarily because they offer just about the only food in the vicinity.

Seasonal rates flourish at almost all hotels here. High-season charges range between 15 and 25 percent more than low-season rates. There are some exceptions, but high season usually runs from mid-December to mid-April, with lower rates applicable from mid-April through mid-December. **Warning**: The most frantic refurbishing and expansion occur just before high season begins and sometimes can detract from one's vacation pleasure.

Extras: Accommodations tax runs 6 percent on EP rates, yet drops to 3 percent for MAP and FAP rates. Many hotels also enforce an energy surcharge of $1 or more, a daily automatic tip ($1.75 per person) for chambermaids, another 15-percent service charge on food bills and room service fees. All these may be added to your bill. Check when you make reservations so that you'll know what to expect.

Free Reservations: For details about a hotel or resort in the Bahamas, and for reservations, call the **Bahamas Reservation Service toll free (800)327-0787 in Canada and the U.S.; phone (305)443-3821 in Miami. In London, England, phone 629-5238, Telex 51-28921.** Be sure to reserve early; tourism is booming and some folks reserve next year's stay while visiting this year. Check to make certain children are welcome. Many hotels have supervised playgrounds, baby-sitters and regularly slated daily activities for youngsters.

All costs are subject to change. Some may drop or rise by 10 to 15 percent. For a quick, free check on standard and package rates of most hotels, call the Bahamas Reservations Service; telephone above.

Other Accommodations

Private homes, cottages, and apartments are often rented to tourists. For details on such rentals, check with the *Bahamas Real Estate Association,* P.O. Box N-8860, Nassau, phone (809)325-4942. The same address can supply information about buying property in the Bahamas. Time-share properties exist here, at minimum rates of about $3,000 per week's ownership. Visitors can buy condos or cottages, arranging for the developer to rent them during specific times. Land can be bought and construction contracted at various costs. However, all such ownership schemes are greatly regulated by the government, and all applicants must be approved before sales are allowed, which can take several months to a year. Because of the commitment and complications involved, I suggest you investigate these possibilities in person, when actually in the Bahamas.

My cost definitions in hotel listings, for two persons in a double room: **Extravagant** $150 and up; **Expensive** $90 - $140; **Moderate** $60 - $89; **Inexpensive** $36 - $59.

Restaurants

Restaurant costs vary but run high because so much food is imported and subject to duty. Also, seafood is costly, even to restaurants: A large grouper bought off a boat at the dock can run $50 or more. Though prices in native restaurants are generally lowest, the cheap lunch and expensive dinner prices noted above in my Costs section are averages for restaurants and hotels where sit-down dining with waiter service is available.

Food is good in the Bahamas, and it's plentiful. Most large hotels and resorts have fine restaurants, with areas like Nassau and Freeport flaunting a few superior dining establishments. The big chain eateries are here, too, supplying fried chicken, ribs, donuts, big burgers, pancakes, and assorted flavors of ice cream and milk shakes. There also are British pubs, pizza places, and street vendors hawking fruits. Bahamian cooks do marvelous things with locally available products, and you can eat well (often for less) by going native. Try one of the cafes or restaurants that's owned, operated, and patronized by Bahamians. (See the opening chapter for more on local foodstuffs.)

Unfortunately, it's often hard to guess the quality of fare by eyeing menu prices or selections, room decor or address. There is, for example, a dining spot named for an internationally famous chef, where management has never met the chef nor undergone the tough training involved in preparing dishes bearing his name. This type of situation seems to stem from the inability of hoteliers and restauranteurs to obtain work permits for experienced chefs of other nationalities. Unless the Bahamian government corrects this, or until locals eventually become sufficiently trained and experienced in the subtleties of gourmet cookery, the tourist may often risk disappointment at some seemingly classy restaurants.

Restaurant prices are based on dinner menus, and are per person, estimating a three-course dinner ordered a la carte, selecting average-priced items on the menu, and not including wine or tip. Lunch will cost about 20 percent less in most restaurants. Here are the categories I have selected for the Bahamas: **Extravagant** $46 and up; **Expensive** $31 - $45; **Moderate** $21 - $30; **Inexpensive** $16 - $20.

Tipping

Porters and bellboys who carry your luggage expect tips of $1 per bag. Taxi and surrey drivers, tour guides, waiters and waitresses expect a minimum of 15 percent. Chambermaids also expect tips, at a minimum of $1 or more a day, and tips are customary at barber and beauty shops and anywhere special services are rendered. Most hotels, resorts, clubs, bars, and restaurants automatically add this minimum tip to your bill, so check it carefully—ask, if uncertain—before digging into your pocket or purse. Should you happen to be displeased with the service, you still must pay the added service charge. If you're especially pleased with the service, however, it's only right to tip a little something over and above the minimum.

Clubs

His Royal Highness, the Duke of Edinburgh, K.G., is the patron of the Bahamas National Trust (BNT), which is dedicated to wildlife protection and conservation and the preservation of places of historic interest and natural beauty. Endangered marine life, flamingos and other birds, turtles, etc., benefit from BNT programs that swank charity affairs help support. Membership runs $5 to $1,500 annually and includes a subscription to the *Journal of Bahamaian Natural History*. The BNT is associated with the World Wildlife Fund and is open to children, adults, clubs, and corporations.

Other Bahamian clubs—from private social groups to bird watchers, animal fanciers, and bridge addicts—welcome foreign members or associates, and joining can enhance your visit here. Service groups are big here, too, including chapters of Kiwanis, Lions, Rotary,

Jaycees, Toastmasters International Inner Wheel and Pilot clubs, American Men's or Women's Club, Canadian Men's or Women's Club, Women's Corona Society, and others. Visitors are welcome at most meetings, and hotels can provide specifics.

Church bazaars, and festivals are held in addition to regular services.

People-to-People is a Ministry of Tourism official program, operating in the Nassau and Freeport areas, which gives tourists and locals a chance to get together and share interests in the professions, sports, hobbies, or the cultural scene. Volunteers register and are matched up by dedicated people, then make their own arrangements to meet. If you want to participate, register well in advance though a travel agent or the Bahamas Tourist Office branch nearest you.

Bahamahost: For personalized tours of sights, night and day spots and such, your best bet lies with a Bahamahost. Certified by the Ministry of Tourism after intensive study of the Bahamas, its history, folklore and culture, plus tourism particulars, the Bahamahost is trained to give professional service at reasonable rates. Many Bahamahosts work independently and have their own limousines; others work for hotels, tour agencies, airlines and taxi companies.

Business Hours

Most Bahamian businesses follow the nine-to-five routine, including those involved in travel, shopping and other tourist interests. Some vary by opening as late as 10 A.M. and closing as late as 7 P.M., but almost all are closed on Sundays and public holidays. As some stores close one afternoon weekly, and as that afternoon can vary, morning shopping sprees assure more browsing time. The straw and native crafts markets generally operate from early morning to dusk.

Larger islands usually have banking hours from 9:30 A.M. to 3 P.M., and extend closing to 5 P.M. on Fridays. Many banks on smaller islands open later and close earlier, and frequently banking facilities are available only once a week. There are several small islands with no banks.

All these hours, by the way, are Eastern Standard Time in winter and Eastern Daylight Time in summer (five hours behind Greenwich Mean Time).

Electricity

Throughout the country, normal electrical current is 120 volts, 60 cycles, AC. North American appliances may be used here. Visitors from Europe and the U.K. will need adapters.

Major utilities firms provide power for New Providence, Grand Bahama and all or part of several smaller islands. However, many small villages and settlements have no electricity unless communities or individuals operate their own generators. Many hotels, resorts and restaurants generate their own current in outlying areas, and most have emergency generators even in the major centers of population.

Water and Drink

"Serious shortage" describes the status of fresh water on many Bahamian islands, including New Providence, which partially depends on supplies brought in regularly from larger, less-populated Andros. Hotels post signs such as "Please don't water the sink" in bathrooms, seldom have stoppers for tubs, and serve water at the table only on request.

Bottled water is sold practically everywhere, but this has more to do with taste than shortages. Wells sunk through limestone rock produce nearly all fresh Bahamian water, which is high in salts. Though purified, filtered and often chlorinated, it occasionally manages to retain a distinct flavor that some can detect and few enjoy. Assorted literature for tourists here proclaims that drinking the tap water causes no ill effects. Yet you're advised to buy the bottled stuff or have the dining room deliver water to your room.

Communications

Telephone, Telex, telegraph and postal services bridge the distance gaps between the Bahamas and the rest of the world. Slowly.

Telephone service can be quite frustrating if you expect speedy connections. Few Bahamian hotels in the Family Islands have direct-dial systems, and it can take up to a half-hour just to raise the operator who's struggling (often single-handedly) with several circuits and dated equipment. Line trouble is an everyday thing throughout the islands, and some remote spots must make do with a single radio line that runs only certain hours a day. In general, when you approach a telephone, expect difficulty, and have a book handy to read while you wait.

Most hotels charge 50 cents for a local call, 25 percent service charges on all long-distance calls, and $2.50 service charge on all credit card or collect calls. Telephone rates can vary throughout the country.

With the Bahamas linked to the North American telephone network via area code 809, Direct Distance Dialing (DDD) has become available for overseas calls from New Providence and Grand Bahama islands, at a savings of 60 percent over operator assisted calls, to the North American continent and some nearby islands. All other inter-island or intercontinental calls must be placed through operators, including all person-to-person, collect, and credit-card calls. Only New Providence, Grand Bahama, Bimini, Andros, Exuma, and Eleuthera can originate DDD calls, and DDD can be dialed within the Bahamas only to parts of Abaco, Andros, Bimini, Eleuthera, Exuma and Grand Bahama; service usually is daytime only. Radiotelephone connections can be made to ships and yachts at sea. See the telephone directory for specifics.

Telegraph service ITT, TRT, Western Union International or CW is available via telephone by dialing 910.

Telex service is available through most major hotels, and there's public Telex service in Nassau and Freeport and at Nassau International Airport; please check locally for latest rates.

Postal services can be extremely fast or excruciatingly slow, within the country and to or from abroad. While an airmail express envelope can reach a stateside address from Nassau in two days, an ordinary airmail letter can take weeks (you could get home first). If you post letters from an Family Island serviced once weekly by mailboat, and you miss a boat, add another couple of weeks to the delivery time. One consolation: Bahamian stamps are attractive.

Air parcel post is available to all destinations, with rates listed at post offices.

Most post offices are open Monday through Friday from 8:30 A.M. to 5:30 P.M., and until 12:30 P.M. Saturdays. Family Island post offices sometimes open only a few hours a day, often erratically. Only Bahamian stamps are valid but, before you trek to a post office, check the hotel desk or gift shop; most sell stamps.

Newspapers, both local and foreign are available. The *New York Times*, the London *Times*, and the *Wall Street Journal* are available at most of the large hotels and newstands, usually a day late. Local newspapers include the *Nassau Guardian*, the *Nassau Tribune*, and the *Freeport News*.

Medical Assistance

Doctors fly to patients in the Bahamas. Literally. If someone's seriously hurt on an isolated Family Island, far from sufficient medical services, a "flying doctor" goes there and, if necessary, escorts the patient back to the Princess Margaret Hospital in Nassau, by air for further aid. Should specialists be needed, there are always flights to Florida. IAMAT (see Travelers' Advisory Planning Ahead) has a doctor and clinic in Freeport.

Pounds and Kilos

Since imports arrive in the Bahamas from around the world, tourists will find merchandise weighed and measured by quarts and liters, pounds and kilos, meters, and inches.

1 centimeter (cm) = 0.4 inch
1 meter (m) = 3.28 feet
1 kilometer (km) = 0.62 miles
1 liter (l) = 0.26 gallons
1 gram (gm) = 0.035 oz.
1 metric ton (t) = 1.1 tons U.S.

1 inch = 2.54 cm
1 foot = 0.31 cm
1 yard = 0.93 km
1 gallon = 3.75 l
1 ounce = 28 g.
1 pound = 450 gm

In short, a liter is very close to a quart, a meter to a yard, and a centimeter to a half inch.

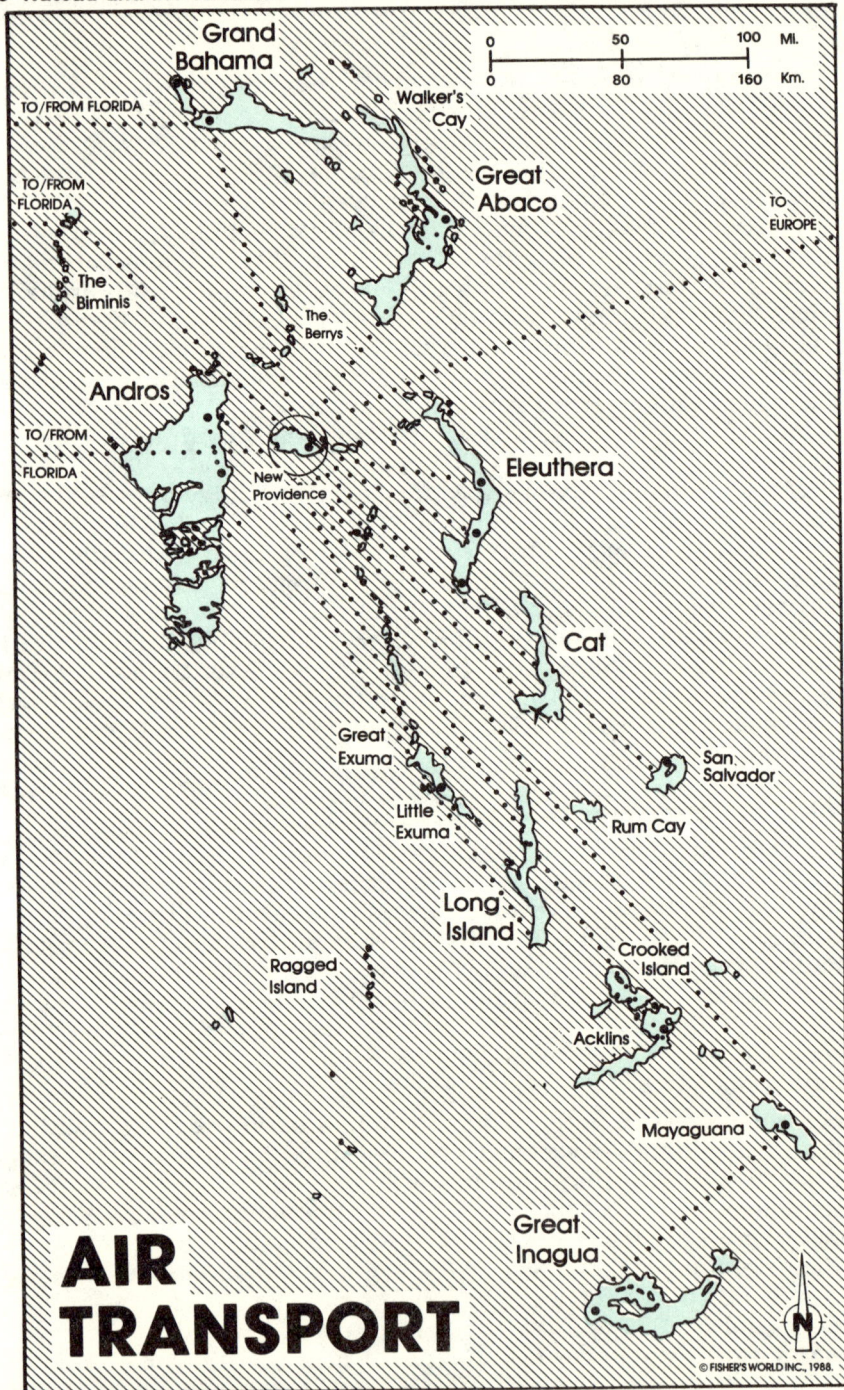

SPECIAL CAUTIONS

Drugs/Weapons

Marijuana and other illicit drugs are strictly illegal in the Bahamas, and law officials do not play games about import, export, or possession. Scrutiny is severe, inspection thorough, and prosecution swift and stringent, with cash fines to $5,000, plus ten years in jail. Possession of illegal firearms also results in grim consequences. Should you have valid authority for possessing or acquiring drugs or guns, only advance government permission can shield you from severe and automatic punishment.

Sun

A boon in careful dosages but a bane otherwise, this mighty tropical sunshine calls for protective measures. Wear a sun hat even if you never wear hats back home, and sunglasses to cut the glare, which can bring eye discomfort. Go for long sleeves and trousers if you're out for lengthy periods. Drink a lot more fluids than usual and use special products to keep your skin healthy before, during and after sunning sessions. Tanning lotions that block harmful rays come in handy, as does lip moisturizer. If you use chemicals to dye or tint your hair, don't expose your hair to the sun. **Note:** overexposure to sun plus heat prostration are the two key tourist ailments.

Insects

Before you find out that the no-see-ums really cannot be seen but their bites can cause extreme itching and discomfort, spray on insect repellent. Creepy crawly insects can invade even the most posh hotel suite. You might want to pack a can of killer spray and use it before dinner—spray your room thoroughly, then close it and air it out on your return. This last precaution is particularly wise for cabins on Family Islands.

Poisons

If you're not familiar with a plant, tree, fish, or marine-life species, avoid it—it could be poisonous. Take care to avoid the poisonwood tree, which is so potent that even water falling off its leaves can raise a rash worse than poison oak and poison ivy.

Beaches

It's wise to wear sneakers or similar footgear on many beaches to avoid nasty cuts from jagged rocks, reefs, and conch shells.

Camera Care

That delicate instrument can go berserk from too much heat or even a little sand or salty water. Keep it in a shady, airy place and keep the

40 Nassau and the Bahamas

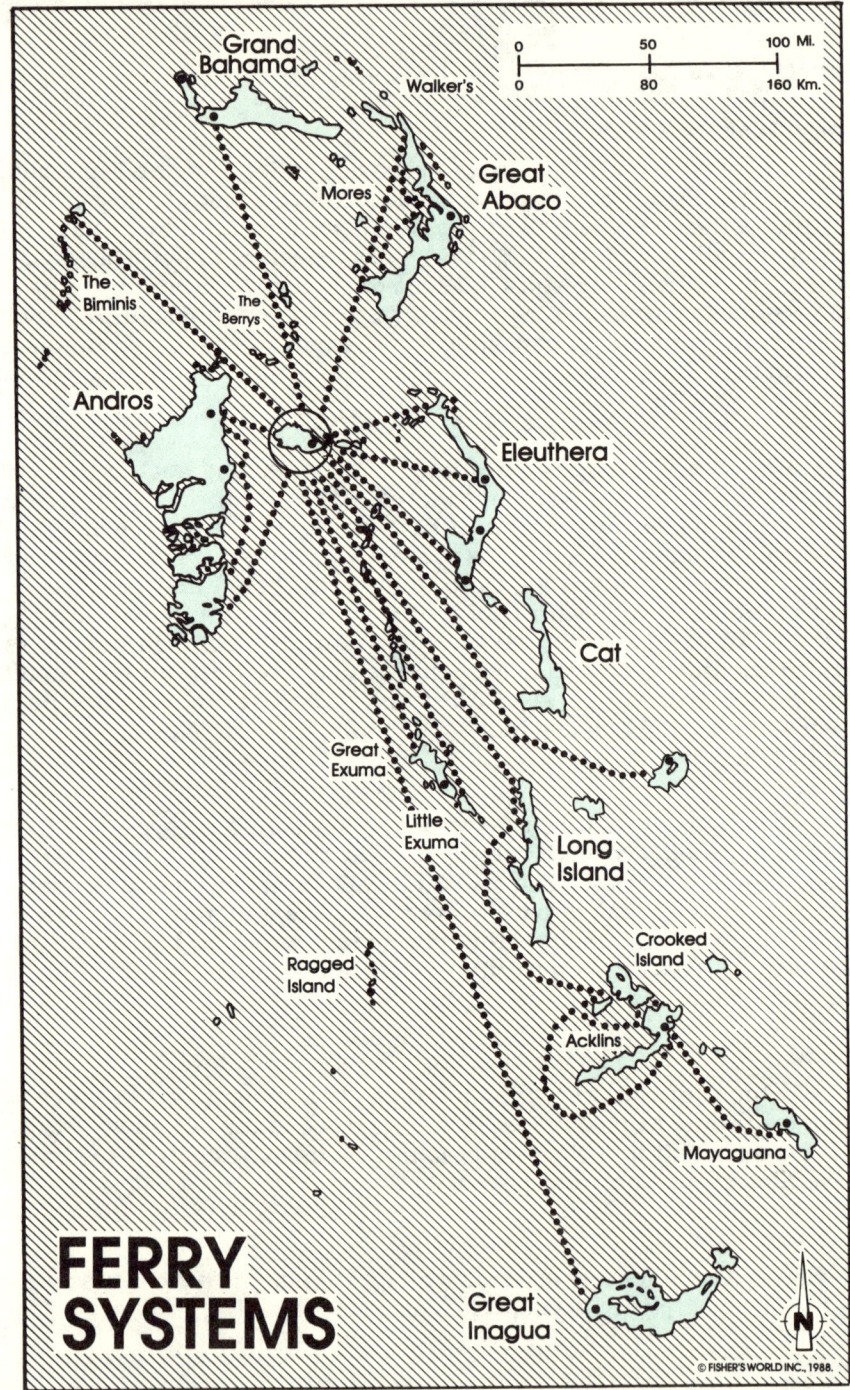

FERRY SYSTEMS

lens cap on and the camera in its case when it's not being used. Note that strong glare from the sun and waters can ruin many a picture; pack and use filters to prevent this. Also, photograpy buffs usually prefer to bring their own film supplies and wait until they're back home to have film developed. (Remember that the heat of X-ray machines at airports destroys chemicals in the film.)

Scuba-Diving Precautions

Scuba divers should take care how high they fly after diving. Experts advise them to avoid heights greater than 1,200 feet above sea level for at least 12 hours after the last dive. This means no commercial jet travel, but small-craft flights can be safe.

You might want to look for a scuba diving instructor certified by one of the following:

National Association of Underwater Instructors (NAUI)
Professional Association of Diving Instructors (PADI)
Associates of Canadian Underwater Council (ACUC)
YMCA Diving Accreditation

Crime

In the Family Islands, honesty is so much a part of living that few locks or keys exist and there's almost no theft much less violent crime. It's different in the bigger cities, particularly Nassau, where the crime rate has risen recently. However, even Nassau has extremely low crime rates compared with cities on the North American continent. (Perhaps because of the relative infrequency of violence here, there is heavy media coverage of what crimes do occur.) By far the biggest problem tourists need worry about is the purse snatcher or pickpocket.

GETTING AROUND THE BAHAMAS

How you do this depends very much on where you go. Island hopping is possible by air and sea; land travel is available via taxi, rental vehicles and jitney buses. Local tour operators slate sightseeing and shopping jaunts, too.

By Air

The national carrier, Bahamasair, has regularly scheduled inter-island flights. A vital service, it's often costly to the carrier, so expect no frills and don't be surprised by delays. Crews are capable and friendly Bahamians, which helps make up for the obvious absence of flight attendant training as rigid as most airlines require. Most planes seat 48 and have boarding steps that fold out onto the tarmac. Family Island airports are tiny buildings, sometimes with nearby snack bars or restaurants, a clutter of private and charter craft on the apron, and a group of locals and cabbies waiting for each landing. Since some islands are serviced only once a week and schedules are subject to change, it's best to book seats well in advance via your travel agent or the airline, then check departures at the last minute. In the *United States* dial **Bahamasair** toll free: (800)222-4262; in *Miami*, dial (305)593-1910. Within the Bahamas, numbers are: *Nassau*, 327-8511; *Freeport*, 352-8341; *Eleuthera*, 332-2196. All numbers are for reservations and to confirm seats (a must) at least 48 hours before flights. Flight schedules are in *Goombay Magazine*, free to visitors.

If scheduled flights can't get you where you want to go when you want to get there, inter-island charter flights are available usually flying daylight hours only, with fees from $170 to $600 per hour depending on craft and capacity. See charter airline listings.

By Sea

Aside from cruise ships, the only inter-island regular routes are plied by Bahamian mailboats. Generally departing from Potters Cay, under Paradise Island Bridge, Nassau (809-323-1064), most visit one or more island docks per trip, with voyages lasting four hours to most of a day. Seldom is a dock visited more than once a week, and it's a big day when the boat chugs in, crammed higgledy-piggledy with mail and provisions, fruit and vegetables, animals and assorted goods for retailers, Bahamians visiting home or friends, and the occasional tourist adventurer.

Traveling on these boats can be fascinating but dicey because of lack of space and tourist facilities. Furthermore, just to get aboard you must get to the dockmaster's office and book passage in person on departure day. If you don't get there early, those lined up ahead of you will secure the most desirable space. You also should pack along some simple snacks and a wrap; some folks take food, Thermos, and blanket. Typically, departure time is revised and re-revised on the spot, resulting in hours of waiting. Fares are minimal: Round trips run approximately $15 to $70.

Other boating ventures come via charter yachts, powered by sail, motor, or both. With costs starting around $300 to $400 a day and rising in tandem with size, value and capacity of vessel, charters come with everything plus captain and crew, or as bareboats, with rentals set by the hour, half-hour, day, week, or month. Travel agents have details. Highly recommended is the *Heritage of Miami*—a tall ship available for charter. Telelphone (305)534-7447. Also recommended is *Fantome*, c/o Windjammer Cruises, P.O. Box 120, Miami Beach, FL 33139, (305)373-2090. *Barefoot Rouge* operates from Freeport to all the islands in the Caribbean.

Small boat rental, for fishing, water-skiing or running between neighboring islands or cays, should be booked when accommodation reservations are made, or you may have to do without. Prices vary widely.

Ferry boats and smaller water taxis usually follow scheduled routes between a large island and its nearby, small, but well-populated cay. Boats hold two to twenty passengers; the service is steady and careful, and the fees are set (quite reasonably). Schedules usually coincide with airline arrivals, so if the plane's late, the ferry is, too.

Official ports of entry:

Abaco: Green Turtle Cay; Marsh Harbour; Sandy Point; Walker's Cay

Andros: Congo Town; Fresh Creek; Mangrove Cay; Nicholl's Town; San Andros

Berry Islands: Chub Cay; Great Harbour Cay

Bimini Islands: Alice Town; North Bimini (yachts); South Bimini (planes)

Cat Island: Cat Cay Club

Eleuthera: Cape Eleuthera; Governor's Harbour; Harbour Island; Hatchet Bay; Rock Sound Airport

Exuma: George Town

Grand Bahama: Freeport; Lucaya; West End

Inagua: Matthew's Town

Jumento Cays (Ragged Island): Duncan Town

New Providence/Nassau: Nassau International Airport; all yacht basins

San Salvador: Cockburn Town

By Car

You can rent an automobile in the Bahamas if you are at least 21 and have a valid driver's license. Rates are $7 to $15 per hour, $47 to $70 and up per day, and $170-$384 and up a week; plus a minimum $150 deposit (unless you are 25 or older and use a major credit card), mileage, fuel, and insurance (buy all you can get). In Nassau, Freeport, and their airports, Hertz, Avis, National and Budget agencies are at your service with European, Japanese, and U.S. models ranging from manual-shift compacts to luxury limousines. Family Islands also have rental cars, available through hotels or local cabbies.

Although you can rent an automobile in the Bahamas, think twice before you do. Rates and fuel are high, safety factors generally low. Grand Bahama Island provides the best driving conditions; Nassau is second, and the Family Islands are far behind. It's the winding, narrow streets, blind crossings, paucity of traffic lights and abundance of vehicles that cause confusion and the call for steely nerves in Nassau town and other areas. And while locals may be accustomed to all this, tourists in rented cars are not. Rented vehicles have special white-tag plates just to warn other drivers to keep clear.

Bahamian roads deserve special mention. In either Grand Bahama or New Providence, many less frequently roads, even those leading to some tourist spots, are partially or totally unpaved. Yet those very back roads would often put an Family Island highway to shame. The farther you get from major populated areas, the less likely you are to find a hard paved road in good repair. It's not that the government doesn't work on the roads (repair teams are constantly employed), but underlying waters plus heavy showers can wash away foundations, and other factors combine to produce incredible potholes. Without precision steering, you'll never maneuver around these obstacles, and if you do, you'll feel you deserve citations for skill and bravery. Frequently, the worst stretches are "scraped"—heavy machinery levels the holes (or tries to) by scaling off the scraps of paving material. It can be easier to drive over rough scraped roads than partially paved ones. That is, until you see another car heading toward you over a road that is wide enough for one and a half cars. Standard practice is for each vehicle to swing partially off the shoulder into the formidable bush, allowing them to pass within kissing distance of each other. Speed limits start at 15 to 25 miles per hour in towns, 35 elsewhere.

These limits apply to motor scooters, too, and some people can travel that fast on scooters in some parts of the country. But as a minimum safety precaution, it's wise to become familiar with the oddities of the rented machine and nearby roads, as well as traffic flow, before raising speed. Poor highway maintenance, potholes, and scraped roads can make scootering dangerous. Despite the mandatory crash helmets, scooter drivers and riders rack up high ratios of spills, scrapes and sore bones. If you rent one, have a driver's license handy, along with some $28 per day or $18 per half-day, including insurance fees. (Weekly rates are available in some places.) Scooters can be rented from hotel desks or streetside sites. The same places usually rent bicycles, which are quite popular, and cost a mere $12 a day plus deposit and theft insurance.

Note: All vehicle rentals should be made early in the morning, or even the night before.

By Taxi

Aside from walking, taxis are by far the most common means of tourist locomotion. In major cities or on Family Island highways, drivers are friendly and courteous. Usually they drive safely, too, not wanting to risk high repair bills. Their fees are government regulated, either by meter or by time. For short rides, be sure the meter is used; for one to two persons, rates are $1.20 for the first quarter-mile, 20 cents for each additional quarter-mile, $1.50 per each additional rider over three years old, plus fees for more than two bags, and for waiting. Hourly rates of $12 to $15 are more economical for lengthy trips or taxi tours. Always negotiate in advance for long trips; often drivers will bargain to $10 per hour for all-day tours.

By Bus

Though no public transport exists, some tour operators provide minibus service to and from airports solely for their package-tour clients. Some hotels operate complimentary minibuses to shift their guests to and from town, beaches and such. Then there are jitney services that ply regular routes between hotels, towns, and residential districts thronged with Bahamians traveling to and from hotel jobs. Join them for a look around the area and a listen to the lingo. (They don't go to the airports, though.) If no stops are marked, ask a passerby where to wait for the minivehicles, or flag one down. They generally run between 6 A.M. and 6 P.M.; fares range from 50 cents to approximately $1.

Note: Bahamians hitchhike. Tourists are generally safe thumbing rides on Family Islands where traffic and transport are minimal and locals live like one big island family, helping everyone out.

GOING HOME

Children under age three are exempt from departure tax when leaving the Bahamas. At the airport, all ticketed passengers pay $5; children age two and under are exempt. Freeport, Grand Bahama Island, also has a $10 per person seaport departure tax.

Customs declarations are available from major hotels and tour or carrier offices. Preparing yours in advance can save awkward airport moments.

United States residents actually clear U.S. Customs at Nassau and Freeport international airports before boarding their flights. Travelers departing from other areas clear customs on arrival in the United States or other country of debarkation.

United States residents, including minors, are allowed duty-free purchases of up to $400 in retail value if they have been out of the country more than 48 hours and have had no similar exemption in 30 days. This exemption can include 200 cigarettes or 100 cigars (not from Cuba) regardless of resident's age, and 33.8 ounces (1 liter) of alcoholic beverages if the traveler is 21 or older. A family may pool exemptions.

Canadian citizens, after 24 hours outside the country, may reenter as often as they like with $20 worth of duty-free goods. After 48 hours abroad, Canadians' duty-free allowance rises to $100 once each calendar quarter, and may include 200 cigarettes, 50 cigars, 2 pounds tobacco and 40 ounces of liquor (for persons 18 or older). Canadians who have been outside the country at least seven days may claim a $300 exemption, even if a $100 exemption was claimed previously; the two cannot be combined.

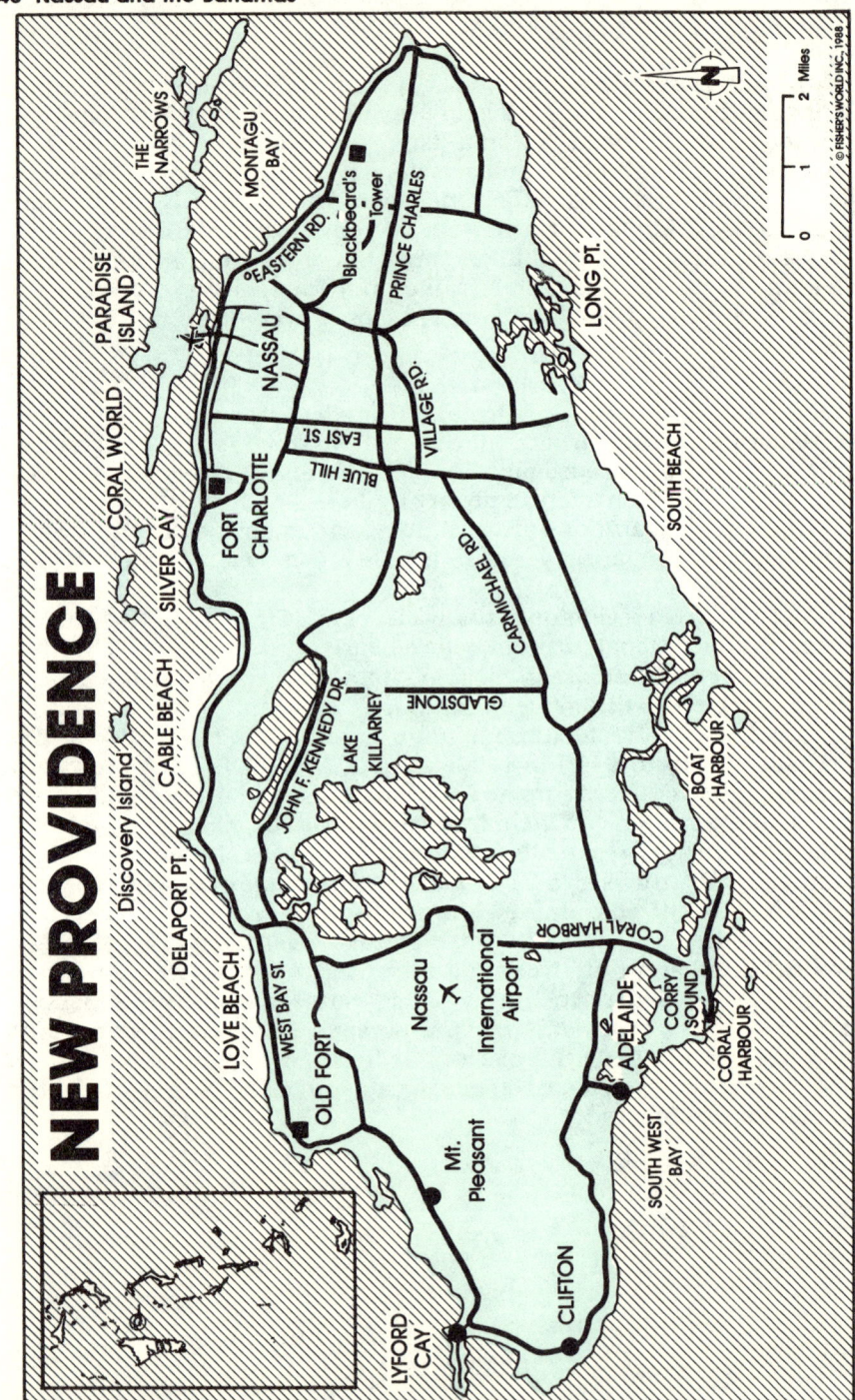

Author's Choice-Bahamas

Note: Hotels without address/phone numbers may be reached through **Bahamas Reservation Service (800)327-0787**

NEW PROVIDENCE:including NASSAU, CABLE BEACH, PARADISE ISLAND

HOTELS

Britannia Towers Paradise Island. Phone (800)321-3000. *Extravagant.*

Buena Vista Hotel & Restaurant Delancy Street, Nassau. P.O.Box N-564. Phone (809)322-2811. *Inexpensive.*

Crystal Palace/Cable Beach Casino Dual Carriageway, Cable Beach. P.O.Box N-4914. Phone (800)822-4200; in Canada (800)631-4200. *Extravagant.*

Graycliff Hotel Across from government house, central Nassau. P.O.Box N-10246. Phone (312)883-1020; toll free (800)423-4095. *Extravagant.*

Nassau Beach Hotel Dual Carriageway, Cable Beach. P.O.Box N-7756. Phone (809)327-7711. *Extravagant.*

Ocean Club & Tennis Resort Paradise Island. P.O.Box N-4777. Phone (800)321-3000. *Extravagant.*

Paradise Island Resort & Casino Britannia Towers, Paradise Towers, Paradise Club. Phone (800)321-3000. *Extravagant.*

The Royal Bahamian Hotel & Villas West Bay Street, Cable Beach. P.O.Box N-7528. Phone (800)822-4200; toll free in Canada (800)631-4200. *Extravagant.*

Sheraton Grand Hotel Paradise Island. P.O.Box SS. Phone (809)326-2011. *Extravagant.*

Wyndham Ambassador Beach Hotel Dual Carriageway, Cable Beach. Phone (800)822-4200; toll free in Canada (800)631-4200. *Extravagant.*

Holiday Inn Paradise Island. P.O.Box 6214. Phone (809)326-2101. *Extravagant.*

Loews Harbour Cove Paradise Island. P.O.Box SS-6249. Phone 326-2561. *Expensive.*

Sheraton-British Colonial Hotel 1 Bay Street, central Nassau. P.O.Box N-7148. Phone (809)322-3301; toll free (800)334-8484. *Extravagant.*

Divi Bahamas Beach Resort & Country Club Formerly the South Ocean Beach Hotel and Golf Club. P.O.Box N-8191. Phone 326-4391; toll free (800)367-3484. Southwest of Nassau Airport. *Extravagant.*

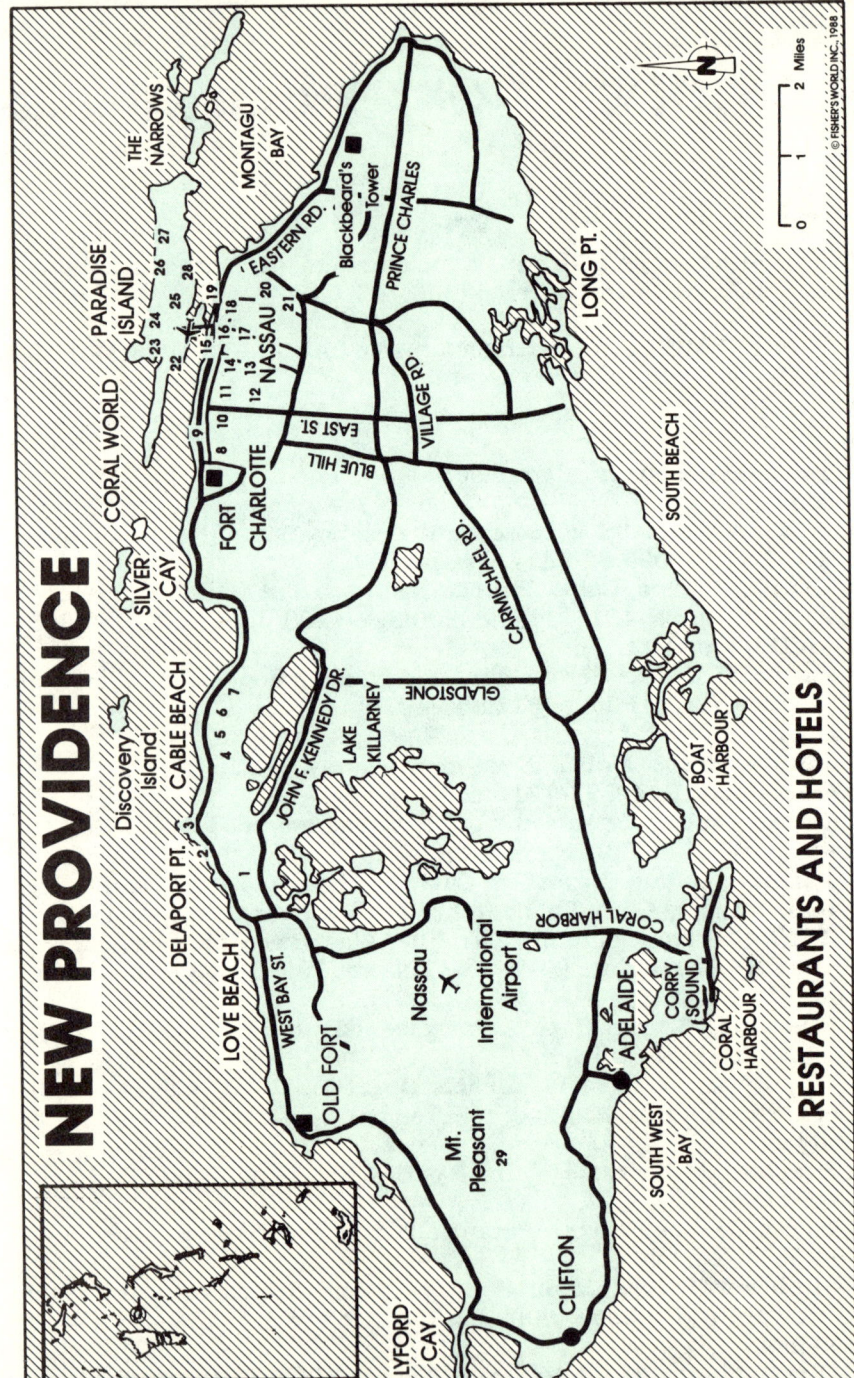

RECOMMENDED RESTAURANTS
NEW PROVIDENCE ISLAND

- 14 Buena Vista
- 4 Baccarat
- 27 Courtyard Tavern
- 12 Graycliff
- 26 Julie's
- 5 Regency Room
- 10 Ristorante Davinci
- 25 Gulfstream
- 23 Neptune's Table
- 5 Sole Mare
- 7 Rib Room
- 21 The Sun And...
- 24 Coyaba
- 13 Liz's
- 18 Parliament Terrace Cafe
- 11 Rose Lawn
- 8 Travellers Restaurant
- 9 Del Prado
- 15 Green Shutters
- 1 Roundhouse

RECOMMENDED HOTELS
NEW PROVIDENCE ISLAND

- 2 Bahamas Beach Inn
- 24 Britannia Towers
- 14 Buena Vista
- 1 Casuarinas
- 22 Cable Beach Manor
- 3 Club Med
- 5 Crystal Palace
- 12 Greycliff Hotel
- 23 Holiday Inn
- 28 Loews Harbour Cove Hotel
- 6 Nassau Beach Hotel
- 19 Nassau Harbour Club and Marina
- 27 Ocean Club & Tennis Resort
- 20 The Orchard
- 25 Paradise Island Resort & Casino
- 18 Parliament Hotel
- 17 Pilot House
- 4 Royal Bahamian
- 16 Sheraton-British Colonial Hotel
- 26 Sheraton-Grand Hotel
- 29 South Ocean Beach Hotel & Golf Club
- 7 Wyndham Ambassador Beach Hotel

Bahamas Beach Inn Formerly the Cable Beach Inn. P.O.Box N-4920. Phone 327-7341. Cable Beach. *Expensive.*

Cable Beach Manor Dual Carriageway, Cable Beach. P.O.Box N-8333. Phone (809)327-7785. *Moderate to Expensive.*

Casuarinas Dual Carriageway, Cable Beach. P.O.Box N-4016. Phone (809)327-7921. *Expensive.*

Nassau Harbour Club Hotel & Marina East Bay Street, Nassau. P.O.Box N-3703. Phone (809)323-3771/8. *Expensive.*

The Pilot House Hotel Box N-4941, Nassau. Phone 322-8431. *Expensive.*

Club Med Paradise Island. P.O.Box N-7137. Phone (809)326-2640. *Modearte.*

The Orchard P.O.Box N-1514. Phone 323-1297. Village Road, Nassau. Near Montague Beach. *Inexpensive.*

Parliament Hotel Nassau. P.O.Box N-7530. Phone (809)322-2836. *Inexpensive.*

Yoga Retreat P.O.Box N-7550. Phone 326-2902. Paradise Island. *Inexpensive.*

RESTAURANTS

Buena Vista Delancey St. Phone 322-2811. *Extravagant.*

Baccarat In Royal Bahamian Hotel. *Extravagant.*

Courtyard Terrace Ocean Club & Tennis Resort on Paradise Island. *Extravagant.*

Graycliff Across from Government House. Phone 322-2796. *Extravagant.*

Julie's Sheraton Grand Hotel. *Extravagant.*

Regency Room Crystal Palace/Cable Beach Casino. *Extravagant.*

Ristorante Da Vinci West Bay Street, central Nassau. Phone 322-2748. *Expensive to Extravagant.*

Gulfstream Paradise Island Hotel & Casino. *Expensive.*

Neptune's Table Paradise Island, Holiday Inn. Phone 326-2101. *Expensive.*

Sole Mare Crystal Palace/Cable Beach Casino. *Expensive.*

The Pasta Kitchen Wyndham Ambassador Beach Hotel. Phone 327-8231. Charming new restaurant with cosy ambiance. Specializes in homemade Italian cuisine. *Moderate to Expensive.*

Sun And... Fort Montague area. Phone 323-1205. *Expensive.*

Coyaba Britannia Towers, Britannia Beach Hotel, Paradise Island. Phone 326-3000. *Moderate to Expensive.*

Liz's Midtown, Elizabeth Avenue. Phone 322-4780. *Expensive.*

Parliament Terrace Cafe Parliament Hotel. *Inexpensive.*

Regata Room Pilot House Hotel. Phone 322-8431. *Moderate to Expensive.*

Roselawn Cafe Midtown, Bank Lane. Phone 325-1018. *Moderate.*

Traveller's Rest West of Cable Beach. Phone 327-7633. *Moderate.*

Del Prado El Greco Hotel. West Bay Street. Phone 325-0324. *Expensive.*

Green Shutters Parliament Street, in central Nassau. Phone 325-5702. *Inexpensive to Moderate.*

Round House Restaurant Casuarinas, Crystal Palace. *Moderate.*

Small Eateries

Back Stage Deli Crystal Palace /Cable Beach Casino.
Bahamian Kitchen Trinity Place, midtown.
Three Queens, Shoal, Poinciana, Fish Net, Reef, F & S Take Away, Jane's Take Away, Casablanca, Captain Nemo's, Smiley's Place, Village Gourmet, Health Corner, Candy Bar.

Pubs and Bars

Rum Keg Bar Nassau Beach Hotel.
Charley Charley's On Delancy.
Green Shutters Downtown.
Poop Deck Near Paradise Island Bridge.
Never Say Never Again Sheraton British Colonial Hotel.

ENTERTAINMENT

Performing Arts

Performances held in auditoriums of large resorts and in the *Dundas Civic Center* (newly renovated) at Mackey Street, phone 322-2728. Many amateur groups. International artists often perform at the invitation of the Nassau Music Society or the Bahamas Music Society. Look for posted notices and in newspapers.

Gambling

Paradise Island Resort & Casino and *Crystal Palace/Cable Beach Casino.* Slots open at 9 A.M. and tables at noon; closing time varies from 4 to 6 A.M. **Note:** Law forbids Bahamians to gamble in these casinos.

Shows and Revues

Drum Beat Club, on West Bay Street near the Sheraton. Best show in town stars "Peanuts" Taylor.

Barbeque & Junkanoo Feast, in the Pineapple Place restaurant, in the Nassau Beach Hotel. Dancing afterwards.

Le Cabaret, adjacent to Paradise Island Casino. Vegas-style revue. Dinner.

Les Fantastiques, at Crystal Palace. Broadway favorites and modern laser light shows.

Discos

The Palace, off Bay Street on Elizabeth Avenue. 9 P.M. to 4 A.M. (except Mondays). Cover charge.

52 Nassau and the Bahamas

Cinnamon's, in the Nassau Beach Hotel, 9 P.M. to 2 A.M. (except Sundays). Cover charge.

Club Pistache, at Britannia Towers on Paradise Island.

Tradewinds Lounge, at Paradise Towers on Paradise Island.

Le Paon, at the Grand Hotel on Paradise Island.

Junkanoo Lounge, same locations as above. Two shows nightly (ex 10:45 P.M., 12:45 A.M. except Sundays) and dance music from 9 P.M.

SHOPPING

Clothing Size Equivalents

Women's Suits and Dresses

American	8	10	12	14
British	10	12	14	16
Continental	38	40	42	44

Women's Hosiery

American	8	8.5	9	9.5
British	8	8.5	9	9.5
Continental	0	1	2	3

Women's Blouses and Sweaters

American	30	32	34	36
British	32	34	36	38
Continental	36	38	40	42

Women's Shoes

American	6	6.5	7	7.5
British	4.5	5	5.5	6
Continental	38	38	39	39

Men's Suits and Overcoats

American	36	38	40	42
British	36	38	40	42
Continental	46	48	50	52

Mens's Shirts

American	14	14.5	15	15.5
British	14	14.5	15	15.5
Continental	36	37	38	39

Men's Socks

American	9.5	10	10.5	11
British	9.5	10	10.5	11
Continental	38-39	39-40	40-41	41-42

Men's Shoes

American	8	8.5	9.5	10.5
British	7	7.5	8.5	9.5
Continental	41	42	43	44

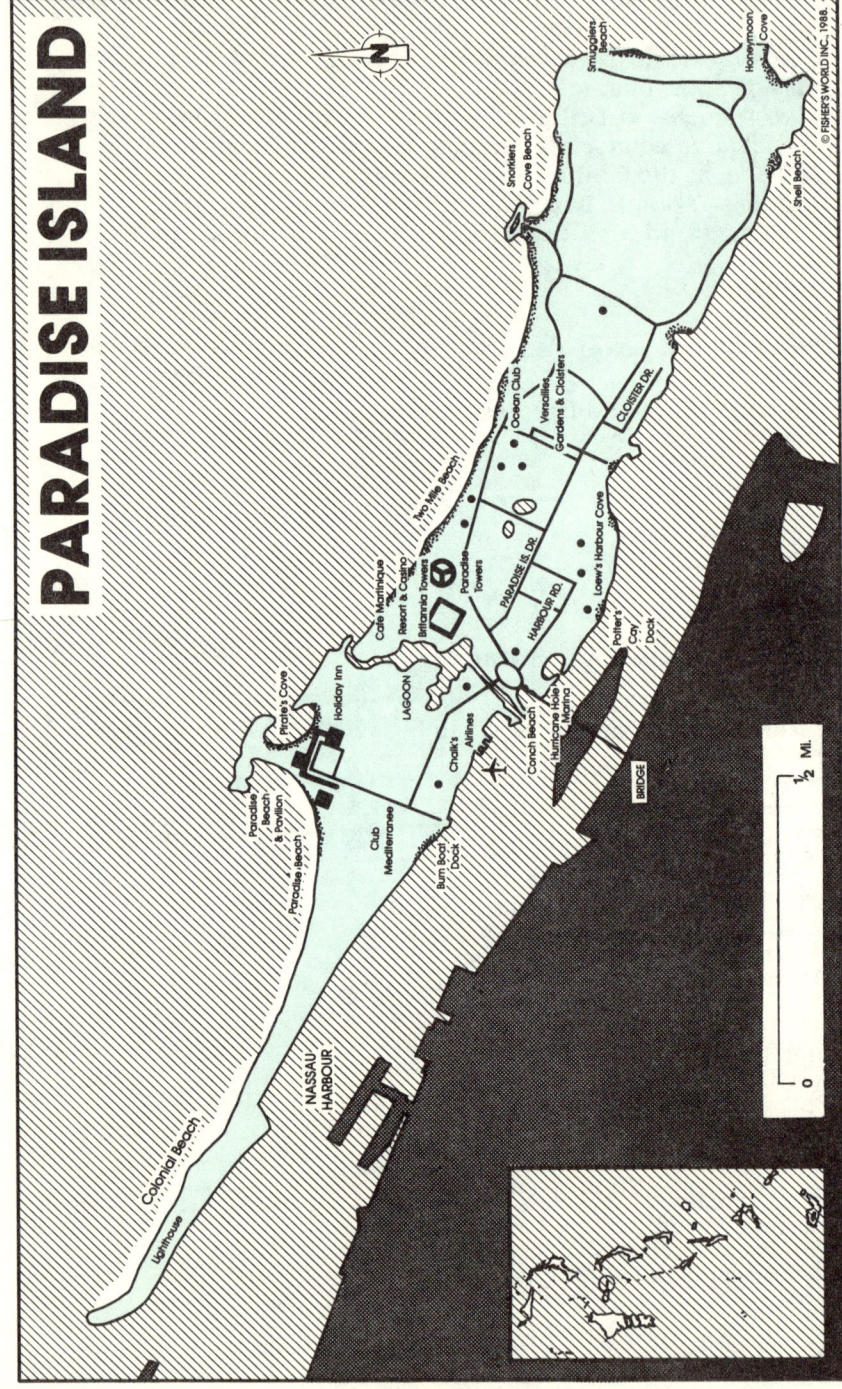

Children's Clothes

American	4	6	8	10
British height(in)	43	48	55	58
Continental height(cm)	125	135	150	155

Antiques: Francis Peek, The Heirloom, Balmain Antiques.
Art: Nassau Glass Art Gallery, Temple Art Gallery.
Books: The Island Shops, Nassau Shop, Anglo-American Book Store, Paradise Island Drug Store.
Brass: Brass & Leather Shop.
Cameras: John Bull, Colombia Emeralds, Jade Dolphin, Pipe of Peace, Patrick's Camera, Watch Shop.
China, Crystal, Giftware: Bernards, Solomon's Mines, Treasure Traders, Crystal Shop, Francis Peek.
Coins and Stamps: Coin of the Realm. The post office, banks.
Cosmetics: Beauty Spot/Perfume Shop, Scottish Shop.
Eyeglasses: Optique Shoppe, Imperial Optical.
Fabrics and Linens: Bahamas Hand Prints, Linen Shop, English Shop, Distinctive Shop.
Jewelry: Coin of the Realm, Nassau Shop, Greenfire Emeralds Ltd., Lords Ltd., John Bull Colombia Emeralds, Black Coral And..., Johnson Brothers Ltd., Sea Garden Shop, Discount Warehouse.
Knitwear: Trader Vic's, Scottish Shop, Ambrosine, Distinctive Shop, Nassau Shop, Island Shops, Amanda's.
Leather: Las Tiendas, Brass & Leather Shop, Scottish Shop, Pipe of Peace, Galaxy Shoes.
Liquors and Spirits: Bahama Blenders, Butler & Sands, Robertson & Symonette, Maury Roberts Co. Ltd.
Men's Wear: Distinctive Shop, Trader Vic's, Scottish Shop, Nassau Shop, Relax-Sir, Island Shops, Caribah Originals, Ambrosine.
Perfumes: Bahamas Fragrance & Cosmetic Factory, Lightbourne's Perfume Centre, Nassau Shop, Perfume Shop, Paris Shop, Island Shops, Beauty Spot.
Prescriptions: City Pharmacy, Cole Thompson.
Straw Work: Market and street vendors; Look for work by Ivy Simms.
Souvenirs: Jackpot, Pyfrom's.
Tobacco: Pipe of Peace, Nassau Shop, Island Shops.
Watches: See stores listed under Jewlery and Cameras.
Women's Fashions: Mademoiselle, Chez Mizpah, Caprice, Coles of Nassau, Caribah Originals, Ambrosine, Nassau Shop, Island Shops, Palm Cottage, Beautiful Woman (sizes 14-32 1/2).

MUSEUMS

Archives, Junkanoo Art Gallery/Museum.

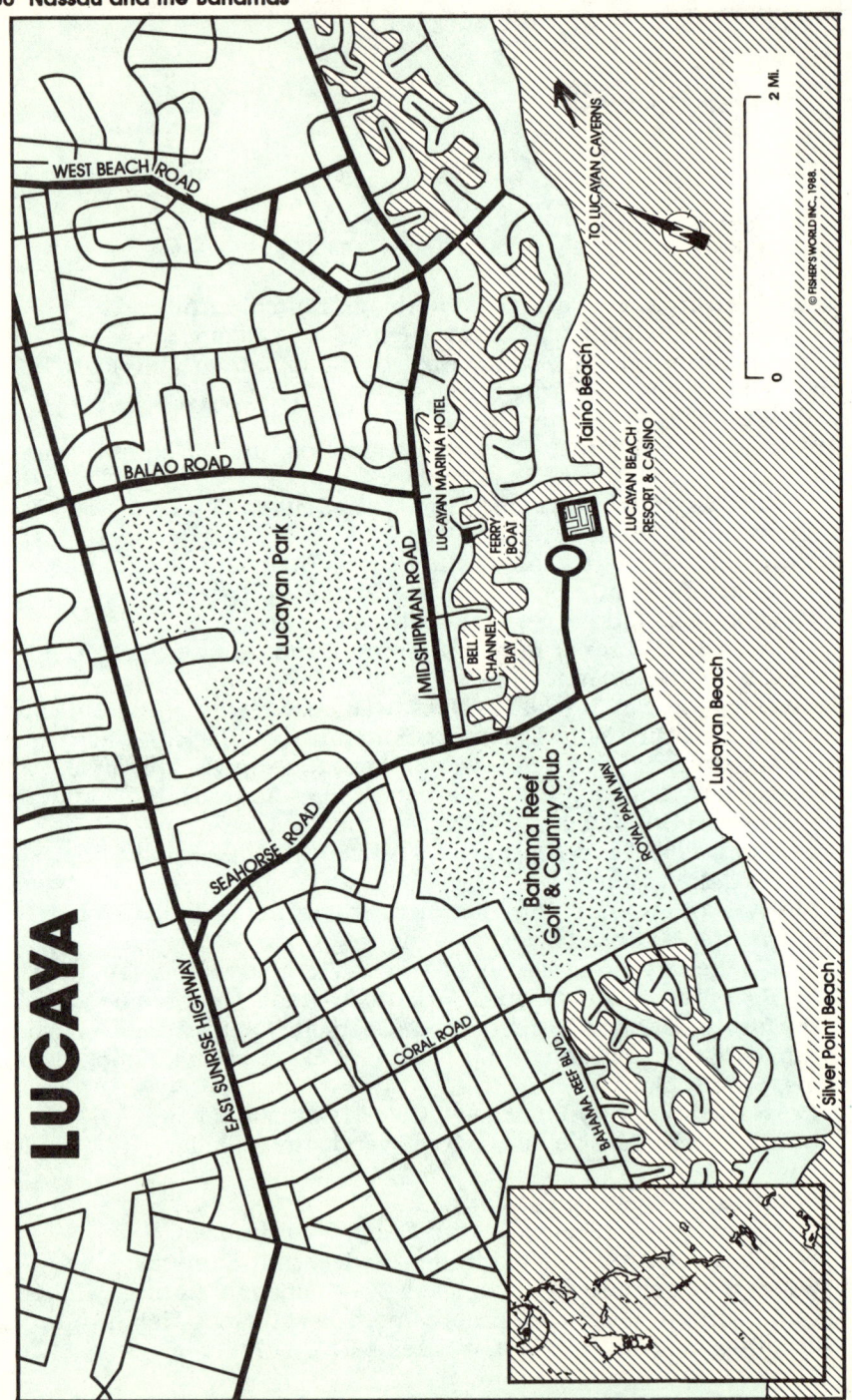

Parks and Gardens

Versailles Gardens and Cloister, on Paradise Island.
Coral World Marine Park, off Bay Street. 328-1036. Admission fee.
Royal Victoria Gardens, opposite the public library in Nassau.
Bush Medicine Gardens, at the YMCA on John F. Kennedy Drive.
Nassau Botanical Gardens, near Fort Charlotte. Open daily 10 A.M.-4 P.M. Admission fee.
Ardastra Gardens, near Fort Charlotte. Open Monday -Saturday, 9 A.M.-5:30 P.M. Admission Fee.

Historic Buildings and Sites

Blackbeard's Tower, Christ Church Cathedral, Fort Charlotte, Fort Fincastle, Fort Montague, Houses of Parliament, Colonial Secretary's Office, Supreme Court, Public Library, Gregory Arch, Grant's Town, Jumbey Village (Angelo's Art Centre), Queen's Staircase, Fort Nassau, Blackbeard's Wall, St. Augustine's Monastery, Woodes Rogers Walk, . Country villages: Adelaide, Carmichael, Fox Hill, Gambier.

Other Sights

Bay Street shopping district, Rawson Square, Seafloor Aquarium, Straw Market. Changing of the Guard, Bahamian Supreme Court Assizes

SPORTS

Boating

East Bay Yacht Basin, 322-3754
Nassau Harbour Club, 323-1771
Nassau Yacht Haven, 322-3601

Golf

Crystal Palace/Cable Beach Golf Club, 327-8231
Paradise Island Golf CLub, 326-3925
Divi Bahamas Beach Resort Golf Club, 326-4391

Horseback Riding

Happy Trails Stable, New Providence Island. Phone 326-1820.

Parasailing

Available at *Nassau Beach Hotel, Crystal Palace/Cable Beach, Paradise Island Resort.*

Scuba Diving and Snorkeling

Bahama Divers Ltd., 326-5644
Peter Hughes at Divi Bahamas Beach Resort, 326-4391
Sun Divers at Sheraton British Colonial Hotel, 322-3301

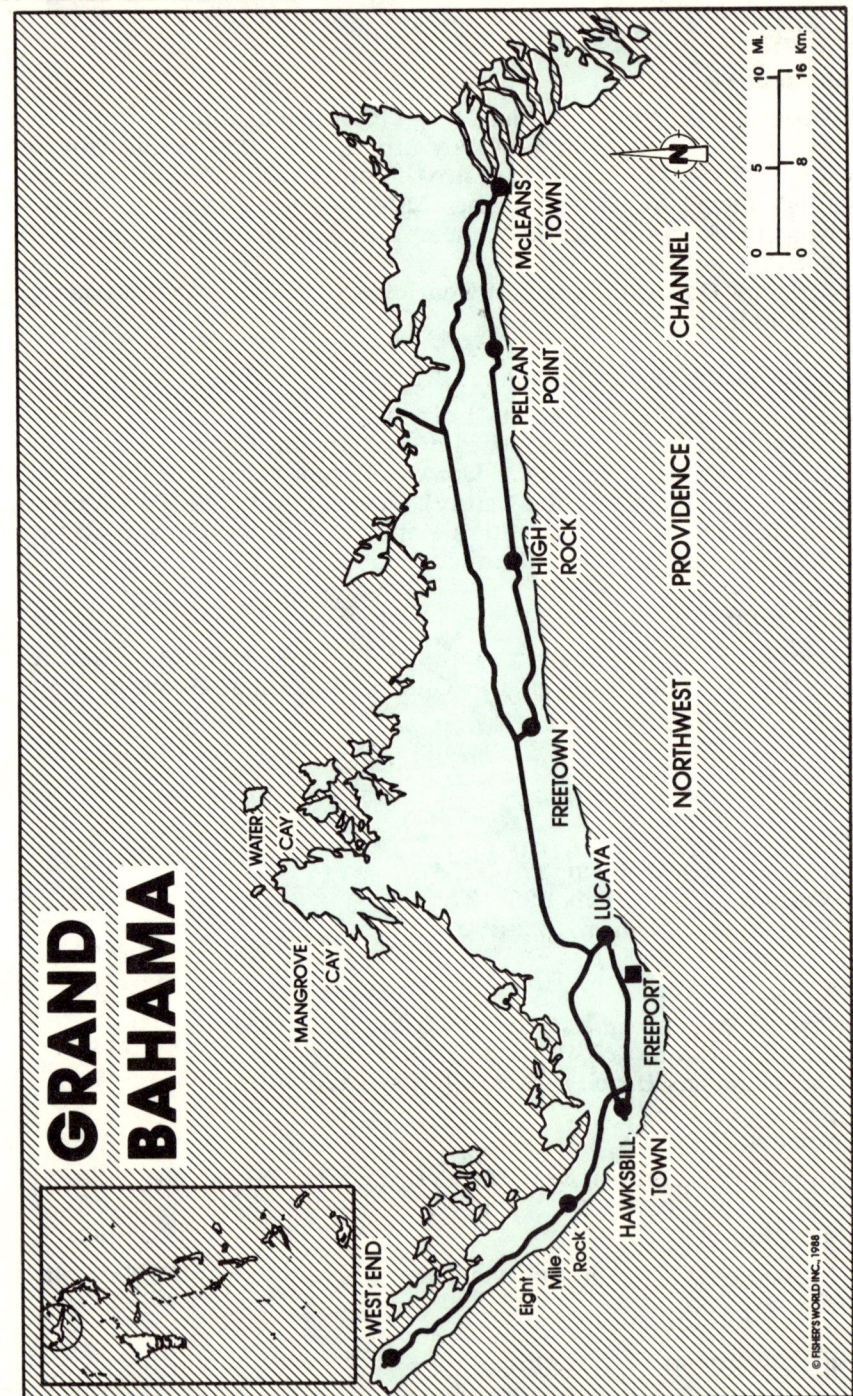

Hartley's Undersea Walk, at Nassau Yacht Haven, 322-8234

Tennis

Britannia Towers: 9 hard
Crystal Palace/Cable Beach Hotel & Casino: 5 clay (4 night lit)
Nassau Beach Hotel: 9 Flexipave (6 night lit)
Ocean Club & Tennis Resort: 9 HarTru (4 night lit)
Paradise Towers (Paradise Island): 3 hard (all night lit)
Royal Bahamian Hotel & Villas: 2 Flexipave (all night lit)
Sheraton Grand Hotel: 4 hard (all night lit)
Wyndham Ambassador Beach Hotel: 8 hard (4 night lit)
Holiday Inn: 4 hard (2 night lit)
Loews Harbour Cove: 2 hard (all night lit)
Sheraton British Colonial Hotel: 3 hard (all night lit)
Divi Bahamas Beach Resort & Country Club: 4 hard (2 night lit)
Bahamas Beach Inn: 2 hard
Club Med: 20 HarTru (9 night lit)

Windsurfing

Available at *Wyndham Ambassador Beach Hotel, Crystal Palace/Cable Beach Hotel & Casino, Paradise Island Resort & Casino.*

Getting Around

Transport unique to Nassau: the horse-drawn surrey. Cost is about $8 to $10 an hour. Carriages easily found at Rawson Square and off Bay Street on Frederick Street.

DIRECTORY

Emergency Telephone Numbers

Police or Fire: 919
Ambulance: 322-2221
Hospital: 322-2861
Bahamas Air Sea Rescue: 322-3877
Electrical Repair: 325-5561.

Diplomatic and Consular Representatives

American Embassy: Queen Street, P.O. Box N-8197, phone 322-4753.

British High Commission:, Bitco Building, 3rd Floor, East Street, P.O. Box N-7516, phone 325-7471; emergencies after hours, 326-6222.

Canadian Consulate: Ground Floor, Out Island Traders Building, East Bay Street, phone 323-2123; emergencies 325-7348.

Freeport

Tourist Information

Nassau International Airport:: phone 327-6833.
At Rawson Square on Bay Street:: phone 3267-9781.

Service Telephone Numbers

Information: 916
Time: 917
Weather: 915
Bahamas Sports Information Center: for information before leaving home, phone toll free (800)32-SPORT.

Religious Services

Christ Church Cathedral (Anglican), King & George streets, phone 322-4186.
St. Francis Xavier's Cathedral (Roman Catholic), West & West Hill Streets, phone 323-3802.
Also, check with tourist information desks or your hotel for other Anglican, Assemblies of God, Bahai, Baptist, Christian Science, Church of God of Prophecy, Greek Orthodox, Jehovah's Witness, Jewish, Methodist, Lutheran, Presbyterian, Roman Catholic, and Seventh Day Adventist houses of worship.

GRAND BAHAMA

HOTELS

Lucayan Beach Resort & Casino P.O.Box F-336, Lucaya. Phone (809)373-7777; toll free (800)772-1227. *Moderate to Expensive.*
Atlantik Beach Hotel P.O.Box F-531. Phone (809)373-1444; toll free (800)622-6770. *Moderate to Expensive.*
Bahamas Princess Hotel and **Princess Tower.** P.O.Box F-207. Phone toll free in US (800)223-1818; toll free in Quebec and Ontario Provinces (800)268-7140; other Provinces (800)268-7176; London (01)439-8027. *Expensive to Extravagant.*
Holiday Inn P.O.Box F-2496. Phone (809)373-1333. *Expensive.*
Xanadu Beach Marina Resort P.O.Box F-2438. Phone (809)352-6782. *Extravagant.*
Lucayan Marina Hotel P.O.Box F-336. Phone (809)373-8888; toll free (800)772-1227. *Moderate to Expensive.*

Specialized Accommodations

Deep Water Cay One-half mile out from the Grand Bahama "mainland". *Expensive.*
Jack Tar Village. West End. Phone toll free (800)527-9299. *Expensive.*

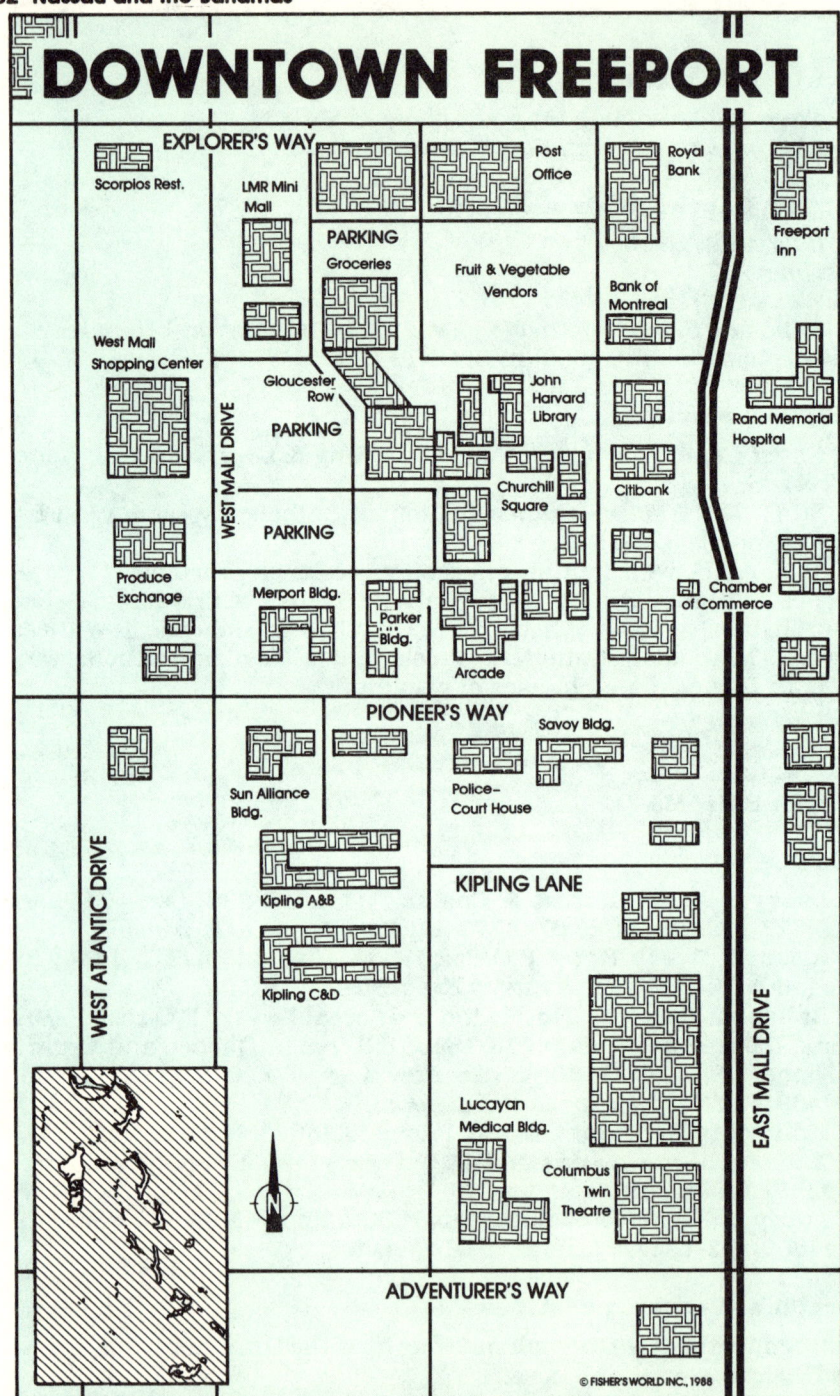

RESTAURANTS

Les Oursins Lucayan Beach Resort. 373-1066. E*xtravagant.*
Cotillion Room In the Princess Tower Hotel. *Extravagant.*
Lucaya Country Club's Famous Dining Room Albacore Street off Sargent Major Drive. *Extravagant.*
The Rib Room In the Bahama Princess Hotel. 352-6721. *Extravagant.*
Ruby Swiss Restaurant At Bahama Princess Hotel's Ruby Golf Course. 352-8507. *Extravagant.*
Beef Cellar In Princess Tower Hotel.*Extravagant.*
Escoffier Room In Xanadu Beach Hotel. 352-6782. *Extravagant.*
Silvano's The Mall, across from the casino. *Moderate.*
Buccaneer Club At Deadman's Reef, Eight Mile Rock. 348-3794. *Expensive.*
Captain's Charthouse One East Sunrise at Beachway Drive, Lucaya. 373-3900. *Expensive.*
Harry's American Bar Deadman's Reef. Lunch only. *Expensive.*
Island Lobster House On the Mall. *Expensive.*
Japanese Steak House International Bazaar. 352-9521. *Expensive.*
Marcella's Italian Village Inn East Mall and Kipling. *Expensive.*
Nino's Fishing Hole Restaurant & Bar Fishing Hole Rd. (Queen's Hwy) on the Bay. *Moderate.*
The Stoned Crab Taino Beach, Lucaya. 373-1442. *Moderate.*
New Peace & Plenty Restaurant Eight Mile Rock. 373-1814. *Inexpensive.*
Freddie's Hunters, just outside Freeport. 352-3250. *Inexpensive to Moderate.*

Pubs

Pub On The Mall *Inexpensive to Moderate.*
Sir Winston Churchill Pub Mall. *Moderate to Expensive.*
Britannia Pub Lucaya Harbour. *Inexpensive to Moderate.*

ENTERTAINMENT

Performing Arts

Watch for posted bulletins. Check Freeport Players Guild in Regency Theatre. The Grand Bahamas Players present plays in Bahamian lingo.

Gambling

Lucayan Beach Casino, beachside. Comcheck allows players to draw against credit cards. *Princess Casino,* in heart of Freeport's tourist area.

Note: Neither Bahamians nor tourists under twenty-one are allowed to gamble in these casinos.

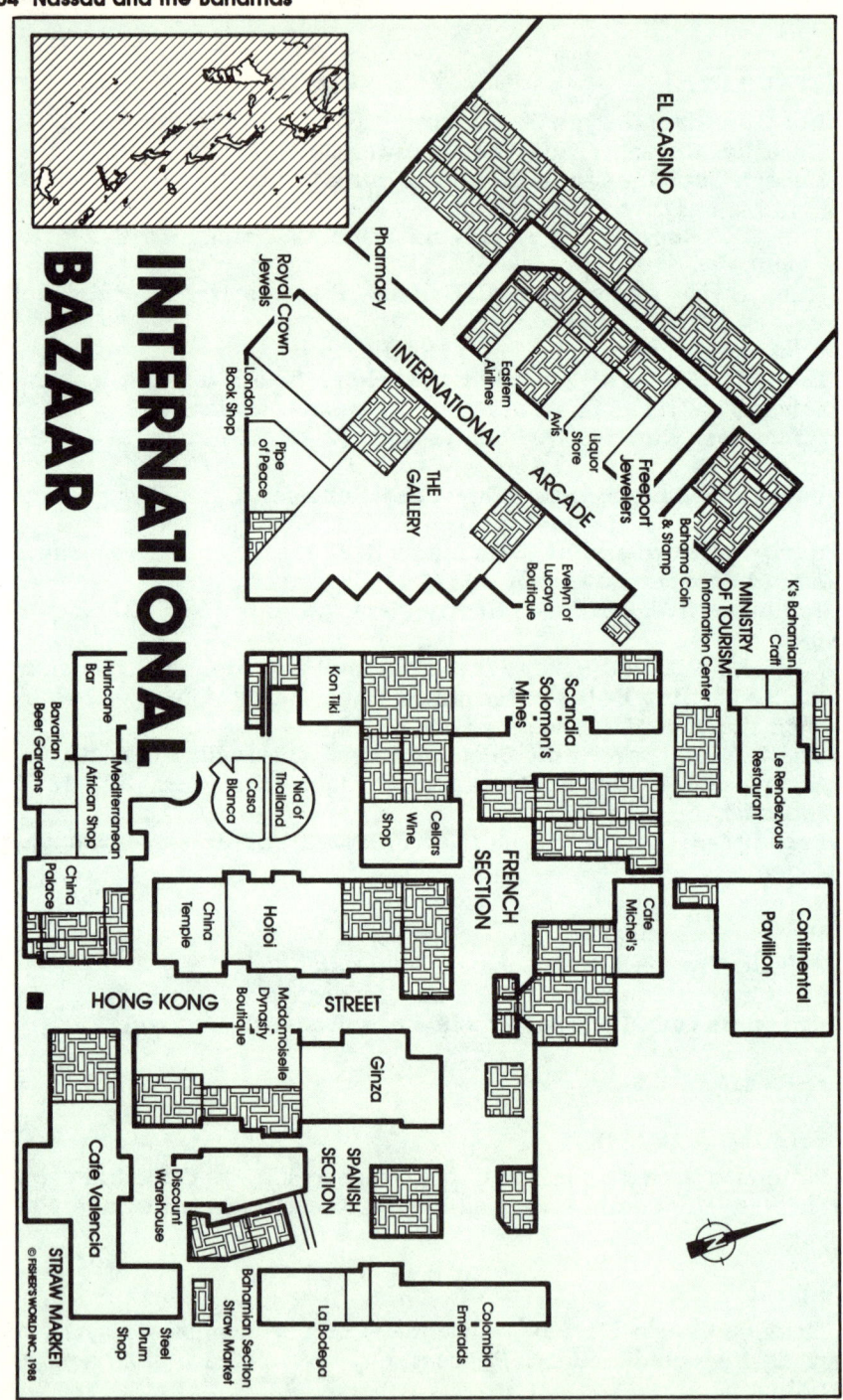

Shows and Revues

Casino Royale Theatre, in Princess Casino. Two shows nightly, except Monday. *Palm Pavillion*, in Bahamas Princess Hotel. Live shows and festival-type productions. Holiday Inn, festive evenings each week. *Pirate's Den*, Lucayan Marina Hotel, native show.

Discos

Tipsy Turtle Disco, Holiday Inn; *Coral Cave Discotheque* at Bahamas Princess Hotel; *Desserts & Disco*, Xanadu Beach; *Sultan's Tent*, Princess Tower Hotel. Dancing at all from 9 P.M. to 3 A.M. All mix disco with live entertainment. Local spots: *Studio 9; Sandpiper; Orbit Club Disco; Village Calypso Disco; The Back Room* serves breakfast, lunch, dinner-offers 25-percent tourist discounts.

SHOPPING

International Bazaar; Hawksbill Shopping Plaza; East Sunrise Shopping Centre; Town Centre, Churchill Square.

Antiques: The Old Curiosity Shop.
Art: The Gallery.
Bahamian Gifts: Straw Market; Beachcomber; Bahama Mama; K's Bahamian Crafts; the Happening; the Linen Shop; Little Sparrow Steel Drum Shop; Rhona's Gift Shop.
Blown Glass: Arcade. Work by Sidney Pratt.
Books: London Bookshop.
Brass: Bombay Bazaar; China Temple; India House; Mid-East Emporium; Sabra Shop.
Cameras: Ernie's Studio & Camera Center, Ltd.(Parker Building, downtown); Ginza; Hotoi Ltd.; Pipe of Peace; Fast Foto Xanadu Beach Hotel Arcade (60-minute color film processing).
Candy: Chocolate Box; Mortimer's Candy Kitchen.
Carvings: Higgs Brothers, China Temple; Colombian Shop; India Houase; Mediterranea; Nid of Thailand.
China, Crystal, Giftware: Scandia (Solomon's Mines); Midnight Sun; Casa Miro; China Temple; Continental Pavillion Jewelry; Tang's Art Work.
Children's Clothing: Cardon's Tots and Teens; Caprice.
Coins and Stamps: Bahama Coin & Stamp Ltd.
Copperware: Casa Simpatico; Colombian Shop; Sabra Shop.
Eyeglasses: Optical Boutique El Casino.
Fabrics and Linens: the Linen Shop; Kon-Tiki.
Gourmet Items: Midnight Sun.
Jewelry: Royal Crown Jewels; Freeport Jewellers Ltd.; Colombia Emeralds; Greenfire Emeralds of Colombia; La Tienda; the Rock Shop (La Tienda II); Continental Pavillion Jewelry Shop; Anata-O Shop; Casa Simpatico; Bombay Bazaar; Bengazi; Charm Chest; El Galleon; El Rondel; Hotoi Ltd.; Mediterranea; Nid of Thailand; the Piaka; Kon-Tiki; Azteca de Oro; Mid-East Emporium; Sabra Shop; Belle Bagaille.

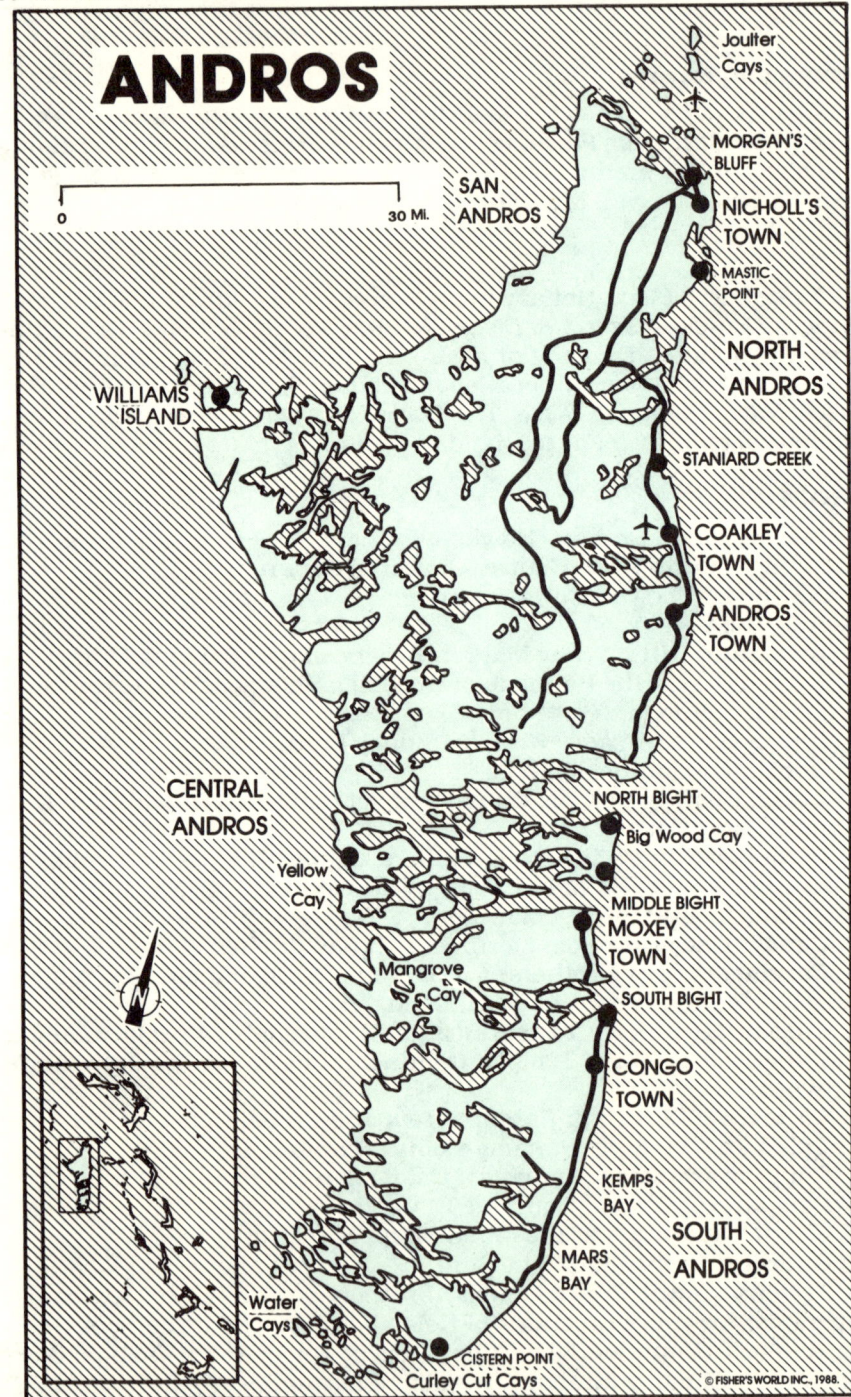

Knitwear: Lee's Hong Kong Shop; London Pacesetter Boutique; Evelyn of Lucaya Boutique.
Leather: Leather & Things; Casa Miro; Fantastico; El Mercado Mexicano; Mediterranea.
Liquors and Spirits: Arcade Liquor Shop; Carib Liquor Store; Cellers Wine Shop.
Lingerie: Continential Pavillion Lingerie Shop; Playgirl Ltd.
Men's Wear: Executive Men's Shop; John Kendrick's Fashions for Men (Churchill Square); R.P.'s Men's Boutique; Caprice; Hong Kong Tailor; the Piaka; Bombay Bazaar; Nid of Thailand; Sabra Shop.
Perfume: Parfums de Paris; Continential Pavillion Perfume Bar.
Pewter: Midnight Sun.
Prescriptions and Sundries: City Pharmacy; Grand Bahama Pharmacy (E. Sunrise Shopping Centre); L.M.R. Drugs (Churchill Square, Town Centre).
Records: Sounds Unlimited.
Silver: Casa Simpatico.
Straw Goods: Straw Market.
Toys: Cardon's Tots and Teen; L.M.R. Drugs; Hawksbill Fashion & Department Stores.
Watches: Mademoiselle Dynasty; Bahama Coin & Stamp Ltd.; Continental Pavillion Jewelry Shop; Ginza; Hotoi Ltd.; Freeport Jewellers Ltd.
Women's Wear: Evelyn of Lucaya Boutique; Caprice; London Pacesetter Boutique; Dynasty; Love Boutique; Sabra Shop; Bahama Mama; Caribana Boutique; Fol-o-Fashions; the PLaka; Bombay Bazaar; Azteca de Oro; El Mercado Mexicano; Colombian Shop; Nid of Thailand; Lee's Hong Kong Shop; Hawksbill Fashion & Department Store (Hawksbill Shopping Plaza).

MUSEUMS

Museum of Underwater Exploration Underwater Explorers Society, Lucayan Bay Hotel.
Royal Crown Jewels, displayed in the International Bazaar.

Parks and Gardens

Garden of Groves, on Lucaya's Shannon Golf & Country Club property. Includes *Fern Gully* and *Groves Museum*.

Tours around Grand Bahama Island

Contact Tourist Information Centres or:
International Travel & Tours Ltd., P.O.Box F-850. Phone 352-6910.
Playasol Travel Sevices Ltd., P.O.Box F-2585. Phone 352-4811.
Bahamas Travel Agency Ltd., P.O.Box F-3778. Phone 352-3141, ext. 1000.
Fun Tours, P.O.Box F-1159. Phone 352-7005.
Cruises via Reefs Tours Ltd., P.O.Box F-2609. Phone 373-5800.

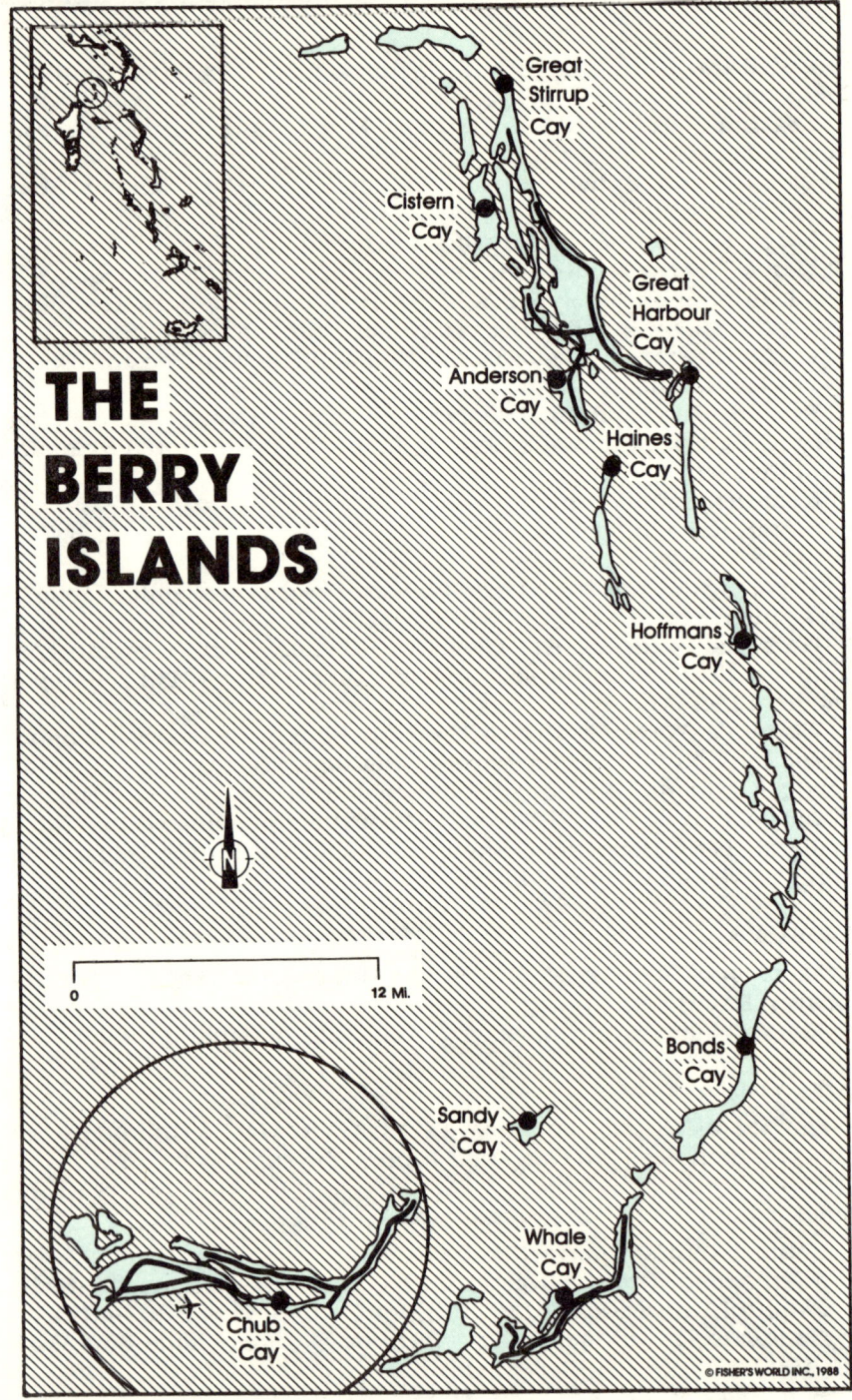

SPORTS

Boating

Freeport/Lucaya area: *Running Mon Marina*, P.O.Box F-565. Phone 352-6834.
Lucayan Harbour Inn Marina, P.O.Box F-2677, phone 373-1677.
Xanadu Beach Hotel Marina, P.O.Box F-2438, phone 362-6780.
On Grand Lucayan Waterway: *Sir Charles Hayward Yacht Club*.
West End: *Jack Tar Village*.

Fishing

See Captain Stan Lockhart at *Lucayan Marine/ Hotel Spa*. Also Captain Alonzo Lowe at *Xanadu Beach Hotel Marina*. Also the Casper at *Running Mon Marina*; *Silver Point Condominium*, phone 373-5018; *Jack Tar Village*.

Golf

Bahamas Princess Hotel, P.O.Box F-207, phone 352-6751 (two courses).
Bahama Reef Golf & Country Club, P.O.Box F-1790, phone 373-1055
Fortune Hill Golf & Country Club, P.O.Box F-2619, phone 373-4500
Lucayan Golf & Country Club, P.O.Box F-333, phone 373-1066.
Jack Tar Village, West End, phone 348-2030.

Horseback Riding

Pinetree Stables, P.O.box F-2915, phone 373-3600.

Parasailing

Available at *Lucayan Beach Resort, Atlantik Beach Hotel; Holiday Inn*.

Scuba Diving and Snorkeling

Underwater Explorers Society, Lucayan Beach Hotel, P.O.Box F-2433, phone 373-1244. Special trips on *Holiday Dream*, phone 373-1333; *TriWind*, phone 373-5880.

Tennis

Bahamas Princess Hotel: 6 hard; 2 night lit
Bahamas Tower: 3 clay; 3 hard (all night lit)
Channel House: 2 hard
Holiday Inn: 4 hard, plus lessons
Shalimar Hotel: 2 asphalt
Silver Sea Lodge: 2 hard
Xanadu: 3 hard (2 night lit)
Jack Tar Village: 16; 6 clay (all night lit) for guests only.

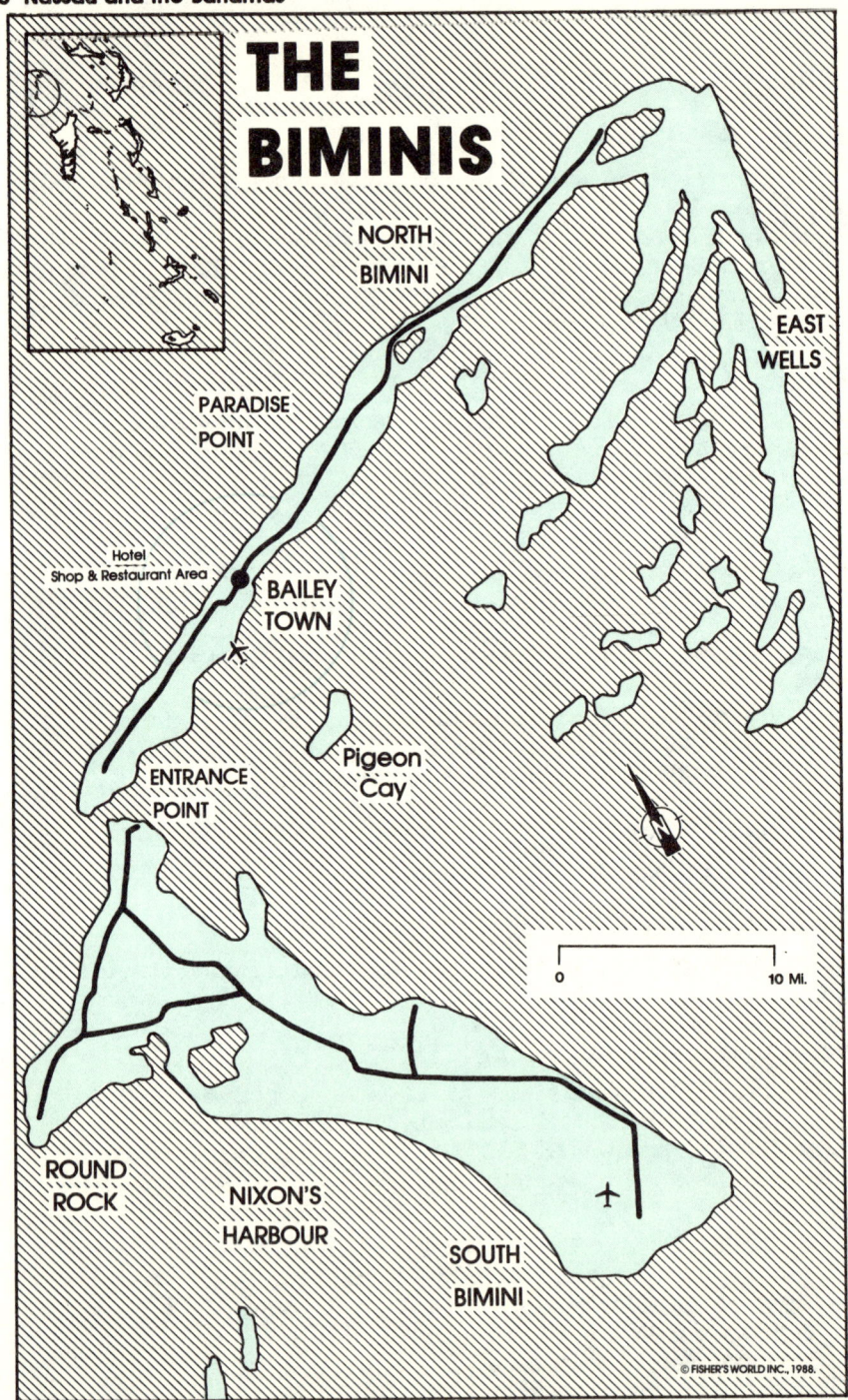

Lucayan Beach Resort: 4 courts (all night lit)

Waterskiing

Holiday Water Sports, at Holiday Inn, phone 373-1458.

Windsurfing

Holiday Water Sports, phone 373-1458.
Atlantic Beach Hotel Windsurfing School, phone 373-1444.

DIRECTORY

Emergency Numbers

Ambulance: 352-2689; 352-6735
Police Department:: International Building, P.O.Box F-82, phone 352-8333.
Air-Sea Rescue: 373-2264, 352-9889
Fire Department: 352-8888
Power/Water: 352-8411

Tourist Information

Ministry of Tourism Information Centre: International Bazaar & International Airport, P.O.Box F-251, phone 352-8044

Service Numbers

Travel Agent: R.H.Curry Ltd., 10 Savoy Building, P.O.Box F-453, phone 352-7234 (IATA & ASTA).
Telegrams : 352-6227
Dry Cleaner: Jiffy, Town Centre Shop, 352-7079

Religious Services

Emanuel Baptist Church, West End at Eleuthera Drive, Hawksbill, phone 352-6461
Christ the King Episcopal Church, E. Atlantic at Pioneers Way, phone 352-5255.
Mary Star of the Sea (Roman Catholic), East Sunrise Highway at Beach Road West, phone 373-3300/3456
Freeport Hebrew Congregation, East Sunrise Highway (no Telephone), services Fridays, 8:30 P.M.

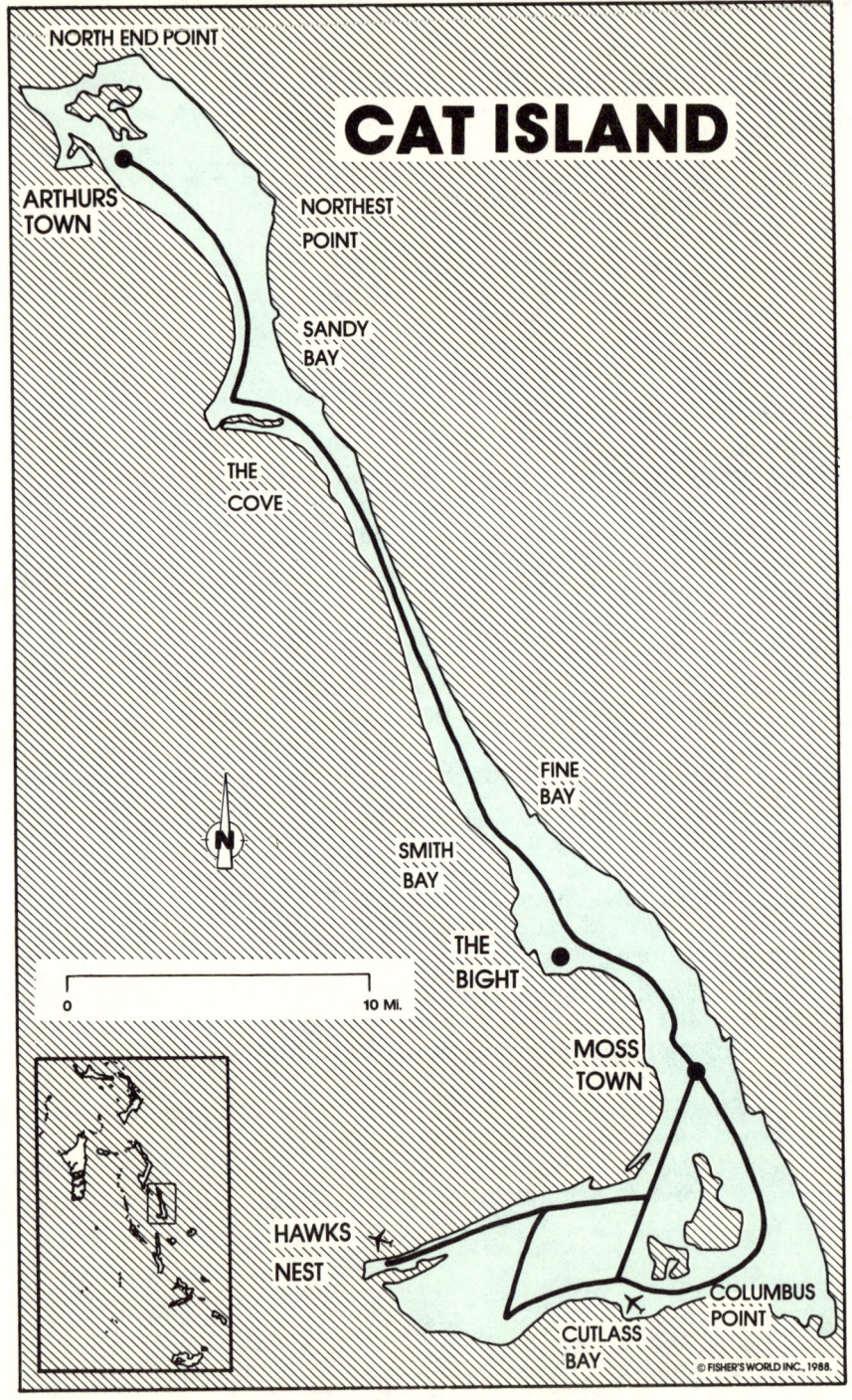

THE FAMILY ISLANDS

ANDROS

Andros, CENTRAL ANDROS

Getting There

From Nassau, Bahamasair regular daily service to and from northern San Andros Airport, Andros Town Central Airport. In south Andros, airstrips at Mangrove Cay and Congo Town. Some resorts have private planes. Seaplanes land at Central Fresh Creek, southern Congo Town and northern San Andros. Mailboats regularly from Nassau-five to seven hours one way.

Hotels

Small Hope Bay Lodge Write P.O.Box 21667, Fort Lauderdale, Fl 33335. Phone (809)368-2014; in FL (305)463-9130; toll free (800)223-6961. *Moderate.*

Andros, CONGO TOWN, south

Las Palmas Beach Hotel P.O.Box 800. Phone (809)329-4661.
Congo Beach Gardens and **Royal Palm** are *Inexpensive* guest houses.

Andros, MANGROVE CAY

Contact through Bahamas Reservations Service: in Little Harbour **Bannister's Guest House** (AP only), **Cool Breeze Cottage, White Sand Beach Hotel, Mangrove Cay Beach Hotel, Moxey's Guest House**, and **Longley's Guest House** in Lisbon Creek.

Andros, NORTH ANDROS

Hotels

Andros Beach Hotel & Villas Nicholl's Town. Phone toll free (800)327-8150. Home of annual Bahamas Freediving Championship.. *Inexpensive to Moderate.*
Tradewind Villas P.O.Box 4465. Phone (809)329-2040. Nicholl's Town. *Inexpensive.*

BERRY ISLANDS

Getting There

Bahamasair offers twice-weekly service to and from the airport at Chub Cay. Privaye planes land at private airstrips. Mailboat *M/V Captain Dean*, from Nassau Tuesdays or Wednesdays.

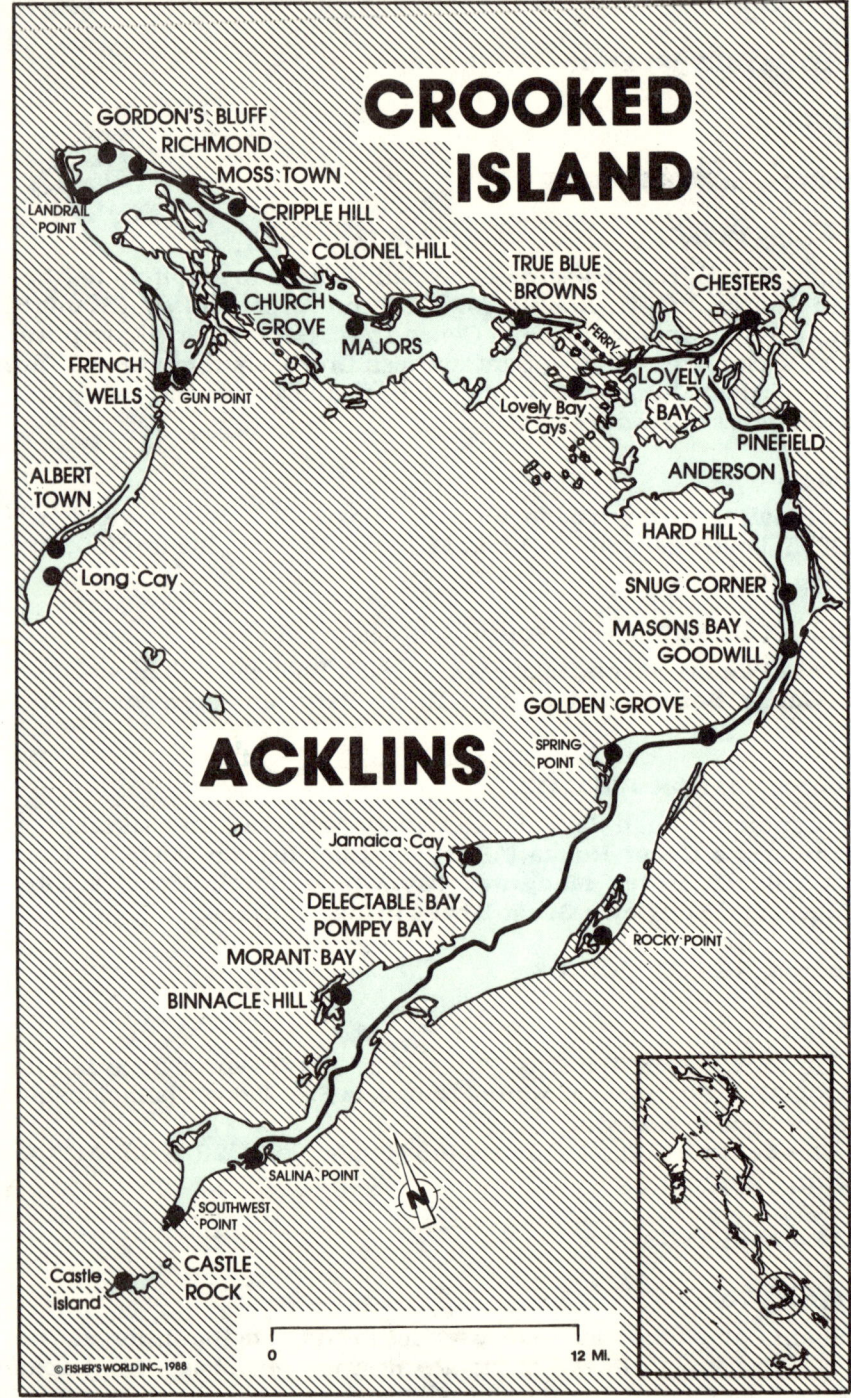

Hotels

Chub Cay Club Phone (809)325-1490. On private island. Admits nonmembers. *Flying Bridge Restaurant. Extravagent.*

THE BIMINIS

Getting There

Chalk's International Airlines has regular seaplane service to North Bimini from Miami and Paradise Island. Also lands on Cat Cay seaplane ramp. Private and charter craft land at South Bimini Airport. Mailboat *M/V Bimini Mack* from Nassau Thursdays to Cat Cay and alice Town (north Bimini).

Hotels

Bimini's Big Game Fishing Club & Hotel P.O.Box 699, Alice Town. Annual Bimini Billfish Tournament. *Moderate to Expensive.*
Bimini's Blue Water Marina P.O.Box 627, Alice Town. Phone (809)347-2166. *Inexpensive to Moderate.*
Compleat Angler P.O.Box 601, Alice Town.

Restaurants

Bimini's Big Game Fishing Club & Hotel, Bimini's Blue Water Anchorage Restaurant, The Compleat Angler.
The Red Lion *Inexpensive to Moderate.*
Fisherman's Paradise Restaurant & Bar *Inexpensive to Moderate.*

Sports

Weech's Bimini Dock; Underwater Adventures.

Historic Sites

Fountain of Youth and *Atlantis*, South Bimini.

CAT ISLAND

Cat Cay Club Private Island. Phone (305)757-6439. *Extravagent*

CROOKED AND ACKLINS ISLANDS

Getting There

Weekly Bahamasair flights between Nassau and Crooked Island Airport, where private planes also land. Airstrip on Acklins Island. Government ferry between Crooked Island and Acklins Island runs between 9:00A.M. and 4:00P.M. Mailboat from Nassau weekly for ports on Crooked Island, Acklins Island, and Mayaguana.

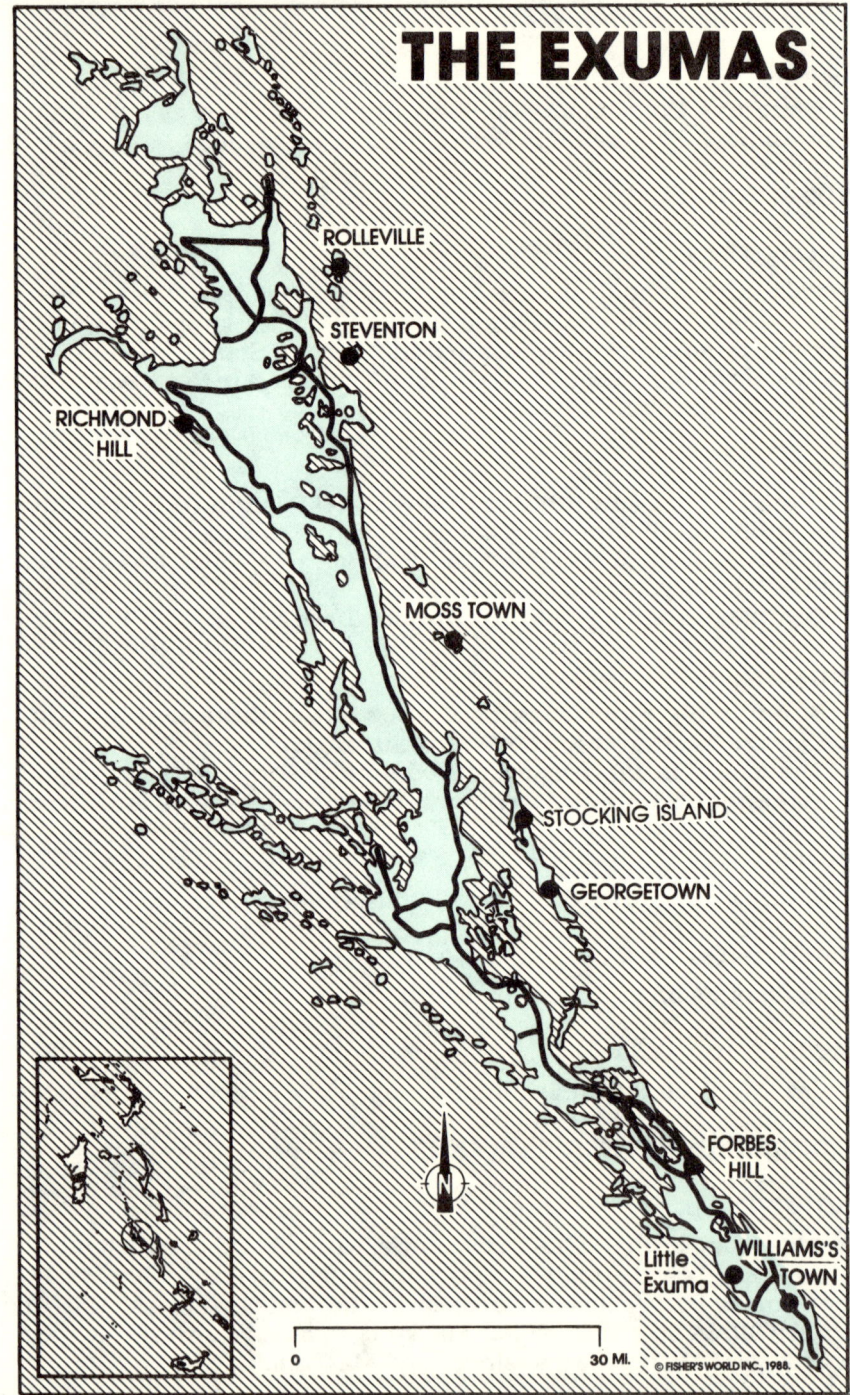

Hotels

Pittstown Point Landings Limited Inn At Landrill Point, Crooked Island.. Closed September. *Expensive.*
Sunny Lea Guest House, Colonial Hill, Crooked Island.
T & S Guest House Cabbage Hill, Crooked Island.
Williams Hilltop On Acklins Island.

EXUMAS

Exumas, GREAT EXUMA

Getting There

Direct service twice-weekly on Bahamasair from Miami. Regular service from Nassau. Private craft also land at George Town Airport. Mailboat from Nassau on Tuesdays for George Town; on Thursdays for Stanial Cay, Black Point, Farmers Cay, and Barraterre.

Hotels

Out Island Inn P.O.Box 49, George Town. Phone (809)336-2171. *Inexpensive to Moderate.*
Peace & Plenty Hotel P.O.Box 55, George Town. Phone (809)336-2551/2; toll free in U.S. and Canada (800)327-5118. *Inexpensive.*
Pieces Of Eight Hotel P.O.Box 49, George Town. Phone (809)336-2600. *Inexpensive to Expensive.*
Pirates Point Villas P.O.Box 23, Kidd Cove. *Inexpensive.*
Regatta Point Kidd Cay. Phone (809)336-2206. *Inexpensive.*
Two Turtles Inn P.O.Box 51, George Town. Phone (809)336-2545. *Moderate.*

Sports

Exuma Divers, George Town 336-2710; *Clifford Dean's Charter Fishing Service,* George Town; *Minns Water Sports,* 336-2604; *Exuma Docking Services,* 336-2578.

Vehicle rentals: *R.R. Maynard Rentals,* George Town; *Sam Gray,* Out Island Inn.

Exumas, STANIEL CAY

Staniel Cay Yacht Club Phone Florida (305)467-6850. FAP only. *Moderate.*

Getting Around

Exuma Flotilla, Ltd., P.O. Box N-910, Nassau.

INAGUA

Ford's Inagua Inn Closed part of the year. *Inexpensive.*
Main House Open year-round. *Inexpensive.*

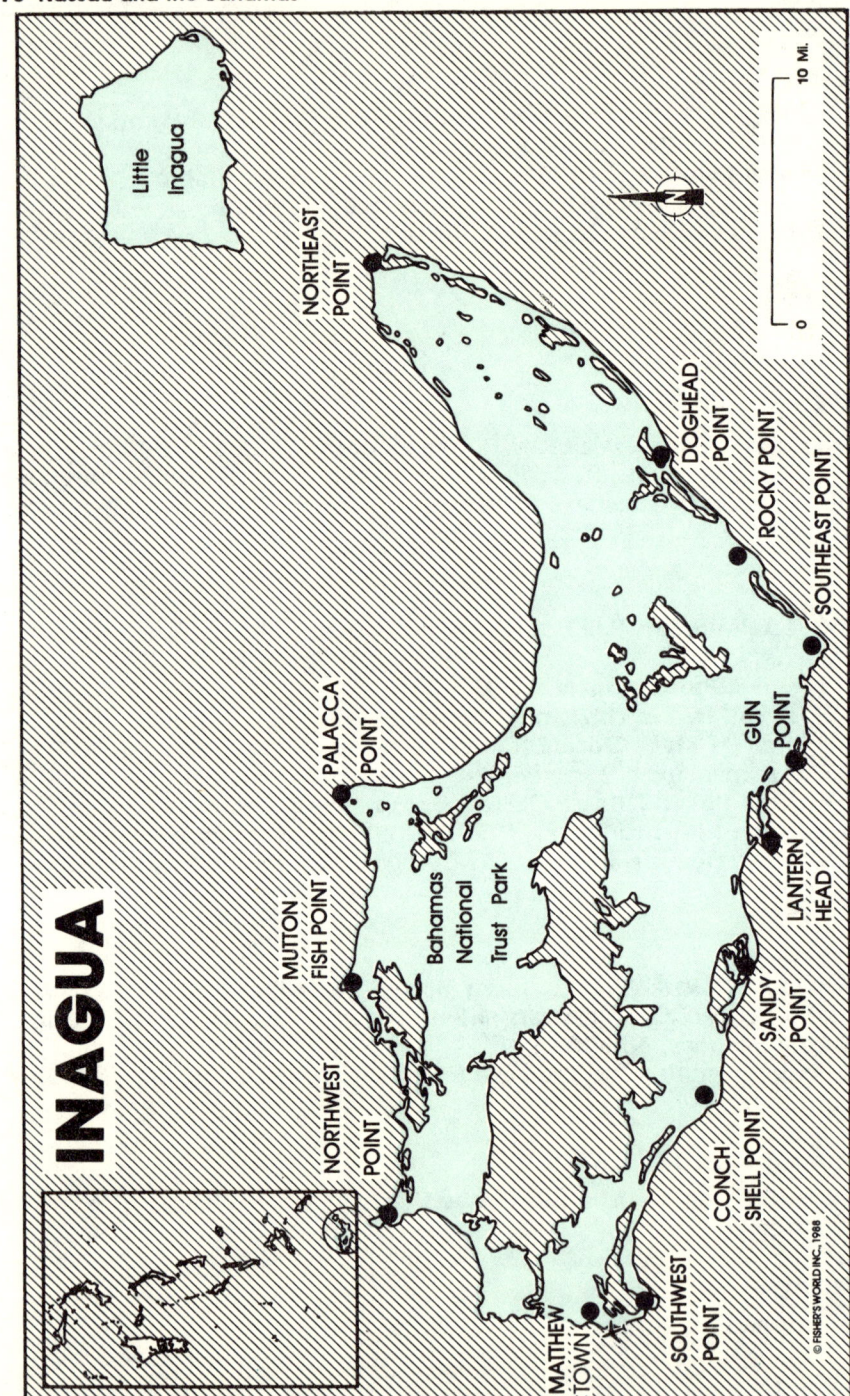

Sports

Matthew Town Dock.

LONG ISLAND

Stella Maris Inn, Marina/Yacht Club and Estates P.O.Box 105, northern Long Island. Phone (305)467-0466. *Moderate to Expensive.*

Restaurants

Hibiscus Inn, Thompson Bay Inn Patio and Grill.

RUM CAY

Rum Cay Club P.O.Box 22396, Fort Lauderdale, FL 33335. Phone FL collect (305)467-8355; toll free (800)334-6869; Bahamas Reservation Service (800)327-0787. FAP. *Moderate to Expensive.*

THE OUTER FAMILY ISLANDS

Note: Most Outer Family Islands hotels, etc., cost notably less than similar facilities in Nassau or Freeport and this is reflected in my rate classifications. I base hotel rate categories on comparable costs of rooms alone (**EP**). However, some establishments supply meals and include food costs in regular rates. Such places are marked (**AP** or **FAP** only, or **MAP** minimum), but food costs were deducted in order to present comparison rate categories. (See Settling Down in Travel Planner).

ABACO

Abaco, ELBOW CAY—including HOPE TOWN

Hotels

Abaco Inn Six miles from Marsh Harbour Airport. Phone (809)367-2666. Closed mid-September through mid-November. *Moderate to Expensive.*

Hope Town Harbour Lodge Elbow Cay. Twenty minutes from Marsh Harbour Airport. Phone (809)366-0095. *Moderate to Expensive.*

Museum

Wyannie Malone Historical Museum Hope Town.

Abaco, GREEN TURTLE CAY

Green Turtle Yacht Club & Marina Green Turtle Cay. Phone (809)367-2572. Affiliated with Royal Yachting Association. Closed September 4 to November 8. *Moderate to Very Extravagant*

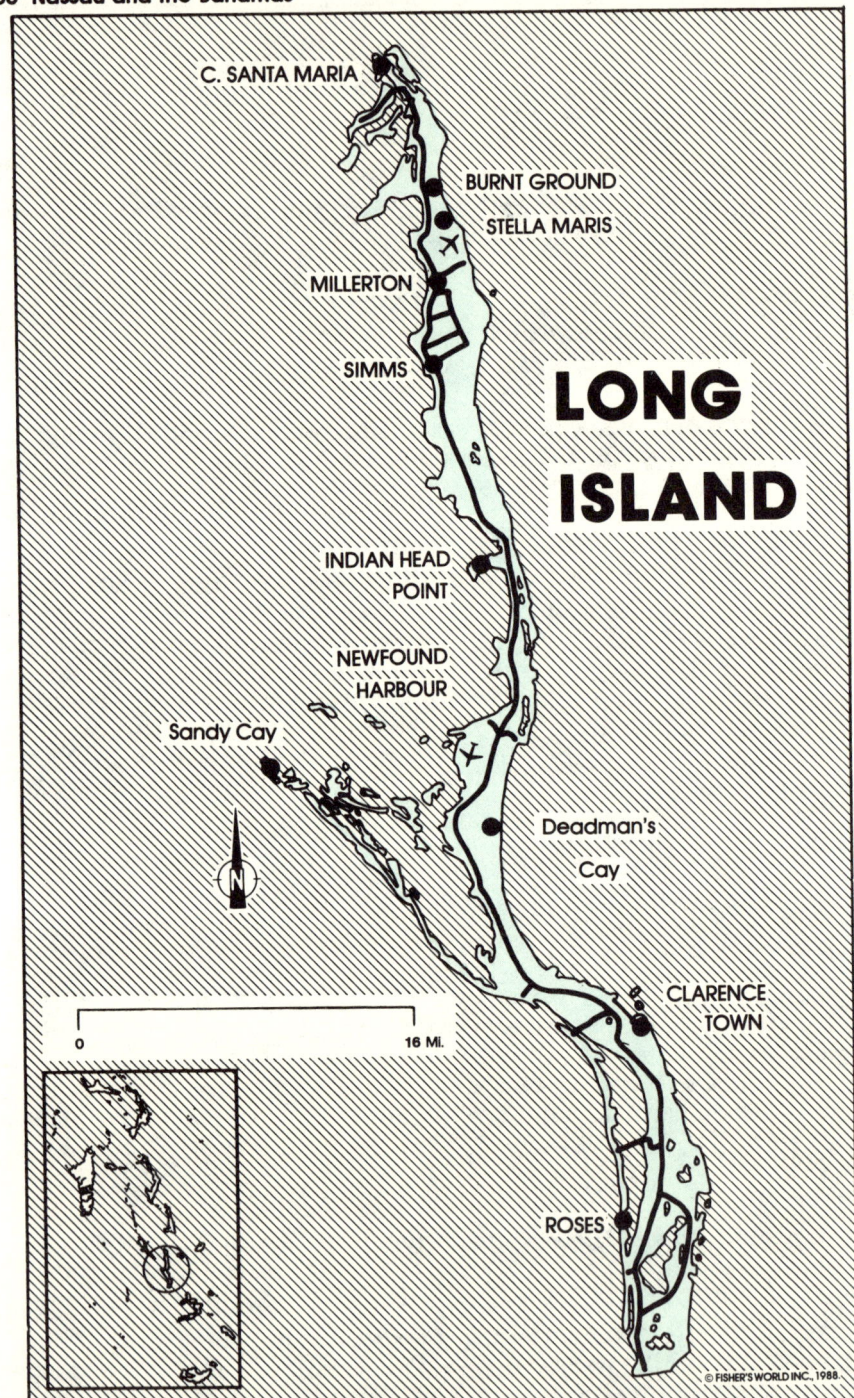

Abaco, GREAT GUANA CAY

Hotels

Bay View Apartments (7 rooms), **Pinder's Cottages** (4), **Guana Beach Resort**(19 rooms)
New Plymouth Club & Inn P.O.Box 462. Phone (809)367-5211 Closed August -September. *Inexpensive.***Bougainvillea Apartments** Closed August. *Inexpensive.*

Spectacles and Displays

Contact **Ministry of Tourism, Sports Division**, phone 322-7500, or write Bay Street, Nassau. Events include Abaco Week; Green Turtle Cay Club/Yachting Club Summer Regatta and Tourney.

Abaco, MARSH HARBOUR

Hotels

Conch Inn Resort & Marina P.O.Box 434, Marsh Harbour. Phone (809)367-2800. *Inexpensive to Moderate.*
Great Abaco Hotel P.O.Box 419, Marsh Harbour. Phone (809)367-2158. Bus service to Treasure Cay golf course. *Inexpensive to Moderate.*

Restaurants

Conch Inn and Great Abaco Hotel Highly recommended. *Moderate to Expensive.*
Kentucky Fried Chicken in town.
The Jib Room Marsh Harbour Marina. Inexpensive to Moderate.
Cynthia's Kitchen In town. Open 8:30 A.M. to 11:00 P.M. *Inexpensive.*
Keys Bakery and Restaurant Closed Sundays. *Inexpensive.*
Mother Merle's Fishnet Restaurant In nearby Dundas Town. Dinner only, 6:00 P.M. to midnight. *Inexpensive.*

Getting Around

Automobile rental: H & L Car Rentals, P.O.Box 507, Marsh Harbour, at Shell station.
Bicycle rental: Western Auto Bicycle Co., P.O.Box507, Marsh Harbour.
Bus service: Jason's Bus Service, P.O.Box 513. From Marsh Harbour to Treasure Cay, Spring City, Dundas Town, Murphy Town; charter available.
Taxis: available by CB from your hotel.
Boat rentals: Junior Roberts, P.O.Box 574, Marsh Harbour. Bahamas Yachting Services, Inc. (BYS). Marsh Harbour Marina, P.O.Box 518. Abaco Bahamas Charters, Ltd., Hope Town.

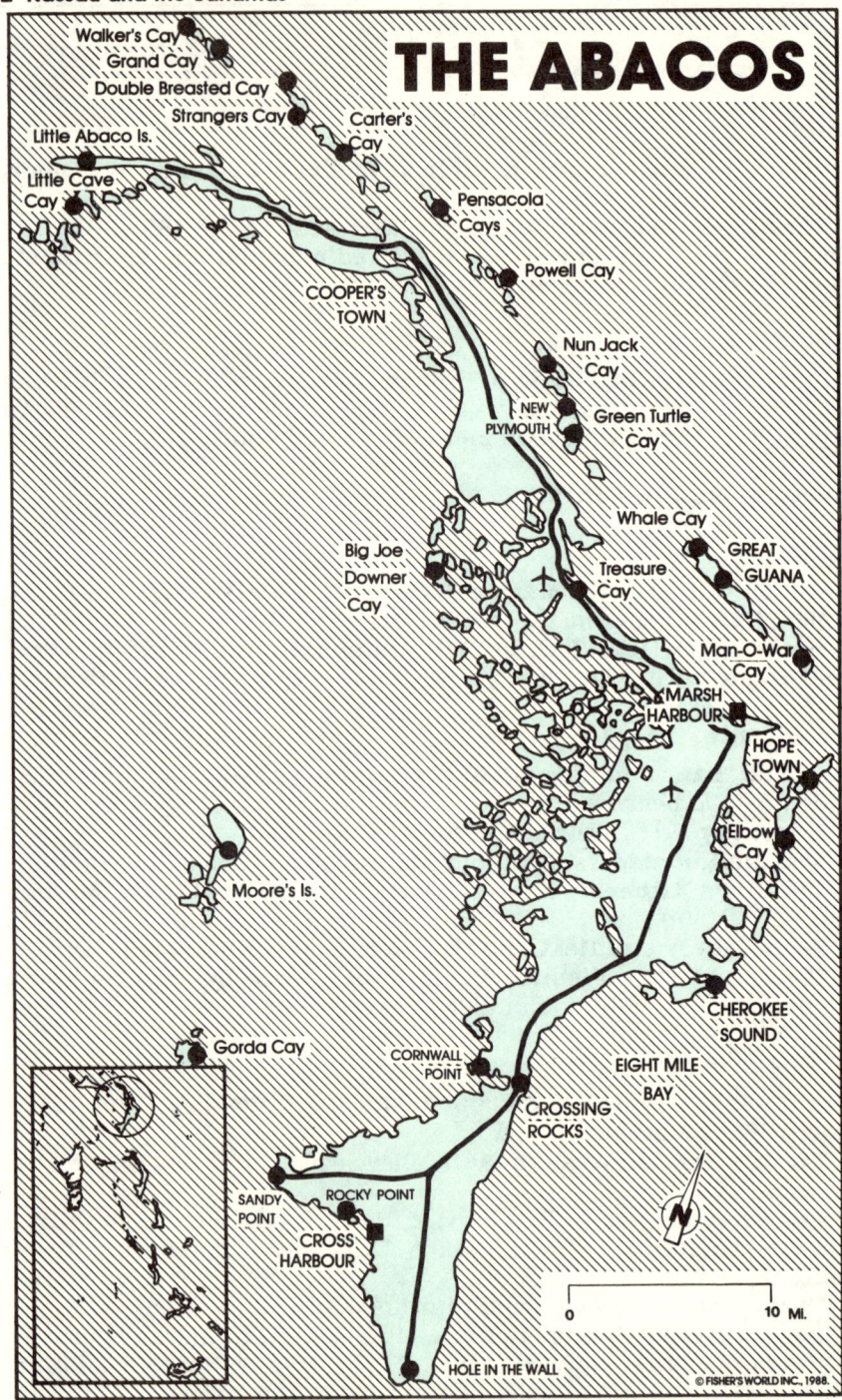

Ferry: Albury's Ferry Service, near Great Abaco Hotel. Regular trips between Marsh Harbour, Hope Town, Guana Cay, Man-O-War Cay. Charters available.

Tours

By land: Contact local taxi guides through hotel.

By Sea: *William H. Albury,* captained by Master Captain Joe Maggio, Conch Inn Marina. $600/person with six passengers.

Nature Reserves: Pelican's Land and Sea Park, between Little Harbour and Tilloo Cay.

Note: Marsh Harbour Rotary meets weekly at Great Abaco Hotel. *Abaco Life* published twice yearly.

Abaco, TREASURE CAY

Treasure Cay Resort Phone FL (305)525-7711; or (800) 432-8257. *Expensive to Extravagant.*

Abaco, WALKER'S CAY

Walker's Cay Hotel and Marina Private island. Self-contained resort at northern point of Abaco. Phone (305)522-1469. *Moderate to Expensive.*

ELEUTHERA

Eleuthera, CAPE ELEUTHERA

Getting There

Bahamasair daily flights from Nassau to North Eleuthera, Governor's Harbour, and Rock Sound. Private airstrip at Cape Eleuthera. Regular mailboat service weekly to Harbour Island, North Eleuthera, Central Eleuthera, Current Island, and Current Village from Nassau-about seven hours one-way.

Hotels

Cape Eleuthera Resort and Yacht Club P.O.Box 48. Phone (809)334-2152.

Eleuthera, GREGORY TOWN

Cambridge Villas, Restaurant, Bar & Grill P.O.Box 1548. Phone (809)332-2269. *Moderate.*

Thompson's Bakery

Eleuthera, GOVERNORS HARBOUR (including South Palmetto Point)

Club Med P.O.Box 80. Reservations direct or through travel agents. Phone (809)332-2270.

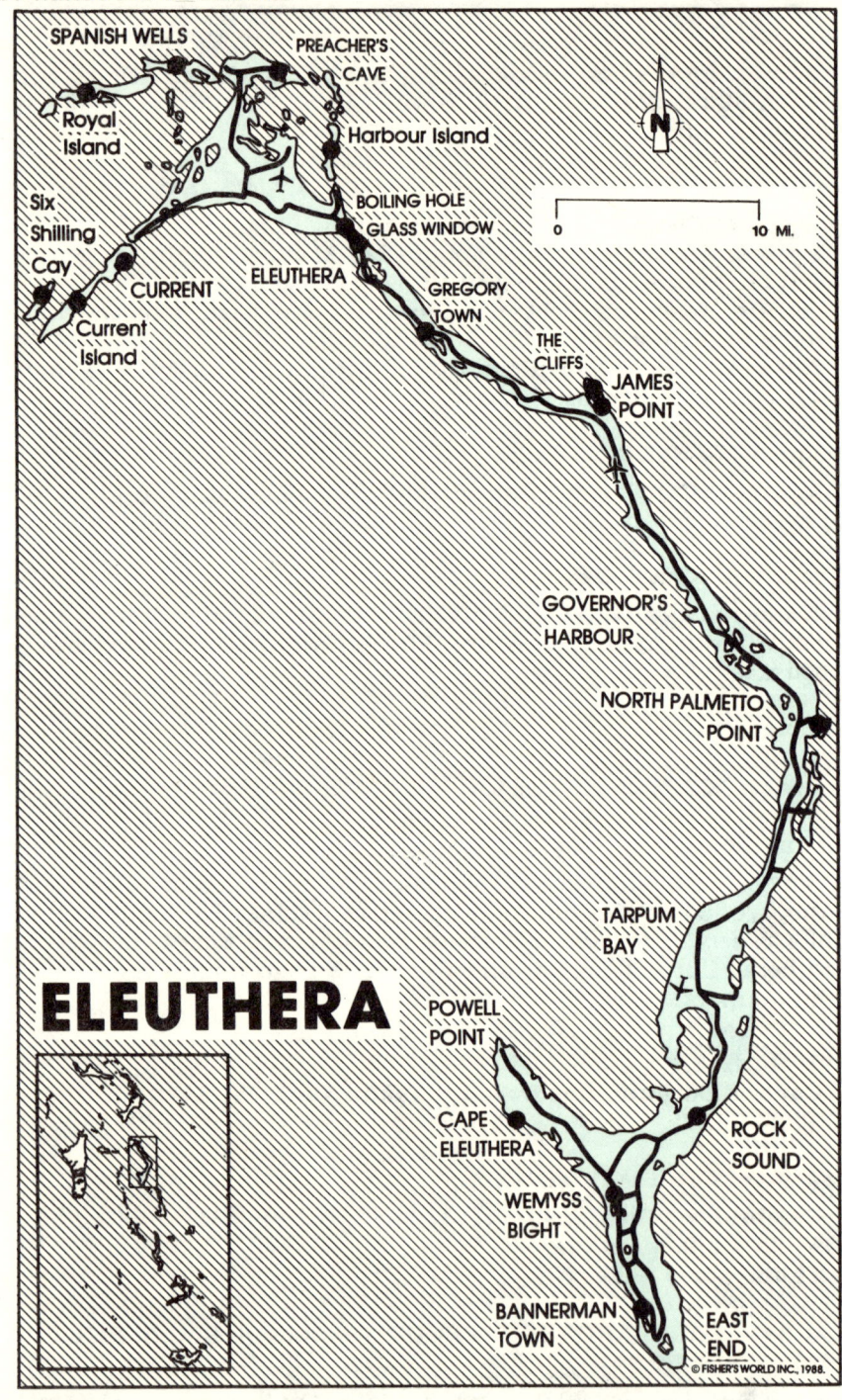

Restaurants

Cigatoo Inn, Muriel's Bakery, The Blue Room, Windermer Club.

Nightlife

Globe Princess movie theater.

Automobile Rental

Ronnie's Rent-A-Car, P.O. Box 118. *Norma's U-Drive-It*, P.O. Box 136.

Eleuthera, HARBOUR ISLAND

Hotels

Pink Sands Phone 333-2030. The site is an Audubon Society designated bird sanctuary. Closed August to November & part of May. Reservations by direct contact. AP only. *Extravagant.*

Dunmore Beach Club Phone 333-2200. Closed May 10 to August 10. Reservations by direct contact. AP only. *Expensive.*

Romora Bay Club Phone 333-2325; or in Florida (800)327-8286. Closed September 15 to Novemmber 1. *Expensive to Extravagant.*

Coral Sands Phone 333-2350. *Moderate.*

Runaway Hills Phone 333-2150. Reservations direct or through travel agent. *Moderate.*

Valentine's Yacht Club & Inn & Dive Center Phone 333-2142. Reservations are direct. *Moderate.*

Restaurants

All clubs and resorts cater to guests. Outside guests encouraged at **Runaway Hill** and **Rock House Picarroon Restaurant. Angela's Starfish Restaurant, Major's Everready Cook Shop.**

Nightlife

Valentine's Nautical Bar, nightly music; **Romara,** weekly disco night; *Pink Sands Lounge,* harborside; **Tingum's Nightclub; Vic-Hum Club; Willie's Sunset Inn Bar, George's Billy the Goat Tavern.**

Eleuthera, ROCK SOUND

Cotton Bay Beach, Golf & Tennis Resort Phone (809)334-2101. FAP only. *Expensive to Extravagant.*

Windermere Island Club Write VSOE Hotels, 1 World Trade Center, NYC, NY 10048. Phone (212)839-0223; toll free in U.S. (800)237-1236; toll free in Canada (800)451-2253. Reservations direct; packages available. AP only. *Extravagant.*

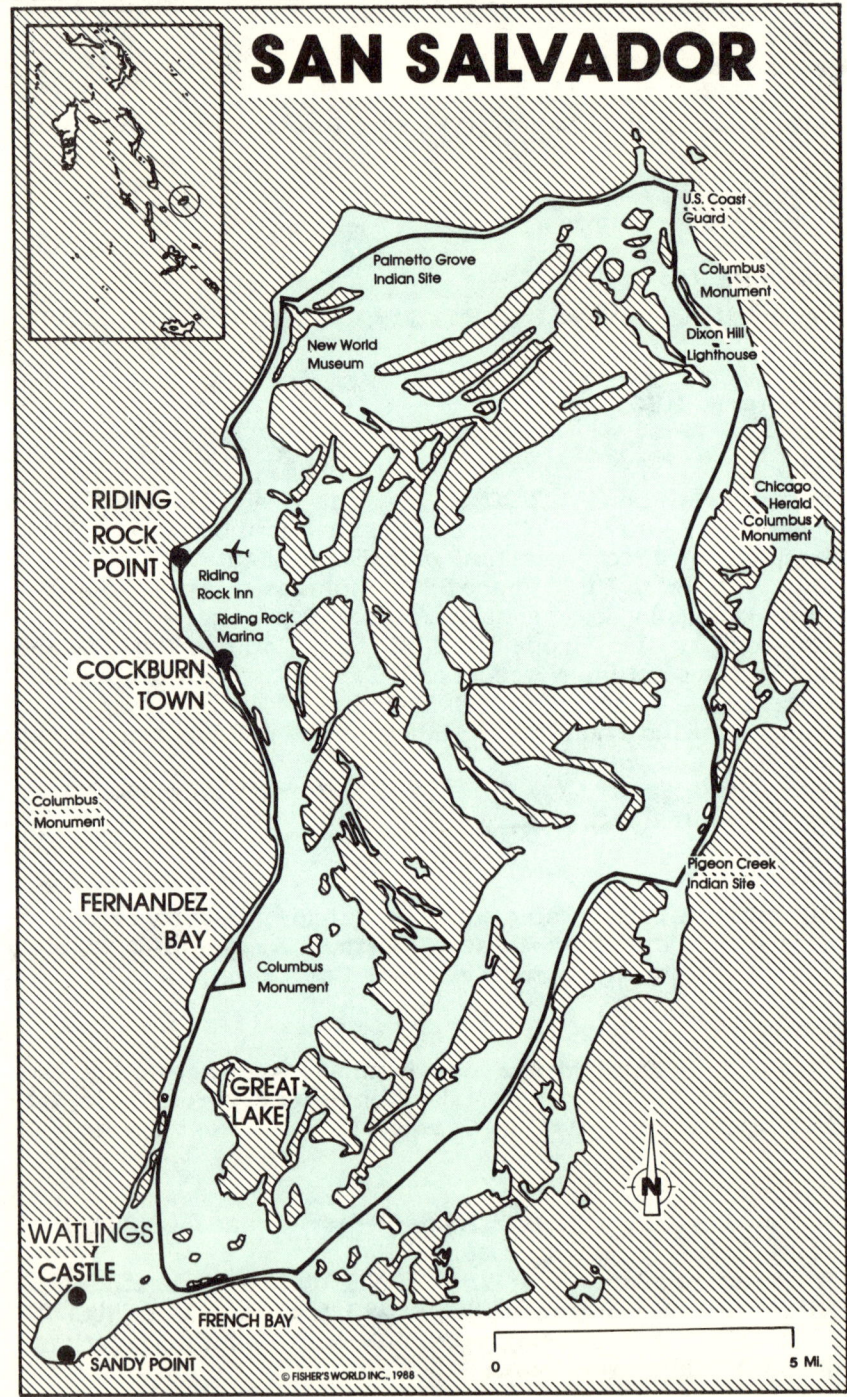

Eleuthera, SPANISH WELLS

Hotels

Spanish Wells Beach Resort and **Spanish Wells Harbour Club** Scuba is the focus here. *Inexpensive.*

Restaurants

Walton's Langousta Restaurant and Bar On the harbor. Open 9A.M. to 3 P.M. and 6 to 10 P.M. Lunch and dinner. *Moderate.*

Snack Bar Open 9 A.M. to 1 P.M. and 5 to 10 P.M.; **Roddy's Place.** Both *Inexpensive to Moderate.*

Shopping

Quilt Shop.

SAN SALVADOR

Riding Rock Inn Phone (809)322-2631. Reservations direct. Focus on scuba, skin diving, snorkeling. Fly Bahamasair or Riding Rock's charter plane from Fort Lauderdale. *Moderate to Extravagant.*